Digital Forensics
for
Enterprises Beyond
Kali Linux

Navigate complex legal frameworks, ensure
digital evidence admissibility, and establish
robust forensics laboratory environments

Abhirup Guha

bpb

www.bpbonline.com

I0049916

First Edition 2025

Copyright © BPB Publications, India

ISBN: 978-93-65895-902

LIMITS OF LIABILITY AND DISCLAIMER OF WARRANTY

To View Complete
BPB Publications Catalogue
Scan the QR Code:

Dedicated to

My father – **Late Hriday Ranjan Guha**

My mom – **Madhumita Guha**

My wife – **Pampa Biswas Guha**

And my little star, my boy – **Ishayu Guha**

About the Author

Abhirup Guha holds a Master of Business Administration in Information Technology from IBMR and a Bachelor of Computer Applications from NSEC College. He also holds a Certified Information Systems Security Professional (CISSP) certification from Charles Sturt University and several cybersecurity certifications from various universities worldwide.

As an accomplished cybersecurity expert, he is passionate about sharing his knowledge and skills with individuals and businesses to help them safeguard their digital assets against emerging cyber threats. With over 15+ years of experience in the industry, he has successfully trained professionals on various topics, including cyber forensics, mobile forensics, and cybersecurity.

Beyond the boardroom, he also serves as an Associate Cyber Security and Cyber Forensic Trainer at a reputed government body, where he delivers comprehensive training on forensic cloning, steganography, and digital evidence management. As a Lead Penetration Tester and Security Auditor at a reputed organization, he helped clients secure their digital infrastructure from a consistently evolving threat landscape.

About the Reviewer

Sanyam Jain is a distinguished Cloud Security Engineer and cybersecurity thought leader with a strong record of securing complex digital ecosystems and safeguarding critical infrastructure. With deep experience across cloud security, security operations, application security, compliance, and security automation, Sanyam has helped global organizations exceed their security objectives through forward-thinking strategies and cutting-edge technology.

His core technical proficiencies span network security, threat detection and response, container and Kubernetes security, data encryption, and identity/access control, with hands-on expertise across leading cloud platforms, including AWS, Azure, and Google Cloud. He brings a DevSecOps mindset to modern development pipelines, designing secure architectures, automating compliance, and embedding security at every layer of software delivery.

Sanyam's research on security vulnerabilities has earned international recognition, featured in Forbes, TechCrunch, ZDNet, Bleeping Computer, and 40+ other prominent publications. His work reflects a relentless drive to improve digital resilience globally.

Beyond the enterprise world, Sanyam actively gives back to the cybersecurity ecosystem. He serves as a Judge for the Globee® Awards for Cybersecurity and Disruptors (2025), Stratus Awards, and the Big Awards for Business, where he evaluates emerging technologies and cybersecurity innovations. He also contributes as a Mentor of Change with NITI Aayog, fostering grassroots innovation and leadership.

As a technical advisor to startups, Sanyam helps shape and secure early-stage ventures, guiding them on cloud architecture, secure coding practices, infrastructure hardening, and regulatory compliance to build defensible businesses from day one.

He contributes to global cybersecurity resilience through partnerships with NGOs like the GDI Foundation and CSIRT.Global, helping safeguard critical internet infrastructure. He's also a technical reviewer for key publications from Apress and BPB, strengthening community access to high-quality learning content.

Sanyam holds a Master's in Technology from BITS Pilani (with distinction) and is a Certified Kubernetes Administrator (CKA). He's mentored thousands of learners via platforms like Udacity, Rooman Technologies, and QwikSkills, empowering the next generation of cybersecurity professionals.

With a unique blend of technical depth, community leadership, and startup advisory, Sanyam Jain is not only defending the cloud but helping define its future.

Acknowledgement

I would like to express my sincere gratitude to all those who contributed to the completion of this book.

First and foremost, I extend my heartfelt appreciation to my family and students for their unwavering support and encouragement throughout this journey. Their love, support, and encouragement have been a constant source of motivation.

I am immensely grateful to BPB Publications for their guidance and expertise in bringing this book to fruition. Their support and assistance were invaluable in navigating the complexities of the publishing process.

I would also like to acknowledge the reviewers, technical experts, and editors who provided valuable feedback and contributed to the refinement of this manuscript. Their insights and suggestions have significantly enhanced the quality of the book.

Last but not least, I want to express my gratitude to the readers who have shown interest in my book. Your support and encouragement have been deeply appreciated.

Thank you to everyone who has played a part in making this book a reality.

Preface

Cybercrimes, data breaches, and online fraud are now daily headlines in today's times, thus triggering the need for professional digital forensics experts. This book is authored from the intersection of technological advancement and the urgent need for investigative skills in the digital space. This book seeks to provide a comprehensive and practical handbook for handling the complex world of digital evidence and cyber investigations.

The handbook on digital forensics is aimed at future practitioners and forensic analysts interested in learning more about digital investigations. The book progresses from simple concepts such as evidence handling and chain of custody to advanced concepts such as malware analysis, cloud forensics, and mobile device analysis. The book follows a step-by-step methodology based on case studies and industry needs. All the chapters are made readable, actionable, and relevant to today's legal and ethical standards.

The content of the handbook on digital forensics has been sourced from years of experience, research, and collaboration with law enforcement, legal, and cybersecurity professionals. It bridges the gap between practice and theory and encourages critical thinking and systematic problem-solving. Whether you are preparing for a certification exam, building internal incident response capacity, or working a case in the field, the advice in these pages will be your trusted guide.

I would like to extend my thanks to the authors who have shared their knowledge, and to the readers who strive to maintain the integrity and efficacy of digital investigations on a daily basis. My hope is that Handbook on Digital Forensics will enable you to reveal the truth concealed in data, and to do so with accuracy, professionalism, and purpose.

Chapter 1: Unveiling Digital Forensics - This chapter introduces major fields of digital forensics. Digital forensics is concerned with the application of scientifically established methods of collecting, gathering, authenticating, identifying, analysing, interpreting, recording, and presenting digital evidence. This digital evidence, gathered from electronic sources, is the foundation for re-creating the past or predicting potential unauthorized activity that can disrupt normal business operations.

Chapter 2: Role of Digital Forensics in Enterprises - The chapter will elucidate the very important role played by digital forensics in most business segments and industries. Organizations today are relying increasingly on digital infrastructure to store, process, and provide data, and hence, the significance of the role played by digital forensics in the management of cybersecurity breaches is invaluable. Its strategic implementation allows organizations to create actionable intelligence that assists them in adjusting and improving their defenses based on the ever-evolving cyber threat landscape.

The ever-changing nature of cyber threats has made enterprise security an imperative with the inclusion of quality threat intelligence at the forefront. To properly address cybersecurity incidents, professional investigators need to utilize digital forensic methods with accuracy and consistency. Digital forensics in this regard is not just a response function but also a preemptive action in safeguarding organizational assets and processes.

Computer forensics has evolved from its initial function of investigating cybercrimes. Now, it has a more extensive function in the whole process of handling cybersecurity incidents. They range from the detection of threats and recovery of compromised data to legal compliance and regulation. Computer forensics has therefore emerged as a critical function in enterprise security measures.

The ongoing use of digital forensics in the digital era is aimed at validating a holistic application of cybersecurity. Not only does it provide for the investigation and containment of incidents, but it also ensures digital environment sustainability. As threat behavior changes in terms of sophistication, the need for forensic processes in safeguarding and maintaining trust in digital infrastructures is heightened.

Chapter 3: Expanse of Digital Forensics - Digital forensics has emerged from conventional computer forensics due to the increased dependency of contemporary businesses on a range of digital technologies. From a cybersecurity perspective, data on these digital devices is identified as digital evidence. The coverage of digital forensics today extends to various aspects of digital activity, both in hardware and network infrastructures. The digital revolution quickly pervades many business operations and hence incessantly highlights the importance of digital forensics. This is significantly propelled by the extensive application of internet technologies to facilitate business processes and address client needs. Digital forensics is also vital in incident response and compliance audits, both of which are essential for organizations to safeguard their reputation and hold a competitive advantage in their markets.

Chapter 4: Tracing the Progression of Digital Forensics - The expanding role of digital transformation has been met with an equivalent expansion of cyberattacks and cybercrimes. These threats to security must be countered effectively through the strategic application of digital forensics. The diversification and sophistication of cybercrimes have, however, enhanced the complexity of forensic investigation. This necessitates the ongoing enhancement of digital forensics to keep up with the development of new technology. The development in the field is now focused on the incorporation of new tools and approaches to forensic simplification. This chapter attempts to examine the development of digital forensics in countering the growing complexity of cybercrime investigation.

Chapter 5: Navigating Legal and Ethical Aspects of Digital Forensics - Value allocation to the digital forensics role in the current digital age requires its correct positioning within applicable legal and ethical standards. These standards are discussed in this chapter in the context of global digitalization, which has created the need to rely increasingly on different digital devices such as smartphones, laptops, and tablets. Instant response to cybercrime and accidents is warranted for protecting organizational assets and maintaining operational continuity. Nevertheless, current cyber attacks are increasingly sophisticated in nature, with malicious groups being behind them in most cases, with the intention to damage the reputation and credibility of firms operating in their own industry.

Chapter 6: Unfolding the Digital Forensics Process - The digital forensic analysis can take a long time, mainly due to the complexity of analyzing the digital devices utilized. This is due to the fact that the devices have a lot of diverse data. The data comes in various forms, in the modern digital age, including documents, emails, pictures, videos, log files, and encrypted files, all of which have to be analyzed in detail in a case of investigation.

Chapter 7: Beyond Kali Linux - Kali Linux is renowned in the field of digital forensics owing to its immense potential in penetration testing and cybersecurity evaluation. Its extensive set of built-in tools makes it a popular operating system among forensic experts. Forensic tools like Autopsy, Wireshark, and Volatility are integrated, and they are capable of performing detailed and efficient forensic analysis. Exclusive reliance on Kali Linux is limiting for cybercrime investigators because there is no single platform that can address all investigative hurdles. The rising popularity of Kali Linux in digital forensics is a reflection of the growing complexity of modern cybercrimes. The chapter continues to introduce a variety of forensic tools employed under varied investigative scenarios.

Chapter 8: Decoding Network Forensics - Modern organizations today are dependent on networks of interconnected digital devices to increase their efficiency and provide uninterrupted customer service. This dependence, however, tends to attract external assailants who attempt to compromise such systems. The opportunity, therefore, for digital forensic investigators to carry out thorough and methodical investigations of the device networks at cybercrime scenes is provided. Forensic investigators will perform different tasks like packet analysis, log examination, incident response, and attack reconstruction. As technology advances and the configuration of device networks within organizations gets more complex, forensic experts are required to resort to specialized tools to probe. Wireshark, Zeek, Snort, Splunk, Forensic Toolkit (FTK), and NetworkMiner are examples of some tools that are very important for this line of inquiry. This chapter focuses on the field of network forensics and the current practices and standards in digital forensics.

Chapter 9: Demystifying Memory Forensics - Memory forensics is crucial to cybersecurity and digital forensics, for it allows investigators to analyze RAM, which is a type of volatile memory, in order to detect evidence of malicious activities. Unlike disk forensics, dealing with persistent storage, memory forensics affords a live view of the state of a system, revealing crucial details about active processes, open connections, encryption keys, and possibly even malware. This chapter discusses different aspects of memory forensics that demonstrate its worth to digital forensic investigators in providing valuable and necessary results for effective investigations.

Chapter 10: Exploring Mobile Device Forensics - Smartphones have become the object of choice for cyber adversaries due to growing dependence on them. These attacks begin on mobile devices, among many modern cybercrimes that target individuals. Following the rise of mobile forensics as an important branch of digital forensics, therefore, comes mobile forensics. Mainly, mobile forensics pertains to the area of digital forensics that concerns itself with the extraction, analysis, and presentation of data on mobile devices that include but are not limited to cell phones, smart tablets, and GPS units. It serves criminal investigations, cybersecurity, and corporate security equally. This chapter focuses on mobile forensics and the techniques and tools employed during evidence acquisition and analysis.

Chapter 11: Deciphering Virtualization and Hypervisor Forensics - Virtualization means running more than one operating system inside one physical machine using hypervisors. It makes digital forensic investigations more complex. Investigating virtualized environments is complicated due to multiple factors such as shared resources, layered data storage, and live migration. All of these factors complicate the forensic process. Hence, knowledge of virtualization and hypervisor forensics is mandatory to overcome these challenges. Typical applications of virtualization are cloud computing, enterprise IT infrastructures, and cybersecurity sandboxes. This chapter examines how the effective interpretation of virtualization and hypervisor forensics is useful to digital forensic investigators in resolving cyberattacks more quickly.

Chapter 12: Integrating Incident Response with Digital Forensics - The organizations have been increasingly dependent on networks of digital devices, and at the same time, they are encountering a greater number of incidents of cybercrime. Complexity in incidents comes with a drastic need for highly sophisticated investigation procedures, as emphasized by the need for digital forensics. The combination of incident response (IR) and digital forensics leads to possession of a much broader and better-managed approach to handling incidents of a security nature by organizations. This aids not only in the resolution of current problems but also in the collection of credible threat intelligence (TI) that will prevent similar incidents from occurring again in the future. The chapter will look into the linkages between incident response and digital forensics in regards to how they can be used to improve the overall actions toward any cybersecurity effort.

Chapter 13: Advanced Tactics in Digital Forensics - Advanced cyber attacks are highly evasive even for most forensic methods. It is fast becoming apparent that classical means cannot simply keep pace with the complexities introduced by advanced cyber threats, their encrypted data, and various anti-forensic techniques designed to hinder investigations. Advanced forensic techniques enable the extraction of hidden evidence and the analysis of complex cyber incidents, thereby helping to strengthen legal cases. The succeeding section shall showcase these advanced digital forensics techniques and their enhancement of the investigative art.

Chapter 14: Introduction to Digital Forensics in Industrial Control Systems - Digital transformation has a truly consequential impact on many critical areas such as energy, manufacturing, water supply, and transportation. With increased penetration of industrial control systems (ICS) into these sectors, these sectors become prone to cyber threats. This chapter discusses the aspects of digital forensics in a protection scheme for ICSes and critical infrastructural security. It examines the vulnerabilities in this area that lead to disruptions, which, if they harm the stakeholders involved, can result in severe repercussions across the vital sectors.

Chapter 15: Venturing into IoT Forensics - The rapid growth of the Internet of Things (IoT) has brought about a transformation in diverse industries, connecting billions of devices across healthcare, transportation, industrial systems, and smart cities. But there is a flip side to this general acceptance of IoT devices - the detection of security loopholes and new forensic challenges, which have made IoT forensics a prime area of interest in digital investigations. Unlike those of traditional computing systems, IoT ecosystems are a heterogeneous group of devices with diverse hardware, operating systems, and communication protocols. For this reason, investigators experience serious difficulties in data acquisition, evidence preservation, and forensic analysis. Furthermore, many IoT devices have limited storage and processing capabilities, which makes this transient data very difficult to analyze forensically. The chapter focuses on IoT forensics and supports the discussion on forensic issues, methods, legal issues, and real-world case studies. In addition, it will present a demonstration of best practices along with tools to perform forensic study inside smart environments so that whenever digital evidence from IoT devices, cloud services, and network logs is collected, it will be efficiently analyzed by forensic professionals.

Chapter 16: Setting Up Digital Forensics Labs and Tools - The establishment of a well-equipped digital forensics lab is important for investigations that are efficient, reliable, and hold space in a court of law. Such labs provide a conducive environment that allows forensic analysts to have access to tools, infrastructure, and security measures for analyzing digital evidence. The lab ensures that the integrity of the forensic investigation is preserved, the chain of custody remains intact, and legal standards are adhered to. Knowledge of the capability of tools and their limitations allows forensic professionals to select the most suitable analysis tool for any particular evidence pertaining to digital objects for an investigative situation. This chapter will give a practical, complete guide on how to establish digital forensics labs and select suitable tools for investigation.

Chapter 17: Advancing Your Career in Digital Forensics - Digital forensics is quickly changing its pace through technology innovations, increasing cyber threats, and gradually complicated legal issues. Organizations are more intensively concentrating on cybersecurity and digital investigations, so the demand for skilled professionals might increase in digital forensics. However, a successful career in this specialization was not an easy journey; it means building a solid technical foundation, gaining hands-on experience, and committing oneself to lifelong learning. Whether working for law enforcement, private security companies, governmental agencies, or corporate cybersecurity, professionals will always be on their toes with the latest tools, investigative methods, and legal requirements. Being equipped with industry certificates and having presented practical experience in forensic investigation may materially advance the career of an individual. In this sense, this chapter reviews interesting career avenues, critical skills and certifications, and trends in the industry as a guide for budding and mature professionals in taking their career advancements in digital forensics.

Chapter 18: Industry best practices in Digital Forensics - Digital forensics is fast-paced and multidimensional, and combines elements from cybersecurity, law enforcement, and corporate investigations. Rising cyber threats have made it more and more common for institutions to rely on digital forensics for evidence collection and increased security. Digital forensics foundation and growth show increasing dimensions in terms of application from simple file recovery techniques of the past to the most up-to-date techniques used today in analyzing cybercrimes and data breaches. The ever-growing digital footprint brought about by technologies such as cloud computing and IoT makes development even more complex. This chapter discusses industry best practices and considers career opportunities that exist in an ever-progressing digital forensics environment.

Coloured Images

Please follow the link to download the
Coloured Images of the book:

https://rebrand.ly/mljjnju

We have code bundles from our rich catalogue of books and videos available at **https://github.com/bpbpublications**. Check them out!

Errata

We take immense pride in our work at BPB Publications and follow best practices to ensure the accuracy of our content to provide with an indulging reading experience to our subscribers. Our readers are our mirrors, and we use their inputs to reflect and improve upon human errors, if any, that may have occurred during the publishing processes involved. To let us maintain the quality and help us reach out to any readers who might be having difficulties due to any unforeseen errors, please write to us at :

errata@bpbonline.com

Your support, suggestions and feedbacks are highly appreciated by the BPB Publications' Family.

Did you know that BPB offers eBook versions of every book published, with PDF and ePub files available? You can upgrade to the eBook version at www.bpbonline. com and as a print book customer, you are entitled to a discount on the eBook copy. Get in touch with us at :

business@bpbonline.com for more details.

At **www.bpbonline.com**, you can also read a collection of free technical articles, sign up for a range of free newsletters, and receive exclusive discounts and offers on BPB books and eBooks.

Piracy

If you come across any illegal copies of our works in any form on the internet, we would be grateful if you would provide us with the location address or website name. Please contact us at **business@bpbonline.com** with a link to the material.

If you are interested in becoming an author

If there is a topic that you have expertise in, and you are interested in either writing or contributing to a book, please visit **www.bpbonline.com**. We have worked with thousands of developers and tech professionals, just like you, to help them share their insights with the global tech community. You can make a general application, apply for a specific hot topic that we are recruiting an author for, or submit your own idea.

Reviews

Please leave a review. Once you have read and used this book, why not leave a review on the site that you purchased it from? Potential readers can then see and use your unbiased opinion to make purchase decisions. We at BPB can understand what you think about our products, and our authors can see your feedback on their book. Thank you!

For more information about BPB, please visit **www.bpbonline.com**.

Join our book's Discord space

Join the book's Discord Workspace for Latest updates, Offers, Tech happenings around the world, New Release and Sessions with the Authors:

https://discord.bpbonline.com

Table of Contents

CHAPTER 1
Unveiling Digital Forensics

Introduction

This chapter will cover digital forensics. Digital forensics is the use of scientifically derived and proven methods to preserve, collect, validate, identify, analyze, interpret, document, and present digital evidence derived from digital sources to facilitate or further reconstruct events or help anticipate unauthorized actions that can be disruptive to planned business operations.

Structure

The chapter covers the following topics:

- Understanding digital forensics
- Rules of computer forensics
- DFRWS investigative model
- Six A(s) of digital forensics
- Skills required for digital forensic investigator
- Digital evidence
- Types of digital forensics

- Digital forensic tools and their purposes
- Primary techniques of digital forensic analysis
- Incident response

Objectives

The objectives of this chapter are to develop a detailed understanding of digital forensics from the perspective of its role in modern-day crime investigation. We will also learn how to be aware of different skills that are required by digital forensic investigators to proceed with digital forensic investigation and develop a basic understanding of digital evidence from multiple perspectives, including legal considerations. We will also learn to acquire a preliminary understanding of incident management from the perspective of the digital world.

Understanding digital forensics

The progress of digital forensics Investigation conforms to different types, but primarily, the concerned principles and procedures remain the same, more or less. This relates to effective analysis of digital evidence to identify the root cause of a cybersecurity incident. The tendency of digital forensic investigators relates to resisting recurrences of cybersecurity incidents within the organizational environment. This leads to the overall success of a digital forensic investigation, relying on the expertise of associated investigators on the effective interpretation of data after using relevant information retrieval tools. The long-term experience of forensic investigators encourages them to select effective tools that can generate reliable results and thereby be considered as trustworthy for upcoming investigation procedures. Digital forensics gradually emerged as the Science of forensics combined with the art of investigation. The observed stages of digital forensics can be categorically represented as follows in *Figure 1.1*:

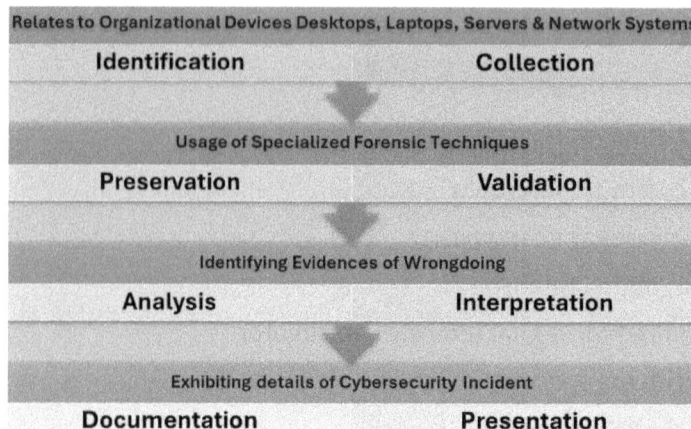

Figure 1.1: Procedure of handling digital evidences in digital forensics

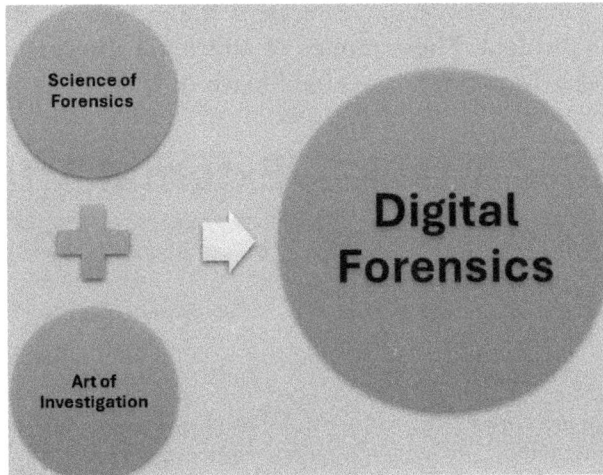

Figure 1.2: Pillars of digital forensics

Digital forensics is the combination of the science of applying appropriate methods and deductive reasoning to data, along with the art of interpreting this data to reconstruct an event as depicted in *Figure 1.2*.

The goal of conducting evidence analysis by investigators relates to finding the facts and thereby using them to reconstruct the true course of an event. The revelation of truth from a forensic investigation relates to discovering and exposing the remnants (traces) of the event left on the system. The remnants in forensic investigation are identified and referred to as artifacts or evidence during legal proceedings. The progress of simple tasks during the creation of artifacts apart from their cleaning that leaves additional artifacts.

Digital forensics investigators must apply the two tests for digital evidence for the aspect of survival in a court of law which includes authenticity and reliability. The importance of the authenticity test for digital evidence relates to uncovering its sources, as shown in the following *Figure 1.3*:

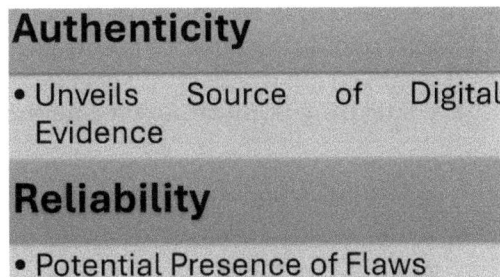

Authenticity

- Unveils Source of Digital Evidence

Reliability

- Potential Presence of Flaws

Figure 1.3: Assessment of digital evidence

Similarly, the importance of reliability for digital evidence relates to assessing the potential flaws present within it.

The detailed digital forensic investigation reveals the modes of attack that resulted in the occurrence of the incident. **These modes of attack are illustrated in** *Figure 1.4.* This includes insider attacks, implying a possible breach of trust from employees within an organization.

Insider Attack   External Attack

Insider Attack	External Attack
Dissatisfaction of employees	Involvement of Market Rivals
Leading to Breach of Trust	Unfair Competitor
Originates from within an organization	Maligning reputation of target company

Figure 1.4: Modes of attack

Otherwise, the occurrence of external attacks relates to hiring hackers by competitors to promote unhealthy market competition. The hired external hackers are instructed by competitors to target and destroy the reputation of their market rivals.

Rules of computer forensics

A good forensic investigator should always abide by specific rules to lead a fruitful forensic investigation procedure, as illustrated in *Figure 1.5*. These include proceeding with the due investigation with duplicate images of evidence instead of the original evidence. This is crucial in terms of refraining from tampering with the digital evidence. This is because the loss of integrity by digital evidence can lead to losing its admissibility in the Court of Law. Furthermore, digital evidence tends to be crucial for crimes in the modern-day digital world. The effective preservation of original digital evidence and thereby using only its image for the investigation procedure is essential to maintain the overall integrity of the evidence. This is because using only the image of digital evidence resists frequent handling of evidence and thereby avoids the possible occurrence of integrity loss.

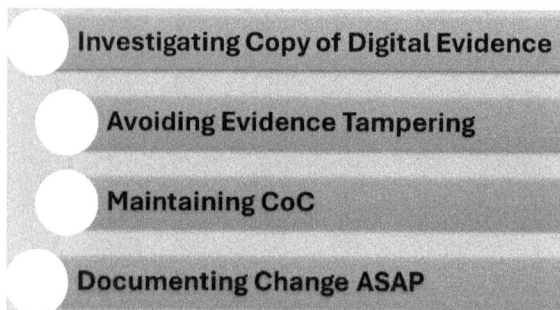

- Investigating Copy of Digital Evidence
- Avoiding Evidence Tampering
- Maintaining CoC
- Documenting Change ASAP

Figure 1.5: Best practices of digital forensics investigation

The rules for leading forensic investigations further include preparing a duly filled-out **Chain of Custody (CoC)** to encourage careful handling of evidence. The importance of maintaining the CoC of Evidence relates to timely documenting changes in evidence during an investigation. This is in addition to implying in the Court of Law that the digital evidence has been handled with due care during the phase of investigation. The importance of these rules for investigation relates to increasing the overall value and defensibility of the concerned case. The detailed documentation of a digital forensic investigation, carried out by a designated team of investigators, is crucial for its verification by another team of investigators, as per the direction of the Court of Law in the future, if needed for the benefit of the case. The forensic investigators are required to face a complex landscape of laws and regulations, and this requires them to meticulously document the details of digital evidence investigation.

DFRWS investigative model

This is a standardized investigative model for the progress of digital forensic investigations, consisting of multiple stages. The uniqueness of this model relates to considering individual digital devices to be a digital crime scene for investigators. The relevant stages of this model are listed as follows, as well as illustrated in *Figure 1.6*.

- **Identification:** The basis of Forensic Sciences is based on the Exchange Principle of Locard, which relates to the exchange of traces. The modern digital world resembles the combination of two systems that result in their exchanging traces. For instance, if an individual browses a website, the web server or web application firewall may record the individual's IP address within a collection log. This principle can guide the identification of potential sources of evidence during an incident. E.g., identifying the root cause of a malware infection requires starting with an analysis of the infected system by searching the firewall connection or proxy logs for any outbound traffic from the infected system to external IP addresses. This may reveal the C2 Server.

- **Preservation**: This subsequent phase, after evidence identification, relates to safeguarding it from any modification or deletion. This is done by enabling the controls to protect the potential evidence, e.g., log files, from removal or modification. Considering the host systems, such as desktops, isolate the potential digital evidence from the rest of the network, either through physical or logical controls, or through network access controls, etc. It is critical that the users not be allowed to access a suspect system to prevent deliberate or inadvertent integrity tampering of evidence. The required preservation of evidence in virtual systems is achieved through snapshotting systems, cloning the system, and saving on non-volatile storage.

- **Collection (media)**: The investigators initiate the actual process of digital evidence acquisition, and during this phase, consider the volatility of the evidence. Considering the network equipment, this could include active connections or log data stored in the device. Specifically, the **Internet Engineering Task Force (IETF)** prepared a document titled, **Guidelines for Evidence Collection and Archiving (RFC 3227)** addressing the order of the volatility of following digital evidence.

- o Registers, Cache
- o Routing Table, ARP Cache, Process Table, Kernel Statistics, Memory
- o Temporary File Systems
- o Disk
- o Remote Logging and Monitoring Data, relevant to the system in question
- o Physical Configuration, Network Topology
- o Archival Media

- **Proper evidence handling:** The intentional as well as inadvertent altering of the original evidence results in their integrity's loss. This encourages the best practice of always working on the image of evidence for investigation.

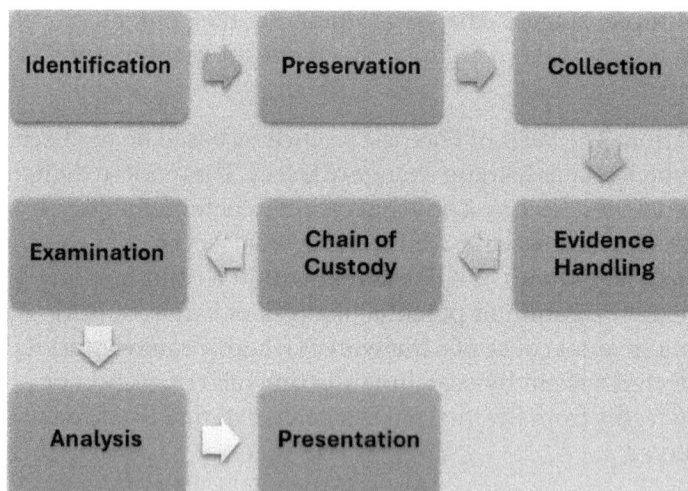

Figure 1.6: Stages of the DFRWS investigative model

- **Documentation**: The appropriate documentation of evidence handling is crucial to ensure maintaining its detailed record of passing through different stages of investigation. This relates to the concept of CoC. This is described as the documentation of a piece of evidence through its life cycle of investigation. It initiates when an investigator first takes custody of the piece of evidence to the incident is finally closed and processed for documentation. The CoC of devices can be maintained both electronically or manually.

- **Examination (data):** This details of evidence examination relate to the specific tools and forensic techniques in order to identify and extract data from the seized evidence, for instance, a C&C Activity. The specific information from the acquired memory image of digital evidence would be considered in this stage of the investigation. For instance, the extraction of Secure Shell traffic from a network capture. The appropriate preservation of evidence is prioritized throughout the evidence examination process.

- **Analysis (information):** Once the investigator extracts the potentially relevant pieces of data, he/she proceeds to analyze the data in light of any other relevant data obtained. For instance, if the analyst has discovered that the compromised host has an open connection to an external IP address, he will then correlate that information with an analysis of the packet capture from the network. Using the IP address as a starting point, the analyst would be able to isolate the particular traffic and, hence, identify the C2 server. It can take many iterations and might include a reduction of the acquired base data set. Other examples include file system analysis, file content analysis, log analysis, etc.

- **Presentation (evidence):** This stage of digital forensic analysis refers to a detailed written report of facts related to a digital forensic case. It needs to be clear and concise, addressing every action and identifying the critical data required. It should be thorough, accurate, and free from any bias or opinion. It aids in determining the root cause of an incident. It is usually presented in a court of law and might require validation from an expert witness.

Six A(s) of digital forensics

The six A(s) of digital forensics are as follows (*Figure 1.7*):

- **Assessment:** You must be able to distinguish between evidence and junk data. For this, you should know what the data is, where it is located, and how it is stored. The differentiation between evidence and junk data is crucial for a digital forensic investigation to maintain a proper course of investigation.

- **Acquisition:** The evidence you find must be preserved in its original state as safely as possible. However, observing any changes made to digital evidence during this phase requires it to be documented and justified by the concerned investigator.

- **Authentication:** At least two copies of the original evidence are taken to proceed with the digital forensic investigation. One of these is sealed in the presence of the device owner and then placed in secure storage. This is the master copy, and it will only be opened for investigation as per order and direction from the court of law. This is in the event of facing a challenge after carrying out forensic analysis on the second copy and presenting it to the court of law.

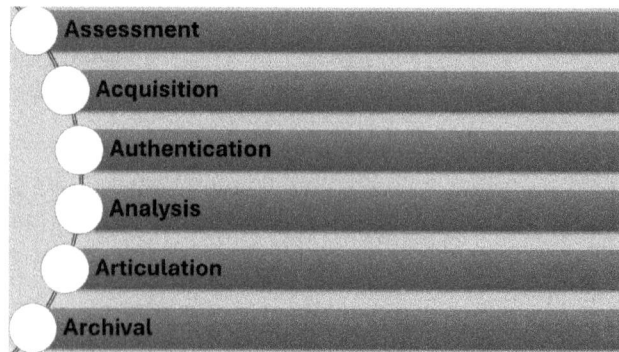

Figure 1.7: 6As of digital forensics

- **Analysis:** The stored evidence must be analyzed to extract useful information and recreate the chain of events leading to the occurrence of the incident.

- **Articulation:** The manner of presentation of findings of a digital investigation is important, and it must be understandable by judges in the court of law. It should thereby be technically correct and credible. A good presenter can help in this respect appropriately.

- **Archival:** After the case closure, the original evidence is sealed and kept in a secure storage location. This is because, by chance of a case reopening after some time or years, it will be required to re-investigate the evidence for production in the court of law.

Skills required for digital forensic investigator

Digital forensic investigators are required to possess three specific categories of skills to effortlessly participate in a digital forensic investigation. The required skills for digital forensic investigators are categorized into technical, interpersonal, and evidence management in *Figure 1.8*:

Technical Skills	Interpersonal Skills	Evidence Management
•Programming or computer-related experience •Understanding of Operating Systems •Strong computer science fundamentals •Knowledge of intrusion tools, cryptography and steganography	•Involvement of Market Rivals •Unfair Competitor •Maligning reputation of target company	•Rules •Handling Best Practices

Figure 1.8: Required skills for potential digital investigators

Potential digital forensic investigators are required to have adequate programming or computer-related experience along with a broad understanding of operating systems and their applications. This justifies the importance of having strong computer science fundamentals for a potential digital forensic investigator. Furthermore, knowledge of the latest intrusion tools, cryptography, and steganography significantly aids digital investigation for an investigator. Besides these technical skills, the digital forensic investigator is required to possess an appropriate interpersonal skillset. The range of Interpersonal Skills that guides a Digital Forensic Investigator during an investigation includes effective communication, paying attention to detail, critical thinking, team collaboration, and being patient and persistent. The importance of possessing effective communication skills by a Digital Forensic Investigator relates to explaining complex areas of investigation to individuals from non-technical backgrounds in the Court of Law. These individuals are crucial for an investigation and include law enforcement officers, lawyers, and judges. The Digital Forensic Investigators are assigned the responsibility of minutely analyzing the digital evidence and thereby meticulously documenting their findings. The skill of critical thinking is crucial for digital forensics investigators in terms of revealing the underlying clues in digital evidence and presenting them in the Court of Law for the effective delivery of justice. This relates to accurately analyzing digital evidence to interpret the stored digital data. Team collaboration is crucial for Digital Forensic Investigators and requires the exhibition of both patience and persistence. Moreover, the potential digital forensic investigators are supposed to possess a strong understanding of the rules of digital evidence and their handling during investigation. This is along with having appropriate analytical skills and system administrative skills.

Digital evidence

The concept of digital evidence is elaborated as information and data of value to a digital investigation. Such data and information tend to be stored, received, or transmitted by an electronic device. This evidence acquisition tends to be during the seizure of electronic devices from crime scenes for detailed digital forensic investigation. According to the National Institute of Justice, *Digital evidence should be examined only by those trained specifically for that purpose.*

Legal considerations

The digital evidence is required to be **Admissible, Authentic, Complete, Reliable,** and **Believable** for acceptance in the Court of Law. The stages of digital evidence are as follows:

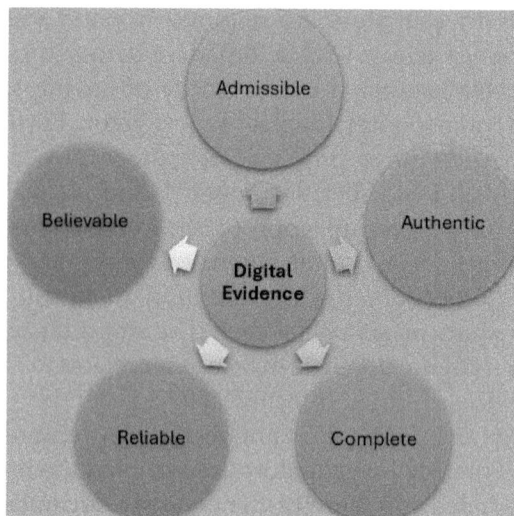

Figure 1.9: Stages of the incident response process

The stages are as follows:

- **Admissible:** Digital evidence must conform to certain legal rules and regulations before it can be produced at the Court of Law

- **Authentic:** Digital evidence must comply with the occurrence of the incident

- **Complete:** Digital evidence is required to depict the entire story of the incident and thereby refrain from only divulging a limited detail of the incident

- **Reliable:** The collection and handling of digital evidence requires transparency to conform to its authenticity

- **Believable:** Digital evidence is required to be believable and understandable by a court of law

Order of volatility

When collecting evidence, investigators should proceed by tackling the volatile first and then the less volatile. The following *Table 1.1* illustrates the volatility level of different evidence categories:

Evidence category	Level of volatility
Registers and Cache	HIGH
Routing Table, ARP Cache, Process Table, Kernel Statistics, Memory	HIGH
Temporary File Systems	MEDIUM
Disk	LOW

Remote Logging and Monitoring Data	LOW
Physical Configuration, Network Topology	LOW
Archival Media	LOW

Table 1.1: Stages of the incident response process

Collection of evidence: Digital evidence can be collected from the relevant device types as depicted in *Table 1.2*:

Output devices	Storage devices	Network devices	Multifunction devices	Contemporary peripheral devices
• Printers • Monitors • Speakers	• External Hard Drives • USB Flash Drives • Memory Cards • Optical Discs (CDs/DVDs)	• Modems • Routers • **Network Interface Cards (NICs)** • Wireless Adapters	• All-in-One Printers • Docking Stations	• Smartphones and Tablets • Wearable Devices (e.g., Smartwatches) • IoT Devices (e.g., Smart Home Assistants)

Table 1.2: Types of devices for digital evidence collection

Output devices include:

- **Printers**: Generating hard copies of documents, print logs, and spool files can reveal document printing history
- **Monitors**: Display visual output, screen artifacts can be a source of incident details
- **Speakers**: Output audio relevant in cases involving sound playback

Storage devices include:

- **External hard drives**: Store large volumes of data containing user files and backups
- **USB flash drives**: Portable data storage devices are often used to transfer files
- **Memory cards**: Used in cameras and mobile devices to store photos, videos, and similar data
- **Optical discs (CDs/DVDs)**: Store data such as media and documents that can be extracted for analysis

Network devices include:

- **Modems**: Facilitate internet connectivity, and thus, their logs can show connection history
- **Routers**: Directs network traffic that can contain logs of connected devices and data flow
- **Network Interface Cards (NICs)**: Enables network connections, indicating possible tracking of MAC addresses
- **Wireless adapters**: Connects to Wi-Fi networks that can reveal access point details and connection times

Multifunction devices include:

- **All-in-one printers**: Combine printing, scanning, copying, and faxing, implying its logs and memory can store various data types
- **Docking stations**: Expand connectivity for laptops to connect multiple peripherals and potentially store connection histories

Contemporary peripheral devices include:

- **Smartphones and tablets**: Serve as both input and output devices that contain extensive user data
- **Wearable devices (e.g., Smartwatches)**: Track health and location data of users and thus can provide timelines of user activity
- **IoT devices (e.g., Smart Home Assistants)**: Record interactions and control smart home functions, and its logs can offer insights into user behavior
- **Game consoles**: Store user profiles, game history, and media that can be relevant to certain investigations

Tools and materials for collecting digital evidence

The collection of digital evidence relates to using multiple tools, such as the following:

- Cameras (Photo and video)
- Evidence stickers, labels, or tags
- Crime scene tape
- Anti-static bags
- Gloves
- Permanent markers
- Evidence inventory logs
- Non-magnetic tools

- Evidence tape
- Paper evidence bags
- Radio frequency-shielding material (*Figure 1.10*)
- Aluminum foil

Figure 1.10: *Faraday bags (radio frequency-shielding material)*

Types of digital forensics

Digital forensic evidence is available in different types (*Figure 1.11*), listed as follows:

- **Disk forensics:** Disk forensics is the interpretation of digital data stored on computer storage devices, such as **hard disk drives** (**HDDs**), **solid-state drives** (**SSDs**), and other media.
- **Mobile device forensics:** Mobile device forensics is defined as the process of extracting and analyzing information which had been stored in mobile devices.
- **Memory forensics:** Memory forensics refers to the analysis of volatile data in a memory dump of devices.

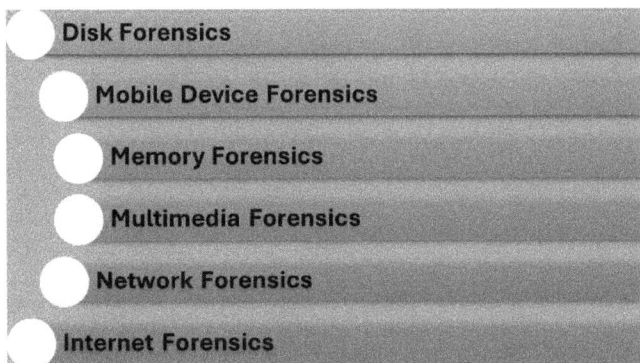

Figure 1.11: *Types of digital forensics evidence*

- **Multimedia forensics:** Multimedia forensics involves the set of techniques used for the analysis of multimedia signals like audio, video, and images. It aims to reveal the history of digital content.

- **Network forensics:** Network forensics looks at network traffic, logs, and other data about network use. It helps solve computer crimes, network problems, and data theft. The main job of network forensics is to find and keep digital proof that can be used in a court of law.

- **Internet forensics:** Internet forensics shifts focus from an individual machine to the Internet at large during the investigation of digital evidence.

Digital forensic tools and their purposes

Digital forensic tools and their purposes are listed in the following *Table 1.3*:

Tool	Operating system	Description	Status of analysis
Registry Recon	Windows	Registry Rebuild, Parsing for in-depth analysis	Static
SANS Investigative Forensics Toolkit (SIFT)	Ubuntu	Digital forensic analysis on different operating systems	Live
Encase	Windows	Gathering and analysing memory dump	Static
PTK Forensics (Programmers Toolkit)	Linux	GUI-based framework for static and live analysis	Both Static & Live
FTK	Windows	Digital analysis and indexing of evidentiary data	Static
Wireshark	Windows/Mac/Linux	Captures and analyses packets	Both Static & Live
The Sleuth Kit	Unix/Windows	GUI and CLI tools for analysis of Unix and Windows systems	Live
Computer Online Forensic Evidence Extractor (COFEE)	Windows	Extracting and analysing live forensic data	Live
X-Ways Forensics	Windows	General-purpose forensic tool with a hex editor	Both Static & Live

Bulk Extractor	Windows/Linux	Extraction of phone numbers, email addresses, URLs, etc.	Live
Open Computer Forensics Architecture (OCFA)	Linux	CLI for distributed computer forensics; used in forensic labs	Live
Memoryze	Windows	Acquires and analyzes RAM images, including the page file on live systems	Live
Volatility Framework	Volatility Systems	Extraction of items from RAM	Live

Table 1.3: Digital forensic tools

Primary techniques of digital forensic analysis

The process of digital forensics analysis resembles the traditional approach of static forensics and live forensics based on evidence handling during a seizure, as seen in *Figure 1.12*:

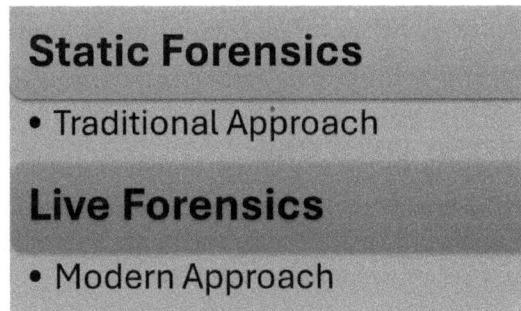

Static Forensics

• Traditional Approach

Live Forensics

• Modern Approach

Figure 1.12: *Types of digital forensics analysis*

The technique selection of digital forensics analysis is determined by the state of the system. This is from the perspective that both these types of approaches are different, but both need to be paired together to complement each other. Both these types of forensic analyses tend to possess advantages and disadvantages:

- **Traditional forensics:** This analytical technique of digital forensics provides incomplete evidentiary data. Besides this, information in volatile memory cannot be effectively recovered by using this technique. Contrarily, the required digital forensics Investigations are carried out exclusively on data at rest. This analysis tactic is suitable for applying to images of evidence.

- **Live forensics:** This approach to digital forensics analysis provides a more accurate and consistent picture of current and previous running processes as it works on live systems in real-time. The inherent advantage of this process relates to the quick completion of analysis, as it excludes the imaging requirement of evidence. This process is applicable for volatile memory, registry keys, open network connections, and system accounts. This relates to the selection of this approach for immediate and active threats, as it does not require any specific process for decryption and unpacking.

Incident response

The concept of incident response relates to additional capability along with existing policies and procedures of organizations, irrespective of their sizes. The digital forensics investigator possesses the ability to efficiently respond to security incidents. this allows the organizations not only to limit the damage of a potential cyberattack but also recover from the corresponding damage that is caused due to the attack. The increment of incident response capability relates to addressing multiple issues. This includes working knowledge of the incident response process that includes general incident flow and general actions taken at each stage of incident response. The organizations tend to be capable of forming incident response teams after formalizing the plan and associated processes. The aspect of having an incident response framework in place requires the concerted plan to be continually evaluated, tested, and improved as new threats emerge. Having appropriate incident response capability positions organizations to be prepared for the reality of incident occurrence that compromises their security.

Incident response process

Preparation: The lack of adequate preparation leads to a subsequent incident response to be disorganized and further degrading the incident. This relates to considering the following components of incident response preparation:

- Incident response plan development (includes processes, procedures, and any additional tools)
- Appropriate team building
- Appropriate staff training
- Integrating hardware forensic tools and forensic software applications
- Regularly conducting training exercises for organizational employees

The process of incident response is illustrated in the following *Figure 1.13*:

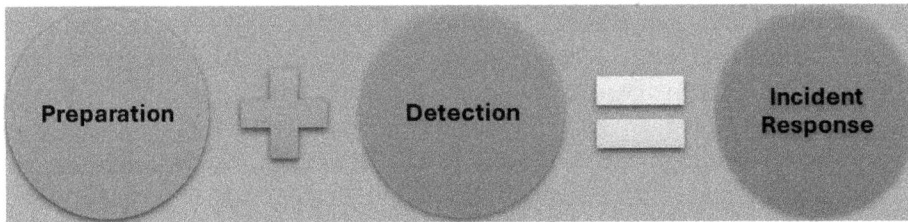

Figure 1.13: *Incident response process*

Detection: The detection of incident response relates to the organization becoming aware of a set of events that indicate possible malicious activity. The detection of potential incidents is a complex endeavor for the concerned incident response team. An organization can have millions of computational events per day. This is coupled with the security controls constantly altering the activity, which makes it difficult to separate malicious incidents from network traffic. This is despite the rapid development of cutting-edge **Security Incident and Event Management (SIEM)** tools due to their irregular updating latest security patches. SIEM technology or other security personnel, such as a security analyst, may receive an alert that a particular administrator account was in use during a period when the user was on vacation. External sources (ISP or law enforcement agencies) may detect malicious activity originating in an organization's network, contact them, and advise them to tackle the situation. Users, such as employees, inform a SOC team that they received an Excel spreadsheet from an unknown source and opened it unsuspectingly. This led to their files on the local system being encrypted suddenly.

Incident detection and response process

The incident detection and response process includes the following phases and is illustrated in *Figure 1.14*:

- **Analysis:** The detection of the incident encourages the initiation of the analysis phase for the concerned incident response team. The team starts with the task of collecting evidence from relevant areas of systems, including:

    o   Running memory

    o   Log files

    o   Network connections

    o   Running software processes

    Depending on the severity of the incident, it might take a few hours to several days to reveal details of the incident occurrence. The corresponding phase of evidence collection relates to its analysis by the incident response team using suitable tools. Such analysis helps in ascertaining details of the incident, as in its impact on organizational infrastructure resources, apart from identifying involved systems as well as detecting possible deletion of confidential data.

- **Containment:** Organizations take measures to limit the ability of threat actors to continue compromising other network resources, communicating with command-and-control infrastructures, or exfiltrating confidential data. The corresponding containment strategies range from locking down ports and IP addresses to a firewall or simply removing the network cable from the back of an infected machine. This indicates that the selection of a containment strategy for an incident depends on its overall uniqueness.

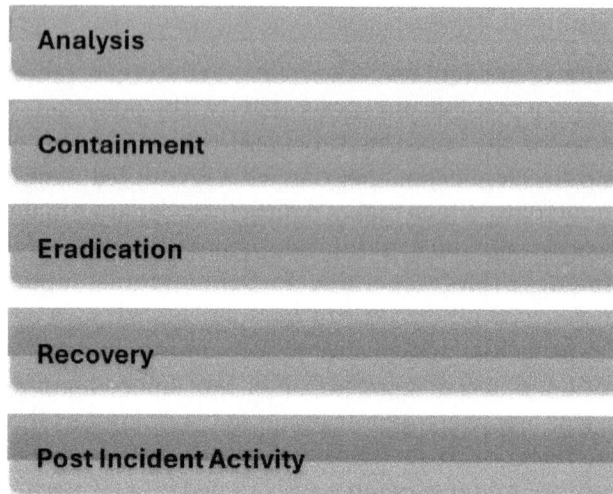

Analysis

Containment

Eradication

Recovery

Post Incident Activity

Figure 1.14: Stages of the incident response process

- **Eradication:** The organizational incident response team removes the threat actor from the impacted network. For instance, in a malware infection, the incident response team can run an enhanced anti-malware solution. This is in terms of reinstalling the operating system on the infected machines. Furthermore, removing or changing compromised user accounts can be effective for required incident response. After the identification of exploited vulnerabilities, vendor patches are applied or software updates are installed to prevent the recurrence of the incident.

- **Recovery:** The relevant recovery activities of incident response are closely aligned with the business continuity or disaster recovery plans of the organization. The process of recovery includes reinstalling the operating system on the concerned devices. The event of data deletion from a device requires its data restoration from backups. The incident response team further proceeds with auditing their existing user and administrator accounts. The incident response team launches a comprehensive vulnerability scan to ensure the removal of all vulnerabilities from infected systems.

- **Post-incident activity:** The range of post-incident activity includes a complete review of all the actions taken during the incident. The incident response team reviews the overall pros and cons of an incident occurrence. This highlights tasks and actions that have a positive or negative impact on the outcome of incident response. The documentation of actions during IR is crucial in the event of including a detailed description of all involved technical jargon. Finally, organizational personnel should update their own incident response processes with the outcome of the incident occurrence to tackle similar incidents in the future.

Conclusion

We have talked about various sections of digital forensic investigation in this chapter. We have introduced how the digital forensic investigation is being executed, its process, methodology besides various kinds of digital evidence, and its preservation and processing. This is further to how digital evidence ultimately becomes permissible for presenting at a court of law.

The upcoming chapter will detail a discussion on the various types of digital forensics and their applications.

Join our book's Discord space

Join the book's Discord Workspace for Latest updates, Offers, Tech happenings around the world, New Release and Sessions with the Authors:

https://discord.bpbonline.com

CHAPTER 2
Role of Digital Forensics in Enterprises

Introduction

This chapter will delve deeper to realize the critical role of digital forensics across enterprises of different business sectors. Modern-day organizations are increasingly becoming dependent on digital devices for their storage, management, and retrieval of data. The engagement of digital forensics for relevant cybersecurity Incident management across the organization results in the generation of appropriate results that can encourage them to strengthen their security posture as per the consistently evolving threat landscape. This changing threat landscape across the digital world results in the increasing importance of consistently bolstering enterprise security by integrating efficient threat intelligence. The effective response to cybersecurity incidents across the organization requires the dedicated application of digital forensics tactics by associated investigators. The effective mitigation of cyber threats, therefore, requires the effective deployment of digital forensics processes along with suitable incident response procedures. The relevance of digital forensics has evolved from solely focusing on the investigation of cybercrimes to the investigation of cybersecurity incident management across the organization. The increasing relevance of digital forensics in the modern era relates to its ability to recover data alongside threat identification and assurance of legal compliance. The constant application of digital forensics in modern days relates to securing the digital world holistically.

Structure

The chapter covers the following topics:

- Overview of digital forensics
- Enhancing security posture
- Case studies of digital forensics
- Challenges and future trends of digital forensics
- Incident investigation
- Digital evidence preservation
- Threat detection
- Threat mitigation
- Compliance and legal requirements
- Business continuity
- Continuous improvement

Objectives

The current chapter progresses by focusing on relevant learning outcomes that aim to shed light on different aspects of digital forensics from the relevant organizational benefits. The chapter attempts to assess the concept of digital forensics and its key components to identify its role in incident response and thereby enhance the security posture of an organization, along with considering multiple case studies of digital forensics applications. The chapter proceeds to analyze relevant challenges and future trends in digital forensics. This chapter proceeds with a detailed analysis of the incident investigation, alongside focusing on effective evidence preservation. The chapter presents adequate descriptions to understand threat detection and its effective mitigation. The chapter continues with analyses related to areas of digital forensics, including compliance and legal requirements, business continuity, and continuous improvement. The overall chapter encourages a detailed understanding of digital forensics in light of increasing cybercrime incidents across different business sectors that result in significant financial loss to concerned organizations.

Overview of digital forensics

The concept of digital forensics is the overall process of collecting digital evidence from the digital crime scene and, thereby, analyzing it to reveal underlying insights. The importance of digital forensics for modern-day crimes relates to the extensive usage of digital devices by individuals in their daily lives. The underlying provision of digital forensics relates to handling digital evidence carefully to ensure its appropriate admissibility in the Court of Law. For instance, the investigation of a data breach from a database of an organization relates to engagement in the digital forensics process. Furthermore, the legal investigation of a murder relates to analyzing the digital devices of the victims, such as smartphones and laptops, to identify clues behind the murder.

Key components of digital forensics

Digital forensics emerged from forensic science, which implies processing digital evidence appropriately. This relates to its **key components,** including the **Identification**, **Collection**, **Analysis,** and **Reporting** of valuable digital information from digital evidence recovered from cybercrime spots (*Figure 2.1*).

Identification	• Evidences related to digital crime • Storage Media, Hardware, Operating System (OS), Network and Application
Collection	• Preservation of Digital Evidence • Ensuring Integrity Preservation of Digital Evidence
Analysis	• Assessment of Collected Evidence • Tracing possible path of crime occurence
Reporting	• Efficient Documentation of Digital Evidence • Paves path for case study in future

Figure 2.1: Steps of digital forensics

The phase of **Identification** relates to spotting evidence that is directly associated with digital crime. These include different types of storage media along with hardware devices, **Operating Systems (OS)**, networks, and applications. The subsequent phase of **Collection** relates to the preservation of spotted digital evidence by ensuring its integrity preservation till presented in the Court of Law. This phase further relates to the retrieval of underlying digital data from the collected digital devices by Digital Forensic Investigators. This requires legal approval by a concerned team of Digital Forensic Investigators. The consequent phase of **analysis** relates to assessing the collected digital evidence by the deployment of relevant tools to trace the occurrence of cybercrime. The last phase of **Reporting** is critical for overall digital forensics investigation as it involves documenting the findings of the digital investigation to be produced in the Court of Law to seek justice for the victim.

Role of digital forensics in incident response

The occurrence of digital crime is considered a cybersecurity incident, irrespective of its place of occurrence. This implies that digital crime can take place in the organizational environment of a reputable company as well as the personal space of an individual *(Figure 2.2).*

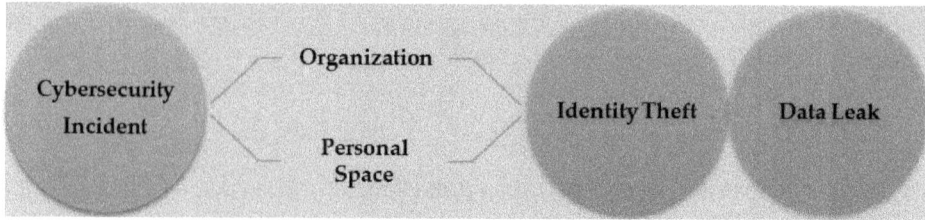

Figure 2.2: Cybersecurity incident

The concept of digital forensics relates to the investigation of digital evidence and, thereby, the reconstruction of cybersecurity incidents appropriately. This relates to applying the different components of digital forensics *(Figure 2.1)* to proceed with addressing the cybersecurity incident. The steady progress of digital investigation results in the identification of root causes of cybersecurity incident occurrence. This relates to the ability of Digital Forensic Investigators to reconstruct cybersecurity incidents using the aid of collected digital evidence. The generation of effective results from a digital investigation results in supporting cybersecurity incident response along with possible legal action in the future. The outcome of the digital investigation of a cybersecurity incident relates to the detection, investigation, and response to cyber threats appropriately. Furthermore, from the point of view of cybercrime, the identification of cybercriminals is simplified by proceeding with a fruitful digital forensic investigation under the guidance of digital forensic experts.

Digital forensics incident response

The concept of DFIR relates to effectively combining two fields of cybersecurity, **digital forensics (DF)** and **incident response (IR)** *(Figure 2.3)*. This thereby aids in streamlining planned threat response along with evidence preservation against cyber criminals.

Figure 2.3: DFIR

Separate conduction of digital forensics and incident response can result in interfering with their generated outcomes. Specifically, incident response can result in integrity loss of digital evidence due to a lack of scope for its careful handling. Furthermore, conducting digital forensics as a standalone procedure can result in ineffective responses to cybersecurity incidents. However, combining these two processes results in effective threat prevention along with no evidence of tampering during threat resolution.

Enhancing security posture

The appropriate conduct of digital investigation results in generating valuable insights into underlying vulnerabilities. This results in effectively strengthening the overall digital security posture of an organization. The components ensuring security posture enhancement of an organization relate to considering multiple areas such as **Security Controls**, **System Monitoring**, **Incident Response**, **Employee Awareness Training**, and **Compliance** *(Figure 2.4)*.

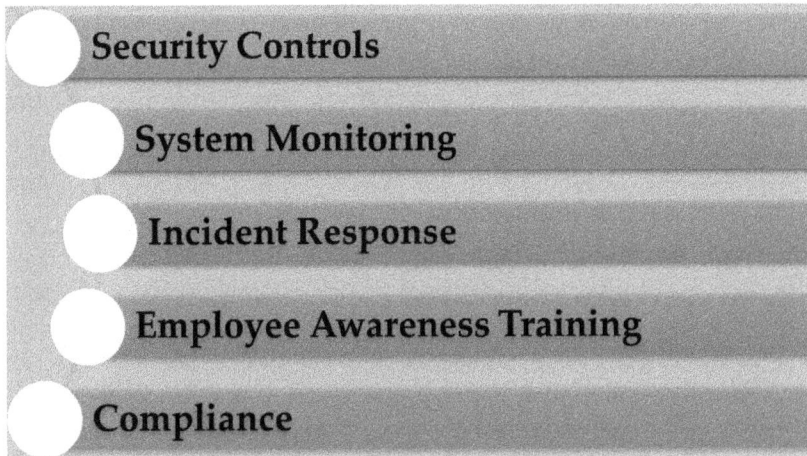

Figure 2.4: Components of organizational digital security posture

Security Controls are a crucial part of cybersecurity due to their being effective mechanisms to prevent, detect, and thereby reduce the scope of cyberattack occurrence. The occurrence of a cyberattack on an organization encourages the concerned organization to utilize the findings of the investigation to update security controls effectively. Consistent **System Monitoring** encourages the quick detection of potential cyberattacks on an organization. This is furthered by the threat intelligence gathered during the investigation of a cybersecurity incident. The application of effective skills and competencies by the **Incident Response Team** of an organization results in minimizing the impact of an incident on the organization significantly. The long-term experience of the members of an Incident Response Team to effectively address a cybersecurity incident leads to appropriate data security of modern-day organizations as per the consistently evolving threat landscape. The commencement of a cyberattack on the organization often begins with the unsuspecting and innocent mindset of employees. This requires them to undergo **Employee Awareness Training** to identify potential signs of a cyberattack quickly. The concerned awareness training can focus on a detailed analysis of emerging threats that target disrupting the digital infrastructures of organizations. This results in enhancing the capability of identifying cyberattacks by the employees of an organization. The effective strengthening of security posture relates to maintaining the trust level of customers and thereby complying with the regulations of data security.

Case studies of digital forensics

The following are some case studies of digital forensics:

- **Pegasus spyware scandal:** The year 2021 saw India get engaged in a controversy about the widespread usage of Pegasus Spyware. The dedicated group of digital forensic experts teamed up to play a crucial role in investigating these allegations about unauthorized surveillance of individuals by proceeding to analyze their mobile devices and thereby trace the presence of spyware within those devices. This case study of digital forensics demonstrated the sheer importance of deploying digital forensics to timely uncover the potential and sophisticated cyber espionage activities. The outcome of this case study further highlighted the importance of maintaining cyber hygiene by individuals in the modern day.

- **IPL spot-fixing scandal:** The digital investigation of the **Indian Premier League (IPL)** spot-fixing scandal of 2013 related to assessing electronic evidence and recovering data from it. The digital forensic investigators proceeded with identifying the individuals involved in the match-fixing along with unlawful betting practices by examining their smartphones, logs of phone calls, and text messages, apart from financial transactions. Digital forensics played a vital role in establishing the underlying communication networks and thereby revealing the complexity of the scandal in the Court of Law.

Challenges and future trends of digital forensics

The evolving threat landscape of modern days indicates the implication of multiple challenges that attempt to hamper the progress of digital forensics investigations. However, the rapid development of technology can ensure the emergence of relevant trends in digital forensics that can boost its effectiveness in reducing the rate of cybercrime *(Figure 2.5)*.

The challenges are as follows:

- **Encrypted data:** The presence of encrypted data within digital evidence, such as devices and networks, results in difficulty for digital forensics. This is in terms of forensic investigators facing critical issues in collecting evidence from crime scenes. This requires additional effort in applying decryption tools and techniques to recover the data from digital evidence.

- **Data destruction:** The possible destruction of digital evidence by the accused can result in challenges for forensic investigators. The process of digital evidence destruction relates to wiping data alongside physically damaging the digital evidence.

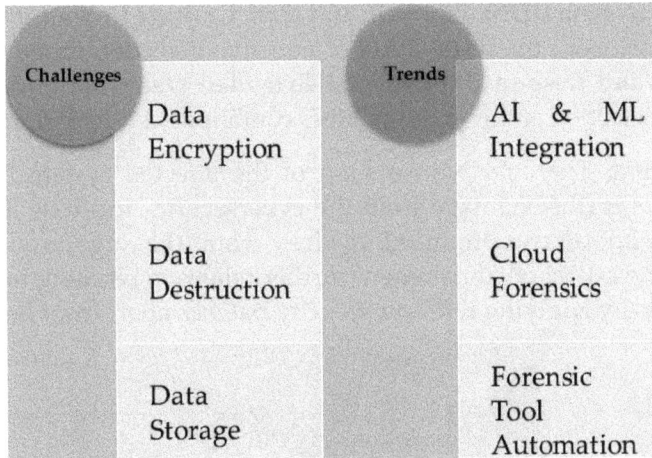

Figure 2.5: *Challenges and future trends of digital forensics*

The future trends are as follows:

- **Integration of AI and ML into digital forensics:** The seamless integration of **artificial intelligence (AI)** and **machine learning (ML)** within digital forensics effectively automates complex tasks, thereby enhancing the overall accuracy of an investigation.

- **Cloud forensics:** The increasing demand for cloud data storage across the organization results in the increasing importance of conducting cloud forensics in the event of a cybersecurity incident. The requirement of involving a cloud environment while conducting a digital investigation relates to facing multiple challenges. These challenges include data volatility, multi-tenant architecture, and jurisdictional issues.

Incident investigation

The target of a timely and effective response to cybersecurity incidents in an organization relates to the identification of root causes. For instance, preventing the recurrence of data breaches within an organization relates to identifying possible exploitation of existing vulnerabilities by adversaries. Such insights are effective for strengthening the security posture of an organization alongside the prevention of incident occurrence and recurrence. Appropriately responding to cybersecurity incidents results in protecting the reputation of an organization within its operating sector. The relevant stages of incident investigation are listed as follows:

- **Detection and identification:** The identification of an incident relates to determining the occurrence of an incident and thereby gathering initial information about its nature. The detection of incidents relates to using multiple monitoring systems such as **Security Information and Event Management (SIEM) Systems, Intrusion**

Detection System (IDS), Firewall, and **Data Leakage Prevention (DLP) software**. This is apart from the installation of effective detection tools, namely **Endpoint Detection and Response (EDR)** and **Extended Detection and Response (XDR)** for rapid detection along with seamless containment *(Figure 2.6)*.

- **Containment:** The effective isolation of the affected system from the network prevents its further damage from the cybersecurity incident. This relates to the disconnection of compromised devices from the organizational network of devices. The aspect of containment further relates to resisting further occurrences of incidents by applying relevant security patches apart from firewall rules.

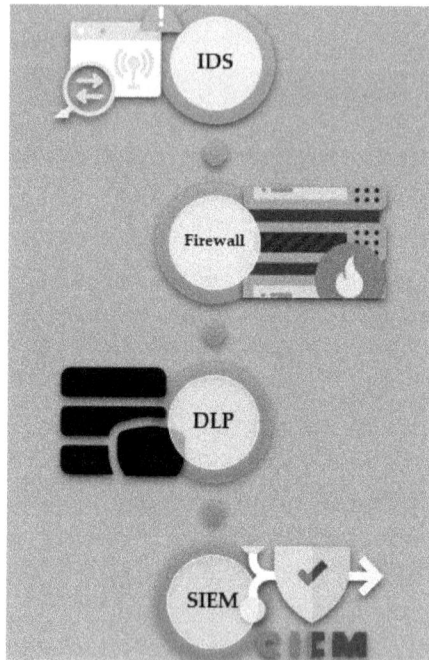

Figure 2.6: Monitoring systems

- **Eradication:** The timely cause identification of an incident is crucial to prevent future occurrences of similar incidents. The common causes of cybersecurity incidents include **malware attacks, vulnerability exploitation,** and **insider threats**. Contextually, monitoring systems detect insider threats and encourage detailed investigation in terms of behavior analysis. The successful root cause identification of vulnerabilities leads to a corresponding procedure for patching vulnerabilities effectively.

- **Recovery:** The process of recovery relates to the restoration of compromised devices and re-integrating them within the organizational network. This relates to verifying the functionality and security of devices prior to positioning them within the network.

- **Post-incident activity:** The importance of conducting Post-Incident Activity relates to a detailed analysis of the incident and thereby documenting the findings. This relates to the effective implementation of measures to prevent the recurrence of the incident. This relates to **policy updating, enhancement of security measures,** and **conducting awareness training to prevent incident recurrence**.

Digital evidence preservation

The primary requirement of evidence preservation relates to maintaining its admissibility in the Court of Law. This relates to maintaining the integrity of the digital evidence throughout the duration of legal proceedings. The appropriate integrity preservation of digital evidence results in the facilitation of accurate analysis. Maintaining the consistency of digital evidence leads to its supporting investigative findings. This relates to the appropriate preservation of digital evidence as per definite steps. The overall process of preserving digital evidence relates to considering the constant expansion of the digital realm in modern days and thereby proportionately increasing the amount of digital data. This justifies the importance of maintaining a detailed plan for handling digital evidence by the investigators. The process of digital evidence preservation relates to multiple stages that are listed as follows:

- **Identification and collection:** The source identification of digital evidence from the cybersecurity scene relates to all the digital devices present in that scene. This implies a wide range of digital devices such as **computers**, **laptops**, **smartphones**, **storage media**, etc., along with specific entities such as network logs *(Figure 2.7)*. The subsequent phase of evidence identification is its collection by the digital investigators to proceed with the remaining stages of forensic investigation. The collection of forensic evidence relates to adopting multiple forensic tools by the concerned investigators. These forensic tools include **FTK Imager** for imaging the evidence and **EnCase** for acquiring data from digital devices.

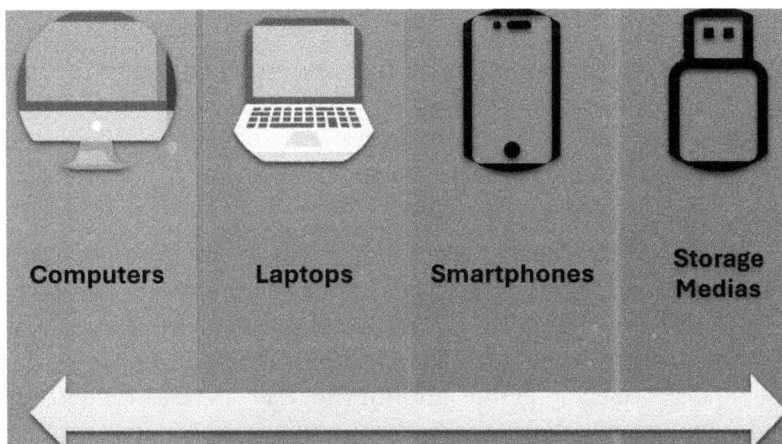

Figure 2.7: Potential tangible sources of digital evidence

- **Imaging and hashing:** The importance of imaging digital evidence relates to its vulnerability of easily altered or copied. This results in their quickly being compromised and losing credibility for presenting in the court of law. The risks of compromise for digital evidence include suspects intentionally deleting data from the evidence. Furthermore, intentional malware attacks can lead to the alteration or encryption of data within the digital evidence. This justifies the importance of imaging and hashing digital evidence before considering it for detailed analysis. The phase of image creation of digital evidence encourages the concerned team of digital investigators to use the hardware, a **write blocker**. This encourages the facilitation of the legal defensibility of a forensic image in the court of law. The entire process of imaging digital evidence is carried out using **FTK Imager** and **Magnet RAM Capture**. Amongst these, FTK Imager is associated with creating images of local hard drives, USB drives, and individual files from different sources of digital evidence. On the other side, **magnet RAM capture** relates to capturing the physical memory of digital evidence. The process imaging is closely followed by the generation of cryptographic hashes such as **Message Digest 5 (MD5)** and **Secure Hash Algorithm 1 (SHA-1)**.

- **Secure storage:** The completion of imaging and hashing of digital evidence encourages safe and secure storage by the concerned team of digital investigators. The required secure storage of digital evidence relates to selecting a controlled environment. This further relates to maintaining its integrity and thereby admissibility in the court of law. The integrity assurance of digital evidence relates to its encrypted storage to protect it from unauthorized access. The controlled environment for secure storage of digital evidence resembles **scrambled storage**, **special locks**, **fingerprint locks,** and **alarm systems**.

- **Documentation:** This phase of evidence preservation is crucial as it deploys a **Chain of Custody (CoC)**. The importance of maintaining the CoC of digital evidence relates to its utilization of multiple descriptive attributes for the digital evidence.

- **Compliance with legal standards:** The assured compliance of digital evidence preservation with relevant legal standards includes **ISO 27037:2012**. The underlying provisions of this standard relate to identifying, collecting, acquiring, and preserving digital evidence to ensure its credibility and thereby appropriate for admissibility in the Court of Law.

- **Regular audits:** The regular auditing of digital evidence during its preservation relates to monitoring its CoC minutely to identify potential instances of unauthorized access. The prime objective of regular audits relates to the accurate and complete filing of the CoC for digital evidence. Apart from the assessment of CoC, the process of regular auditing further includes analyzing access logs of digital evidence to timely identify the potential occurrence of unauthorized access. The phase of regular audit by the experts includes integrity checking of digital evidence. This phase relates to comparing current hash values with the hash values recorded during the phase of digital evidence acquisition. The regular auditing of digital evidence involves assessing additional environmental factors such as temperature, humidity, and potential data corruption risk.

Threat detection

The detailed process of threat detection relates to the undertaking of the following precautions:

- **Establishment of baseline:** The establishment of a baseline for cybersecurity threat detection relates to the undertaking of multiple steps. These steps include **risk assessment and threat modelling, data collection** for threat intelligence, **defining thresholds,** and **implementation of monitoring tools** *(Figure 2.8)*. The importance of threat detection further relates to unmasking fraud and financial offences within a company.

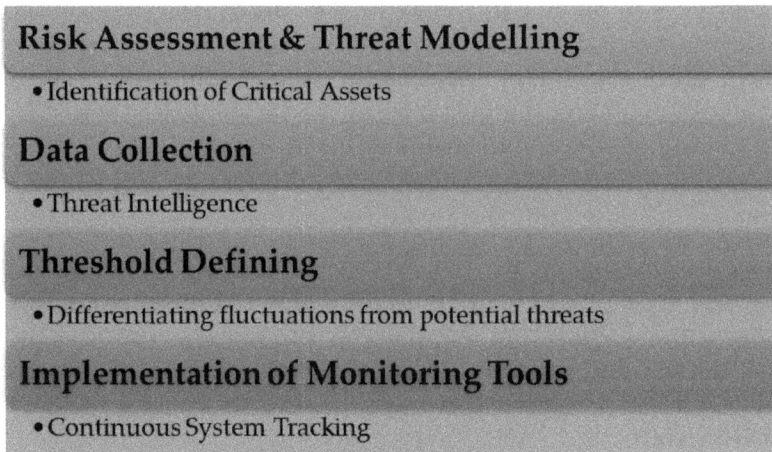

Risk Assessment & Threat Modelling
- Identification of Critical Assets

Data Collection
- Threat Intelligence

Threshold Defining
- Differentiating fluctuations from potential threats

Implementation of Monitoring Tools
- Continuous System Tracking

Figure 2.8: Steps of baseline establishment

- **Implementation of threat detection tools:** The efficient implementation of Threat Detection Tools relates to maintaining robust cybersecurity by an organization. The key tools for threat detection include IDS, **SIEM Tool, EDR, Firewall**, and **TI platforms**. Apart from such tactics, engaging in effective **User and Entity Behaviour Analytics (UEBA)**.

- **Threat intelligence (TI) integration:** The timely detection of threats at the organization is crucial to initiate their mitigation procedure along with limiting their adverse impact on the organizational infrastructure. This relates to quickly identifying anomalies in the traffic and thereby isolating the **Indicators of Compromise (IoC)** at the earliest possible. The aspect of the proactive approach leads the incident management team to undertake pre-emptive measures and thereby foil the attempt of adversary.

- **Anomaly-based detection:** The procedure of anomaly-based detection relates to timely identifying deviations of traffic from normal patterns of behavior. The benefit of this threat detection procedure, as opposed to the Signature-based detection process, relates to seamlessly detecting unknown threats. This implies the protection of organizational networks from emerging threats of malware attacks that can seamlessly bypass Signature-based detection systems.

- **Real-time alerts:** The benefits of real-time alert generation encourage the containment of threats prior to their escalating to the next level. The outcome of this relates to reducing the overall window of exploitation for the adversaries. This, in turn, reduces the impact of potential security breaches on the market reputation of a company. This benefit catalyzes the overall security posture of an organization in response to a consistently evolving threat landscape.

- **Incident response integration:** The observed outcome of incident response tends to be an appropriate source of threat intelligence that can be utilized to tackle the occurrence of similar incidents in the future. The application of a unified approach by the incident response team leads to effective responses to incidents and their quick resolution. The incident response integration fosters enhanced communication among the members of the Incident Response Team due to the timely sharing of critical information. This aspect combines both threat detection and response efforts that encourage organizations to streamline their security process.

- **Continuous improvement**: The fast-evolving threat landscape relates to an increasingly wide range of emerging risks such as **Ransomware Resurgence**, **IoT Insecurity,** and **AI-powered threats**. This encourages enhanced threat detection capabilities by the Incident Response Team of reputed organizations. The continuous improvement further leads the security systems to adapt to emerging threats efficiently.

Threat mitigation

The process of threat mitigation tends to proceed as per the following steps:

- **Risk assessment:** The process of risk assessment leads to the evaluation of organizational cybersecurity defenses as a top-down approach. The phase of risk assessment leads to the identification of potential vulnerabilities, threats, and weaknesses within the organization to encourage their fast resolution prior to exploitation by adversaries. The importance of risk assessment relates to safeguarding the intellectual properties of a company to encourage its efficient market performance. The robust risk assessment for effective threat mitigation relates to the completion of relevant stages, including **Identification of Assets and Threats**, **Vulnerability Assessment**, **Impact Determination**, and **Likelihood Evaluation** *(Figure 2.9).*

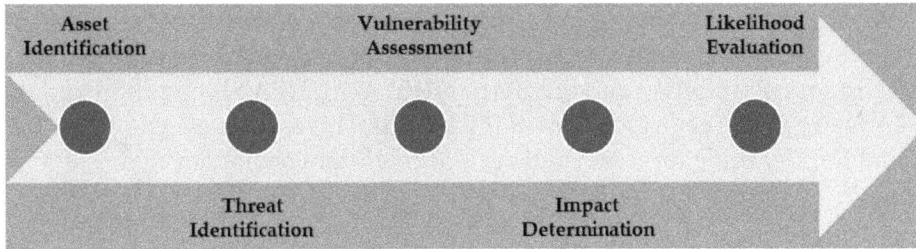

Figure 2.9: *Stages of risk assessment*

- **Implementation of security controls:** The effective implementation of security controls leads to restricting unauthorized access to sensitive information. This leads to their security from external and internal threats. This results in minimizing or eliminating risks to the possible extent.

- **User education and training:** The end users of the organizational network are the employees required to change their behavior by using common sense and maintaining awareness. The tendency to introduce change in the behavior of employees can result in the generation of temporary resistance from them. However, the long-term benefit of resisting employee misconduct and related technological misuse.

- **Incident response planning:** Effective incident response planning leads to reducing the impact of security events. The outcome of this relates to limiting operational, financial, and reputational damage to an organization.

- **Continuous monitoring:** The concept of continuous monitoring leads to facilitating proactive threat mitigation. This is by identifying potential vulnerabilities and suspicious activities well in advance of their escalating into critical security incidents.

- **Vulnerability management:** This aspect relates to identifying and fixing potential security issues well in advance of their transforming into critical cybersecurity concerns for the company. The practice of vulnerability management is associated with the prevention of potential data breaches, thereby ensuring reputational benefit for the company.

- **Data protection:** The aspect relates to implementing multiple strategies and tools to secure access to sensitive data of an organization. The assured data protection using firewalls, encryption, and vulnerability patching leads to the prevention of cyberattacks well in advance of their occurrence. The tendency of an organization to classify its data according to its importance for business objectives leads to the first stage of data protection.

- **Policy and compliance:** The assured policy and compliance ensure effective threat mitigation by establishing an efficient framework for security practices. The concept of policy and compliance relates to adhering to laws, regulations, and industry standards. Modern-day companies are required to comply with multiple regulations, such as the **General Data Protection Regulation (GDPR)**, the **Health Insurance Portability and Accountability Act (HIPAA),** and the **Payment Card Industry Data Security Standard (PCI-DSS)**. This assures effective data protection and thereby mitigates specific threats such as data breaches.

- **Third-party risk management:** The benefit of third-party risk management for effective threat mitigation relates to in-advance identification of risks. Third-party risk management is assigned to entities such as vendors, service providers, and contractors. The ability of the third-party vendors to comply with the business objectives of a company ensures parallelly comply with its security standards and regulatory requirements.

Compliance and legal requirements

The compliance and legal requirements of organizations relate to the following different stages:

- **Collection and preservation of digital evidence:** The process of digital forensics is closely associated with carefully handling digital evidence. The overall process of handling digital evidence relates to its collection and preservation without compromising its integrity *(Figure 2.10)*. This is crucial as integrity loss of digital evidence results in its inadmissibility in the Court of Law. The compliance and legal requirements for handling digital evidence as part of digital forensics relate to using specialized tools for imaging and underlying data extraction. The tendency to use a write blocker to reduce the scope of evidence tampering during its imaging further ensures adherence to compliance. The consistently increasing proliferation of technology and its integration within modern businesses leads to its spontaneous inclusion within legal matters.

- **Incident response:** The occurrence of a security breach and its identification in the form of a cybersecurity incident requires the application of the digital forensic procedure. Suspecting cybersecurity incidents leads to the isolation of concerned digital evidence from the network of digital devices *(Figure 2.10)*. The process of incident response relates to identifying the scope and impact of a breach, parallel to identifying an **Incident of Compromise (IoC)**. The relevance relates to identifying loopholes within existing security frameworks of the organization that need to be tackled effectively.

- **Regulatory compliance:** The underlying provisions of regulatory compliance relate to protecting sensitive data and thereby reporting data breaches to relevant supervisory authorities within a stipulated timeframe. This is apart from initiating an effective incident response process to minimize the impact of data breaches on the reputation of the company within its operating market. These incident response processes further relate to fulfilling provisions of regulations such as GDPR and HIPAA.

- **Legal admissibility:** The legal admissibility of digital evidence relates to its appreciated collection and preservation as per ongoing legal standards. This relates to the collection and preservation of digital evidence as per forensically sound techniques, such as using CoC. The tendency to prepare a detailed report relates to explaining the findings from the analysis and thereby stating the processes used for progressing the analysis.

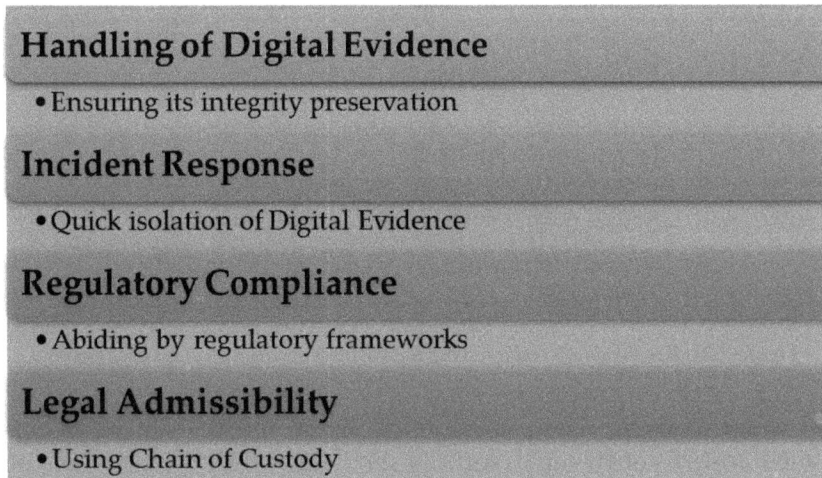

Handling of Digital Evidence

- Ensuring its integrity preservation

Incident Response

- Quick isolation of Digital Evidence

Regulatory Compliance

- Abiding by regulatory frameworks

Legal Admissibility

- Using Chain of Custody

Figure 2.10: Compliance and legal requirements of digital forensics

Business continuity

The relevance of business continuity for organizations is stated as follows:

- **Rapid incident response:** The application of the digital forensics procedure ensures a quick response to cybersecurity incidents and thereby limits the possibility of financial losses and operational disruptions *(Figure 2.11)*. This represents the agility of digital forensics that contributes to the required business continuity of the concerned organization. The detailed analysis of cybersecurity Incidents from the perspective of digital forensics leads to the formulation of multiple preventive measures that can protect an organization from the occurrence of similar incidents in the future.

- **Data recovery:** The competency of digital forensics experts extends to the quick recovery of lost and corrupted data from the concerned digital devices. This is relevant for the concerned businesses in terms of reducing their downtime appropriately *(Figure 2.11)*. The application of digital forensics techniques for data recovery leads to the recovery of accurate data that can catalyze the fast resumption within the affected organizations. Alongside data breaches, the occurrence of data loss further increases the financial loss of a company. Thus, effective recovery of data can protect the affected organization from facing such extended financial loss.

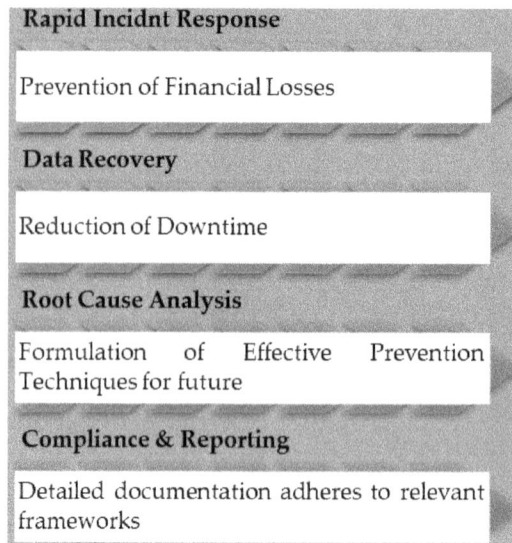

Figure 2.11: Benefits of digital forensics for business continuity of an organization

- **Root cause analysis:** The procedure of digital forensics leads to engaging in a detailed analysis of the cybersecurity incident and thereby ensures performance root cause analysis. The benefit of this aspect results in the formulation of an effective systematic approach that can encourage this organization to handle the outcome of the incident and mitigate similar occurrences of the incident in the future *(Figure 2.11)*.

- **Compliance and reporting:** The application of the digital forensics procedure leads to a detailed investigation of a cybersecurity incident along with its appropriate documentation. This demonstrates effective compliance with multiple compliance frameworks, including GDPR and HIPAA *(Figure 2.11)*. The occurrence of a cybersecurity incident within an organization requires the creation of detailed reports about the impact of the incident and making it to the associated stakeholders. These stakeholders include external regulatory bodies, customers, and internal management committees.

Continuous improvement

The continuous improvement for an organization relates to the following aspects:

- **Lesson from cybersecurity incident:** The occurrence of a cybersecurity incident within an organization implies the possible presence of loopholes within its existing infrastructures *(Figure 2.12)*. The detailed investigation of the cybersecurity incident from the perspective of digital forensics relates to pinpointing such shortcomings and mitigating them at the earliest possible. This thereby leads to continuous security improvement of the digital infrastructures of a company.

- **Proactive threat mitigation:** The benefit of digital forensic analysis relates to timely uncovering the vulnerabilities along with potential threats that can result in significant issues. This leads to businesses undertaking pre-emptive measures and thereby enhancing their overall digital security posture *(Figure 2.12)*. The target of proactive threat mitigation for an organization relates to constructing a proficient digital forensics squad.

- **Policy updating:** The immediate outcome of digital forensics analysis results in updating the policies of the organization. An instance, detecting possible attempts of data theft in an organization relates to the creation of rules in the SIEM tool as per the observed IoC from the digital forensics investigation. The target of enhancing the security resilience of a company relates to updating internal processes in terms of their alignment with industrial best practices of the concerned operating sector *(Figure 2.12)*.

- **Employee training and awareness:** The occurrence of a cybersecurity incident within an organization relates to a lack of security awareness amongst its employees *(Figure 2.12)*. This encourages them to undergo detailed training sessions to gather knowledge about the latest security threats. This relates to illustrating real-world case scenarios that can encourage these individuals to adhere to the updated security policy of the organization. The outcome of such training initiatives results in enhancing their capability to recognize potential threats while working with the digital infrastructures of their employer organization.

Lesson from Cybersecurity Incident	• Plugging existing loophole
Proactive Threat Mitigation	• Timely uncovering of vulnerabilities and threats
Policy Updating	• Aligning with Security Best Practices of Operating Industry
Employee Awareness & Training	• Enhancing knowledge of employees about latest cybersecurity threats

Figure 2.12: Influence of digital forensics for continuous improvement of an organization

Conclusion

This chapter progresses with a deeper look at the concept of digital forensics from an enterprise perspective. The detailed analysis of this chapter indicated the relevant benefits of digital forensics that encourage compliance of organizations with relevant data security frameworks. The chapter further presented a detailed analysis of cybersecurity incident management across organizations from the viewpoint of digital forensics. The chapter indicated that digital forensics plays a vital role in the continuous development of an organization as per the prevailing security best practices within its background operating sector.

The upcoming chapter will proceed with an expanse of digital forensics, implying its crucial role in the digital security of modern-day businesses.

Join our book's Discord space

Join the book's Discord Workspace for Latest updates, Offers, Tech happenings around the world, New Release and Sessions with the Authors:

https://discord.bpbonline.com

CHAPTER 3
Expanse of Digital Forensics

Introduction

Digital forensics gradually originated from traditional computer forensics due to the increasing dependence of modern businesses on a wide range of digital devices. The materials present within digital devices gain an identity as digital evidence from a cybersecurity perspective. The expanse of digital forensics includes its presence across different areas of digital operation, including devices and networks. The fast integration of digital transformation across different areas of business operations leads to the consistently increasing importance of digital forensics. This is because of the extensive adoption of Internet technology by companies to manage their businesses and client requirements. The importance of digital forensics further relates to incident responses and compliance auditing for the reputational benefit of modern organizations that prioritize securing adequate market share within their operating environment.

Structure

The chapter covers the following topics:

- Overview of digital forensics
- Traditional digital forensics
- Evolution of digital forensics

- Digital forensics and its fundamentals
- Digital forensics process and methodologies
- Tools and techniques for digital forensics
- Applications of digital forensics in various fields
- Emerging trends and technologies in digital forensics
- Future developments of digital forensics
- Case studies on digital forensics

Objectives

The current chapter on the expanse of digital forensics relates to delving deeper into the world of digital forensics. The chapter presents details about the evolution of digital forensics by including relevant instances of technological advances. The detailed analysis of digital forensics indicates that its growth and development relate to the consistent integration of the latest technological advancements. The chapter presents detailed processes and methodologies of digital forensics. These methodologies relate to focusing on error-free assessment of digital evidence and, thereby, generation of expected results. The chapter includes details of different tools and techniques that are readily adopted by digital forensic investigators to complete an investigation appropriately. The chapter states details of applying digital forensics across various fields. This relates to the extensive adoption of digital devices by individuals for their personal and professional requirements. The steady progress of this chapter relates to different branches of digital forensics, along with emerging trends and technologies in digital forensics. The chapter proceeds to include relevant insights about different branches of digital forensics, such as computer forensics, mobile device forensics, and network forensics. The chapter includes relevant challenges and future directions in the expanse of digital forensics. The inclusion of relevant case studies indicates the increasing importance of digital forensics for modern-day organizations that are required to consistently focus on their business and operational progress within the surrounding market.

Overview of digital forensics

Digital forensics is a branch of cybersecurity that focuses on the recovery and investigation of evidence present in digital devices that are recovered from the cybercrime scene. The importance of digital forensics is closely associated with upholding legal standards to the fullest extent. The acceptance of digital forensics relates to specific stakeholders in the industry, including law enforcement agencies in criminal and civil cases, and **incident response** (**IR**) teams of organizations. The former uses digital forensics to investigate digital evidence as an effective aid to support criminal and civil cases. The range of legal cases that require considering the benefits of digital forensics includes murder trials and civil cases. On the other side, the IR teams of organizations are required to quickly respond to cyberattacks and thereby indulge in a detailed analysis of the digital evidence to enhance the scope of **threat intelligence** (**TI**) for the concerned organizations.

Traditional digital forensics

Digital forensics tends to be a synonym of computer forensics, and it has expanded to a detailed investigation of all devices that are capable of data storage and retrieval. The concept of digital forensics resembles the perspective of computer forensics despite having significant differences. The primary difference between computer forensics and digital forensics relates to the former being related to specific computing devices, such as computers, tablets, and mobile phones, whereas the latter resembles a wide range of digital devices, such as networking devices *(Figure 3.1)*. The success of digital forensic investigation relates to following complex and fool-proof procedures to uncover details from authentic digital evidence. The aim of digital forensic investigators relates to re-tracing the occurrence of cybercrime by following a 4-fold process, including identification, preservation, analysis, and documentation.

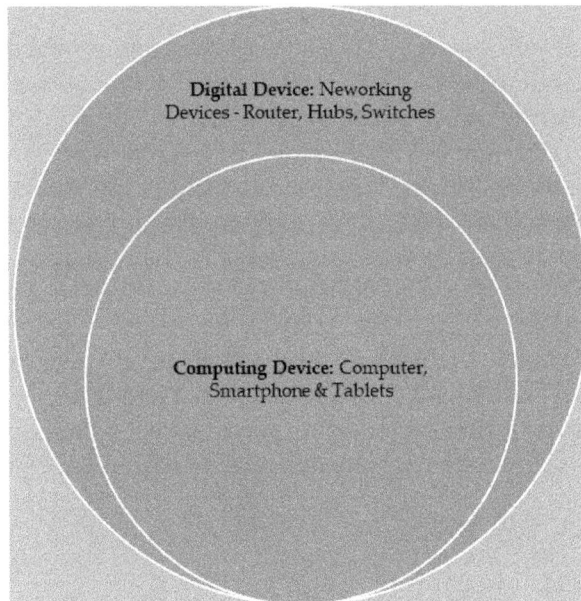

Figure 3.1: Subset representation of digital device and computing device

The concepts of digital forensics and computer forensics further differ as the former involves pinpointing the source of cyberattack and the latter limits the retrieval of data from computer devices *(Figure 3.2)*. The benefits of digital forensics relate to the deployment of different tools and techniques that can simplify the overall process and seamlessly generate the desired findings. The aspect of quickly generating results from digital forensics investigation is crucial for legal cases in terms of delivering justice to victims.

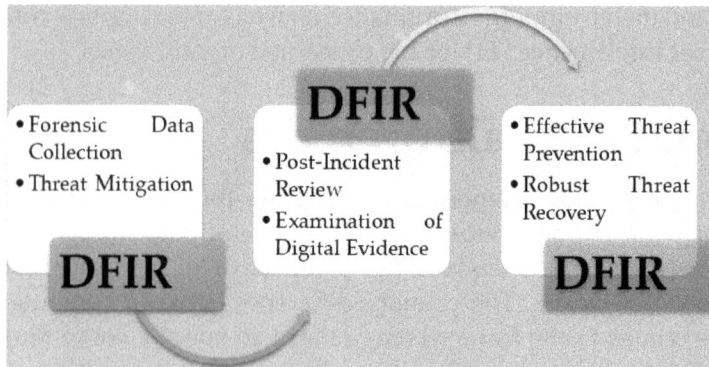

Figure 3.2: Benefits of DFIR

Importance of digital forensics in the modern world

Digital forensics is closely associated with quickly resolving cybersecurity challenges for individuals and organizations. For instance, digital forensics gained recognition as an essential security control for financial organizations. This is due to its involvement in the recovery and investigation of information and data associated with cyber incidents observed in the core application of concerned financial organizations. The reliability of a Court of Law on the digital forensics procedure relates to the involvement of a team of specialists and experts, having detailed knowledge of the process of digital forensics and types of digital devices that can be considered as digital evidence during a digital forensic investigation. The importance of digital forensics for effective law enforcement relates to deploying an effective method to analyze digital evidence from electronic devices. Digital forensics plays a crucial role in legal investigations for effective law enforcement. This is because digital forensics ensures detailed corporate investigations and national security. This is owing to its dedicated step of evidence collection from the crime scene and thereby deployment of suitable tools and techniques for their detailed analysis.

Evolution of digital forensics

The steady evolution of digital forensics relates to the early beginnings of digital forensics from traditional forensics to the digital realm. The **1970s** witnessed the emergence of digital data from mainframes and minicomputers. This evolved to the development of personal computers in the **1980s,** which related to enhancing the need for methods to investigate computer-related crimes. The digital forensics during this phase primarily focused on analyzing only personal computers to recover evidence. The increasing importance of digital devices for personal and professional usage during the **1990s** resulted in the establishment of relevant techniques along with tools for digital forensics. The relevant law enforcement organizations, along with cybersecurity experts, tend to focus on developing protocols and methodologies for the appropriate investigation of digital crimes. This was during the early 1990s, and during the late 1990s, the internet became accessible to desired users, and thus, cybercrime emerged as a major concern. Thus, digital forensics is required to face challenges associated with various crimes committed using internet facilities, such as hacking, identity theft, and online fraud. The commencement of the early 2000s relates to reputed authorities such as the **International Association of Computer Investigative Specialists (IACIS)** and the **National Institute of Standards and Technology (NIST)** initiated availing relevant guidelines and best practices for conducting digital investigations. The mid-2000s observed increased usage of mobile devices and digital media that further enhanced the scope of digital forensics. This is owing to digital forensics, which requires the extraction of digital evidence from a wide variety of digital devices, such as mobile devices, USB drives, and memory cards. The late 2000s further observed the advent of cloud computing and virtualization presented new challenges for digital forensics. This includes the decentralized nature of data storage along with the complexity of the virtual environment. The commencement of the 2010s proceeded with the explosion of big data alongside the usage of advanced technologies such as **machine learning (ML)** and **artificial intelligence (AI)** that impacted digital forensics significantly. However, such technologies further encouraged efficient analysis of large data volumes to uncover patterns and insights. The phases after the 2010s primarily focused on the evolution of the technology landscape in terms of data encryption, usage of the **Internet of Things (IoT)**, Blockchain, and other emerging technologies. The advancement of these technologies has resulted in creating both challenges and benefits for digital investigators.

The relevant milestones in the development of digital forensics include the availability of the Magnetic Media Program by the FBI in 1984. The phase between the 1980s to 1990s further witnessed the development of the **Computer Analysis and Response Team (CART)** along with the development of early forensic software tools. The aspect of professionalization in digital forensics further relates to the establishment of renowned organizations such as the **International Organization on Computer Evidence (IOCE)** in 1995. The mobile and cloud era of the 2000s to 2010s resembles the emergence of cloud forensics to tackle distributed and virtualized systems. The range of milestones in the evolution of digital forensics further included the formulation of guidelines by the NIST in the 2000s. The recent development of digital forensics resembles the application of ML for pattern recognition and anomaly detection.

The direct impact of technological advances on digital forensics includes expanding its scope of application to a wide variety of devices. This is in addition to streamlining as well as simplifying the overall process of digital forensics. The effective technological advancement led to the formulation of innovative solutions such as Forensic Case Management Systems. The benefits of using such innovations include effectively equipping investigators to tackle the impending challenges of digital forensics and ensuring the delivery of justice to victims.

Digital forensics and its fundamentals

Some of the key concepts and terminologies used in digital forensics are listed as follows:

- **Digital evidence:** The concept of digital evidence from the perspective of digital forensics relates to data having probative value that tends to be stored or transmitted in digital form. This tends to contain e-mail and documents to logs, and images. The increased dependency of modern-day individuals on digital devices leads to the creation of digital fingerprints in the form of digital evidence that needs to be collected and analyzed by experts to reveal the traces of relevant digital activity.

- **Chain of Custody (CoC):** The perspective of CoC relates to the effective handling of digital evidence from its collection from the cybercrime scene till it is presented at the Court of Law to deliver justice to victims. The CoC is a detailed logbook that tracks the overall activities performed on the digital evidence.

- **Bit-stream copy:** The integrity preservation of digital evidence is a critical requirement to ensure its admissibility in the Court of Law. This requires creating an exact replica of the collected digital device from the cybercrime scene and proceeding with its detailed analysis. This is crucial in terms of refraining from tampering with the original device.

- **Write blockers:** The use of such software during the investigation of digital evidence restricts its potential tampering and thereby loss of integrity. The relevant benefit of using Write blockers relates to the effective imaging of digital evidence without compromising its integrity.

The different types of digital evidence are stated as follows:

- **Computer-based evidence:** These are the traditional types of digital evidence that include data stored on a variety of devices such as desktops, laptops, and servers. Examples of computer-based evidence include documents, emails, and system logs.

- **Mobile device evidence:** This is the wealth of information stored within smartphones and tablets that tends to be crucial for investigations. The typical mobile device evidence includes call logs, text messages, photos and videos, and app data.

- **Network evidence:** The overall data transmitted over the networks is subject to interception and analysis. The network evidence includes packet captures, firewall logs, and **Intrusion Detection System (IDS)** logs.

- **Cloud-based evidence:** The abundant quantity of data stored across the remote cloud servers acts as Cloud-based evidence. The relevant evidence includes stored data and service logs.

- **Internet evidence:** The overall web platform acts as a source of providing a significant quantity of digital evidence. The range of evidence includes web browsing history, cookies, and social media activity.

- **Multimedia evidence:** The wide range of multimedia evidence, such as images, videos, and audio files, tends to contain a wide quantity of hidden data that can reveal vital insights for a digital forensic investigation. This requires the application of appropriate tools and techniques by the concerned forensic investigator during analysis.

- **Internet of Things (IoT) device evidence:** The increasing dependency of individuals on smart devices leads to their consideration for digital investigation. The smart devices that are a source of digital data for forensic investigation include smart home devices, wearable technology, and automotive systems.

- **Encrypted data:** The widespread tendency of data encryption across multiple digital devices acts as a challenge for forensic investigators while analyzing digital evidence. The process of assessing such encrypted data relates to its decryption by forensic investigators using suitable techniques and strategies.

- **Deleted data:** The principle of digital forensics implies that deleted files from a digital device can be seamlessly recovered by applying suitable tools and strategies. The relevant strategies and techniques for the recovery of deleted data include file carving and slack space.

The legal and ethical considerations of digital forensics relate to ensuring the admissibility of digital evidence while presenting it to the Court of Law. This is because digital evidences tend to be a crucial source of information that catalyzes the significance of a legal case. Apart from legal considerations, ethical consideration of digital evidence relates to balancing privacy and investigation needs appropriately.

Digital forensics process and methodologies

The relevant steps in the digital forensics process are listed as follows:

1. **Investigation lifecycle:** This step proceeds with incident identification and thereby response generation. The entire digital forensic process initiates with identifying resources and devices that need to be subjected to further analysis. The subsequent stage of incident identification relates to the acquisition of associated evidence and thereby its preservation for realizing further stages of digital forensic investigation. The range of digital evidence that is related to forensic processes includes laptops, smartphones, servers, and network devices.

2. **Analysis and examination:** The effective analysis and examination of digital evidence leads to the revelation of insights that can ensure delivering justice to the victim. The forensic investigator applies relevant methods for extracting, analyzing, and interpreting digital evidence. Such relevant methods for digital

investigation include reverse steganography and data carving. The process of reverse steganography relates to extracting hidden information by considering the hash or character string associated with an image. The process of deleted file recovery is recognized as data carving, and it is used to identify and retrieve deleted files from remaining traces. Some of the case studies as examples of digital forensic investigations are listed here:

- **BTK serial killer:** This infamous serial killer case in the US involved a forensic investigation of the floppy disk. This investigation led to the tracing of a computer device at the local church and thereby arrest of the killer.

- **Take down of Silk Road:** The infamous Silk Road tended to be an online black market that sold drugs, weapons, and related illegal goods. The importance of digital forensic investigation for taking down this online black market relates to tracing the flow of money and other communications through anonymous networks that were a part of this black market

3. **Reporting and legal proceedings:** The successful completion of a digital forensic analysis relates to appropriate documentation and presentation of findings. The aspect of appropriately presenting findings to the Court of Law implies ensuring their admissibility in the Court of Law. The phase of digital forensic reporting relates to considering its CoC that documents the detailed handling of the digital evidence, from its collection from the crime scene, and progressing to detailed analysis. The reporting phase of a digital forensics investigation is crucial for associated legal proceedings due to its target of tracing the occurrence of incidents. This relates to tracing a detailed chronology of concerned incidents such as data breaches, data leaks, financial crime, and cyber espionage. The overall phase of digital forensics analysis relates to applying appropriate legal standards to comply with admissibility requirements in the Court of Law. The admissibility of digital evidence in the Court of Law requires the presence of a relevant certification about its authenticity.

Tools and techniques for digital forensics

The selection of appropriate tools and techniques in digital forensics investigation relates to selecting from either open-sourced Software Tools or proprietary tools. The open-sourced software tools that can contribute to digital forensics analysis include Kali Linux, Volatility, Wireshark, Autopsy, Bulk Extractor, and Network Miner. On the other hand, the proprietary tools for digital forensics analysis include EnCase Forensic, Magnet AXIOM, Exterro, IBM QRadar SIEM and Forensics, LogRhythm, and CyberTriage. Apart from tools, the application of efficient techniques, powered by existing tools, can result in a fast generation of expected results from the concerned analysis. The range of techniques that are extensively deployed by digital forensics investigators includes reverse steganography, stochastic forensics, cross-drive analysis, live analysis, and deleted file recovery. These techniques are elaborated as follows:

- **Reverse steganography:** This technique of digital forensics includes unveiling the hidden data in a file by analyzing its content thoroughly. The process of content analyzing the file requires its hashing by suitable techniques.

- **Stochastic forensics:** This technique of digital forensics satisfies the requirement of not using any digital artifacts in a digital forensic investigation. This process is thereby useful for the detection of data breaches and insider threats, thereby restricting their potential spread within the network.

- **Cross-drive analysis:** The professional digital forensics investigator uses this technique of digital forensics to correlate data collected from a wide range of digital devices associated with the concerned crime. This effective correlation of data leads to the successful identification of suspicious activities.

- **Live analysis:** This technique of digital forensics analysis relates to the investigation of RAM or cache while the device is still functioning. The adoption of this procedure by the investigators relates to using the forensic lab for the maintenance of evidence.

- **Deleted file recovery:** This forensic investigation procedure relates to partially or fully recovering deleted files from a device. The concerned procedure implies tracing the file from the fragments spread across systems and memory.

The increasing complexity and sophistication of modern cybercrime encourage digital forensic investigators to deploy appropriate hardware tools to catalyze the process of digital forensics. The relevant hardware tools that boost the speed of digital forensics investigation include **Forensic Recovery of Evidence Device (FRED)**, Cellebrite **Universal Forensics Extraction Device** (**UFED**), Oxygen Phone Manager, and Radio Tactics Aceso. These tools are further detailed as follows:

- **Forensic Recovery of Evidence Device (FRED):** This hardware tool for digital forensic investigation effectively analyzes a significant amount of data, retrieved from a wide range of media types. This workstation for digital forensic investigation encourages the extraction of data from mobile devices.

- **Cellebrite Universal Forensics Extraction Device (UFED):** This mobile device is associated with accessing and extracting data from multiple devices such as smartphones, tablets, and GPS devices.

- **Oxygen phone manager:** This specialized digital forensic device resembles a software tool that is used to manage data from mobile phones. Besides managing data, this tool encourages the backing up of data from mobile phones that can benefit an ongoing digital forensic investigation.

- **Radio Tactics Aceso:** The prime benefit of this device is its portability, which encourages fast capture of data from mobile phones and SIM cards. This tool encourages the collection of evidence-based data from a variety of digital devices, SIMs, and Media Cards.

The role of AI and ML in aiding the process of digital forensics is significant as it catalyzes the overall process. This is in terms of increasing the overall efficiency of the digital evidence collection stage within the investigation. Such integration assures the precision of digital forensics investigation to a larger extent. This is specifically from the perspective of image and text analysis, network analysis, and the implication of machine-powered decision-making. The tendency of digital forensics investigation relates to assessing an enormous quantity of data that can require a significant amount of time. However, integration of these technologies can result in simplification of the overall process, thereby streamlining the result generation.

The process of digital forensics tends to face relevant challenges due to existing limitations that can hamper its consistent progress and thereby the generation of expected results. Some of these challenges are listed as follows:

- **Change of technology:** The change in technology leads to corresponding changes in encryption methods and thereby hampers the progress of digital forensics investigation. The process of encryption typically results in accessing the data on a digital device by the concerned digital forensics investigator.

- **Misleading cyber evidence:** The increasing tendency to rely on digital evidence for serving justice at the Court of Law can result in the presence of misleading digital evidence at the cybercrime scene. Furthermore, inconsistency and complexity of the digital evidence can lead to its rejection at the Court of Law, thereby altering the direction of a legal case.

- Apart from the observed challenges, the process of digital forensics faces issues due to existing limitations. Some of these limitations are stated below:

- **Increasing number of digital devices:** Digital devices play a vital role in the daily life of modern-day individuals. This results in an increasing number of digital devices that tend to be associated with cybercrime. However, assessing such a large number of digital devices poses a significant challenge for digital forensics investigators.

- **Lack of efficient tools:** The formulation of efficient digital forensics tools is disproportionate to the increasing complexity of digital forensics. Specifically, sorting the huge volumes of digital data from devices to identify exact digital evidence within a limited time results in a cumbersome task for digital forensics investigators due to a lack of efficient tools.

Applications of digital forensics in various fields

The application of digital forensic techniques relates to the following fields:

- **Law enforcement:** The increasing rate of cybercrime across different parts of the world requires the appropriate application of digital forensics procedures to serve justice in the Court of Law. The inherent association of digital devices with modern-day cybercrimes requires their solution by using effective digital forensic tools and techniques.

- **Tracking cybercrimes:** The timely tracking of cybercrime in modern days is crucial to prevent repeated occurrences of such crimes in the future. Digital forensic investigators typically trace the footprints of cyber criminals to identify the root cause of cybercrime and accordingly proceed with preventing its further occurrence.

- **Corporate investigations:** Cybersecurity issues tend to hamper the performance efficiency of companies in the corporate world. The occurrence of data breaches results in adversely impacting the reputation of companies across different business sectors. This leads to the application of effective digital forensics procedures to address the incident. The extended implication of digital forensics relates to conducting internal investigations to track intellectual property theft within an organization. The presence of experts within the team of digital forensic investigators results in mitigating insider threats appropriately.

- **Cybersecurity:** The increasing rate of cybersecurity issues across different business and industrial areas requires the conduct of digital forensics consistently. The process of digital forensics plays a crucial role in counter-terrorism and espionage. This further requires cross-border collaboration between different teams of digital forensic investigation teams to proceed with digital investigations.

- **Academia and research:** The consistent application of digital forensics for relevant fields of academia and research relates to a wide range of areas. These areas include cybersecurity research, legal studies, technological innovation, and educational programs. Cybersecurity research relates to studying cyberattacks and thereby developing effective defense mechanisms. The relevance of digital forensics for legal studies implies the development of guidelines and best practices for the collection and analysis of digital evidence by a team of digital investigators. Digital forensics relates to catalyzing technological innovation by encouraging the development of tools for data recovery, analysis, and encryption. The relevant digital forensics case studies encourage the development of suitable educational programs for careers in cybersecurity, law enforcement, and corporate security.

Emerging trends and technologies in digital forensics

The relevant emerging trends and technologies in digital forensics are listed as follows:

- **Preliminaries of computer forensics:** The concept of computer forensics relates to the careful collection of digital evidence from various digital devices by using suitable strategies that can ensure their admissibility in the Court of Law. This process involves performing a structured investigation along with maintaining related documents such as the CoC for the concerned digital devices. The benefit of these aspects relates to tracing the details of cybercrime occurring and the activities of individuals responsible for it. This is because the CoC of digital evidence is maintained from the collection of the evidence from the cybercrime scene, and for the entire duration of the digital forensic investigation. The development of computer forensics as a dedicated part of digital forensics relates to its invention and fast acceptance within the base of users. The inherent connection of digital devices with modern-day crime results in requiring their effective collection and handling to ensure the preservation of data and metadata. This relates to ensuring the admissibility of digital evidence in the Court of Law. The investigations of computer forensics require adequate knowledge of fundamental concepts such as OS, information security, programming language, and network security. Alongside these technical requirements, possessing knowledge about legal guidelines can encourage digital forensic investigators to proceed with computer forensic analyses effortlessly. The seamless procedure of computer forensics indicates the use of specific tools by the concerned digital forensic investigator. These technical tools are used for a wide range of devices, such as laptops, memory, and mobile devices. Precisely, digital forensic investigators use COFFEE, the Coroner's Toolkit, and The Sleuth Kit to analyze laptops and PCs. Amongst these, COFFEE is a tool suite used for performing forensic analysis on the Windows Operating System of Microsoft. On the other hand, digital forensic investigators use the Coroner's Toolkit to perform Unix Analysis. The Sleuth Kit is beneficial for digital forensics investigators in terms of acting as a library of tools for both Unix and Windows. The benefits of computer forensics is used by digital forensics investigators to analyze intellectual property theft, industry espionage, fraud, and bankruptcy investigations. The advantage of using computer forensics as a tool to aid cybercrime investigations is to produce relevant evidence in the Court of Law that can serve justice to the victim. The relevant benefit of computer forensics for reputed organizations relates to identifying underlying loopholes in their digital network of devices and encouraging their quick mitigation

- **Introduction to network forensics:** The concept of network forensics relates to assessing specific areas such as network traffic, logs, and related data about the network. The motive of digital forensic investigators to be involved in Network Forensic Analysis relates to tracing overall communication amongst the digital devices within a network. Their investigation reveals the exchange of data between different endpoint devices of the network. The benefits of network forensics imply solving a variety of issues, such as cybercrime, network problems, and data theft. The process of network forensics relates to the application of multiple tools for the generation of desired results quickly. These tools include packet-capturing tools, full packet capture tools, log analysis tools, NetFlow analysis tools, **Security Information and Event Management (SIEM)** tools, digital forensics platforms, and IDS tools. These tools are used by the digital forensics investigator in terms of extracting information from different parts of the digital network, such as routers and servers. The benefit of conducting a detailed investigation related to network forensics relates to revealing the existing issues within a network and mitigating them appropriately. The timely mitigation of vulnerabilities in a network leads to restricting the occurrence of a critical cyberattack on the infrastructure of an organization.

- **Introduction to cloud forensics:** The concept of cloud forensics relates to conducting detailed investigations about cloud environments. The increased adoption of cloud computing by modern-day organizations for the relevant benefit of their business leads to their increased threat from cloud-related cybersecurity attacks. Cybercriminals tend to attack their target by using a cloud environment as a medium. Forensic experts are assigned the responsibility of detecting the responsible groups or individuals by effectively using their skills and competencies. Digital forensic investigators tend to use specific tools for their investigation of cloud environments, such as **The Sleuth Kit (TSK)**, Autopsy, and Volatility. Digital forensic investigators use TSK to extract underlying information from hard disks and related storage devices. These digital forensic investigators use Autopsy to examine the hard disks that contain data on OS, users, applications, and internet history. Digital forensic investigators use the open-source framework, Volatility, to analyze computer memory. The target of conducting cloud forensics requires the concerned digital forensic investigators to focus on specific computing resources such as servers, networks, applications, storage, and databases. However, the target of proceeding with cloud forensics results in digital forensic investigators facing relevant challenges. These challenges include jurisdiction complications, physical access, and instability. This is because the aspect of jurisdiction complication relates to cloud services being hosted across different states or countries, as compared to the user location. The traditional technique of digital forensics relates to freezing the infrastructure for proceeding with the investigation. However, this is impossible for a public cloud environment and thereby creates a challenge for the concerned investigation. The seamless progress of digital forensic investigation relates to physically assessing the cloud environment. However, this is challenging for digital forensic investigators as cloud hosting companies tend to apply strict security to safeguard their data centers. The deployment of such strict security for data centers results in limited scope for physical access by digital forensics investigators. The benefit of cloud forensics relates to rapid deployment and thereby encourages aiding time-limited investigations. The presence of scope for remote access leads to investigators accessing data effortlessly, irrespective of their physical location. Cloud forensics tends to be associated with a reduction of both cost and maintenance requirements as opposed to other forms of digital forensics. This encourages their consistent application across different investigation scenarios.

- **Introduction to mobile device forensics:** The constant evolution of mobile devices to be appropriate for both personal and professional usage leads to them playing a crucial role in modern-day cybercrime. The overall compactness of mobile devices leads to storing vital and sensitive information such as contact details and appointments, electronic correspondence, and electronic document conveying. This implies the possible scope of such devices being a primary source of digital evidence for digital forensic investigators. The procedure of mobile forensics is widely used for military applications, corporate investigations, and law enforcement. The relevance of mobile forensics for military applications includes a collection of data that can boost the efficient planning of military operations. The extensive usage of smartphones by the employees of reputed organizations leads to their being subjected to mobile device forensics in terms of identifying potential attempts at data breach. The process of mobile device forensics covers the extraction of data from related devices such as smartphones and tablets. Digital forensic investigators tend to utilize a wide variety of tools and techniques to interpret the OS of mobile devices. Despite this, they face challenges as specific OS tend to be closed, such as **iPhone OS (iOS)** as opposed to widely used open-source OS such as Android.

- **Introduction to IoT forensics:** The continuous technological enhancement has led to the prevalence of areas such as the IoT. Contrarily, the emergence of IoT led to the prevalence of cybercrimes that are coordinated to attack the interconnected devices of a device network. The target of IoT forensics is to restrict the recurrence of cyber attacks on interconnected devices. Digital forensic investigators target relevant layers of the IoT that include sensors, internal networks, and the cloud. The concept of IoT forensics is segregated into three specific layers, namely cloud forensics, network forensics, and device forensics. The aspect of cloud forensics relates to targeting the application layer, consisting of **Amazon Web Services (AWS)** IoT, IoT Core, and IoT Device Defender. The middle position of network forensics between cloud forensics and device forensics relates to focusing on the network layer. Device forensics relates to a network of different IoT devices that are used for communication by individuals in the organization.

- **Introduction to social media forensics:** The increasing acceptance of social media as a reliable platform for communication encourages a proportional increase in the number of cybercrimes. The prime role of digital forensic investigators is to collect publicly available information for the identification and detention of cybercriminals. Digital forensic investigators tend to focus on specific areas such as posts, messages, comments, likes, and shares. These insights are crucial for a cybercrime investigation in terms of establishing connections and thereby proceeding to resolve the crimes at the earliest. Digital forensic investigators tend to use OSINT Tools to target the collection of adequate insights about a cybercrime. The constantly evolving social media platform leads to the availability of a wide range of features for the communication benefit of users. The aspect of social media forensics requires adhering to adhere with legal frameworks in terms of abiding by the underlying provisions of relevant legal frameworks, applicable across different areas. The tendency of users on social media platforms to share sensitive information leads to their appropriate linking to relevant civil and criminal cases. The detailed analysis of social media content results in revealing the behavioral tendencies of an individual and thereby encourages identifying their potential contribution to cybercrime.

- **Introduction to multimedia forensics:** The evolution of multimedia in the modern world relates to mixing a wide array of items such as audio, video, image, and text. Such a combination of multiple items results in increasing the overall complexity of multimedia and thereby concerns digital forensics investigators facing critical challenges. The process of multimedia forensics proceeds with analyzing the active image authentication. The process of active image authentication relates to assessing the embedded codes on images during their generation from the source. The process of digital forensics Investigation further relates to active image investigation. This process indicates assessing the integrity of the image by the concerned digital investigator. The process of multimedia forensics relates to considering the concept of digital fingerprints. This process relates to the safe delivery of multimedia content from the sender to the receiver across the Internet. The drawback of this process relates to concerned validity of digital fingerprints expiring after delivery to the receiver. However, forensic investigators tend to consider tracing the delivery of the multimedia content from sender to receiver and assessing the access control of the receiver. The outcome of multimedia forensics relates to encouraging the concerned users to realize the legal boundaries of the modern-day virtual world.

- **Introduction to digital forensics in industrial control systems:** The fast adoption of industrial control systems by businesses relates to their enhancing operational efficiency in the market. This is beneficial as industrial control systems tend to be composed of diverse and proprietary systems. However, this tends to be a challenge for digital forensic investigators to proceed with investigating relevant scenarios. This encourages tailoring relevant tools and techniques by digital forensic investigators to proceed with their desired investigation. Cybercriminals tend to attack the **Programmable Logic Controllers** (**PLCs**) to disrupt the industrial control systems significantly. The importance of digital forensics in this regard is to acquire and analyze relevant control logic to assess the attack and determine its impact on the physical processes of the organization. Digital forensic experts tend to use the concept of digital twins to proceed with their investigation requirements. The digital twins tend to be an exact replica of existing physical controls. The overall forensic readiness relates to adapting existing models to the relevant areas of industrial control systems. The appropriate collaboration between industrial control system manufacturers and forensic investigators results in addressing relevant threats within the industrial control system environment.

The different branches of digital forensics tend to be influenced by the latest technological advancements, such as AI and ML. Such emerging trends in digital forensics are listed as follows:

- **AI and ML in digital forensics:** The application of AI relates to using advanced AI Algorithms along with relevant ML techniques to aid the investigation and analysis of digital evidence. This relates to the programming of different tools that can boost the overall process of digital forensics analysis. The application of AI within digital forensics analysis further relates to automating repetitive tasks and thereby reducing the workload on the concerned digital forensic investigators.

- **Quantum computing shaping digital forensics:** The benefits of quantum computing result in catalyzing the process of digital forensic investigation appropriately. The long-term implication of this benefit relates to speeding up the digital forensics procedure, aiding in the quick detection of cyberattacks, and proceeding to quick data recovery.

- **Evolving threat landscape:** The consistent evolution of the threat landscape relates to the rising nuances of deepfakes across the internet platform. Furthermore, modern-day cybercriminals tend to use sophisticated hacking techniques to realize their attack and manipulate the victims accordingly. The evolving threat landscape relates to the rising number of cybercrimes worldwide.

Challenges in the expanse of digital forensics

The relevant challenges in the expanse of digital forensics are listed as follows:

- **Encryption and anti-forensic techniques:** The complicated encryption of data within the digital evidence results in concerned digital forensic investigators facing critical challenges. The effective encryption of sensitive data within a device acts as a source of data safety. However, this poses a critical challenge for digital forensic investigators in their efforts of evidence. The detailed analysis of the anti-forensic technique relates to the efforts of cyber criminals to hinder the efforts of digital forensic investigators to trace their wrongdoings on the internet platform. The range of anti-forensics techniques that are widely used by cybercriminals includes disk wiping, file encryption, steganography, malware, and compression.

- **Balancing privacy rights and investigative needs:** The responsibility of digital forensic investigators relates to unveiling underlying data within digital evidence and presenting it in the Court of Law. This is because the overall admissibility of digital devices is crucial for serving justice in cybercrime in the Court of Law. The concerned digital forensic investigators are required to focus on existing legal frameworks, ethical practices, data minimization, and security measures. The importance of implementing security measures relates to the safe and secure storage of digital evidence during the phase of the investigation. This is in terms of reducing the scope of integrity loss for the concerned digital evidence.

Future developments of digital forensics

The rising number of cybercrimes requires adequate future development of digital forensics. These future developments are discussed from the following perspectives:

- **Predictions and forecasts:** The increasing dependence of companies on cloud architecture relates to predicting demand for the enhancement of cloud forensics. The adequate development of cloud forensics relates to cloud architecture being complex and thereby requiring specialized tools and methodologies for effective extraction and analysis of data. This relates to the relevant forecasting of standardizing the international legal frameworks to efficiently simplify cross-border data retrieval.

- **Challenges and opportunities:** Despite having adequate requirements for development within the field of digital forensics, the effort of requirements tends to face critical challenges. The relevant challenges are stated here:

  o **Exponential data growth:** The exponential generation of data from different sources in modern days results in challenges, the sole purpose of effective data extraction and analysis within the field of digital forensics.

  o **System complexity:** The increasing dependence of individuals and organizations on the modernization of computers results in their increased complexity. These complexities include data encryption and proprietary data artifacts. The system complexity further relates to the presence of an intricate web of interconnecting devices and systems that are widely adopted across different business sectors.

  Despite the presence of such challenges, relevant opportunities for development exist within the field of digital forensics. These opportunities are listed as follows:

  o **Development of AI and ML:** The relevant development of the latest technologies, such as AI and ML, can aid in simplifying the existing complexities of digital forensics investigations. This relates to automating the repetitive tasks of digital forensics investigation and thereby reducing the workload on the concerned investigators. The long-term benefit of this aspect relates to the associated investigators focusing on the sophistication of cyberattacks seamlessly.

  o **Legal and regulatory support:** Digital forensics tends to ensure aiding legal and compliance requirements appropriately for a prolonged duration. This encouraged the legal and regulatory sectors to target adequate enhancement of the digital forensics field. This is in terms of encouraging collaboration between different agencies for a smooth investigation.

- **The evolving role of digital forensics professionals:** The roles and responsibilities of digital forensic professionals play a vital role in the generation of effective results from digital forensics investigations. Digital forensics professionals are required to be well-versed in emerging areas of digital forensics such as cloud forensics, mobile forensics, and IoT forensics. This is in terms of tackling the underlying challenges of such fields that pose critical challenges during sophisticated cyberattacks.

Case studies on digital forensics

Some of the high-profile cybercrime cases involving dedicated applications of digital forensics are discussed here, stating the learned lessons and future implications:

- **High-profile cybercrime case 1: The Waifu Hacker Case:** This cybercrime involved the adversary gaining unauthorized access to the databases of 165 companies and demanding a ransom worth a significant amount. These databases contained sensitive data about the company and its stakeholders. The digital forensic investigators tracked the IP address of the adversary along with analyzing the data transfer.

- **High-profile cybercrime case 2: Health Service Ransomware Attack of Ireland:** The **Health Service Executive** (**HSE**) of Ireland faced a critical ransomware attack in 2021. This attack disrupted its operation significantly. The application of the digital forensic investigation procedure resulted in the analysis of server logs and tracking of IP addresses to block further penetration of cybercriminals in the organizational network.

- **Lessons Learned from past investigations:** The detailed analysis of the abovementioned case studies revealed that the timely initiation of digital forensics investigation plays a vital role in reducing the impact of the cyberattack on the sensitive assets of concerned organizations. The enhancement of relevant infrastructure for the initiation of digital forensics Investigation results in the quick generation of desired results.

- **Future implications:** The outcome of a digital forensics investigation relates to strengthening the overall digital security posture of an organization. The efficiency of digital forensic investigation ensures plugging the existing loopholes of an organization's network using suitable tactics. This relates to patching the existing vulnerabilities along with the upgradation of security hardware. Furthermore, digital forensics investigation encourages proactive threat detection within an organization.

Conclusion

The increasing complexity in the threat landscape encourages appropriate development in the field of digital forensics. The relevant development includes the integration of relevant threat intelligence, derived from past cybercrime investigations. This is apart from integrating the latest technological developments across the different digital forensics procedures to ensure their quick application by companies and individuals to seek safety and security against critical cybercrimes. The continuous enhancement of digital forensics is crucial due to increased instances of sophisticated cyberattacks by adversaries on critical assets of an organization. Modern-day cyberattacks tend to proceed without any visible IoCs and hence require appropriately enhanced digital forensics procedures.

The upcoming chapter focuses on tracing the progression of digital forensics in terms of detailing its different areas. This includes historical improvement of digital forensics that spans its early approaches. The aspect of emerging technologies that tends to influence the progress of digital forensics. The chapter will shed light on the evolution of digital forensics in terms of standards and best practices.

Join our book's Discord space

Join the book's Discord Workspace for Latest updates, Offers, Tech happenings around the world, New Release and Sessions with the Authors:

https://discord.bpbonline.com

CHAPTER 4

Tracing the Progression of Digital Forensics

Introduction

The increasing impact of digital transformation leads to proportionately increasing occurrences of cyberattacks and cybercrimes. The effective resolution of such cybersecurity incidents relates to the application of digital forensics. The increasing variation of cybercrimes results in complicates the course of digital forensics investigation. This indicates that the relevant advancement of digital forensics implies its continuous progress as per the latest technological developments. Such progress implies the integration of the latest technologies to simplify the process of digital forensics analysis. The current chapter attempts to trace the progress of digital forensics from the aspect of increasing complexities in the cybercrime investigation procedure.

Structure

The chapter covers the following topics:

- Overviewing progression of digital forensics
- Early approaches to digital forensics
- Emerging technologies and impact on digital forensics
- Digital forensics standards and best practices
- Role of AI and ML in digital forensics

- Automation and efficiency streamlining digital forensics processes
- Challenges and limitations in digital forensics
- Future of digital forensics

Objectives

The objectives of this chapter are to list the early approaches to digital forensics in terms of disk imaging to file carving. These traditional approaches to digital forensics relate to tackling the limited complexity of cybercrime cases. The chapter includes emerging technologies and their impact on digital forensics. The chapter proceeds to trace the evolution of digital forensics standards and best practices. The chapter focuses on the role of **artificial intelligence** (**AI**) and **machine learning** (**ML**) in digital forensics. The wide adoption of such technologies within digital forensics results in increasing complexity of the digital infrastructure and thereby poses challenges for digital forensics Investigators. The chapter indicates automation and efficiency from the perspective of streamlining digital forensics Processes to cater to its increasing demand against the backdrop of digital transformation. The chapter includes relevant challenges and limitations in the progression of digital forensics. The relevant predictions and possibilities relate to indicating the relevant future of digital forensics.

Overviewing progression of digital forensics

Digital forensics is a field of forensic science that consists of different processes to examine digital evidence and aid in solving cybercrime incidents. The concerned process involves multiple steps of recovering, preserving, analyzing, and presenting electronic data. The outcomes of digital forensics aid in tracing the origin and progress of specific cybercrimes, such as data breaches and various legal disputes. The concept of digital forensics emerged between the late 1970s and 1980s due to an increase in the number of personal computer users. Primarily, law enforcement and military organizations realized the need to examine digital evidence to tackle criminal investigations. The initial recognition of digital forensics was by the term computer forensics. The benefits and significance of digital forensics have evolved over time due to its playing a significant role in solving cybercrimes and tracking adversaries involved in cyberattacks. The 1980s focused on computer-related crimes such as hacking and data theft. This required the development of primary tools to recover deleted files and analyze floppy disks (*Figure 4.1*):

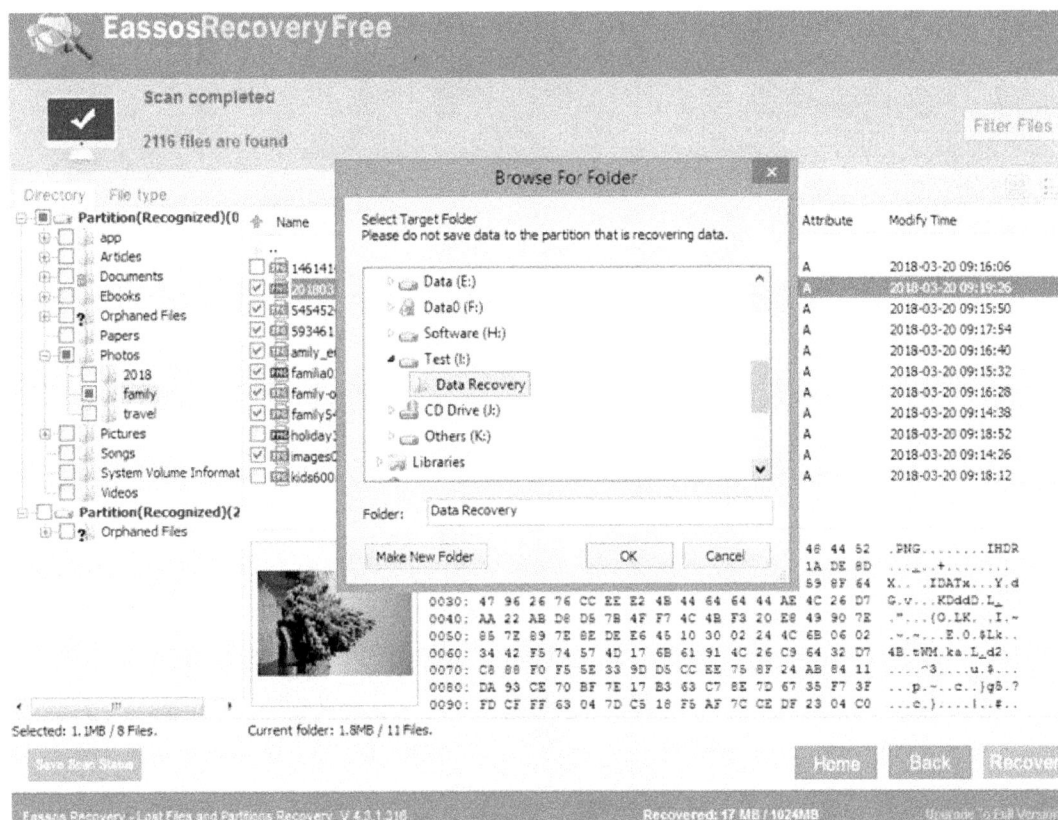

Figure 4.1: *Deleted data recovery*

The subsequent commencement of the 1990s witnessed the rapid growth of the internet and widespread digital communication. Parallelly, this duration led to increased instances of cybercrimes such as online fraud and phishing. This encouraged digital forensic investigators to use specialized software solutions for digital investigations, such as EnCase *(Figure 4.2).*

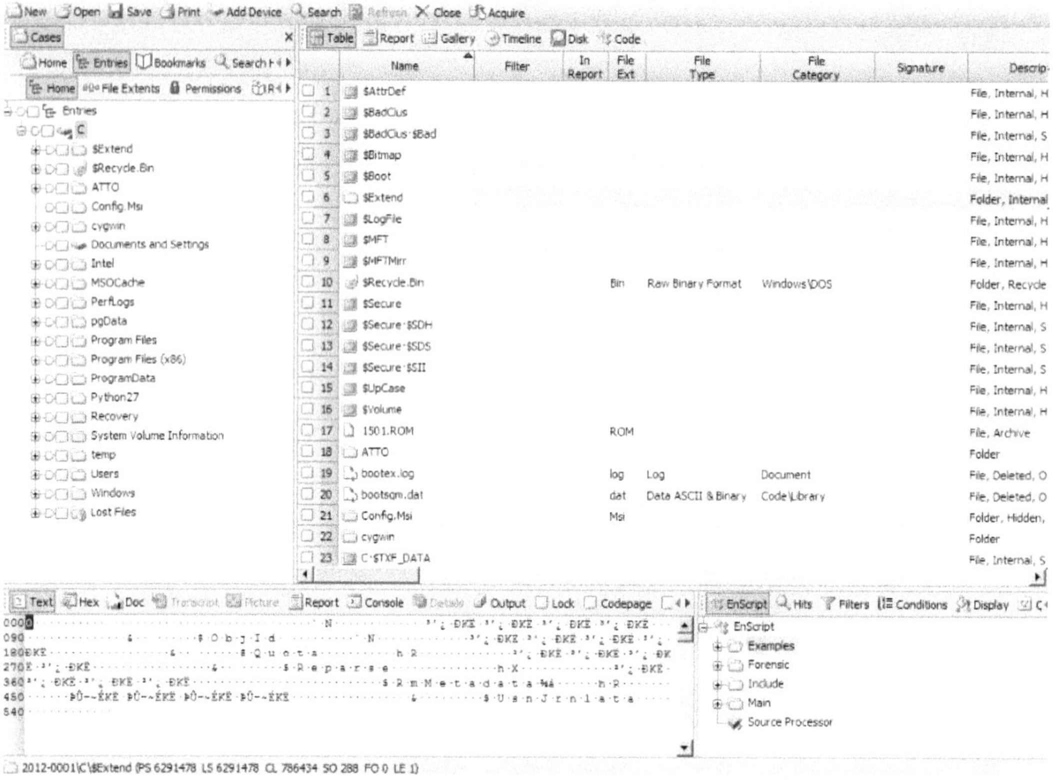

Figure 4.2: Interface of EnCase

The commencement of the 21st century, since the 2000s, witnessed the emergence of smartphones, tablets, and similar portable digital devices. This thereby resulted in relevant challenges for Digital Forensic Investigators dealing with encrypted and cloud-stored data. This duration further signifies the establishment of international standards to handle digital evidence. The importance of legal frameworks lies in aiding different digital forensics investigations. This led to the development of relevant laws and policies, including the **Computer Fraud and Abuse Act (CFAA)** in the U.S. This phase related to the recognition of digital forensics as admissible evidence in the Court of Law. The vast expanse of modern digital forensics includes different areas such as cloud forensics, network forensics, and IoT device investigations. The increased number of cybercrimes and, thereby, the generation of huge volumes of data encouraged the use of AI and ML to tackle such large volumes of digital evidence. The procedure of digital forensics focuses on privacy concerns and ethical issues.

Despite encouraging relevant developments, modern-day digital forensic investigators tend to face challenges such as rapidly changing technologies as well as encryption techniques. The increased number of digital device usage leads to concerned digital forensic investigators facing the challenge of handling data from multiple devices and platforms. Digital forensic investigators further need to balance privacy rights and the needs of the investigation. The increasing influence of digital transformation leads to the effective integration of automation and AI within digital forensic investigations. Digital forensic investigators tend to address the inherent challenges associated with decentralized systems such as blockchain. The vast spread of cybercrimes across different physical borders encourages collaboration across international borders for cybercrime investigations.

Early approaches to digital forensics

Digital forensic investigators realized the importance of extracting and preserving electronic data during the phases of the 1980s and 1990s. The initial focus of digital forensic investigators related to the involvement of personal computers in tackling issues such as fraud and hacking. The earlier approaches to digital forensics are stated as follows:

- **Disk imaging: Foundation:** The concept of disk imaging from a digital forensic perspective involves creating exact copies in terms of bit-by-bit, of the concerned storage device, such as the hard drive, to proceed with evidence preservation. The importance of disk imaging points to ensuring the digital integrity of the concerned evidence during an investigation by resisting any change to the original device. The process of disk imaging proceeds with specific tools such as Norton Ghost, early disk cloning software *(Figure 4.3)*, and dd, a Unix/Linux tool for creating raw disk images *(Figure 4.4)*.

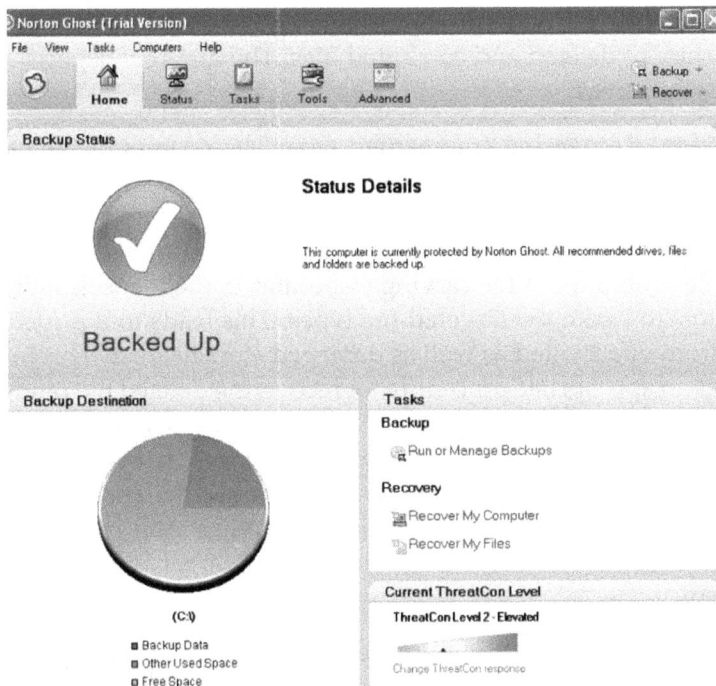

Figure 4.3: Interface of Norton Ghost

```
$ cat disk_clonning4.sh ; ./disk_clonning4.sh
#!/usr/bin/env bash
lsblk /dev/sda /dev/sdb
sudo dd if=/dev/sda of=/dev/sdb bs=1M
lsblk /dev/sda /dev/sdb
NAME    MAJ:MIN RM   SIZE RO TYPE MOUNTPOINT
sda       8:0    0    30G  0 disk
├─sda1    8:1    0   512M  0 part /boot/efi
├─sda2    8:2    0    1K   0 part
└─sda5    8:5    0 29.5G   0 part /
sdb       8:16   0    30G  0 disk
30720+0 records in
30720+0 records out
32212254720 bytes (32 GB, 30 GiB) copied, 96.8382 s, 333 MB/s
NAME    MAJ:MIN RM   SIZE RO TYPE MOUNTPOINT
sda       8:0    0    30G  0 disk
├─sda1    8:1    0   512M  0 part /boot/efi
├─sda2    8:2    0    1K   0 part
└─sda5    8:5    0 29.5G   0 part /
sdb       8:16   0    30G  0 disk
├─sdb1    8:17   0   512M  0 part
├─sdb2    8:18   0    1K   0 part
└─sdb5    8:21   0 29.5G   0 part
```

Figure 4.4: *Execution of the dd command in Linux*

The inherent benefits of disk imaging include allowing forensic analysts to work on copies of original digital evidence without compromising its integrity. The extended benefits include the recovery of deleted and corrupted files. The different aspects of disk imaging include the following areas:

- **File carving: Recovering fragmented data:** The process of file carving involves the effective reconstruction of files from raw data on a storage device. The benefit of file carving is reducing dependence on filesystem metadata. The process of file carving takes place by identifying file headers and footers to locate specific file types. The procedure of file carving elaborates to the identification of the headers and footers to locate the targeted file types. This leads to the successful recovery of data from unallocated as well as damaged storage areas. This indicates that file carving is an appropriate procedure for recovering deleted files and fragments. The extended application of this procedure is extracting data from damaged drives or corrupted systems. However, the related challenges in this regard include dealing with fragmented files spread across different sectors and identifying file types without relevant metadata. This process played a vital role in the extraction of data from a disk drive or storage device without largely depending on the original file system.

- **Early forensic tools:** The traditional forensic tools were designed for relevant tasks such as disk imaging, file recovery, and file carving. These tools include EnCase, **Forensic Toolkit (FTK)** *(Figure 4.5),* and **The Sleuth Kit (TSK)** *(Figure 4.6).*

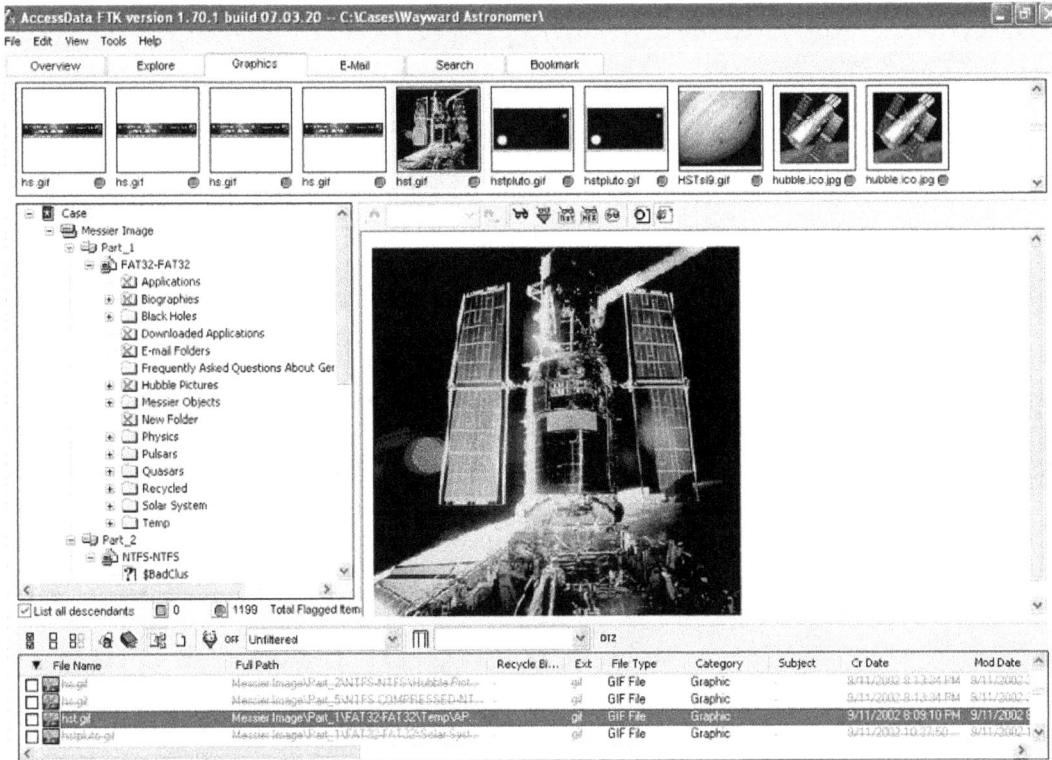

Figure 4.5: Interface of forensic toolkit

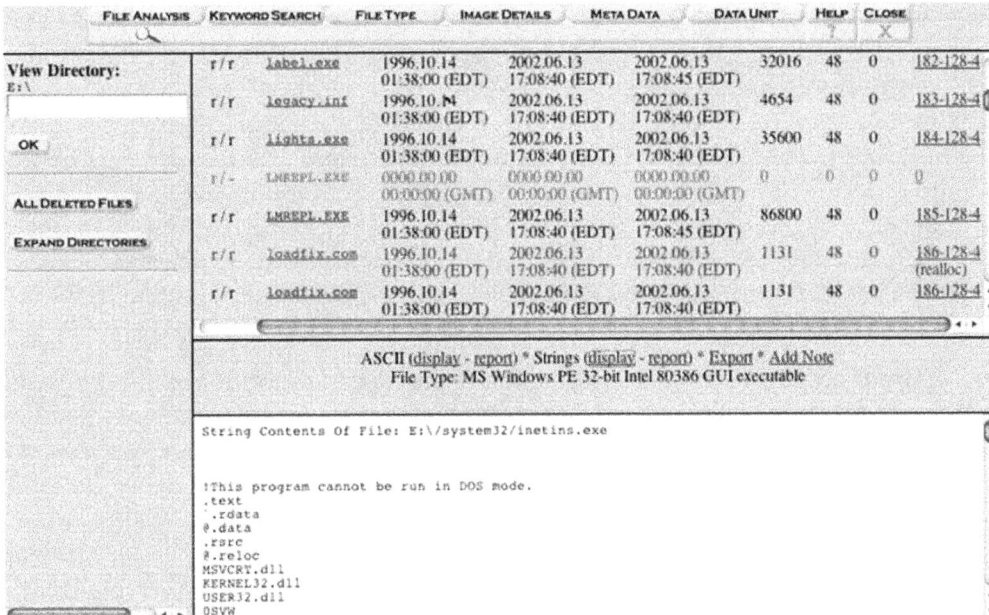

Figure 4.6: Interface of The Sleuth Kit

The benefits of EnCase for digital forensics analysis include seamless disk imaging and analysis. Digital forensic investigators use FTK to index and analyze digital evidence. Digital forensic Investigators use the open-source suite TSK to investigate file systems and carve files. The extensive usage of these traditional digital forensic Tools led to relevant groundwork for modern digital forensic solutions. However, using these tools led to digital forensic investigators facing a wide range of challenges, such as hardware limitations, manual effort, and incomplete data recovery. The adverse impact of these challenges further signifies the lack of standardization. The related legal and ethical considerations in this regard highlight the need for strict protocols to ensure evidence admissibility in court. The legal and ethical consideration of early forensic tools further expands to challenges in maintaining the **chain of custody** (**CoC**) and ensuring data authenticity. The legacy and impact of traditional forensic tools on modern digital forensics include disk imaging and file carving, remaining fundamental techniques in digital forensics even today, and the continuous development of more advanced tools and algorithms improving speed, accuracy, and automation in these processes.

Emerging technologies and impact on digital forensics

The relevant emerging technologies that induce significant effort in the field of digital forensics are stated as follows:

- **AI and ML:** The wide range of emerging technologies that impact digital forensics includes AI and ML. The combined application of AI and ML in digital forensics results in automating data analysis to process large datasets efficiently. This is apart from pattern recognition in malware, fraud detection, and identifying anomalies. The implication of such a combination of the latest technologies further points to speech and image recognition for analyzing multimedia evidence. The related benefits in this regard include reducing the time required for manual analysis. Despite having this benefit, the related challenge includes the presence of potential bias in AI algorithms. This is further to the need for transparency in AI-driven decision-making.

- **Cloud computing and cloud forensics:** The increasing adoption of cloud computing by organizations to enhance their operational efficiency results in evidence often stored in distributed cloud environments such as **Amazon Web Services** (**AWS**) and Microsoft Azure. The prevalence of **as-a-service** models further complicates data recovery for digital forensics investigators. The associated challenges in this regard include multi-tenancy and shared environments, increased complexity, apart from jurisdictional issues due to data being stored across multiple countries. Contrarily, the emerging solutions in this regard include the development of cloud-specific forensic tools to acquire and analyze evidence remotely.

- **Internet of Things (IoT) devices:** The modern-day IoT devices play a vital role in evidence gathering in digital forensics investigations. The evidence is collected from a wide range of devices, such as smartphones, wearables, and smart home devices that generate voluminous amounts of data. The importance of considering such IoT devices for digital forensics analysis indicates their availability of critical evidence in criminal investigations, including activity logs or location data. Digital forensics investigators tend to face challenges such as diverse device ecosystems and proprietary protocols, apart from data volatility and limited storage on IoT devices. The effective tackling of such challenges refers to the implementation of standardized frameworks for the extraction and preservation of IoT data.

- **Blockchain and cryptocurrencies:** the relevance of cryptocurrencies to digital forensics concerns their aiding in illegal transactions, such as money laundering. On the other side, blockchain is relevant to a lack of scope for tracing transactions due to pseudonymity. The emerging tools for blockchain analysis include chain analysis to trace and interpret transactions. The related challenges include proceeding with privacy-centric cryptocurrencies like Monero or Zcash, apart from verifying authenticity in decentralized environments.

- **Quantum computing:** The potential impact of quantum computing corresponds to its breaking traditional encryption that poses risks to data integrity. However, its relevant advances can result in faster decryption of encrypted evidence. The associated challenges include adapting current forensic techniques to quantum-safe cryptographic standards apart from high cost and limited access to quantum systems.

- **Big data analytics:** The impact of big data analytics on digital forensics includes handling vast amounts of structured and unstructured data from diverse sources such as emails, logs, and social media. The use of data analytics encourages identifying connections and trends within datasets. The related benefits of big data analytics for digital forensics include faster correlation of evidence across multiple platforms. The related challenges of big data analytics include maintaining accuracy while processing large volumes of data.

- **Advanced encryption and privacy tools:** The impact of advanced encryption on digital forensics includes widespread use of encryption in terms of full-disk encryption. Encrypted messaging apps tend to complicate evidence extraction. The implication of privacy tools on digital forensics includes relevant privacy-preserving technologies such as **The Onion Router (TOR)** and **Virtual Private Networks (VPNs)** that hinder the tracking of suspects. The emerging solutions include collaboration with technology providers for lawful access, apart from the development of tools to bypass or decrypt protected systems while maintaining legal and ethical standards.

- **Autonomous vehicles and smart cities:** The emerging sources of evidence from autonomous vehicles include the generation of logs and sensor data that are useful in accident investigations. Smart cities produce data from surveillance systems, traffic sensors, and public networks. The emerging challenges in this regard include the integration of diverse data sources into forensic workflows, as well as ensuring real-time evidence preservation in dynamic environments.

- **Virtual reality (VR) and augmented reality (AR):** The emerging role of VR and AR Devices in digital forensics includes creating unique data types, including session logs, user interactions, and virtual environments. The relevant potential for recreating crime scenes for digital forensics analysis and presentation of digital evidence in the Court of Law. The challenges include the extraction and interpretation of data from proprietary VR/AR systems. This is apart from ensuring the admissibility of VR-generated reconstructions in legal proceedings.

- **Future of digital forensics:** The relevant integration of technologies within digital forensics includes cross-disciplinary solutions combining AI, IoT, cloud, and blockchain. The relevant focus is required to be on the standardization of forensic techniques for emerging technologies and training professionals to stay updated with technological advancements. The ethical and legal considerations of the future development of digital forensics include balancing the need for advanced investigations with privacy and civil liberties.

Digital forensics standards and best practices

The evolution of digital forensics standards and best practices is stated as follows:

- **Early challenges in standardization:** The early digital forensic practices during the 1980s and 1990s lacked uniformity. This is due to informal and ad hoc methods for evidence collection and analysis along with limited recognition of digital evidence in legal systems.

- **Recognition of the need for standards:** The increased instances of cybercrime highlighted inconsistencies in forensic methodologies. This is apart from the growing demand for standardized approaches to ensure evidence integrity and admissibility in the Court of Law. This implies the importance of developing industry-specific and international frameworks.

- **Development of forensic standards:** The **Scientific Working Group on Digital Evidence (SWGDE)** as a forensic standard was established in 1998 to create guidelines for handling digital evidence. This standard further connects to publishing documents on best practices for acquisition, analysis, and reporting. The implementation of ISO/IEC 27037 indicated guidelines for identifying, collecting, and preserving digital evidence. The realization of ISO/IEC 27042 indicated guidelines for the analysis and interpretation of digital evidence. The **National Institute of Standards and Technology (NIST)** indicates published standards for forensic tools and processes, along with the development of methods to test and validate digital forensic software.

- **Evolution of best practices:** The use of write blockers and disk imaging leads to maintaining evidence integrity during digital evidence preservation. The related importance of CoC during evidence preservation results in tracking of evidence handling. The validation of forensic tools implies the requirement to test forensic software against known datasets and adherence to reproducibility and reliability in forensic results. The application of relevant reporting standards emphasizes clear, detailed, and unbiased reports for legal proceedings. The selection of suitable reporting standards indicates the use of standardized templates for forensic documentation.

- **Legal and ethical considerations:** The legal and ethical considerations primarily focus on admissibility in the Court of Law and related ethical practices. The aspect of admissibility in the Court of Law associates with establishing criteria for scientific evidence. The admissibility in the Court of Law further associates to indicating the importance of documented procedures to withstand legal scrutiny.

- **Role of training and certification:** The long-term role of training and certification links to the development of multiple certifications for digital forensic professionals such as **Certified Computer Examiner (CCE)**, **GIAC Certified Forensic Analyst (GCFA)**, and **Certified Forensic Computer Examiner (CFCE)**. The importance of continuous education pertains to keeping up with emerging technologies.

- **Emerging challenges for standards:** The emerging challenges for standards in digital forensics include rapid advancements in technology, such as the IoT, cloud, and blockchain, that are outpacing existing frameworks. The varying laws across international jurisdictions result in difficulty in managing digital evidence across international jurisdictions for digital forensics investigators. The existing standards lack adaptability to address privacy regulations such as the **General Data Protection Regulation (GDPR)**.

- **Collaboration and cross-border efforts:** The effective formation of international bodies, such as INTERPOL and Europol, harmonizes digital forensics standards. The aspect of collaboration between the private sector, law enforcement, and academia results in the development of unified practices.

- **Future trends in digital forensics standards:** The assurance of greater emphasis on automation and AI to handle large-scale investigations. The effective standardization for emerging fields like cloud forensics, IoT forensics, and quantum computing can result in effective digital forensics investigations. The enhanced focus on cybersecurity integration within forensic practices can result in the generation of effective practices. The benefit of progressing cross-border investigations requires creating global and universally accepted standards.

- **Legacy and ongoing importance:** The evolving standards and best practices have improved credibility and reliability in digital forensic investigations. The continued development is critical to address technological advancements and legal complexities.

Role of AI and ML in digital forensics

AI simulates human intelligence, while ML allows systems to learn from data and improve performance. This is relevant for digital forensics in terms of enhancing the efficiency, accuracy, and scalability of forensic investigations. The inherent roles of AI and ML from the perspective of digital forensics analysis are stated as follows:

- **Automation of evidence analysis:** The relevant automation of evidence analysis applies to data sorting and filtering, and pattern recognition. Data sorting and filtering concern the automated processing of large datasets such as emails, logs, and multimedia to identify relevant information. Pattern recognition is relevant to identifying trends, anomalies, and correlations in cybercrime cases. The effective detection of repetitive behavior in fraud or phishing attacks.

- **Advanced threat detection:** Advanced threat detection includes malware analysis and IDS. Malware analysis ties into AI-based tools that classify and analyze malware by examining code and behavior. The benefits of ML models relate to detecting zero-day threats by identifying unusual patterns. The IDS is powered by ML algorithms for monitoring network traffic for suspicious activity. Furthermore, adaptive learning enables the **Security Operations Centre** (**SOC**) to respond to evolving threats.

- **Digital evidence recovery:** The process of digital evidence recovery is relevant to the application of multiple strategies, such as file reconstruction and forensic image and video analysis. AI aids in recovering fragmented or deleted files by recognizing file signatures. ML models analyze images for object detection, facial recognition, and scene reconstruction. Video analytics tools automate the search for specific events or objects in surveillance footage.

- **Natural Language Processing (NLP):** The concept of NLP links to the utilization of varied concepts such as text and speech analysis, along with sentiment and keyword analysis. This helps analyze communication data, such as emails and messages, to identify key phrases or topics. The transcription and analysis of audio evidence catalyze investigation purposes. The sentiment and keyword analysis is used to detect intent in communication, such as threats or coercion.

- **Predictive analytics and behavioral profiling:** The increasing complexity within the digital forensics field encourages the utilization of predictive analytics and behavioral profiling. Cybercrime prediction uses predictive models to identify potential threats based on historical data. Contextually, AI helps create behavioral profiles of cybercriminals for proactive measures. Fraud detection corresponds to anomaly detection in financial transactions and online activities.

- **Chain of Custody (CoC) and documentation:** The process of automated tracking applies to AI systems that manage and log the chain of custody for digital evidence, ensuring integrity. The report generation aspect pertains to AI and assists in creating detailed forensic reports and summarizing findings effectively.

- **Challenges and limitations:** The bias in algorithms related to ML models may produce biased results due to training on skewed datasets. The complexity of interpretability is the difficulty in understanding how AI systems arrive at decisions ("black-box" issue). The admissibility in court ensures AI-generated evidence meets legal standards for reliability and transparency. The high costs related to advanced AI / ML tools and infrastructure may be costly to implement.

- **Ethical and privacy concerns:** Data sensitivity connects to AI tools that must balance evidence analysis with privacy regulations such as the GDPR. The potential for misuse includes AI systems that can be exploited if not properly secured.

- **Future trends:** The improved forensic tools include the development of AI-driven tools for real-time analysis of IoT, cloud, and blockchain data. Federated learning is associated with the use of decentralized AI models to analyze data across different jurisdictions while maintaining privacy. The AI for digital twins recreates digital environments for simulation and investigation. The integration of quantum computing results in AI could revolutionize forensic data analysis.

Automation and efficiency streamlining digital forensics processes

Automation refers to the use of technology to perform repetitive, time-intensive forensic tasks with minimal human intervention. Its purpose is to enhance efficiency, reduce errors, and enable faster analysis of large volumes of data. The automation and efficiency aspects of the digital forensics process can be stated as follows:

- **Key areas of automation in digital forensics:** The aspect of data acquisition applies to automated tools for imaging hard drives, mobile devices, and cloud storage. The use of scripts to gather evidence from multiple sources simultaneously. Evidence processing is related to the automated parsing of log files, emails, and network traffic. The process leads to categorizing files based on type, size, or relevance.

- **Efficiency in managing large data volumes:** Big data solutions links to different tools that are designed to handle terabytes of data from enterprise systems or cloud environments. De-duplication engages with the automated identification and removal of duplicate files to streamline analysis. Prioritization aligns with systems that rank evidence based on relevance to the investigation.

- **Automation tools and technologies:** The forensic platforms include tools like EnCase, FTK, and Cellebrite, which offer built-in automation for evidence acquisition and analysis. The scripting and customization relate to using Python, PowerShell, or Bash scripts to automate repetitive tasks.

- **Benefits of automation:** The effective acceleration of evidence collection, processing, and reporting leads to the benefits of digital forensics investigation.

- **Challenges in implementing automation:** The overall reliability of digital forensics tools bears upon ensuring that automated tools produce accurate and reproducible results.

- **Chain of custody and documentation:** The process of automation helps track and log evidence-handling processes to maintain the chain of custody. The automatic report generation ensures detailed and consistent documentation for legal proceedings.

- **Legal and ethical considerations:** The admissibility of automated findings reflects on ensuring evidence processed through automated systems meets legal standards. The ethical concerns relate to balancing speed and efficiency with data privacy and the rights of involved individuals.

- **Future trends in automation:** The process of cloud-based automation resonates with the integration of operational areas with cloud platforms to streamline evidence collection and analysis from remote environments.

Challenges and limitations in digital forensics

The relevant challenges and limitations in the progression of digital forensics are as follows:

- **Volume and complexity of data:** The rapidly growing digital storage capacities make evidence collection and analysis time-consuming in terms of massive data volumes. This corresponds to managing and analyzing terabytes of data from multiple sources like devices, servers, and cloud systems. The associated data complexity indicates diverse file formats, proprietary systems, and encrypted data add layers of difficulty.

- **Encryption and privacy measures:** The widespread use of full-disk encryption and encrypted communication apps such as Signal and WhatsApp challenges evidence extraction. The increased usage of privacy-preserving tools such as TOR, VPNs, and blockchain tends to hinder the tracking and identification of evidence. Balancing privacy and forensics requires the investigators to navigate privacy laws such as the GDPR while collecting digital evidence.

- **Emerging technologies:** The distributed storage of data using cloud architecture results in complicating evidence retrieval and jurisdictional issues. Digital forensics must account for fragmented and volatile data from diverse IoT devices. The aspect of pseudonymity and the decentralized nature of blockchain transactions make tracing activities difficult for digital forensics. Investigating AI systems or understanding decisions made by "black-box" algorithms adds complexity.

- **Lack of standardization:** The lack of standardization across digital forensics aligns with the prevalence of inconsistent practices in terms of varying forensic methodologies across jurisdictions and organizations.

- **Rapidly evolving technology landscape:** The aspect of frequent updates of digital forensics implies continuous advancements in hardware, software, and networks that outpace forensic tool development. The wide prevalence of proprietary systems reflects on the emergence of critical challenges in accessing and analyzing data from proprietary platforms and applications. The presence of legacy systems results in inherent difficulties in extracting evidence from outdated or obsolete technologies.

- **Resource limitations:** The aspect of technical expertise across the field of digital forensics field connects to the shortage of skilled forensic professionals to handle complex cases.

Future of digital forensics

The future of digital forensics in terms of predictions and possibilities is listed as follows:

- **Advancements in AI and ML:** The aspect of advancements in AI and ML encompasses AI-driven automation and deep learning models. Specifically, the relevance of AI-driven automation involves AI streamlining evidence analysis, pattern recognition, and anomaly detection. This is further to the automated sorting and categorization of large datasets with minimal human intervention by using the aid of AI. On the other side, the application of deep learning models addresses enhanced capabilities to analyze complex data like images, videos, and audio. Moreover, real-time digital forensics can be powered by adaptive AI algorithms.

- **Cloud and distributed forensics:** Cloud and distributed forensics indicate cloud-based investigations and edge and fog computing. The cloud-based investigations related to forensic tools will integrate with cloud environments for faster evidence collection. The application of specialized methods for handling multi-jurisdictional data and ensuring compliance with data sovereignty laws. Edge and fog computing relate to evidence acquisition from decentralized systems like IoT devices and edge servers, along with tools designed for low-latency analysis in distributed ecosystems.

- **IoT and embedded systems forensics:** The concept of IoT and embedded systems forensics draws upon different perspectives, such as the explosion of IoT devices, forensics of embedded systems, and challenges in volatility. The explosion of IoT devices correlates with an increased focus on analyzing data from interconnected devices such as smart homes, wearables, and vehicles. The Forensics of embedded systems deals with relevant investigative approaches for devices with proprietary firmware and constrained resources. The associated challenges in volatility relate to addressing issues with ephemeral and fragmented IoT data.

Conclusion

The course of this chapter indicates the overall importance of advancements across the field of digital forensics. Accordingly, this chapter thoroughly indicates the increasing importance of AI and ML for relevant development within the field of digital forensics. The integration of such technologies within the field of digital forensics involves tackling the increasing complexities within the field of digital forensics. The chapter further focused on indicating that integration of the latest technologies can simplify repetitive tasks of digital forensics investigation and thereby catalyze the generation of desired results from such investigations.

The upcoming chapter proceeds with detailing the legal and ethical aspects of digital forensics.

Join our book's Discord space

Join the book's Discord Workspace for Latest updates, Offers, Tech happenings around the world, New Release and Sessions with the Authors:

https://discord.bpbonline.com

CHAPTER 5

Navigating Legal and Ethical Aspects of Digital Forensics

Introduction

Realizing the benefits of digital forensics in the modern digital world results in its effective alignment with the relevant ethical and legal aspects. The current chapter proceeds with realizing such legal and ethical aspects as per the backdrop of worldwide digital transformation, increasing the dependency of individuals on a wide variety of digital devices such as smartphones, laptops, and tablets. The timely solving of cybercrimes and the resolution of incidents across the organization are crucial for appropriately safeguarding their assets. However, modern-day cybercrimes and cyber incidents resemble sophisticated efforts of adversaries to target the market reputation of their target within the business background operating sector.

Structure

The chapter covers the following topics:

- Legal and ethical considerations
- Understanding the legal framework
- Privacy rights and data protection
- Chain of custody and evidence handling
- Consent and authorization

- Intellectual property and trade secrets
- Expert testimony and reporting
- Legal challenges and preparing for litigation
- The Indian Information Technology Act of 2000
- Challenges and opportunities

Objectives

The current chapter attempts to introduce legal and ethical considerations in digital forensics from the perspective of enterprises. The chapter looks into detail about the legal frameworks from different aspects of laws, regulations, and compliance. The steady progress of this chapter relates to privacy rights and data protection in terms of balancing investigative needs and individual rights. The chapter includes a detailed understanding of the **chain of custody** (**CoC**) and evidence handling to ensure the admissibility and integrity of digital evidence in the Court of Law. The chapter indicates the importance of consent and authorization in terms of obtaining proper permissions for forensic investigations. The chapter discusses **intellectual property** (**IP**) and trade secrets in terms of safeguarding sensitive information during forensic processes. The chapter implies the overall importance of expert testimony and reporting from the perspective of presenting digital evidence in legal proceedings. The chapter proceeds with detailing relevant legal challenges and thereby preparing for litigation. The chapter proceeds to include underlying key provisions for digital forensics as a part of the Indian Information Technology Act of 2000. The chapter states relevant challenges and opportunities in Cross-Border Digital Forensics Investigations in India.

Legal and ethical considerations

The purpose of digital forensics pertains to investigating and reconstructing cybersecurity incidents by collecting, analyzing, and preserving digital evidence. This task of reconstruction is done from the traces left by the concerned threat actors, such as malware files and malicious scripts. The benefit of such incident reconstruction concerns pinpointing the root causes of attacks and thereby identifying of culprits. The importance of legal considerations in digital forensics for enterprises includes aligning the course of investigations to the related laws and regulations. The aspect of ethical consideration in digital forensics for enterprises resembles the application of definite principles, including **Objectivity**, **Confidentiality**, **Integrity**, and **Competence** (*Figure 5.1*).

Objectivity	• Avoiding partiality and bias • Based on Factual Evidence
Confidentiality	• Careful handling of sensitive information • Protecting priacy of individuals
Integrity	• Essential Integrity Preservation of Digital Evidence • Proper Chain of Custody (CoC)
Competence	• Possesing required skills • Continuous Professional Development

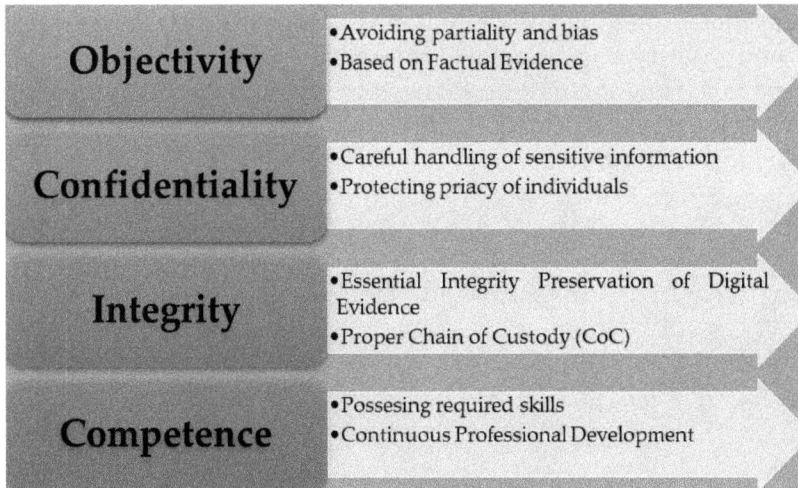

Figure 5.1: *Principle of ethics*

Digital forensic investigators tend to perform investigations on relevant ethical standards to maintain fairness in their roles and responsibilities. The legal and ethical considerations, along with challenges and best practices, are stated as follows:

- **Legal considerations:** The legal considerations include relevant areas such as laws and regulations, jurisdiction issues, admissibility of evidence, and CoC. The appropriate overview of key laws is listed as follows:

  o **General Data Protection Regulation (GDPR):** The underlying provision of GDPR includes granting individuals relevant rights to access their data and point out any mistakes in the record of their data for their timely rectification. Non-compliance with the GDPR can result in them paying a significant amount of fine, worth €20 million or 4% of the global annual turnover of the organization, whichever is higher. The adherence of companies to the GDPR leads them to possess several rights, such as processing the personal data of EU residents. This is essential for a wide number of businesses operated across the EU by companies from several parts of the world. Furthermore, companies that are GDPR compliant can transfer the personal data of their customers across the border after ensuring adequate data protection measures and facilitating international business operations.

  o **California Consumer Privacy Act (CCPA):** The formulation of the CCPA refers to tackling the multiple data breaches across well-known organizations that have inadequately defined access controls and privacy management. The benefit of the CCPA connects to encouraging users' rights to trace their data in terms of its being collected as well as sold, and thereby proceed to opt out of it accordingly. The application of CCPA refers to all for-profit organizations that are required to collect the personal data of consumers and generate annual revenue exceeding US$25 million. The relevance of CCPA further associates with granting a wide range of consumer rights to Californian residents. These rights include the right to know, the right to delete, the right to opt out, the right to non-discrimination, the right to correct, and the right to limit use and disclosure *(Figure 5.2)*.

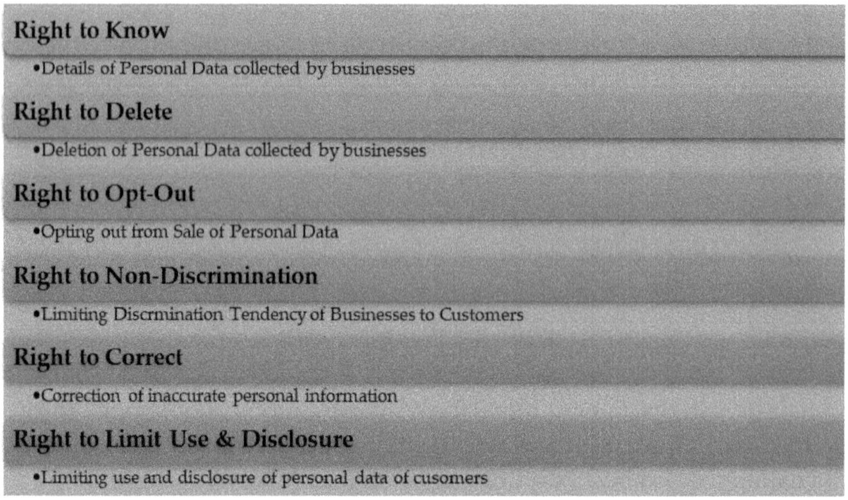

Right to Know
- Details of Personal Data collected by businesses

Right to Delete
- Deletion of Personal Data collected by businesses

Right to Opt-Out
- Opting out from Sale of Personal Data

Right to Non-Discrimination
- Limiting Discrmination Tendency of Businesses to Customers

Right to Correct
- Correction of inaccurate personal information

Right to Limit Use & Disclosure
- Limiting use and disclosure of personal data of cusomers

Figure 5.2: Provisions of California Consumer Privacy Act (CCPA)

The long-term influence of these rights indicates ensuring complete control of their personal data by customers and its handling by the businesses.

o   **Computer Fraud and Abuse Act (CFAA):** This Act is formulated to impose a stipulated amount of criminal penalties on individuals who intentionally attempt to access protected digital devices without having the required authorization. These cybercriminals tend to access protected digital devices by escalating relevant privileges. The multiple amendments of this Act by the concerned legal authority led to its appropriateness for the ongoing evolution of technology. The underlying provisions of this Act relate to prohibited conduct that focuses on prohibiting multiple computer-oriented conduct. These conduct includes unauthorized access to digital devices, collecting national security information, and committing fraud. The Act applies to the protected computers of reputed institutions such as the US Government and Financial Institutions. The violation of the **Computer Fraud and Abuse Act (CFAA)** results in both civil and criminal penalties in the form of fines and imprisonment.

Apart from the laws and regulations, relevant jurisdiction issues further tend to contribute to the legal considerations of digital forensics for enterprises. These issues are significant for handling cross-border data and legal conflicts. This is typically due to the datacenter location of countries being located across international borders. The admissibility of digital evidence in the Court of Law plays a vital role in the associated ongoing legal cases. This aspect encourages maintaining proper documentation of the digital evidence using the CoC technique to maintain the integrity of the concerned digital evidence.

- **Ethical considerations:** The ethical consideration of digital evidence for enterprise-related benefits resembles four specific areas: privacy concerns, consent and authorization, bias and objectivity, and data minimization. The privacy concern corresponds to balancing employee rights and corporate security. The combination of consent and authorization ensures proper approvals before investigations. The importance of bias and objectivity is relevant to avoiding conflicts of interest in forensic analysis. The significance of data minimization ties into collecting only necessary data to protect individuals' rights.
- **Challenges and best practices:** The prevalence of critical challenges results in adhering to relevant legal and ethical considerations of digital forensics for the business benefit of enterprises. This applies to frequently observed pitfalls within the scope of digital forensics. These pitfalls include the use of anti-forensics techniques, technical challenges, resource constraints, documentation and presentation, skill gaps, and legal challenges *(Figure 5.3)*.

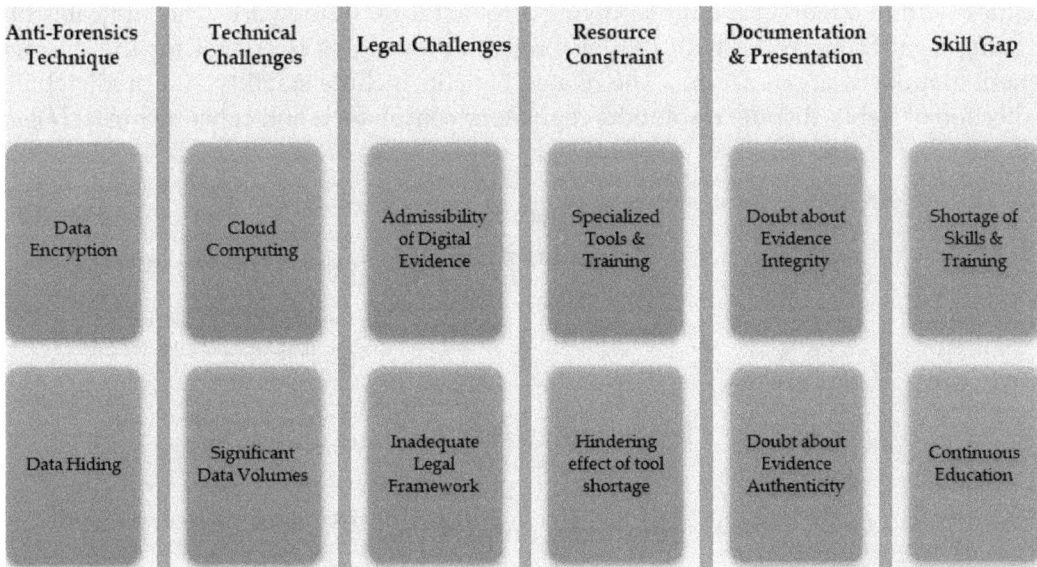

Anti-Forensics Technique	Technical Challenges	Legal Challenges	Resource Constraint	Documentation & Presentation	Skill Gap
Data Encryption	Cloud Computing	Admissibility of Digital Evidence	Specialized Tools & Training	Doubt about Evidence Integrity	Shortage of Skills & Training
Data Hiding	Significant Data Volumes	Inadequate Legal Framework	Hindering effect of tool shortage	Doubt about Evidence Authenticity	Continuous Education

Figure 5.3: Challenges

The aim of tackling the observed challenges of digital forensics and thereby utilizing its benefits for the cybersecurity requirements of enterprises resembles the application of suitable best practices. These best practices include the implementation of corporate digital forensics policy along with employee training and development. Furthermore, the aspect of employee training and development aligns with specifically focusing on building an efficient forensic team consisting of skilled individuals with the appropriate set of competencies. Such teams require efficiency in specific areas of digital forensics, such as compliance and ethics.

The reconstruction of the cybercrime situation as an essential requirement of cyber forensics investigation engages with the dedicated application of effective skills and competencies. The progress of digital forensics investigation steadily resembles adhering to relevant legal and ethical standards and best practices. The adequate development of legal and ethical principles for benefiting digital forensics investigations corresponds with catering to the needs of ongoing worldwide digital transformation across different business sectors. However, this requires tackling the inherent challenges of digital forensics, such as skill gaps, and using effective best practices, such as continuous training and development of employees. The relevant focus on the development of digital forensics from legal and ethical aspects applies to integrating proactive compliance and ethical responsibility.

Understanding the legal framework

The operation of business by companies within a market results in significantly influences the surrounding social and economic areas. The steady stability and predictability of a business within a market require applying a robust legal framework. This indicates that aligning legal frameworks with digital forensics procedures is crucial for the business benefit of modern organizations. The related benefits include stability and predictability, protection of rights, dispute resolution, regulatory compliance, and consumer trust *(Figure 5.4)*.

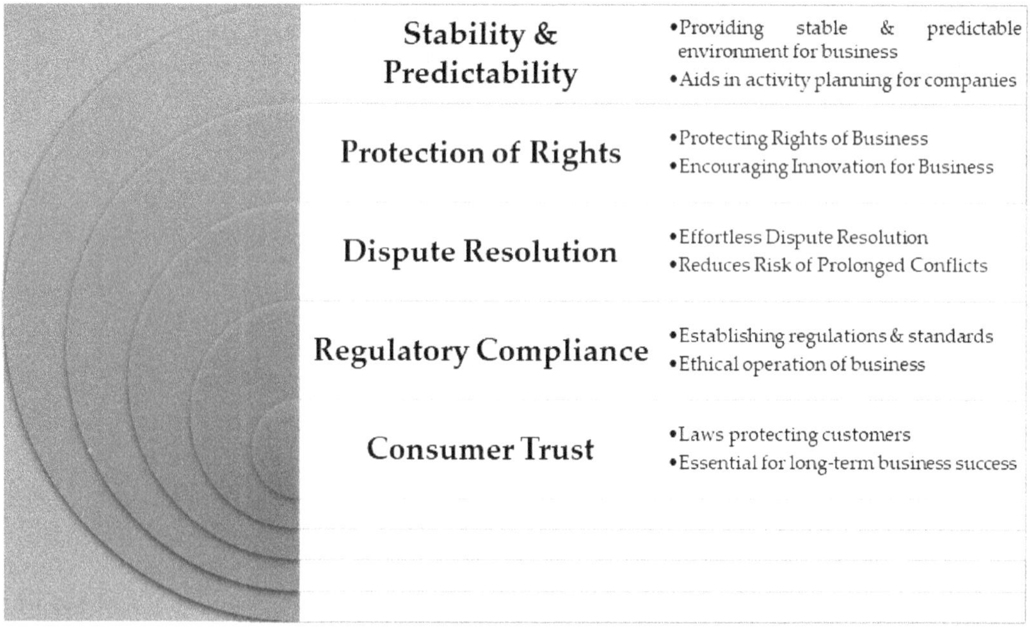

Stability & Predictability	•Providing stable & predictable environment for business •Aids in activity planning for companies
Protection of Rights	•Protecting Rights of Business •Encouraging Innovation for Business
Dispute Resolution	•Effortless Dispute Resolution •Reduces Risk of Prolonged Conflicts
Regulatory Compliance	•Establishing regulations & standards •Ethical operation of business
Consumer Trust	•Laws protecting customers •Essential for long-term business success

Figure 5.4: Importance of a robust legal framework for business

Apart from business benefits, legal frameworks are crucial for businesses for their governance requirement. This is in terms of the rule of law, accountability and transparency, protection of rights and freedom, economic development, and social order and stability *(Figure 5.5)*.

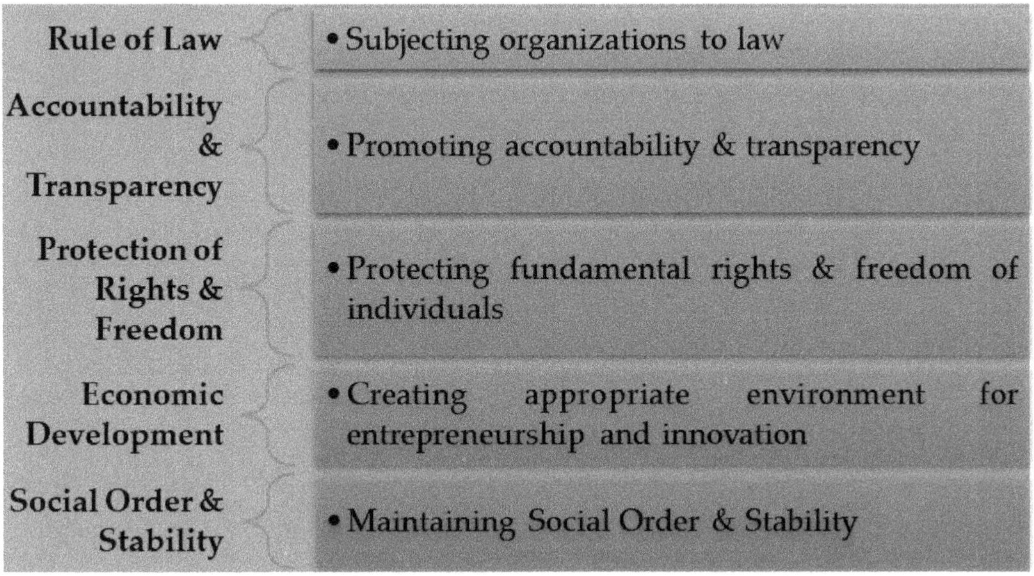

Rule of Law	• Subjecting organizations to law
Accountability & Transparency	• Promoting accountability & transparency
Protection of Rights & Freedom	• Protecting fundamental rights & freedom of individuals
Economic Development	• Creating appropriate environment for entrepreneurship and innovation
Social Order & Stability	• Maintaining Social Order & Stability

Figure 5.5: *Importance of a robust legal framework for governance*

The combined impact of laws and regulations plays a critical role in ensuring compliance and accountability for businesses across multiple sectors. The companies adhere to laws and regulations to fulfill compliance requirements in terms of identifying effective guidelines and standards to follow. Similarly, the adherence of companies to laws and regulations connects to accountability assurance in terms of gaining stakeholder confidence and abiding by the ethical culture. The requirement of understanding legal frameworks requires focusing on the following areas:

- **Key legal concepts:** The overall difference between laws and regulations encourages companies to abide by them accordingly. The laws are specific rules of conduct established by concerned legislative bodies, such as the national or state government. This is contrary to regulations, which are specific rules and standards issued by government agencies or regulatory bodies to implement and enforce the laws. The importance of compliance varies as per the development of different industrial sectors *(Figure 5.6)*.

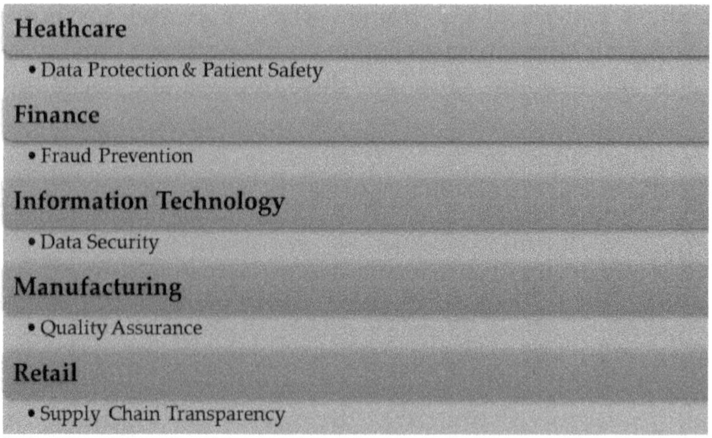

Figure 5.6: *Importance of compliance for various industries*

The enforcement of different bodies is crucial for observing the adherence of different companies to regulatory frameworks *(Figure 5.7)*.

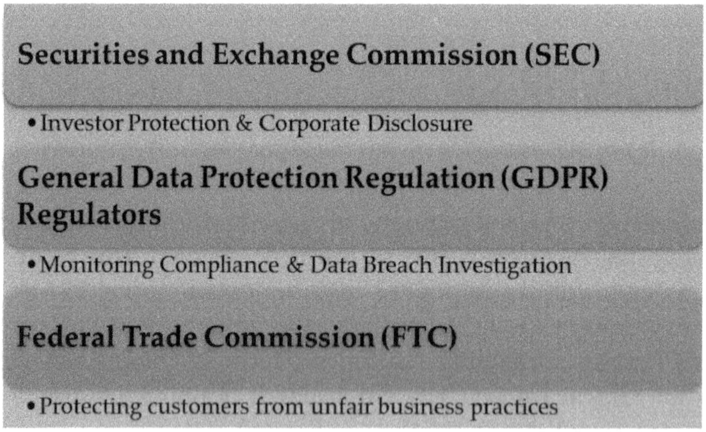

Figure 5.7: *Different regulatory authorities*

- **Major laws and regulations:** The aspect of major laws and regulations is relevant to detailed focusing on data protection laws, financial compliance, cybersecurity regulations, and employment and workplace laws. The focus on specific laws includes the GDPR, the CCPA, and the **Health Insurance Portability and Accountability Act (HIPAA)**. The related financial compliance includes the **Sarbanes-Oxley Act (SOX)**, **Anti-Money Laundering (AML)**, and Basel III. The associated cybersecurity regulations include the **National Institute of Standards and Technology (NIST)**, ISO 27001, and the Cybersecurity Act. The corresponding employment and workplace laws include the **Occupational Safety and Health Administration (OSHA)**, the **Fair Labor Standards Act (FLSA)**, and anti-discrimination laws.

- **Compliance requirements and challenges:** The compliance requirements and challenges include obligations for organizations, penalties for non-compliance, and challenges in compliance. The observed obligations for organizations include areas such as documentation, audits, and reporting. The relevant penalties for non-compliance for organizations include paying fines, facing lawsuits, and repairing reputational damage. However, the relevant challenges in compliance include the evolution of laws, cross-border regulations, and the cost of compliance.

- **Best practices for compliance:** The reputed companies tend to introduce relevant best practices for compliance for their overall operational benefit. These best practices include establishing a compliance framework and corporate governance policies. The conduct of regular audits and risk assessments within the operational areas of the company leads to its appropriateness for compliance. The enterprises subject their base of employees to relevant training and awareness programs. The enterprises proceed with selecting relevant compliance technology and automation.

The changing, evolving digital infrastructure of different business sectors leads to highlights the overall importance of staying updated with regulatory changes for companies. The detailed analysis of compliance frameworks implies their inherent strategic advantage for businesses.

Privacy rights and data protection

The rising influence of digital transformation on the professional and personal lives of individuals worldwide leads to critical outcomes for their privacy rights. This is due to the increasing amount of shared data along with online processing. Thus, the importance of privacy rights and data protection links to the protection of data from data misuse and the safeguarding of personal freedom on the online platform. This directly implies striking a relevant balance between investigative needs and individual rights. The detailed discussion in this regard engages with the following areas:

- **Key privacy and data protection laws:** The notable privacy and data protection laws include GDPR, CCPA, HIPAA, and the CFAA. The GDPR is relevant to the provision of the Right to privacy and data minimization. The CCPA states the consumer's rights over personal data. The HIPAA implies the protection of medical data. The CFAA is concerned with the prevention of unauthorized access.

- **Investigative needs vs. individual rights:** The inherent difference between investigative needs and individual rights draws upon different perspectives. These perspectives include law enforcement and corporate investigations, the right to privacy and consent, and jurisdiction. The importance of law enforcement and corporate investigations resembles the overall need for access to digital evidence. The right to privacy states the importance of protecting personal data and confidentiality. The related consent and justification state the procedure of legal data collection.

- **Ethical and legal challenges:** The wide range of ethical and legal challenges includes overreach and surveillance, data retention and minimization, and cross-border data issues. The overreach and surveillance resemble relevant risks of excessive monitoring. The challenge of data retention and minimization involves limiting the collection of data to a limited extent. The presence of conflicting privacy laws in different jurisdictions leads to relevant cross-border data issues.

- **Best practices for balancing interests:** The presence of underlying challenges requires the application of best practices for the effective balancing of interests. These practices can include implementing clear data governance policies, apart from ensuring transparency and accountability in investigations. Enterprises can focus on using **privacy-enhancing technologies** (**PETs**) to limit unnecessary exposure. The relevant authority requires training investigators and employees on legal and ethical considerations.

The increased complexity of the modern digital world and the extended influence of worldwide digital transformation on enterprises require a balanced approach to protect both security and privacy. This is in addition to continuous adaptation to evolving legal and technological landscapes.

Chain of custody and evidence handling

CoC from the perspective of digital forensics is defined as the concept of documenting, handling, and preserving digital evidence to maintain its integrity and admissibility before presenting it at the Court of Law. The benefit of this procedure from the digital forensics perspective coincides with ensuring its authenticity since the collection from a cybercrime scene and presenting it in a Court of Law. The aspect of proper evidence handling of digital evidence for legal admissibility reflects upon maintaining its integrity and authenticity. The assured CoC Compliance resembles different factors such as details of the collector, timestamp of assessment and transfer, and evidence analysis. The presence of a gap in the CoC about digital evidence leads to credibility questions in terms of evidence tampering. The detailed discussion about CoC and evidence handling hinges on the following areas:

- **Understanding CoC:** The CoC is recognized as a documented process tracking evidence from collection to court. This phase is crucial for digital forensics due to its attempt to prevent tampering, thereby ensuring the authenticity and maintaining the credibility of the digital evidence.

- **Key steps in CoC:** The key steps in CoC relate to identification and collection, documentation, storage and preservation, transfer and access control, and presentation in court. The identification and collection of digital evidence refers back to the application of proper techniques for acquiring digital evidence. The documentation phase links with logging timestamps, handlers, and actions taken. The storage and preservation of digital evidence are addressed using secure methods to prevent data alteration. The transfer and access control of digital evidence restricts unauthorized access to digital evidence. The presentation of digital evidence in the court of law involves demonstrating an unbroken CoC to establish reliability.

- **Challenges in digital evidence handling:** The relevant challenges faced by the digital forensic investigators during the phase of investigation relate to data volatility, encryption and security, and cross-jurisdiction issues. The issue of data volatility encompasses the risk of accidental modification or corruption. The challenge of encryption and security corresponds to handling protected files lawfully. The significant issue related to cross-jurisdiction implies the prevalence of different legal standards for CoC across different parts of the world.

- **Best practices for ensuring evidence integrity:** Forensic investigators tend to face a wide range of challenges while progressing digital forensic investigations, and thereby adopt relevant best practices. These best practices include using forensic tools for data acquisition, such as EnCase and **The Sleuth Kit** (**TSK**). This is apart from maintaining detailed logs and audit trails, as well as ensuring that digital evidence is stored in secure, tamper-proof environments. This is in addition to training forensic teams on CoC protocols and legal requirements.

The increasing complexity of digital forensic investigation leads to reinforcing the need for strict adherence to CoC. The digital forensic investigators are required to assess the overall impact of improper handling on investigations and legal proceedings. The relevant continuous updates to forensic policies as per evolving digital threats can result in relevant benefits for the associated digital forensics investigators.

Consent and authorization

The legal and ethical considerations are crucial to ensure that the concerned digital evidence is collected, analyzed, and presented in a lawful, fair, and professional manner. This applies to consent and authorization, playing a critical role in protecting individual rights and ensuring compliance. The detailed discussion to comprehend consent and authorization in terms of obtaining proper permission for forensic investigation associated with the following areas:

- **Understanding consent and authorization:** The concept of consent pertains to voluntary agreement by an individual or entity to allow forensic examination. On the other side, the perspective of authorization concerns legal or institutional approval, granting permission for an investigation. Thus, the key difference between these two concepts includes their context of requirement and overall legal implications.

- **Legal framework and compliance:** The adherence to a wide range of legal frameworks and compliance requires data protection laws, employment and corporate investigations, and law enforcement considerations. The relevant data protection laws include GDPR, CCPA, and HIPAA, and they are required for obtaining the required consent. The associated employment and corporate investigations relate to phases when employer monitoring is permissible. The appropriate law enforcement considerations include warrants, subpoenas, and legal justifications.

- **Challenges in obtaining proper permissions:** The process of obtaining proper permission refers to concerned digital forensic investigators facing critical challenges. These challenges include a lack of awareness, emergence versus consent, and jurisdictional variations. The elaboration of emergence versus consent connects to handling urgent cases without prior approval. The lack of awareness is the employees and stakeholders failing to realize their rights within the operational areas of an organization. The challenge of jurisdictional variations for obtaining proper permissions corresponds to different legal standards prevailing across various regions of the world.

- **Best practices for consent and authorization:** The successful mitigation of observed challenges to obtain proper permission includes the implementation of clear policies on digital investigations. The requirement of ensuring transparency with employees and stakeholders as a best practice for consent and authorization further applies to using legally binding agreements and documented approvals. The regular training on forensic ethics and legal compliance enhances the overall chances of speedily obtaining consent and authorization.

The necessity of effectively balancing investigative needs with individual rights links to adhering to the importance of maintaining legal and ethical integrity in forensic procedures. This concerns adapting to the evolving regulations for responsible digital investigations.

Intellectual property and trade secrets

The increasing dependency of organizations on IP and trade secrets for the generation of business profitability is relevant to the crucial role of digital forensics in investigating IP theft and data breaches. The understanding of IP and trade secrets from the perspective of safeguarding sensitive information during forensic processes ties into the following areas:

- **Understanding IP and trade secrets:** The concept of IP includes patents, copyrights, trademarks, and trade secrets. Specifically, trade secrets are confidential business information having competitive value. The legal protections include laws such as the **Defend Trade Secrets Act (DTSA), Trade-Related Aspects of Intellectual Property Rights (TRIPS)**, and the **Economic Espionage Act (EEA)**.

- **Risks to sensitive information in forensic processes:** The relevant risks to sensitive information in forensic processes include unauthorized access, data leakage, and legal challenges. The aspect of unauthorized access indicates risks of exposure during forensic investigations. The risk of data leakage resembles accidental or intentional disclosure of confidential files. The legal challenges indicate ensuring compliance with privacy and IP protection laws.

- **Best practices for safeguarding sensitive information:** The application of best practices by the digital forensic investigators is crucial to tackle the observed risks. These best practices include access control, secure handling and storage, **non-disclosure agreements (NDAs)**, data minimization, and compliance with legal Frameworks. The strategy of access control engages by restricting forensic access to authorized personnel only. The best practice of secure handling and storage resembles encrypting and protecting forensic data repositories. The importance of NDAs resonates with ensuring that forensic investigators maintain confidentiality. The strategy of data minimization aligns with collecting only necessary evidence to limit exposure. The target of complying with legal frameworks resembles adhering to IP laws and corporate policies.

- **Challenges in balancing forensic needs and IP protection:** The procedure of balancing forensic needs and IP protection results in facing critical challenges for the concerned forensic investigators. These challenges include forensic integrity versus confidentiality, cross-border investigations, and internal threats. The forensic integrity versus confidentiality resembles ensuring integrity safeguarding during the phase of digital forensics investigations. The significance of cross-border investigations is due to the different IP laws prevailing in global jurisdictions. The challenge of internal threats touches on leaks from employees, having forensic access.

The overall importance of securing IP during digital forensic investigations concerns the inherent need for strict protocols, legal compliance, and ethical handling. This further encourages the overall importance of continuous adaptation to new threats and evolving IP laws.

Expert testimony and reporting

The increasing complexity of digital crimes in modern days requires the presence of expert testimony and reporting from the specific perspective of presenting digital evidence in legal proceedings. The critical role of forensic experts in the presentation of digital crime cases in the Court of Law includes explaining the technical findings to the best possible extent. The details of expert testimony and reporting from the perspective of presenting digital evidence in legal proceedings relate to the following areas:

- **Understanding expert testimony in digital forensics:** The expert witness is recognized as a qualified professional with specialized forensic knowledge. The digital forensic investigators tend to consider relevant legal standards, such as the Daubert and Frye standards, as expert testimony for digital evidence admissibility in the Court of Law. The relevant responsibilities of an expert witness include objectivity, credibility, and clarity in presenting findings at the Court of Law.

- **Preparing and presenting digital evidence:** The aspect of Forensic Reporting applies to structuring clear, concise, and legally sound reports. The CoC links to demonstrating proper evidence handling to maintain integrity. The required simplifying technical information resonates with using non-technical language for judges and juries. The related visual aids and demonstrations include charts, timelines, and digital reconstructions for clarity.

- **Challenges in presenting digital evidence:** The related challenges in presenting digital evidence include technical complexity, cross-examination risks, and credibility and bias concerns. The technical complexity corresponds with overcoming misunderstandings by legal professionals. The cross-examination risks include handling challenges from opposing counsel. The relevant credibility and bias concerns include ensuring neutrality and professional integrity.

- **Best practices for effective expert testimony:** The application of best practices to ensure expert testimony and reporting is crucial for modern-day digital investigators. These best practices include adhering to legal and ethical standards. The best practice of comprehensive documentation includes maintaining accurate forensic records. Effective communication skills are important for explaining the findings in a structured and clear manner. Courtroom preparedness connects with anticipating possible questions and legal challenges.

The importance of expert testimony in ensuring justice and legal accuracy is associated with fulfilling the need for forensic professionals to stay updated on legal and technical standards. The continuous improvement in reporting and testimony techniques is linked with effective evidence presentation.

Legal challenges and preparing for litigation

The importance of legal preparedness in digital forensics and cybersecurity cases reflects on its inherent complexity. This thereby justifies the critical role of forensic evidence in both defense and prosecution for cases involving the role of digital forensics. The related areas in this regard include the following:

- **Common legal challenges in digital litigation:** The common legal challenges faced by digital investigators in digital litigation include the admissibility of evidence. This is intended to ensure compliance with legal standards as per Daubert or Frye. Further observation of challenges includes CoC issues that pertain to risks of tampering, improper documentation, or data integrity loss. The jurisdictional conflicts include handling cross-border data and differing legal frameworks. The associated privacy and compliance relate to balancing investigative needs with suitable privacy laws, such as the GDPR and the CCPA.

- **Strategies for effective litigation preparation:** The strategies for effective litigation preparation include comprehensive evidence collection, proper documentation and reporting, expert testimony readiness, and legal and technical collaboration. The strategy of comprehensive evidence collection resembles using legally sound forensic methods. The strategy of proper documentation and reporting resembles maintaining accurate and defensible records. The best practice of expert testimony readiness corresponds to engaging qualified forensic experts for court proceedings. The legal and technical collaboration resembles working closely with legal teams to strengthen case arguments.

- **Defense strategies in litigation:** The appropriate defense strategies in litigation include challenging evidence integrity, questioning CoC gaps, and demonstrating alternative explanations. The challenging evidence integrity is elaborated as identifying flaws in opposing forensic methods. The questioning of CoC gaps bears upon highlighting improper evidence handling. The demonstration of alternative explanations connects with providing counterarguments based on forensic analysis.

- **Prosecution strategies in litigation:** The appropriate prosecution strategies in litigation relate to presenting strong digital evidence. This is in terms of using clear, well-documented forensic findings. The strategy of building a transparent narrative involves simplifying technical details for judges and juries. The effective cross-examination of opposing experts pertains to identifying inconsistencies in their testimony.

The importance of strategic legal preparation for both prosecution and defense refers to the evolving nature of digital evidence and legal precedents. This is further to the necessity of continuous training for legal and forensic professionals.

The Indian Information Technology Act of 2000

The **Information Technology (IT)** Act, 2000, is the primary cyber law of India. The importance of this law lies in regulating digital crimes and forensic investigations. The detailed assessment of this Act from the beneficial perspective of digital forensics is discussed as follows:

- **Key objectives of the IT Act, 2000:** The key objectives of this Act include the legal recognition of electronic records and digital signatures. The intermediary objective of this Act is linked to the prevention of cybercrimes and the enforcement of cybersecurity measures. The key provisions of this Act result in establish legal frameworks for electronic governance and transactions.

- **Relevant provisions for digital forensics:** The underlying provisions within this Act for the perspective of digital forensics include Sections 43, 65, 66, and 66B-D, 67 and 67A, 69, and 79. Section 43 of this Act reflects upon unauthorized access, data theft, and penalties. Section 65 of this Act resembles tampering with computer source documents. Section 66 of the Act correlates with hacking and identity theft. Sections 66B, 66C, and 66D relate to punishments for data theft, identity fraud, and impersonation. Sections 67 and 67A of the Act imply regulation of obscene or offensive content. Section 69 of the Act gives the government the power to intercept, monitor, and decrypt information. Section 79 of the Act refers back to intermediary liability and safe harbor provisions.

- **Role of digital forensics in IT Act enforcement:** The significant role of digital forensics in IT Act enforcement includes investigating cybercrimes using forensic techniques. This is apart from ensuring the integrity and admissibility of digital evidence in courts. The effective collaboration between law enforcement and forensic experts for cybercrime cases.

- **Challenges in implementation:** The relevant challenges in the implementation of the Act include balancing cybersecurity enforcement with individual privacy rights. The wide range of challenges further includes rapid technological advancements, creating legal gaps. The relevant challenges further extend to cross-border jurisdiction issues in cybercrime investigations.

The evolving nature of the IT Act to address emerging cyber threats corresponds to the importance of continuous legal updates and forensic advancements. The provision of this Act further includes the need for awareness and training in digital forensics and cyber law compliance.

Challenges and opportunities

The growing cyber threats and the need for cross-border digital forensics indicate the importance of international collaboration in cybercrime investigations. The detailed analysis of the challenges and opportunities in cross-border digital forensics investigation in India is stated as follows:

- **Key challenges in cross-border digital forensics:** The key challenges include jurisdictional conflicts, data privacy laws, **Mutual Legal Assistance Treaties (MLATs)**, cloud data storage issues, encryption and anonymity, and lack of standardized forensic procedures. The jurisdictional conflicts indicate the presence of different legal frameworks across countries. The data privacy laws include compliance with the GDPR, the IT Act 2000, and the CCPA. The MLATs relate to the lengthy legal processes for evidence sharing. The cloud data storage issues relate to challenges in accessing data stored overseas. The challenge of encryption and anonymity ties into difficulties in tracking cybercriminals using VPNs, Tor, and encryption. The lack of Standardized Forensic Procedures affects evidence integrity.

- **Opportunities in cross-border digital forensics:** Despite having multiple key challenges in cross-border digital forensics, the presence of relevant opportunities leads to effective benefits for the Digital Forensic Investigators. These opportunities include international cooperation that strengthens agreements with agencies like Interpol, the **United Nations Office on Drugs and Crime (UNODC)**, and **Computer Emergency Response Teams (CERTs)**. The benefit of forensic technology advancements applies to the application of AI-driven investigations and blockchain-based evidence tracking. The relevant cybercrime conventions relate to the participation of India in global initiatives such as the Budapest Convention. The advantage of public-private partnerships encourages collaboration between law enforcement and tech companies for data access.

- **Strategies for overcoming challenges:** The application of relevant strategies for overcoming challenges is crucial for the associated digital forensic investigators. These strategies include strengthening bilateral and multilateral treaties for faster evidence exchange. The target of aligning Indian cyber laws with global standards further simplifies the investigation situation for the investigators. The appropriate enhancement of capacity-building programs for forensic professionals leads to their confidently tackling cybercrime cases. The presence of suitable strategies leads to encouraging cross-border forensic research and technology sharing.

The need for developing robust legal and technical frameworks for digital forensics in India requires proactive global cooperation in combating cyber threats. The consistently developing cyber ecosystem of India requires adequate development of digital forensics.

Conclusion

The current chapter provided a detailed analysis of introducing legal and ethical considerations in digital forensics for enterprises. The increasing complexity of digital crimes in modern days requires the involvement of efficient digital forensics experts to ensure the generation of effective results that can be utilized for the seamless growth and development of this field.

The upcoming chapter refers to the unfolding overall process of digital forensics.

Join our book's Discord space

Join the book's Discord Workspace for Latest updates, Offers, Tech happenings around the world, New Release and Sessions with the Authors:

https://discord.bpbonline.com

CHAPTER 6
Unfolding the Digital Forensics Process

Introduction

The process of digital forensics investigation is a prolonged procedure depending on the complexity involved in the assessment of the involved digital devices. This complexity relates to the volume and variety of data derived from digital devices. The storage of data in modern days involves multiple formats such as documents, e-mails, images, videos, logs, and encryption files.

Structure

The chapter covers the following topics:

- Introduction to the digital forensics process
- IR and preparation
- Identification and collection of digital evidence
- Preservation and documentation
- Acquisition and imaging
- Data recovery and reconstruction
- Analysis and examination
- Forensic tools and techniques

- Timeline and event reconstruction
- Correlation and link analysis

Objectives

This chapter looks at the process of digital forensics in detail. This results in a detailed and step-by-step overview of multiple stages involved in the digital forensics procedure. The chapter includes adequate details about **incident response** (**IR**) and preparation from the perspective of digital forensics investigation. The chapter implies effective identification and collection of digital evidence in terms of locating and securing potential evidence sources. The chapter focuses on detailed and appropriate preservation and documentation of digital evidence. This is crucial in terms of ensuring the integrity and traceability of the concerned digital evidence. The detailed analysis of the acquisition and imaging process of digital evidence pertains to creating forensically sound copies of digital media. The concerned process of data recovery and reconstruction of digital evidence implies extracting and reassembling information from the collected digital artifacts. The phase of analysis and examination of digital evidence connects to uncovering and interpreting digital evidence. The chapter details relevant forensic tools and techniques that digital forensic investigators use to solve cases of digital forensics. The importance of an efficient timeline and event reconstruction links to establishing the sequence of events in a Digital Incident. The effective correlation and link analysis as an essential part of digital forensics corresponds to the effective identification of relationships.

Introduction to the digital forensics process

The procedure of digital forensics involves investigating digital devices by considering diverse and evolving technologies. The process of digital forensics is typically associated with the investigation of cyber incidents, fraud, and security breaches. The stepwise overview of Digital Forensics involves considering the following areas:

- **Definition of digital forensics:** Digital forensics is a detailed procedure of identifying, collecting, analyzing, and preserving electronic data to investigate cybersecurity incidents, security breaches, fraud, and legal disputes. The growing importance of digital forensics in the corporate environment concerns IR and threat mitigation. This is elaborated as investigating cyberattacks, unauthorized access, and data breaches to determine the cause and prevent future incidents. Digital forensics is important for investigating a wide variety of cyberattacks, such as Malware Infections, Ransomware, phishing, and **denial-of-service** (**DoS**) attacks. This is crucial in terms of identifying the attack vector and thereby tracing the action of the attacker. The digital forensics investigation of unauthorized access to systems, accounts, or corporate networks leads to the successful tracking of intrusion attempts along with the detection of privilege escalation. The importance of digital investigation for data breaches is associated with determining the source of the breach and thereby recovering lost or stolen data.

- **Objectives of digital forensics:** The relevant objectives of digital forensics include the identification of key goals related to evidence collection, analysis, preservation, and reporting. The careful collection of digital evidence from the cybercrime scene ties into ensuring the integrity, reliability, and admissibility of its underlying data for both legal and corporate investigations. The analysis of digital evidence is relevant to revealing its underlying data and thereby establishing the facts and the associated timeline of the events. Digital forensics investigators typically focus on reconstructing the who, what, when, where, and how of a cyber incident. The effective preservation of digital evidence resonates with maintaining its overall integrity and authenticity to reduce the chance of data alteration, corruption, or destruction. The reporting of findings from digital forensics investigations applies to ensuring clarity and accuracy in findings. This is crucial in terms of improving future IR and cybersecurity measures.

- **Importance of a structured process:** The application of a structured process for digital forensics analysis involves generating methodical and legally sound research. The importance of a methodical and legally sound approach in forensics corresponds with ensuring evidence integrity and authenticity. This aligns with applying write-blocking tools, cryptographic hashing, and forensic imaging that ensure the integrity preservation of the evidence during its admissibility in the Court of Law. The aspect of a structured process touches on maintaining a transparent **Chain of Custody (CoC)** that guarantees the integrity and preservation of the evidence till the completion of the investigation procedure. The Court of Law and relevant regulatory bodies require appropriate documentation to accept the digital evidence. The occurrence of any procedural error, such as ineffective evidence handling, leads to the dismissal of evidence at the Court of Law.

- **Step-by-step overview of the process:** The overall procedure of digital forensics Analysis resembles the completion of intermediate steps. These steps are as follows:

  1. **Identification:** The timely identification of digital evidence from the cybercrime scene is crucial to managing the overall progress of a digital forensic investigation.

  2. **Preservation:** The effective preservation of digital evidence connects with securing and protecting data from alteration.

  3. **Collection:** The effective gathering of relevant digital artifacts is linked with gathering relevant digital artifacts systematically.

  4. **Examination:** The examination, as a part of digital forensics, bears upon filtering and processing collected data for analysis.

  5. **Analysis:** The interpretation of digital forensics findings reflects on reconstructing events.

6. **Documentation:** The documentation of findings from digital forensics connects with effectively reporting them at the Court of Law.

7. **Reporting:** The presentation of findings by the digital forensic investigator reflects on presenting in a transparent and legally defensible manner

- **Legal and ethical considerations:** The specific role of corporate policies and legal frameworks for digital forensics investigation ties into adhering to CoC and privacy regulations. The relevant legal frameworks relate to the Federal Rules of Evidence (U.S.), the UK **Police and Criminal Evidence Act** (**PACE**), and the EU **General Data Protection Regulation** (**GDPR**). The corresponding ethical consideration deals with integrity and objectivity. Contextually, digital forensics professionals are required to maintain neutrality and avoid bias in digital forensics investigations.
- **Real-world relevance:** The Uber Data Breach Cover-Up (2016) resembles the company experiencing a data breach where hackers accessed the personal data of 57 million riders and drivers. The security team of Uber paid the hackers an amount of $100,000 to keep it secret and delete the data. The role of digital forensics in this case study refers to digital forensics investigators uncovering the breach during an internal audit after a leadership change at Uber in 2017.

IR and preparation

The presence of a well-prepared **IR strategy** is essential for handling digital security breaches and ensuring a smooth forensic investigation. This engages in proper preparation, which enables organizations to detect, contain, and analyze security incidents effectively while preserving crucial digital evidence. The effective IR and preparation resemble the procedures for digital forensics investigation. This is associated with considering the following areas:

- **Understanding IR in digital forensics:** The IR is the structured approach organizations take to detect, investigate, contain, and recover from cybersecurity incidents such as data breaches, malware attacks, insider threats, and unauthorized access. It plays a critical role in minimizing damage, preserving digital evidence, and ensuring business continuity. The role of IR in cybersecurity deals with rapid threat detection and containment that identifies cyber threats early to prevent their further escalation. The role of IR in forensic investigations involves preserving digital evidence to ensure that logs, files, and system data are collected without alteration. This is because the process uses forensic imaging and write-blocking techniques to maintain integrity. A well-prepared IR plan ensures that organizations can detect, contain, and recover from cybersecurity incidents quickly and efficiently. This is because, without the presence of a structured response, cyber threats such as ransomware attacks, data breaches, and insider threats can escalate, causing severe financial, operational, and reputational damage.

- **Importance of preparation:** The rapidly evolving threat landscape discourages the organization from waiting till an attack occurs to undertake suitable mitigation strategies. This resembles a reactive response rather than a proactive action. However, early threat detection prevents its escalation as proactive monitoring allows organizations to identify security threats before they become full-scale incidents. The proactive action of organizations further coincides with the introduction of **Security Information and Event Management (SIEM)** tools, **Intrusion Detection Systems (IDS)**, and endpoint protection to help detect anomalies in real time. The inherent benefit of a Structured **Incident Response Plan (IRP)** reflects upon faster detection and containment of threats, along with the minimization of financial and operational losses.

- **Key components of an IRP:** The relevant key components of an IRP relate to the following areas:

  o **Detection and identification:** This component of the IRP ties back to recognizing security incidents and potential threats.

  o **Containment:** This component of IRP revolves around isolating affected systems to prevent further damage.

  o **Eradication:** This component of IRP implies removing threats and vulnerabilities.

  o **Recovery:** This component of IRP indicates restoring systems and data integrity.

  o **Lessons learned:** This component of IRP corresponds to analyzing the incident to improve future response efforts.

- **Roles and responsibilities in an IRT:** The Security analysts play a critical role in an **Incident Response Team (IRT)** in terms of threat detection and monitoring, along with incident analysis and investigation. The forensic investigators within an IRT identify and preserve digital evidence by ensuring proper CoC to maintain evidence integrity. The roles and responsibilities of legal advisors within an IRT relate to ensuring legal and regulatory compliance by advising on cybersecurity laws, data protection regulations, and industry compliance standards such as GDPR, HIPAA, **Payment Card Industry Data Security Standard (PCI-DSS)**, and ISO 27001. The IT administrators within an IRT proceed with threat monitoring and detection in terms of continuously monitoring network activity, system logs, and security alerts for suspicious behavior.

- **Essential tools and technologies for IR:** The essential tools and technologies for IR include SIEM systems, **Endpoint Detection and Response (EDR)** tools, and forensic imaging and data preservation tools.

- **Establishing a forensic-ready environment:** The establishment of a forensic-ready environment impacts implementing policies for logging, monitoring, and access control. This further associates to training employees to recognize and report security incidents to ensure that legal compliance and data retention policies are in place.

- **Simulating and testing response plans:** The practice of conducting tabletop exercises and penetration testing results in effective simulation and testing of response plans. This further corresponds to regular updates and refinement of response strategies.

- **Real-world example:** Maersk, a global shipping giant, fell victim to the NotPetya ransomware attack in June of 2017. The malware quickly spread across its network, disrupting operations in 76 ports worldwide, shutting down over 4,000 servers, and crippling its IT infrastructure. Despite the massive scale of the cyber incident, Maersk's well-coordinated response strategy enabled a successful recovery. The immediate containment measures of IRT relate to the immediate isolation of infected systems to prevent further spread of the ransomware.

Identification and collection of digital evidence

The commencement of a digital forensic investigation influences the first critical step of identifying and collecting digital evidence from various sources. This digital evidence includes files, logs, emails, metadata, and system traces that help reconstruct cyber incidents. The detailed identification and collection of digital evidence in terms of locating and securing potential evidence sources indicate the following areas:

- **Understanding digital evidence:** Digital evidence refers to any information or data stored, transmitted, or processed in a digital format that can be used as evidence in a forensic investigation. The range of digital evidence includes files, emails, logs, metadata, network activity, and digital artifacts found on computers, mobile devices, cloud storage, and other electronic systems. The volatile evidence implies that its underlying data exists only temporarily and is lost when a device is powered off or altered. The non-volatile evidence indicates that its stored data remains unchanged even when a system is powered off. The integrity of digital evidence refers to ensuring that digital evidence remains unchanged from the time of collection to its presentation in an investigation. Any alteration can compromise its reliability. The admissibility of digital evidence determines whether digital evidence can be used in legal or corporate investigations.

- **Identifying potential evidence sources:** The effective identification of potential evidence sources is connected with the following:
  - **Computers and servers**: Hard drives, system logs, and file systems.
  - **Mobile devices**: Calls, messages, app data, and location history.
  - **Network infrastructure**: Routers, Firewalls, logs, and packet captures.

- o **Cloud storage and SaaS applications**: Emails, shared files, and backups.

- o **Removable media**: USB drives, external hard disks, and memory cards.

- o **IoT and smart devices**: Security cameras, smart assistants, and wearables.

- **Collection best practices:** The best practices for the collection of digital evidence relate to ensuring forensic soundness by avoiding data alteration. The best practices include imaging and cloning digital evidence by using forensic tools to create bit-by-bit copies. The difference between live and dead acquisition associates to capturing volatile data and capturing non-volatile data, respectively. The importance of CoC bridges to documenting every step, from the collection of digital evidence to its analysis.

- **Legal and compliance considerations:** The legal consideration is interwoven with the following company policies, data privacy laws, and industry regulations. This is further to ensuring proper authorization of digital evidence before its collection from the cybercrime scene.

- **Tools and techniques for evidence collection:** The disk imaging tools include FTK Imager, EnCase, and Autopsy. The memory forensics tools include Volatility and Rekall. The range of tools for network packet analysis includes Wireshark and tcpdump.

- **Challenges in evidence collection:** Digital forensics investigators tend to face relevant challenges during evidence collection. This is due to encrypted and hidden data as well as underlying complexity during remote/cloud-based evidence retrieval. The tendency to use anti-forensics techniques is extensively increasing amongst adversaries across the globe.

- **Real-world case example:** The reputed retail giant, Target Corporation, suffered one of the largest data breaches in corporate history in the year 2013. The hackers infiltrated the target's network and stole the credit and debit card details of over 40 million customers, along with the personal information of 70 million individuals. The attack resulted in hundreds of millions of dollars in financial losses and damaged the reputation of the company. The progress of the digital forensics investigation resulted in flagging unusual network activity in the security system of the company weeks before the breach was publicly disclosed. The analysis of the security logs further revealed suspicious file transfers within the device network of the company. The digital forensic analysts identified the malware, a RAM scraper that was collecting payment card data in real-time.

Preservation and documentation

The strategy of digital evidence preservation bridges to the process of securing and protecting digital evidence to prevent tampering, corruption, or loss. This ensures that the evidence remains authentic and unaltered from collection to presentation in the Court of

Law. The importance of ensuring the integrity of evidence shares a connection with digital data being highly fragile, as it can be modified or erased unintentionally. Contextually, forensic investigators use different hashing techniques, such as MD5 and SHA-256, along with write-blockers and forensic imaging techniques to maintain the integrity of the digital evidence. The process of preservation and documentation of digital evidence is associated with the following areas:

- **Importance of evidence preservation:** Evidence preservation in digital forensics refers to the process of securing and protecting digital evidence to ensure its authenticity, integrity, and admissibility throughout an investigation. It involves preventing data alteration, loss, or corruption while maintaining a verifiable chain of custody from collection to analysis and legal proceedings. The importance of maintaining the authenticity of digital evidence correlates with the exact requirement of the Court of Law about the unchanged state of the evidence since its collection from the cybercrime scene. The aspect of evidence preservation impacts relevant compliance regarding the CoC. The effective handling and documentation of digital evidence influence its definite CoC. This maintenance of CoC revolves around demonstrating that the evidence remained unaltered and uncompromised since its collection from the cybercrime scene and its presentation at the Court of Law.

- **Methods for preserving digital evidence:** The effective preservation of digital evidence hinges on using write-blocking techniques, forensic imaging, hashing algorithms, and cold storage solutions. The application of write-blocking techniques addresses preventing data modification during analysis. The relevance of forensic imaging deals with creating bit-by-bit copies using tools like FTK Imager or EnCase. The importance of hashing algorithms such as **Message Digest** (**MD5**) and **Secure Hash Algorithm** (**SHA-256**) connects with ensuring evidence authenticity by generating digital fingerprints. Cold storage solutions are important for securely storing evidence to prevent its tampering by external entities.

- **Tracking evidence handling:** The CoC refers to the documented and unbroken process of handling, storing, and transferring digital evidence from the moment it is collected until it is presented in a Court of Law. It ensures that the evidence remains authentic, untampered, and legally admissible throughout an investigation. The key elements include digital investigators collecting the digital evidence from the cybercrime scene. The effective handling of digital evidence resonates with maintaining detailed logs and proper documentation of the digital evidence.

- **Legal and compliance considerations:** The legal and compliance considerations of digital evidence resemble adhering to corporate policies, GDPR, HIPAA, and other data protection regulations. The legal and compliance considerations further concern understanding the consequences of improper handling, such as evidence dismissal in a Court of Law.

- **Documentation best practices:** The effective documentation best practices include case notes, photographic evidence, incident timelines, and final forensic reports. The case notes include detailed descriptions of evidence collection and analysis steps. The photographic evidence engages with capturing images/screenshots of digital evidence. The incident timelines relate to creating a structured timeline of forensic activities. The final forensic report resembles preparing a clear and legally sound document summarizing findings.

- **Challenges in evidence preservation:** The relevant challenges in evidence preservation include handling encrypted or volatile data, ensuring logs are not altered by adversaries, and managing cloud-based evidence preservation.

- **Real-world case example:** The proceeding of *State v. Smith*, a U.S. criminal case, corresponds with the dismissal of digital evidence because investigators failed to document the CoC properly. The case involved e-mail fraud, and key evidence was a laptop containing incriminating emails. The evidence dismissal aligns with a lack of documentation, along with unsecured storage and unverified integrity.

Acquisition and imaging

Digital forensics corresponds to acquisition, and imaging is a crucial step that ensures investigators collect authentic and unaltered copies of digital evidence for examination. Forensic imaging involves creating an exact bit-by-bit replica of storage media, preserving not only active files but also deleted data and metadata. The acquisition and imaging of digital evidence in terms of creating forensically sound copies of digital media pertains to the following areas:

- **Understanding acquisition and imaging in digital forensics:** The definition of data acquisition from the perspective of digital forensics engages with the process of collecting, extracting, and preserving digital evidence from electronic devices while ensuring its integrity and admissibility in legal or investigative proceedings. This applies to the collection of data from a wide range of storage media, such as hard drives, mobile devices, and cloud services. The process involves the deployment of forensically sound methods to avoid the chances of data corruption.

- **Types of digital forensic acquisition:** The relevant types of digital forensics acquisition include live acquisition, dead acquisition, physical acquisition, logical acquisition, targeted acquisition, sparse acquisition, and remote acquisition. The process of live acquisition resembles performing digital forensics on a running system to capture volatile data (RAM, network traffic, and running processes). The process of dead acquisition includes conducting digital forensics procedures on a powered-off device to extract non-volatile data from storage. The physical acquisition indicates creating a bit-by-bit copy (forensic image) of an entire storage device, including deleted files and unallocated space. Logical acquisition indicates extracting active files and directories from a storage device without capturing deleted data or unallocated space. The targeted acquisition indicates collecting only specific files, folders, or data of interest rather than the entire storage media. The sparse acquisition implies capturing a portion of a drive, including file system metadata and fragments of deleted files. The remote acquisition corresponds with collecting digital evidence from a system over a network, often used in corporate environments.

- **Forensic imaging techniques:** The relevant forensic imaging techniques include bit-by-bit imaging, logical imaging, and snapshot-based imaging. Bit-by-bit imaging concerns itself with full duplication of storage, including deleted and hidden data. Logical imaging resembles copying specific partitions or file structures. The process of Snapshot-based imaging is linked with capturing system states at a specific point in time.

- **Ensuring the integrity of acquired data:** The assured integrity of acquired data includes hashing such as MD5, SHA-256, and SHA-512, using write-blockers and CoC documentation. The process of hashing touches on generating unique digital fingerprints before and after imaging. The process of using write-blockers indicates specific hardware or software tools that prevent data modification during acquisition. The CoC documentation implies recording every step from the collection to the analysis of digital evidence.

- **Tools used for acquisition and imaging:** The relevant tools that are used by digital forensics investigators include FTK Imager *(Figure 6.1)*, EnCase, dd and dc3dd, and Guymager *(Figure 6.2)*. The FTK Imager concerns creating forensic images and verifying their integrity. The EnCase resembles industry-standard tools for evidence collection. The dd and dc3dd are Linux command-line tools that are used for low-level disk imaging. The **Guymager is an** open-source forensic imaging tool.

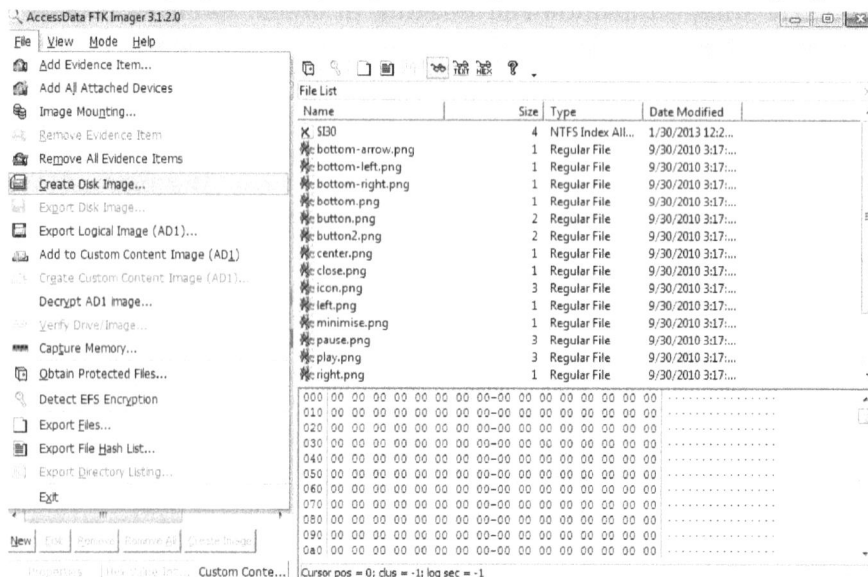

Figure 6.1: Screenshot of FTK Imager

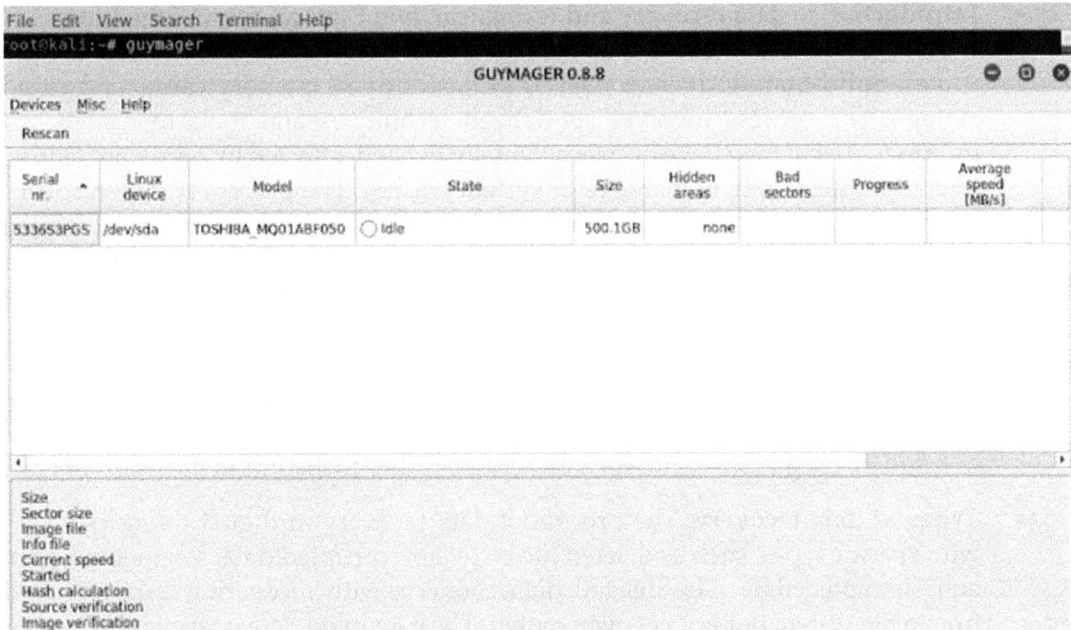

Figure 6.2: Screenshot of Guymager

- **Challenges in data acquisition:** The relevant challenges in data acquisition include encrypted or password-protected drives that imply methods for decrypting or bypassing encryption. The challenge of damaged or corrupted storage is relevant to recovery techniques for partially accessible data. The cloud-based evidence engages with legal and technical challenges in acquiring remote data.

- **Real-world case example:** The reputed financial organization, Morgan Stanley, faced a significant data breach when it failed to decommission outdated IT equipment properly, including servers and hard drives containing sensitive customer data. The company hired a third-party vendor to erase and dispose of these assets. However, due to improper forensic imaging and handling, some of the decommissioned devices were later found to still contain unencrypted personal data. The aspect of ineffective disk imaging led to the incorrect capture and verification of all stored data before decommissioning the hardware. This resulted in incomplete wiping and residual data exposure.

Data recovery and reconstruction

Data recovery and its reconstruction play a critical role in uncovering hidden, lost, or fragmented information from digital devices in the modern, ever-evolving field of digital forensics. Forensic analysts rely on specialized techniques to extract and reassemble digital artifacts for investigating cybercrimes, corporate fraud, or accidental data loss. The detailed analysis of data recovery and reconstruction in terms of extracting and reassembling information from digital artifacts aligns with the following areas:

- **Introduction to data recovery and reconstruction:** Data recovery is the process of retrieving deleted, corrupted, or damaged data from digital media, such as hard drives, **Solid-State Drives (SSDs)**, USB flash drives, memory cards, and cloud storage. The process involves specialized techniques and tools to restore lost information that may have been accidentally deleted, affected by hardware failure, or compromised due to malware or system crashes. The process of data recovery within digital forensics involves extracting potential evidence while maintaining data integrity and authenticity. Data reconstruction is the process of piecing together fragmented, incomplete, or corrupted data to restore its original form and derive meaningful insights. This technique is essential in digital forensics, where analysts work to reassemble deleted files, recover broken database records, or reconstruct digital activity from log files, metadata, and system artifacts. The inherent importance of recovering key evidence in cyber incidents, data breaches, or fraud investigations connects with serving justice to victims in the Court of Law.

- **Types of data recovery:** The process of data recovery in digital forensics aligns with specific types, such as deleted file recovery, corrupted data, fragmented data, and encrypted data. The deleted data connects with recovering data removed from a file system but not yet overwritten. The corrupted data deals with restoring damaged files due to system crashes, power failures, or malware. Fragmented data encompasses reassembling data split across multiple storage sectors, such as e-mail chains and documents. The encrypted data is associated with overcoming encryption barriers to recover and analyze protected information.

- **Techniques for data recovery:** The effective techniques for data recovery include file carving, data mining, journal recovery, and partial reconstruction. File carving aligns with extracting files from unallocated space using file signatures, such as carving JPEGs or DOCXs. Data mining resembles searching large data sets to identify valuable or relevant information. The journal recovery uses metadata or logs to reconstruct the sequence of events or transactions. The partial reconstruction **resembles** rebuilding data from incomplete or fragmented records, such as e-mails and database entries.

- **Tools for data recovery:** The appropriate tools for data recovery are R-Studio, PhotoRec, X1 Search, and EnCase forensic. The R-Studio ensures a comprehensive data recovery tool for various file systems. The PhotoRec corresponds with open-source file recovery software for missing or corrupted files. The X1 Search is a tool for searching and recovering specific files across various media. The EnCase Forensic is used for recovering and analyzing data in forensic investigations.

- **Challenges in data recovery:** The relevant challenges in data recovery include overwritten data, encrypted or password-protected data, damaged storage media, and cloud data retrieval. The overwritten data indicates deleted files being overwritten by new data and making their recovery difficult or impossible. Encrypted or password-protected data resembles the challenge of accessing protected or encrypted information. The issue of damaged storage media includes techniques for dealing with physically damaged hard drives or flash storage. Cloud data retrieval aligns with issues around obtaining cloud-based data while maintaining legal and privacy concerns.

- **Reconstructing digital artifacts:** The reconstruction of digital artifacts is linked with focusing on data timestamps, deleted communication, and application data. Data timestamps indicate analyzing creation, modification, and access timestamps to piece together a timeline of events. Deleted communication resembles reconstructing deleted emails, messages, or chat logs through server data or backup systems. The **application data includes** rebuilding information from browser caches, application logs, and local databases.

- **Legal and ethical considerations:** The legal and ethical consideration associated with data recovery indicates complying with privacy laws and corporate policies. The specific ethical consideration reflects on maintaining the integrity and admissibility of recovered evidence in legal proceedings.

- **Real-world case example:** The reputed energy company, Enron Corporation, collapsed due to widespread accounting fraud, hiding debt off the books and inflating profits. The aspect of data recovery and reconstruction played a vital role in this investigation, as the associated investigators recovered **deleted emails and financial documents** from servers and employee hard drives of Enron. These emails contained internal discussions about fraudulent financial strategies and evidence of executives knowingly deceiving investors.

Analysis and examination

The concept of digital evidence includes emails, log files, metadata, financial records, and encrypted data. The overall importance of digital evidence connects with its critical role in criminal investigations, corporate fraud detection, cybersecurity incidents, and legal proceedings. The importance of analyzing and examining digital evidence reflects on tackling a wide range of issues, such as data encryption, deletion, manipulation, and large volumes of data requiring forensic tools. The aspect of analyzing and examining digital evidence in terms of uncovering and interpreting it deals with the following areas:

- **Introduction to digital evidence analysis and examination:** The **analysis** of digital evidence is the process of interpreting and making sense of digital data collected during the forensic investigation of a cybercrime case. The overall process of examining digital evidence resembles a series of steps where the associated investigators assess the evidence in detail and thereby look for hidden insights. The importance of this stage is in building a coherent narrative from fragmented or obscure data.

- **Analysis techniques:** The relevant analysis techniques relate to data correlation, metadata analysis, timeline reconstruction, keyword searching, and file signature analysis. The process of data correlation addresses identifying patterns by linking different data points from multiple sources, such as logs, devices, and networks. The metadata analysis resembles analyzing timestamps, file attributes, and user activity metadata to uncover hidden actions. The process of timeline reconstruction coincides with building a chronological sequence of events based on file access, modifications, and communications. The aspect of keyword searching implies searching for specific terms or phrases across collected data to uncover relevant evidence. The file signature analysis identifies file types and determines whether files are intact, modified, or deleted.

- **Forensic examination of devices and media:** The forensic examination of digital devices and media involves file system analysis, live system analysis, application data analysis, and network analysis. The process of file system analysis addresses understanding how files are organized and identifying deleted or hidden files. The aspect of live system analysis refers to analyzing active memory, running processes, and volatile data from live systems. The application data analysis involves investigating communication and activity from installed applications such as browsers and chat apps. The network analysis coincides with reviewing logs, packets, and network traffic to uncover unauthorized activities or data exfiltration.

- **Using forensic tools for data analysis:** The relevant forensic tools used for data analysis include Autopsy, X1 Search, EnCase Forensic, and Wireshark. The Autopsy tool is used as an open-source digital forensics platform for analyzing disk images and file systems. The X1 search resembles a tool used for indexing and searching large volumes of data to uncover evidence. The EnCase forensic tool is widely used for in-depth analysis and examination of digital media. Wireshark is a network protocol analyzer for examining network traffic in forensic investigations.

- **Challenges in evidence analysis:** Digital forensic investigators tend to face multiple challenges during evidence analysis. This is due to the wide usage of obfuscation techniques. These techniques relate to challenges posed by encryption, steganography, and data hiding techniques. This is apart from the requirement of managing and analyzing large datasets, especially in cases involving cloud or enterprise systems. The requirement of data integrity hinges on ensuring that the analysis does not alter or compromise the evidence.

- **Interpreting evidence for investigations:** The effective interpretation of evidence for investigation correlates with contextualization, behavioral analysis, and link analysis. The process of contextualization revolves around understanding the broader context of the data, such as user intent and business operations. Behavioral analysis resembles analyzing user behavior, including access patterns, to detect malicious activities or policy violations. Link analysis impacts mapping relationships between entities such as users, devices, and transactions to reveal connections.

- **Reporting findings:** The effective reporting of findings includes preparing a clear and coherent report that explains findings, methodologies, and conclusions. The relevant translation of complex technical findings into an effective format leads to effective understanding by non-technical stakeholders or legal professionals. The legal admissibility is associated with ensuring that evidence analysis is presented in a way that is legally defensible at the Court of Law.

- **Real-world case example:** The importance of effectively analyzing digital evidence is demonstrated in the Case of the BTK Killer. *Dennis Rader*, infamously known as the **Bind, Torture, Kill (BTK)** killer, terrorized Wichita, Kansas, for over three decades. He committed a series of murders between 1974 and 1991, taunting law enforcement with letters and messages detailing his crimes. After years of inactivity, he resurfaced in 2004 by sending communications to the media and police, ultimately leading to his capture. Contextually, the digital forensic investigators recovered metadata from a deleted Microsoft Word file on the floppy disk. The metadata revealed that the document had been edited by a user named *Dennis* on a computer registered to *Christ Lutheran Church*. This led to the arrest of the infamous killer and presenting to the Court of Law.

Forensic tools and techniques

The overall threat landscape of cybercrime is fast evolving, leading to the rampant occurrence of corporate fraud and digital threats. Digital forensic investigators tend to rely on specialized tools and techniques to uncover, analyze, and interpret digital evidence. This indicates that **digital forensics** plays a critical role in criminal investigations, cybersecurity breaches, intellectual property theft, and regulatory compliance, making the selection and application of forensic tools a vital aspect of the investigative process. The current chapter indulges in an in-depth analysis of multiple forensic tools and techniques from the following areas:

- **Introduction to forensic tools and techniques:** Forensic tools and techniques relate to relevant software, hardware, and methodologies that are used to collect, analyze, and preserve digital evidence. The overall importance of these tools is connected with ensuring that digital investigations are thorough, consistent, and legally defensible.

- **Categories of digital forensics tools:** The relevant categories of digital forensic tools include imaging tools, analysis tools, recovery tools, network forensics tools, mobile device forensics tools, and memory forensics tools. The use of digital forensics imaging tools includes FTK Imager and dd for creating exact bit-by-bit copies of digital devices.

- **Key forensic techniques:** The consideration of analysis tools such as **EnCase Forensic**, **Autopsy**, and **X1 Search** for inspecting and analyzing data on digital media. The adoption of tools such as **R-Studio** and **PhotoRec** results in recovering lost, deleted, or corrupted data. The network forensics tools, such as Wireshark and

NetworkMiner for capturing and analyzing network traffic. The usage of mobile device forensics tools such as Cellebrite UFED and XRY by forensic investigators impacts the extracting of data from mobile devices. The forensic investigators tend to use memory forensics tools such as Volatility and Rekall for analyzing system memory (RAM).

- **Popular forensic tools and their uses:** The popular forensics tools used by digital forensic investigators for investigation purposes include EnCase, **Forensic Toolkit (FTK)**, Autopsy, Wireshark, Volatility, and Cellebrite UFED. The EnCase is an industry-standard tool for disk imaging, analysis, and reporting. The FTK is a powerful tool for data analysis, including email, web browsing, and file metadata. The Autopsy is an open-source platform for disk analysis and case management. Wireshark is a network protocol analyzer for capturing and analyzing network traffic. Volatility is a framework for memory forensics, extracting data from RAM to analyze active system processes. The Cellebrite UFED is a tool for mobile forensics, extracting data from phones and other mobile devices.

- **Advantages and limitations of forensic tools:** The advantages of forensic tools include automated data collection and analysis tasks. The range of advantages further includes increased efficiency in processing large datasets, along with standardization across investigations for consistency. However, the limitations include that the majority of tools support all device types or **operating systems (OS)**. Furthermore, the usage of specific tools can require added training for the investigators. The usage of some of the tools can result in additional budget and licensing limitations.

- **Choosing the right tool for the task:** The requirement of choosing appropriate tools for a forensic digital investigation is associated with different considerations. These considerations include the type of device or media. This includes computer, mobile, and cloud. Furthermore, the overall scope of a forensic investigation plays a major role. This corresponds to data recovery, network analysis, and mobile forensics. The associated legal and compliance requirements include tools that are effectively certified for legal proceedings. The importance of using multiple tools in a comprehensive investigation.

- **Challenges and emerging trends in digital forensics:** The challenges and emerging trends in digital forensics include encryption, cloud forensics, IoT forensics, and anti-forensics. Encryption deals with encrypted data and bypassing security mechanisms. Cloud forensics requires tools and techniques for acquiring evidence from cloud environments. IoT forensics influences the analysis of data from emerging IoT devices. Anti-forensics implies techniques employed by attackers to evade detection, such as data wiping and steganography.

- **Real-world case example:** The Enron Scandal (2001) tended to be one of the most infamous corporate fraud cases in history. Enron, an American energy company, collapsed due to accounting fraud, leading to one of the largest bankruptcies in

U.S. history. Forensic tools played a crucial role in uncovering hidden evidence that exposed the fraudulent activities of company executives. The investigators used EnCase to recover deleted emails and financial records from hard drives, revealing attempts to destroy evidence. The FTK helped analyze large volumes of electronic data, including hidden and encrypted files related to fraudulent transactions. Furthermore, investigators retrieved thousands of internal emails showing knowledge of the executives about the fraud and their efforts to cover it up.

Timeline and event reconstruction

The process of digital forensics indicates that accurately reconstructing the sequence of events is critical to understanding how an incident unfolded. In the process of investigating a cyberattack, a data breach, or insider misconduct, establishing a clear timeline provides investigators with a structured narrative of the incident. This process, known as **timeline and event reconstruction**, enables forensic analysts to piece together digital artifacts, correlate disparate data sources, and identify key moments that reveal the cause, impact, and potential perpetrators of an event. The timeline and event reconstruction are bound to establishing the sequence of events in a digital incident and share a connection with the following areas:

- **Introduction to timeline and event reconstruction:** Timeline reconstruction is defined as the process of establishing a chronological sequence of events based on digital evidence. Its importance is interwoven with helping to clarify the sequence of actions, the scope of the incident, and key actors involved in a digital security breach or cybercrime.

- **Creating a digital timeline:** The effective creation of a digital timeline involves deploying a wide range of components. These components include data sources, timestamp analysis, file system events, log files, and user activity. Data sources deal with identifying sources for timeline construction, such as file system metadata, logs, email metadata, and browser history. The process of timestamp analysis resembles analyzing creation, modification, and access timestamps on files and system logs to identify key actions. The file system events relate to understanding specific file operations, such as creation, deletion, and access, that are recorded in file systems. The log files are associated with examining system, application, and security logs to establish when specific actions occurred. These actions include login attempts and network connections. The user activity indicates tracking user activity through event logs, application logs, and system monitoring tools.

- **Event reconstruction techniques:** The relevant event reconstruction techniques relate to metadata analysis, artifact analysis, transaction logs, and forensic tool data. Metadata analysis involves analyzing metadata such as EXIF data from images and document properties to reconstruct the flow of events. Artifact analysis references reviewing transaction logs, such as database logs and access logs, to trace system activities or unauthorized actions. Forensic tool data resembles data from forensic tools (e.g., EnCase, FTK) to validate actions or correlate with system logs.

- **Key components of a timeline:** The key components of a timeline include incident start, critical actions, incident end, and discovery of evidence. The incident start speaks to identifying when the incident began. This is the first sign of a breach, system compromise, or malicious activity. The critical actions relate to pinpointing key activities such as data exfiltration, account compromise, or system exploitation. The Incident End involves determining when the incident was contained or mitigated, such as system shutdown or user account lockout. The discovery of evidence coincides with establishing the timestamp of evidence discovery and analysis.

- **Tools for timeline and event reconstruction:** The application of relevant tools for timeline and event reconstruction include Plaso, Log2Timeline, X1 Search, Autopsy and **Elasticsearch, Logstash, Kibana Stack (ELK)**. The Plaso tool is used as a framework for extracting and analyzing timestamps from a variety of file systems and devices. The Log2Timeline resembles a tool used for creating detailed event timelines from forensic artifacts. The X1 Search is a tool used for indexing and analyzing files across multiple devices, helping piece together event sequences. The **Autopsy** is a platform that can integrate various data sources to assist in event reconstruction. The ELK is a toolset for processing large-scale log data to generate detailed incident timelines.

- **Challenges in timeline and event reconstruction:** The relevant challenges in timeline and event reconstruction include inconsistent or missing data, data manipulation, and the volume of data and complex systems. The inconsistent or missing data involves gaps in logs or missing files that can make timeline construction difficult or incomplete. The data manipulation addresses investigating potential tampering of timestamps or log files by attackers. The volume of data tends to be a challenge, despite managing large volumes of data from various systems and sources, which can result in inaccurate timelines. The complex systems relate to handling timelines from cloud systems, distributed networks, and IoT devices with unique time records.

- **Interpreting the timeline for legal and investigative purposes:** The effective interpretation of a timeline for legal and investigative purposes coincides with the specific areas, such as contextualizing the timeline, reporting, visualization, and legal implications. The aspect of contextualizing the Timeline draws upon understanding the context of actions, such as the authorization state of the user or the nature of the action in terms of maliciousness, accidentality, or routine. The reporting and visualization relate to communicating findings clearly through visual timelines, graphs, or reports that convey the scope and sequence of the incident. The associated legal implication indicates ensuring that the reconstructed timeline is presented in a manner that can be used in court, if necessary.

- **Real-world case example:** The Sony Pictures Hack (2014) revolves around suffering a devastating cyberattack that led to the exfiltration of sensitive corporate data, leaked emails, and the destruction of critical IT infrastructure. The attackers, later identified as the North Korean-backed group Lazarus Group, used sophisticated techniques to infiltrate Sony's network, steal valuable information, and deploy destructive malware. Investigators traced the attack back to a phishing campaign that targeted Sony employees. Using forensic tools like Splunk and Wireshark, analysts reconstructed the sequence of network intrusions and identified malware-laden emails as the initial attack vector.

Correlation and link analysis

The perspective of correlation and link analysis from the perspective of digital forensics correlates with the application of critical techniques for effective identification of relationships between disparate data points. The long-term benefit of correlation and link analysis refers back to helping digital investigators uncover hidden connections, reconstruct events, and attribute malicious activities to specific actors. The correlation and link analysis correlate with connecting the missing dots between multiple data sources, such as logs, e-mails, transactions, and social media. The detailed analysis of correlation and link analysis ties back to the following areas:

- **Introduction to correlation and link analysis:** The process of **correlation analysis** is the process of identifying relationships between different pieces of digital evidence. This indicates that **link analysis** is the mapping of connections between individuals, devices, or activities to uncover patterns. The importance of this aspect hinges on helping digital forensic investigators establish causality, detect anomalies, and uncover hidden connections in cyber incidents.

- **Understanding correlation in digital forensics:** The different types of correlation existing within the field of digital forensics include event correlation, temporal correlation, behavioral correlation, and cross-device correlation. The event correlation resembles connecting different events, such as login attempts, file modifications, and malware execution, to establish patterns in a cybercrime incident. The temporal correlation reflects upon analyzing timestamps across multiple data sources to reconstruct a timeline of related activities. The behavioral correlation draws upon identifying unusual or suspicious user behavior across systems and logs. The cross-device correlation implies linking activities across multiple digital devices, such as linking an IP address from a laptop to mobile device usage.

- **Link analysis in digital investigations:** Link analysis in digital forensics revolves around identifying relationships, mapping communications, tracing financial transactions, and analyzing social networks. The identifying relationships impact mapping relationships between users, devices, and data interactions. Mapping communications involves analyzing email headers, chat logs, or phone records to identify connections. The tracing of financial transactions is the linking of fraudulent transactions to accounts, IP addresses, or geolocations. Social network analysis is associated with examining digital communication networks to uncover associations in cybercrimes or insider threats.

- **Techniques for correlation and link analysis:** The techniques for correlation and link analysis relate to graph analysis, pattern recognition, keyword matching, and geospatial analysis. Graph analysis involves using graphs to visualize connections between people, systems, and events. Pattern recognition is connected with identifying recurring behaviors, such as repeated access to restricted files. Keyword matching is bound to searching for repeated use of specific phrases, filenames, or code fragments. The geospatial analysis bridges to mapping locations of login attempts, transactions, or device movements.

- **Forensic tools for correlation and link analysis:** Digital forensic investigators tend to utilize relevant forensic tools for correlation and link analysis. These tools include Maltego, IBM i2 Analyst's Notebook, Splunk, ELK Stack, and Wireshark. Maltego is a powerful tool for mapping relationships between individuals, organizations, and digital footprints. The IBM i2 Analyst's Notebook is used for visual link analysis in cyber investigations. Theunk is a log analysis tool that helps correlate system events and security incidents. The ELK Stack tool is used for large-scale event correlation and log analysis. The Wireshark tool helps correlate network traffic to identify communication patterns.

- **Challenges in correlation and link analysis:** Digital forensic investigators tend to face multiple challenges in correlation and link analysis. These challenges include data overload, obfuscation by attackers, false positives, and legal and ethical considerations. The challenge of data overload associated with managing and filtering large datasets to extract meaningful connections. The obfuscation by attackers resembles Threat actors using **Virtual Private Networks (VPNs)**, proxies, or encryption to hide their tracks. The issue of false positives correlates with avoiding incorrect correlations that can lead to the misinterpretation of evidence. The legal and ethical considerations deal with ensuring compliance with data privacy laws when analyzing relationships.

- **Applying correlation and link analysis in investigations:** The relevance of applying correlation and link analysis during digital forensics investigations correlates with tackling the existing issues of the cybersecurity field. These include insider threat detection, cybercrime investigations, fraud detection, and nation-state attacks. Insider threat detection impacts uncovering unauthorized access or suspicious employee activities. Cybercrime investigations relate to mapping ransomware or phishing attack networks. Fraud detection involves identifying fraudulent transactions through financial and user behavior correlation. The nation-state attacks relate to linking cyberattacks to state-sponsored threat groups through forensic artifacts.

- **Real-world case example:** The U.S. FBI, in collaboration with international law enforcement agencies, dismantled AlphaBay, one of the largest dark web marketplaces for illicit goods, including drugs, stolen data, and hacking tools, in 2017. Link analysis played a crucial role in tracing cryptocurrency transactions, identifying key administrators, and ultimately leading to the arrest of Alexandre Cazes, the site's alleged creator. Specifically, Digital Forensic Investigators used **blockchain analysis tools** like **Chainalysis** to trace Bitcoin transactions, identifying clusters of wallet addresses tied to illicit activities. The link analysis helped correlate transactions between **AlphaBay vendor accounts and real-world financial accounts**.

Conclusion

The detailed analysis of the digital forensic process in this chapter is related to comprehending its underlying step-by-step. The relevant analyses indicated that digital forensics plays a critical role in tackling cybersecurity incidents across organizations and crime. The chapter indicated that digital forensic investigators tended to face multiple challenges while involved in conducting cybercrime investigations. The efficient analysis of digital evidence plays a critical role in solving cybercrimes in a timely manner and thereby serving justice to the innocent in the Court of Law. The findings from digital forensics investigations result in enhancing threat intelligence for a company.

The upcoming chapter draws upon demystifying Kali Linux in terms of diversifying the toolbox.

Join our book's Discord space

Join the book's Discord Workspace for Latest updates, Offers, Tech happenings around the world, New Release and Sessions with the Authors:

https://discord.bpbonline.com

CHAPTER 7
Beyond Kali Linux

Introduction

The recognition of Kali Linux in the world of digital forensics relates to its powerful penetration and testing capacity. The presence of a wide range of tools encourages its acceptance as a forensics platform for digital forensic investigators. Kali Linux is preloaded with various tools such as Autopsy, Wireshark, and Volatility for conducting seamless forensic investigations. Despite this, solely relying on Kali Linux for progressing digital forensic investigations can be limiting for the concerned cybercrime investigators. The growing importance of Kali Linux for Digital Forensic Investigations relates to the dynamically changing complexity of modern-day cybercrimes. The current chapter progresses by analyzing different types of forensic tools.

Structure

The chapter covers the following topics:

- Introduction to cyber forensic tools
- Open-source alternatives
- Windows-based forensic tools
- Mac-based forensic tools

- Mobile device forensic tools
- Network forensic tools
- Cloud forensic tools

Objectives

The current chapter proceeds with introducing different types of cyber forensics tools that expand beyond Kali Linux. This includes open-source alternatives of Kali Linux, such as Sleuth Kit, Volatility, Encase, Autopsy, etc. The chapter includes adequate details about Windows-based forensic tools such as *Nmap, Recuva, Encase, Volatility, AMPED Five, MAGNET AXIOM,* etc. This is in terms of leveraging Windows-specific solutions for progressing Cybersecurity Investigations. The chapter focuses on different Mac-based forensic tools such as *ArtEx* and *iLEAPP*. This relates to the increasing dependency of modern-day individuals on macOS. The chapter includes adequate details about mobile device forensic tools such as *Oxygen Forensic* and *MOBILedit*. This relates to extending cyber forensics investigations to smartphones and tablets. The chapter looks into details about different network forensic tools such as Wireshark and Network Miner. This is in terms of enhancing cyber forensics capabilities across network environments. The details about cloud forensic tools in this chapter include SleuthKit to investigate digital crimes in cloud computing environments.

Introduction to cyber forensic tools

Cyber forensic tools help investigators analyze digital evidence, recover lost data, and trace cybercriminal activities. This is because these tools aid in network forensics, memory analysis, disk forensics, malware investigation, and log analysis. While **Kali Linux** *(Figure 7.1)* is a well-known platform for digital forensics and penetration testing, relying solely on it can be limiting for digital forensic investigators while investigating complex cybercrime scenarios. This encourages selecting tools for cybercrime investigation by the digital forensic investigators beyond Kali Linux. Specifically, different types of complex investigations require tools tailored for Windows, Mac, cloud environments, or mobile forensics. This establishes the importance of specialized forensic needs in terms of digital forensic tools.

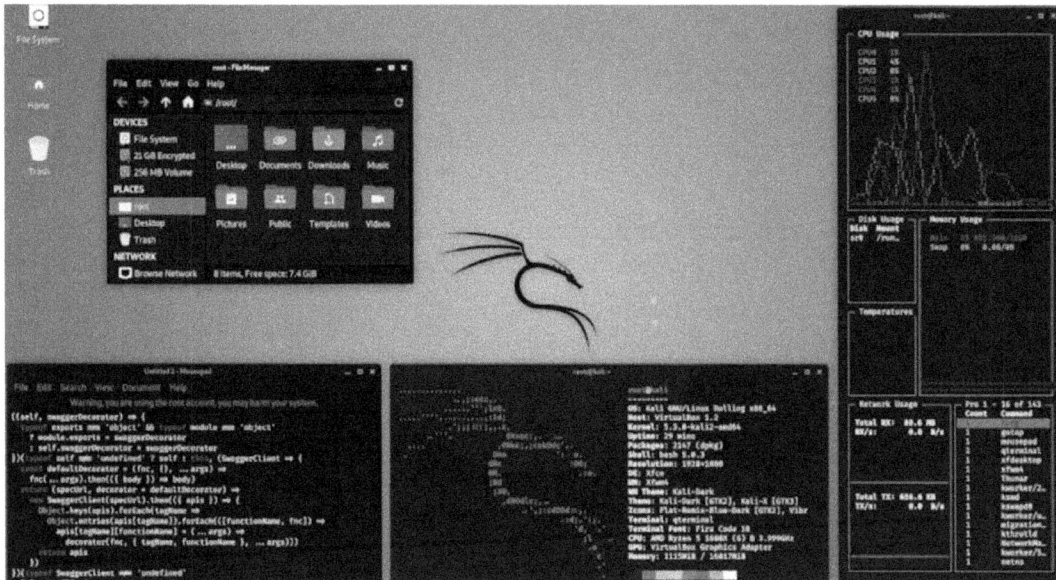

Figure 7.1: *Interface of Kali Linux*

Relevant commercial and cloud-based tools provide superior automation and reporting features, indicating their advanced analytical capabilities. Depending on the overall sensitivity of a legal case, court-admissible digital evidence is crucial, which requires the contribution of specialized tools. The alternative and complementary forensic tools to Kali Linux are stated in the following table *(Table 7.1)*:

Areas of digital forensics	Alternative digital forensics tools
Windows and disk forensics	• FTK (Forensic Toolkit) • X-Ways Forensics • Magnet Axiom
Memory and malware analysis	• Volatility • Redline • Cuckoo Sandbox
Cloud forensics	• AWS CloudTrail • Microsoft Azure Sentinel • Google Chronicle
Mobile and IoT forensics	• Cellebrite • Oxygen Forensic Suite

Network and log analysis	• Wireshark *(Figure 7.2)* • Splunk • Zeek
Blockchain and cryptocurrency investigations	• Chainalysis • CipherTrace

Table 7.1: Digital forensics alternatives to Kali Linux

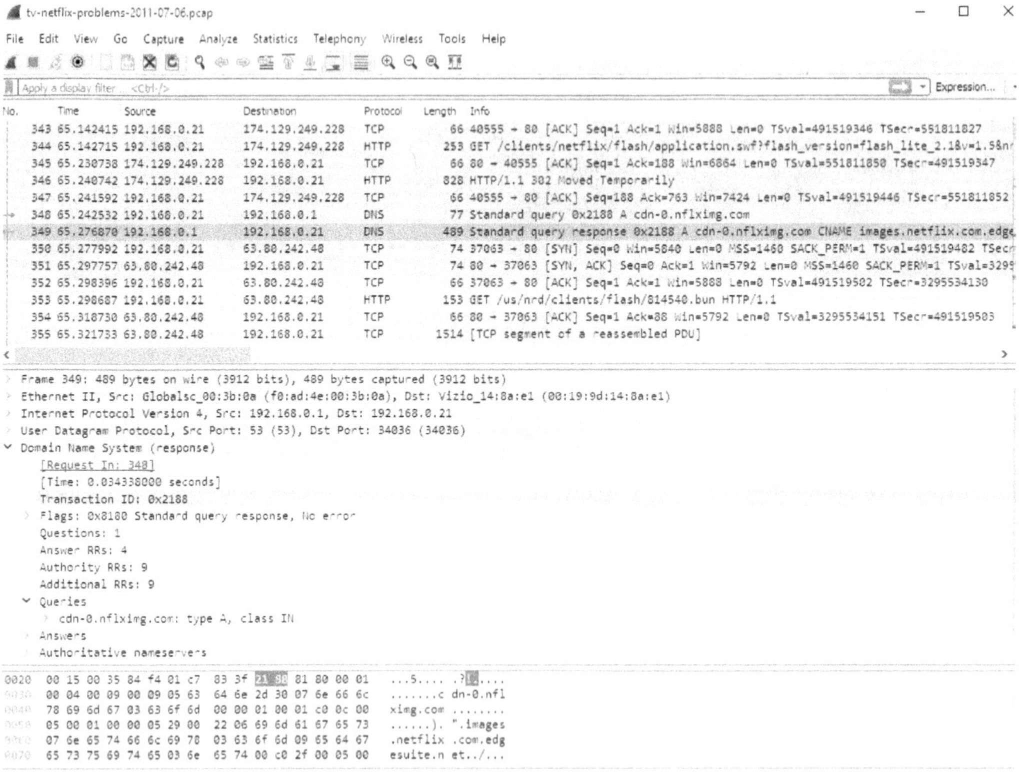

Figure 7.2: Interface of Wireshark

The consideration of relevant factors for the selection of forensic tools by digital forensic investigators plays a crucial role in their digital investigation procedures. These factors include the scope of investigation, usability and learning curve, legal admissibility, and integration and automation. The scope of investigation relates to matching tools with case requirements. This is because the choice of cybersecurity tools tends to differ for cloud breaches and local disk forensics. The factor of usability and learning curve relates to comparing open-source and commercial tools having user-friendly interfaces. The legal admissibility of a digital forensics tool relates to ensuring that the tools follow forensic best practices and maintains evidence integrity. The aspect of integration and automation relates to using suitable tools that streamline investigation workflows and reporting.

Open-source alternatives

Despite Kali Linux having adequate popularity amongst the digital forensic investigators for aiding them in complex investigation procedures, relying solely on its pre-installed tools can be limiting and delay the expected progress of the digital forensics investigation. Contrarily, open-sourced forensic tools provide cost-effective, flexible, and community-driven solutions for forensic investigations. Thus, forensic professionals use specialized tools beyond Kali for disk analysis, memory forensics, mobile forensics, and network investigations. The key open-sourced digital forensics tools for the benefit of digital forensics investigations include the following:

- **Sleuth Kit:** This command-line toolkit is ideal for disk and file system forensics in terms of performing disk image analysis, file recovery, and timeline reconstruction.

- **Autopsy:** This tool acts as a user-friendly **graphical user interface** (**GUI**) for the Sleuth Kit, offering forensic analysis of drives, deleted files, and metadata. This tool is widely used in law enforcement, corporate investigations, and cybercrime cases (*Figure 7.3*).

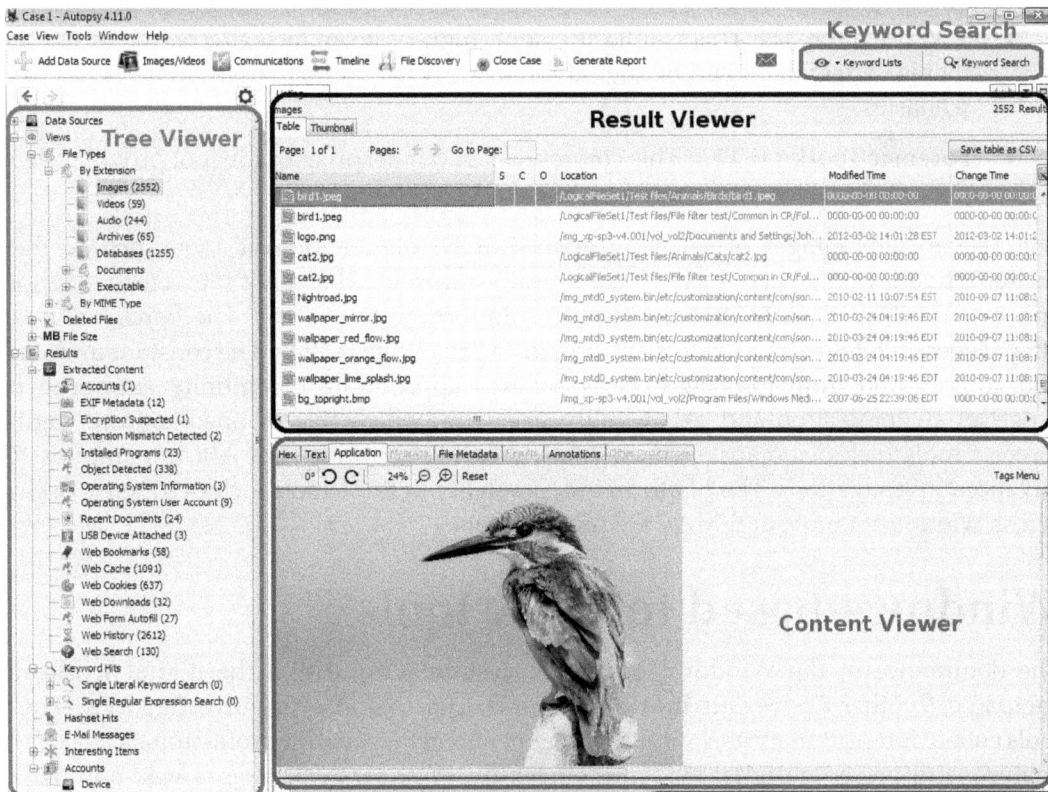

Figure 7.3: Interface of Autopsy

- **Volatility:** This tool is used by digital forensics investigators to perform memory forensics. This is a leading open-source tool for **RAM analysis**, extracting processes, network connections, and hidden malware. This tool is essential for investigating **Advanced Persistent Threats** (APTs), rootkits, and fileless malware attacks. *(Figure 7.4)*

- **Wireshark:** This packet analysis tool is used for monitoring and analyzing network traffic as a part of network forensics. This tool helps detect suspicious activity, intrusion attempts, and data exfiltration. *(Figure 7.2)*

- **Magnet AXIOM (Community edition):** This tool is ideal for cloud and mobile forensics as it possesses open-source cloud and mobile forensic capabilities. *(Figure 7.6)*

- **Cellebrite UFED (limited free version):** This tool is appropriate for cloud and mobile forensics as it extracts data from mobile devices for forensic analysis.

- **EnCase:** This Industry-standard forensic tool is suitable for deep disk analysis and evidence collection. Despite not being a fully open-sourced tool, this is widely used by digital forensic investigators.

- **X-Ways forensics:** This is a lightweight, high-performance alternative to EnCase that is widely deployed by digital forensic investigators to investigate cybercrime scenarios.

- **Forensic Toolkit (FTK):** This commercial and enterprise-grade tool provides deep disk analysis, registry analysis, and email investigations.

The relevant advantages of selecting open-sourced digital forensic tools include their cost-effectiveness, the presence of community support, the ability to customization, and extensibility, apart from being largely platform-independent. The benefit of cost-effectiveness relates to having no provision to pay the licensing fee. The constant updating and contribution from forensic experts ensures appropriate community support. The aspect of customization and extensibility from the perspective of open-sourced digital forensic tools includes many of these tools allowing scripting and API integrations for advanced investigations. The platform independence of these tools includes their working across Windows, Linux, and MAC OS environments.

Windows-based forensic tools

The dominance of the Windows **operating system** (OS) within the digital world, as compared to other OS, results in it playing a crucial role in cyber investigations. These tools enable forensic analysts, law enforcement, and cybersecurity professionals to extract, analyze, and preserve digital evidence efficiently. Windows OS stores a vast number of forensic artifacts crucial for investigations. Such is detailed as follows:

Components of Windows OS	Type digital evidence
Windows Registry	• User activities • Installed programs • System configurations
Event Logs	• Records system and security events • User logins • Application errors
Prefetch Files	• Recently accessed applications and files
NTFS Metadata and Shadow Copies	• Traces of deleted or modified files
Pagefile and Hibernation Files	• Memory snapshots

Table 7.2: Windows components storing digital evidence

Windows, being the most widely used OS in modern days, makes it a prime target for cybercriminal activities. Digital forensic investigators must leverage Windows-specific tools to analyze system artifacts, recover data, and trace malicious activities. The following tools play a crucial role in Windows forensic investigations across different domains:

• **Nmap (Network Mapper):** This digital forensic tool is widely used for network and port scanning. Specifically, this tool is used for scanning networks, identifying open ports, and detecting vulnerabilities. Thus, this tool helps trace unauthorized connections and potential entry points for attackers *(Figure 7.4)*.

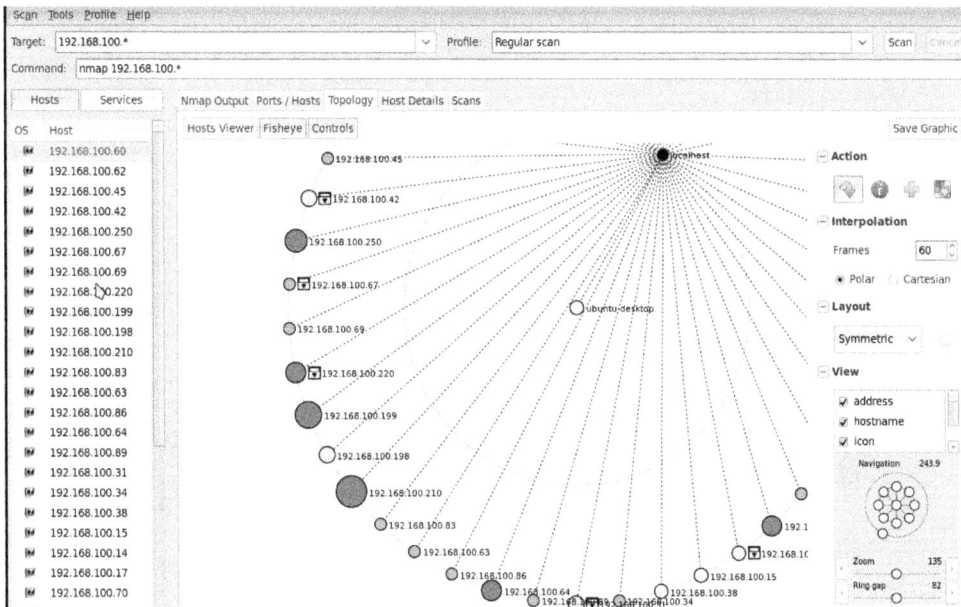

Figure 7.4: Windows interface of the Nmap tool

- **Recuva: This tool is ideal for** Data recovery and file analysis. This tool specializes in recovering deleted files from hard drives, **Solid State Drives** (**SSDs**), and **Universal Serial Bus** (**USB**). This tool is useful for retrieving lost evidence, including documents and images.

- **MAGNET AXIOM:** The digital forensic investigators use this tool to proceed with data recovery and file analysis. This is an advanced forensic suite that recovers and analyzes deleted files, chat logs, and browsing history. This tool supports deep analysis of Windows registry and event logs.

- **Volatility:** This tool is ideal for memory and malware forensics. This is an open-source tool for analyzing volatile memory (RAM). The tool detects malware injections, hidden processes, and active network connections.

- **EnCase forensic:** This Industry-standard tool for disk and memory forensics aids the digital forensic investigators to proceed with memory and malware forensics. This tool is used in law enforcement and corporate investigations for comprehensive evidence collection *(Figure 7.5)*.

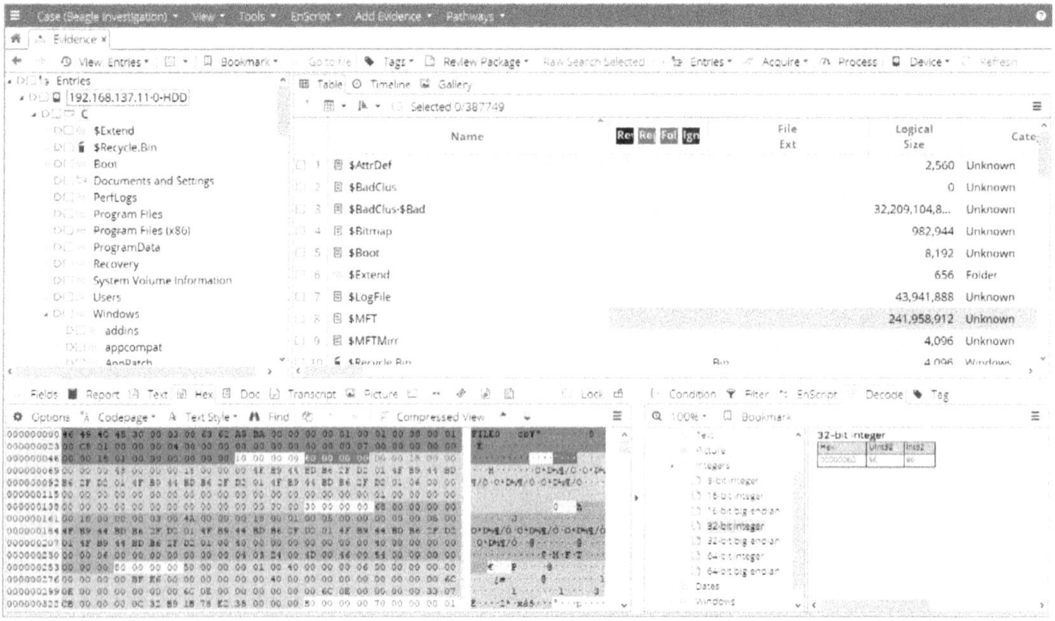

Figure 7.5: Interface of EnCase forensic

- **AMPED Five:** This tool is widely used for video and multimedia forensics. The tool specializes in forensic video analysis and image enhancement. The tool helps extract evidence from CCTV footage and digital images *(Figure 7.6)*.

Figure 7.6: Interface of AMPED Five

- **Windows Event Viewer and Log Parser:** The digital forensic investigators use this tool to proceed with log and event analysis. This tool is essential for reviewing system logs to detect unauthorized access and system anomalies. The tool is used in correlation with other forensic tools for deeper event timeline reconstruction.

Mac-based forensic tools

Digital forensics plays a crucial role in investigating cybercrimes, data breaches, and security incidents. The macOS devices, such as MacBook and iPhone, continue to gain popularity among individuals and enterprises, and the need for specialized forensic techniques and tools for this ecosystem has grown significantly. This is because macOS from Apple is widely used in professional settings, particularly among creative professionals, developers, and businesses that prioritize security. The increasing market share of Mac computers necessitates dedicated forensic methodologies tailored to macOS-specific file systems, encryption protocols, and security mechanisms. However, contrary to Windows-based systems, macOS incorporates advanced security measures such as Gatekeeper, **System Integrity Protection** (**SIP**), and Secure Enclave, which can pose challenges for forensic investigations. On the other hand, FileVault encryption ensures robust data protection, making forensic data acquisition more complex without specialized tools. The introduction of proprietary hardware by Apple, such as the T2 security chip and M1/M2 processors, has further altered forensic approaches, requiring updated forensic strategies. MacOS maintains logs, system artifacts, and unique file structures such as APFS snapshots, unified logs, and the KnowledgeC database that can serve as critical sources of forensic evidence. Thus, understanding macOS-specific user activity data, including application usage, connected devices, and browsing history, is essential in forensic analysis.

Cybercriminals increasingly use macOS devices to perpetrate malicious activities such as cyber fraud, hacking, and insider threats. Thus, investigating threats like malware, unauthorized access, and data exfiltration on macOS systems requires specialized forensic tools and expertise. Contextually, Mac-based forensic tools help in identifying attack vectors, tracking user behavior, and recovering deleted or encrypted data crucial for legal proceedings.

The difference between MacOS and Windows Forensic Approaches is represented as follows:

Differentiating Parameters	Mac Operating System (OS)	Windows Operating System (OS)
File system differences	• **Apple File System (APFS)** • **Hierarchical File System Plus (HFS+)**	• **New Technology File System (NTFS)** • **File Allocation Table (FAT32)** and **Extended File Allocation Table (exFAT)**
Security mechanisms and challenges	• **System Integrity Protection (SIP)** • T2 Security Chip and Secure Enclave • FileVault Encryption • Gatekeeper and XProtect	• BitLocker Encryption • **User Account Control (UAC)** • Windows Defender and Security Logs
Forensic artifacts and evidence locations	• Unified Logs • KnowledgeC Database • Finder and Spotlight Metadata • Plist Files and SQLite Databases • iCloud and continuity artifacts	• Event Logs • Registry Hives • Jump Lists and Prefetch Files • Recycle Bin and Volume Shadow Copies • UserAssist and LNK Files

Data acquisition methods	• **Target Disk Mode (TDM)** • Live Acquisition Challenges • Logical and File-Based Acquisition	• Disk Imaging Tools • Memory Dump Analysis • Remote Forensics
Cloud and backup considerations	• iCloud Syncing • Time Machine Backups	• OneDrive Synchronization • Volume Shadow Copies

Table 7.3: Difference between MAC OS and Windows OS

The suitable forensics tool for MAC OS Analysis plays a crucial role in data acquisition, analysis, and reporting. The relevant tools are stated as follows:

- **ArtEx:** This tool is beneficial for analyzing macOS artifacts. These tools are capable of extracting and interpreting macOS system artifacts. This results in availing key forensic insights provided by this tool to establish the truth at Court of Law (*Figure 7.7*).

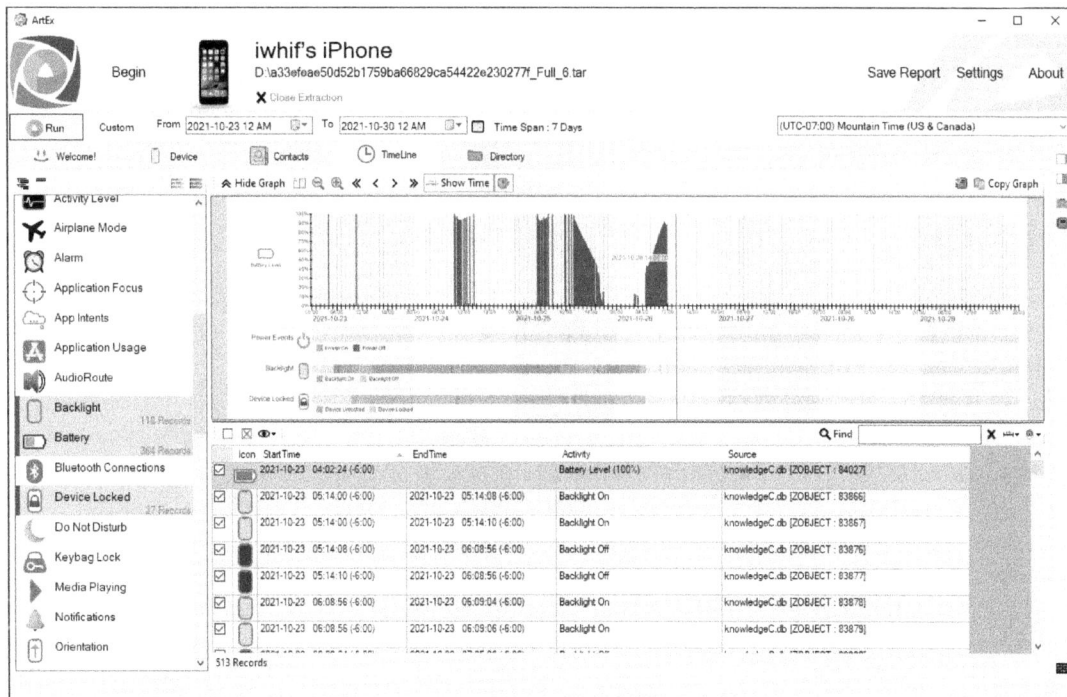

Figure 7.7: Interface of ArtEx

- **iLEAPP:** This tool is widely used for investigating logs of iOS and MAC OS. This tool plays a crucial role in parsing logs and gathering digital evidence. The importance of these generated logs for forensic investigation relates to aiding the reconstruction of the forensic timeline *(Figure 7.8)*.

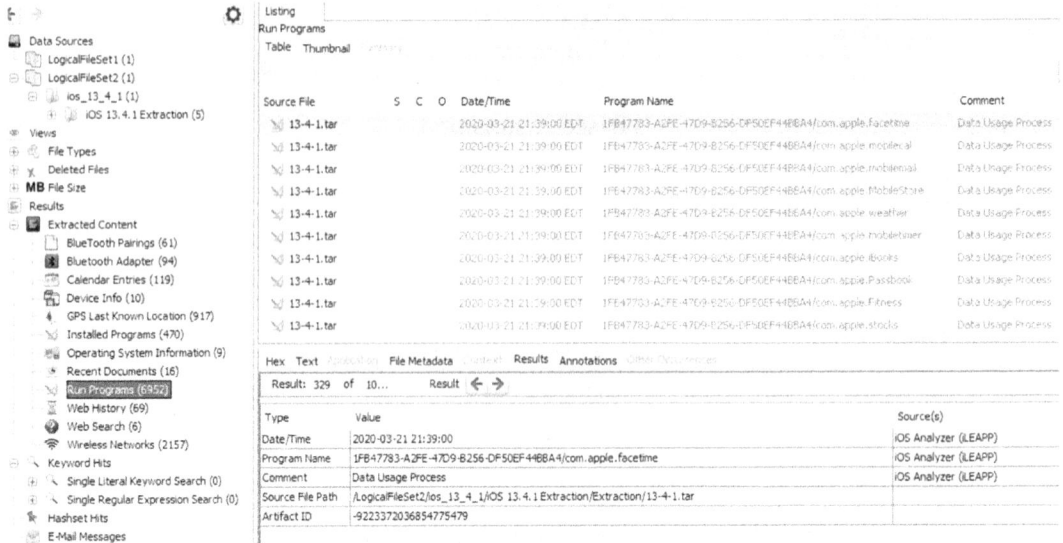

Figure 7.8: Interface of iLEAPP

The significance of MAC forensic tools in digital forensics investigation relates to real-world applications in cybercrime investigations. This is apart from complying with legal and forensic standards.

Mobile device forensic tools

The increasing impact of digital transformation results in mobile device forensics playing a critical role in modern digital investigations. These devices store vast amounts of personal, business, and communication data, making them valuable sources of evidence in criminal, civil, and corporate investigations. The pervasiveness of mobile devices is established by the observation that billions of smartphones are in use worldwide as they serve as primary communication tools for individuals and businesses. Individuals use smartphone devices for calls, messaging, emails, banking, social media, and location tracking, making them rich data repositories for investigations. The need for specialized forensic tools for digital forensic investigations relates to extracting and analyzing data from locked, encrypted, or damaged mobile devices. This is further to addressing the diversity of mobile operating systems such as iOS and Android. The well-known mobile forensics tools are detailed as follows:

- **Oxygen forensic suite:** This tool encourages advanced data extraction from mobile devices, cloud storage, and applications. The tool can recover deleted messages, GPS locations, and encrypted app data *(Figure 7.9)*.

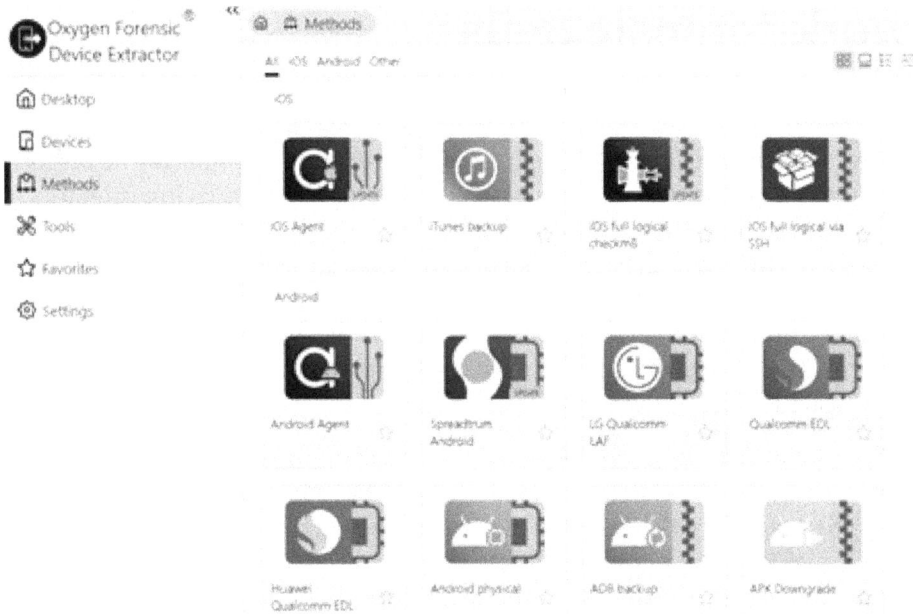

Figure 7.9: Interface of Oxygen Forensic Suite

- **MOBILedit forensic:** This tool supports a wide range of devices and offers deep analysis of mobile content. The features of this tool include SIM card extraction, call logs, messages and application data retrieval *(Figure 7.10)*.

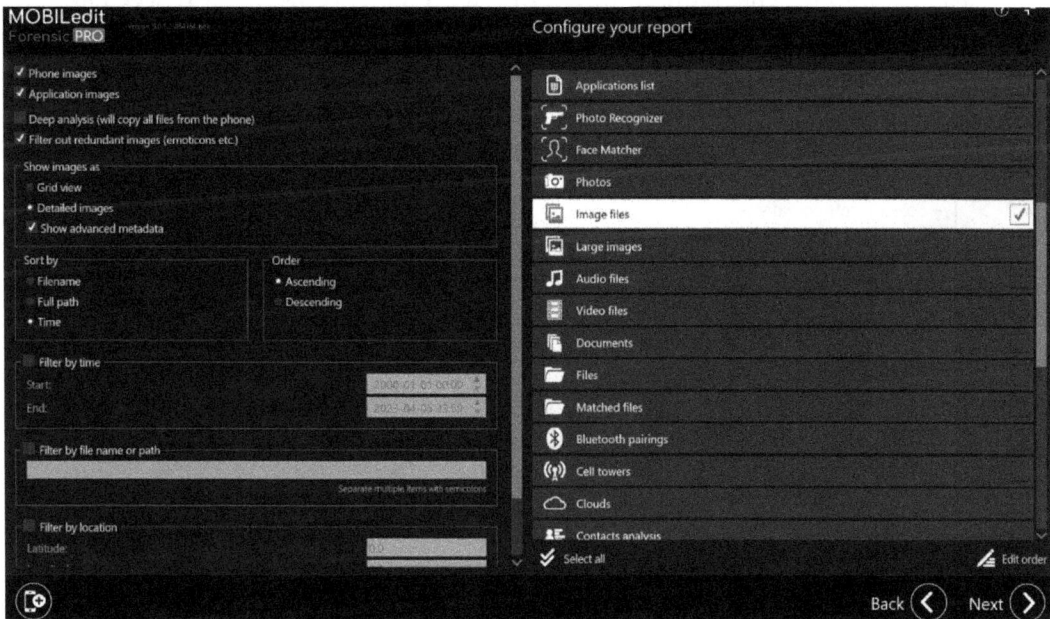

Figure 7.10: Interface of MOBILedit Forensic

Network forensic tools

Network forensics is the branch of digital forensics focusing on capturing, analyzing, and investigating network traffic. The application of network forensics is essential for detecting cyber threats, investigating security breaches, and ensuring compliance. The importance of selecting a suitable network forensics tool is to help digital forensics investigators identify malicious activities, unauthorized access, and data breaches. The selection of a suitable network forensics tool supports cybersecurity teams in incident response and evidence collection. The role of a network forensics tool in cyber forensics includes enabling real-time and post-event traffic analysis. This is further to assist the digital forensics investigators in reconstructing attack scenarios and attributing threats to attackers. The commonly used network forensics tools are elaborated as follows:

- **Wireshark:** This is a powerful packet analyzer for capturing and inspecting network traffic *(Figure 7.2)*. This tool can capture live network traffic from wired and wireless networks. It supports various network interfaces, including Ethernet, Wi-Fi, and Bluetooth, among others. Wireshark can capture packets in real time or read from saved capture files. The tool supports hundreds of network protocols, including TCP, UDP, HTTP, FTP, and DNS, amongst others. It automatically decodes protocol layers and presents them in a readable format.

- **Network Miner:** This is a passive network sniffer for extracting information from packet captures *(Figure 7.11)*. It helps security analysts and incident responders analyze network traffic for forensic investigations and threat detection. This tool can capture packets without interfering with network traffic. It works with both live network traffic and pre-captured PCAP files. Its inherent benefits include not generating its own network traffic, thereby reducing detection risk.

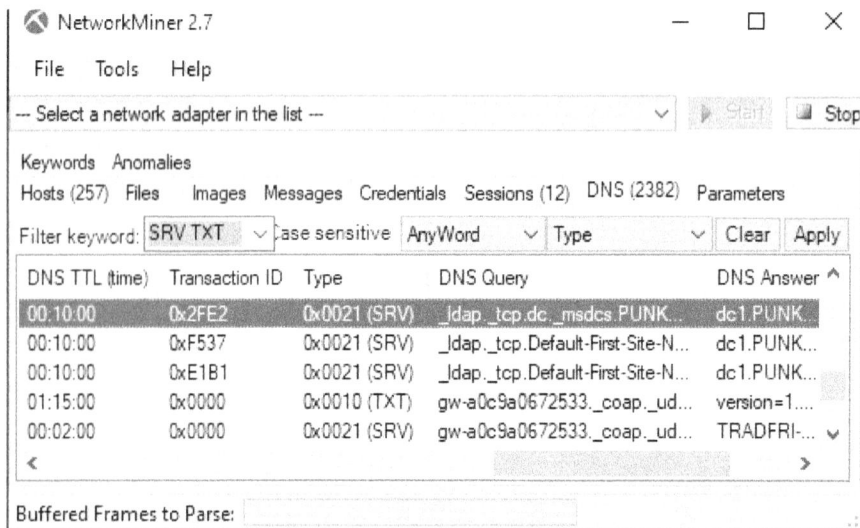

Figure 7.11: Interface of Network Miner

Cloud forensic tools

Cloud forensics is a branch of digital forensics that focuses on investigating, analyzing, and preserving digital evidence in cloud computing environments. It involves the application of forensic techniques to cloud-based data, services, and infrastructure to uncover cybercrimes, unauthorized access, data breaches, and other security incidents. Cloud forensics combines elements of traditional digital forensics with specialized approaches tailored to the distribution of cloud, multi-tenant, and virtualized architecture. It involves three primary domains, namely, data forensics, network forensics, and system forensics. Data forensics implies investigating cloud-stored data and identifying traces of cybercriminal activity. Network forensics involves analyzing cloud-based network traffic and logs for malicious behavior. The aspect of system forensics involves examining virtual machines, containers, and cloud-based applications for forensic evidence. The well-known cloud forensics tool, Sleuthkit, is elaborated as follows:

- **Sleuthkit:** SleuthKit is an open-source digital forensic toolkit designed for analyzing disk images, file systems, and recovering deleted data. It is widely used by forensic investigators for in-depth analysis of digital evidence. Its underlying features include file system analysis, disk image and partition analysis, and deleted file recovery. The aspect of file system analysis indicates support for a wide range of file systems, including NTFS, FAT, ext3/ext4, HFS+, and APFS. It can analyze disk partitions, extract metadata, and identify file system structures. It helps investigators trace file modifications, access timestamps, and file ownership. The perspective of Disk Image and Partition Analysis relates to supporting forensic analysis of raw disk images (`.dd`), EnCase images (`.E01`), and AFF images (`.aff`). It extracts partition tables and identifies hidden or deleted partitions. It allows recovery of formatted or lost partitions. The aspect of deleted file recovery relates to identifying and recovering deleted files and directories from various file systems. It involves detecting file slack space and residual data fragments left after deletion. It implies reconstructing partially overwritten files, aiding forensic recovery efforts.

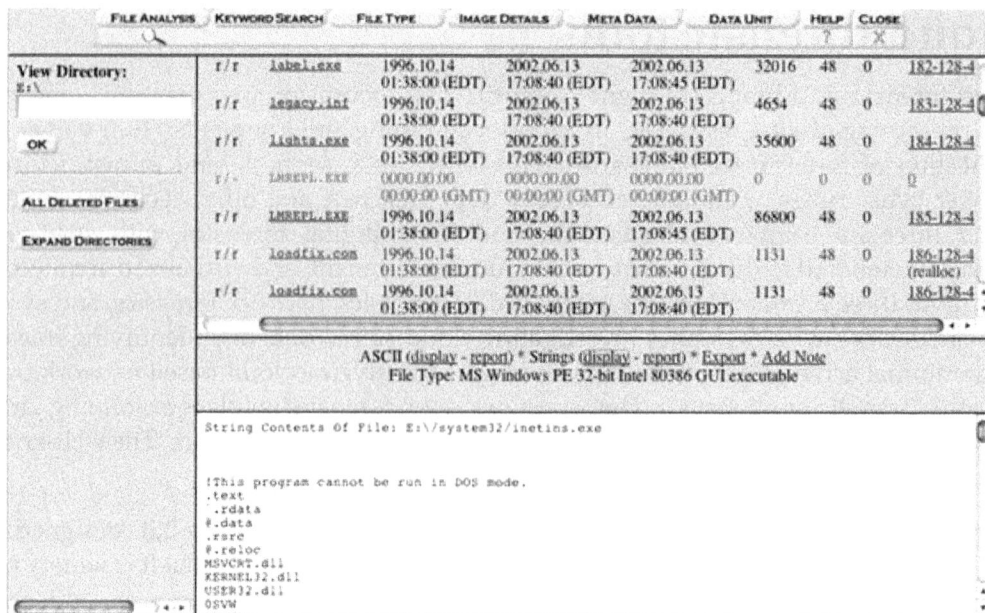

Figure 7.12: *Interface of Sleuthkit*

Conclusion

This chapter elaborated on different digital forensics tools to imply that relying on them by digital forensic investigators can reduce their sheer dependency on pre-installed tools of Kali Linux. The inherent features of different digital forensics tools indicate that they can be selected to aid in critical and complex digital forensic investigations. The detailed analysis of these tools implies that the application of different digital forensics tools tends to focus on the overall complexity of an investigation situation. This resembles the selection of digital forensics tools based on the existing OS of a digital device.

The upcoming chapter focuses on a further detailed analysis of network analysis.

Join our book's Discord space

Join the book's Discord Workspace for Latest updates, Offers, Tech happenings around the world, New Release and Sessions with the Authors:

https://discord.bpbonline.com

CHAPTER 8

Decoding Network Forensics

Introduction

The modern-day business requirement resembles connecting multiple digital devices in a network to enhance their efficiency in serving customers effortlessly. This dependency of organizations on network-based connectivity of devices encourages external adversaries to launch an attack on such a network of devices by deploying relevant threat actors. This allows the digital forensics investigators to indulge in the detailed and forensically sound analysis of the device network at the cybercrime scene. The digital forensic investigators indulge in relevant tasks such as packet analysis, log analysis, **incident response (IR)**, and attack reconstruction. The consistent advancement of technologies leads to a complicated structure of device networks across different organizations. This involves the deployment of specific tools by digital forensic investigators, such as Wireshark, Zeek, Snort, Splunk, **Forensic Toolkit (FTK)**, and NetworkMiner. The current chapter focuses on detailing network forensics as per current standards of digital forensics.

Structure

The chapter covers the following topics:

- Introduction to network forensics
- Network traffic analysis
- Packet capture and analysis

- Log analysis
- Network device forensics
- Malware analysis and detection
- Role of network forensics in incident response
- Application of network forensics in insider threat investigations
- Network forensics in data breach investigations

Objectives

The chapter introduces network forensics as an exploration of its crucial role in bolstering enterprise security. Modern-day enterprises are largely dependent on maintaining a dedicated network of their devices. The chapter includes details about **network traffic analysis** (**NTA**) in light of its revealing valuable insights through studying network communication patterns. The chapter focuses on effective **packet capture** (**PCAP**) and analysis, as it is the art of intercepting and scrutinizing network data. The concept of log analysis is well elaborated in this chapter, as mining pertinent information from network logs. The chapter includes adequate information about network device forensics as a means of conducting thorough investigations on network devices for evidential purposes. The chapter focuses on effective malware analysis and detection in terms of pinpointing and neutralizing network-based malware threats. The chapter states that the role of network forensics in IR is to harness network data to probe cybersecurity breaches. The chapter further focuses on the application of network forensics in insider threat investigations to detect and respond to internal security violations. The chapter implies that network forensics in data breach investigations traces the trajectory of data exfiltration.

Introduction to network forensics

The current era implies sophisticated and frequent growth of cyber threats as enterprises face an ever-evolving challenge of safeguarding their digital assets. Such a situation implies that traditional security measures such as firewalls and antivirus software are no longer sufficient to combat complicated situations such as APTs, insider attacks, and zero-day exploits. This emphasizes the deployment of network forensics as a critical discipline within digital forensics, thereby enabling organizations to detect, investigate, and mitigate security breaches in real time. Network forensics is defined as the practice of capturing, analyzing, and interpreting network traffic to uncover evidence of malicious activities. Network forensics plays a pivotal role in **IR**, helping security teams trace cyberattacks, identify intrusions, and understand how adversaries penetrate enterprise networks. The effective reconstruction of attack timelines by network forensics provides invaluable insights into attacker **Tactics, Techniques, and Procedures** (**TTPs**) and thereby strengthens the defensive posture of an organization. The benefits of network forensics are indispensable for modern-day enterprise security from the following perspectives:

- **Threat detection beyond perimeter security:** The installation of a Firewall and **Intrusion Detection System (IDS)** ensures providing baseline protection to an enterprise. Modern-day sophisticated attackers often bypass these defenses using sophisticated techniques such as encrypted communication, lateral movement, and file less malware. Contextually, network forensics provides visibility into these hidden threats by analyzing traffic patterns and identifying deviations from normal behavior.

- **Incident investigation and response:** The occurrence of a security breach triggers network forensics analysis, thereby enabling investigators to trace the origin of a cyberattack, reconstruct the activities of an attacker, and determine the scope of compromise. This is termed forensic intelligence, and it is crucial for containing threats, recovering compromised systems, and preventing future incidents.

- **Behavioral analysis and anomaly detection:** The continuous monitoring of network traffic leads to forensic systems tending to establish baselines of normal network behavior and detect anomalies that may indicate malicious activity. As an instance, an unusual spike in outbound traffic from a server could signal data exfiltration by an insider threat or an external adversary.

- **Forensic evidence and compliance:** The data from network forensic analysis serves as vital digital evidence in legal and regulatory contexts. This indicates that organizations need to adhere to compliance standards such as the **General Data Protection Regulation (GDPR)**, the **Health Insurance Portability and Accountability Act (HIPAA)**, and the **Payment Card Industry Data Security Standard (PCI DSS)**. Such adherence of organizations to compliance requires deploying robust monitoring and incident investigation capabilities. This is in terms of proper forensic procedures, ensuring that evidence is collected, preserved, and analyzed in a legally admissible manner.

- **Ransomware attack:** Ransomware emerged as one of the most pervasive and damaging cybersecurity threats to enterprises. Contrary to traditional malware that focuses on data theft or system compromise, ransomware encrypts critical business files and systems, rendering them inaccessible until payment of a hefty ransom amount. Modern ransomware attacks, such as double extortion schemes, lock down data and exfiltrate sensitive information, threatening public disclosure in the event of non-payment of the ransom demand. The prevalence of effective network forensics results in the timely detection of potential ransomware attacks through network anomalies. Attackers often conduct reconnaissance before deploying ransomware. Network forensic analysis helps identify unexpected **Server Message Block (SMB)**, **Remote Desktop Protocol (RDP)**, or **Secure Shell (SSH)** traffic, which may indicate an adversary exploring internal systems.

Network forensics is a cornerstone of modern cybersecurity in terms of bridging the gap between traditional security defenses and advanced threat intelligence. It provides deep visibility into network activity, besides empowering enterprises to detect, investigate, and respond to security incidents with greater accuracy and speed.

Network traffic analysis

The modern world resembles an interconnected digital landscape where network traffic serves as a vital source of forensic intelligence. It offers a detailed footprint of communication activities within an environment. NTA plays a crucial role in modern digital forensics across a wide range of areas, such as investigation of cybercrime, detecting unauthorized access, or uncovering signs of data exfiltration. The target of systematically examining network packets, flow data, and communication patterns aids the digital forensic investigators in reconstructing incidents, identifying malicious actors, and strengthening cybersecurity defenses. NTA in digital forensics refers to the process of capturing, monitoring, and analyzing network communications to detect security threats, investigate cyber incidents, and reconstruct digital events. NTA involves examining network packets, traffic flows, and communication patterns to identify malicious activity, unauthorized access, or data exfiltration. This implies the importance of studying network communication patterns for cybercrime investigations, IR, and threat detection. NTA relates to aiding digital forensic investigators in identifying anomalies, intrusions, and data exfiltration. The different components of NTA include the following:

- **Packet analysis:** This process relates to examining individual packets for headers, payload, and anomalies using tools such as Wireshark.

- **Flow analysis:** The process of analyzing aggregated network flows using tools such as NetFlow and sFlow results in detecting patterns of activity.

- **Deep Packet Inspection (DPI):** The aspect of DPI resembles extracting metadata and payload information to detect suspicious activity.

- **Anomaly detection:** The aspect of anomaly detection relates to identifying deviations from normal traffic patterns using behavioral analytics.

The common use cases of NTA in digital forensics are as follows:

- **Incident investigation:** The aspect of incident investigation relates to tracing security breaches, malware infections, and unauthorized access.

- **Threat attribution:** The perspective of threat attribution relates to identifying sources of cyberattacks, including IP tracing and geolocation.

- **Data exfiltration detection:** Data exfiltration detection relates to spotting unauthorized data transfers and insider threats.

- **Malware Command and Control (C2) communication:** This use case relates to detecting hidden backdoors and persistent threats.

The well-known tools used for performing NTA are stated as follows:

- **Wireshark**: This tool is effective for PCAP and analysis. The digital forensic investigators capture network packets in real-time from both wired and wireless interfaces. The tool supports multiple capture formats, such as PCAP files. *(Figure 8.1):*

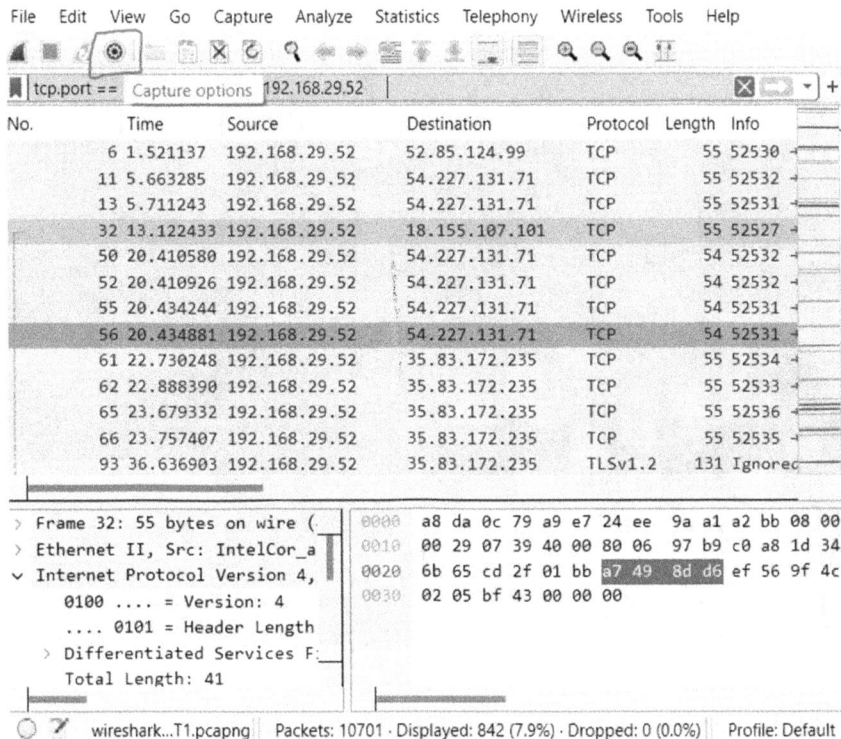

Figure 8.1: Interface of Wireshark

- **Zeek (Bro)**: This tool is suitable for continuous network monitoring and security analytics. The tool supports passive network monitoring as it passively captures network traffic without interfering with operations. The tool works across the Network Layer 3 to the Application Layer 7 to extract detailed metadata.

- **Suricata/Snort**: This is an **Intrusion Detection and Prevention System (IDS/IPS)**. The key features of this tool include Signature-Based Intrusion Detection and Prevention, DPI, and protocol analysis. The concept of signature-based intrusion detection and prevention relates to using rule-based detection to identify known threats. The detailed analysis of DPI and protocol analysis relates to inspecting packet payloads for malicious content. It supports detailed analysis of protocols such as **Hypertext Transfer Protocol (HTTP)**, **Domain Name System (DNS)**, **Secure Socket Layer/Transport Layer Security (SSL/TLS)**, **SMB**, **File Transfer Protocol (FTP)**, and **Simple Mail Transfer Protocol (SMTP)**.

- **Splunk/ Elasticsearch, Logstash, and Kibana (ELK) Stack**: This tool is ideal for Log analysis and visualization. The relevant features of Splunk or ELK Stack include centralized log management and data ingestion, apart from advanced search and query capabilities. The centralized log management and data ingestion imply Splunk uses the **Search Processing Language** (**SPL**) for fast and flexible log queries. The ELS Stack uses the Elasticsearch Query DSL and KQL of Kibana for log searches *(Figure 8.2)*:

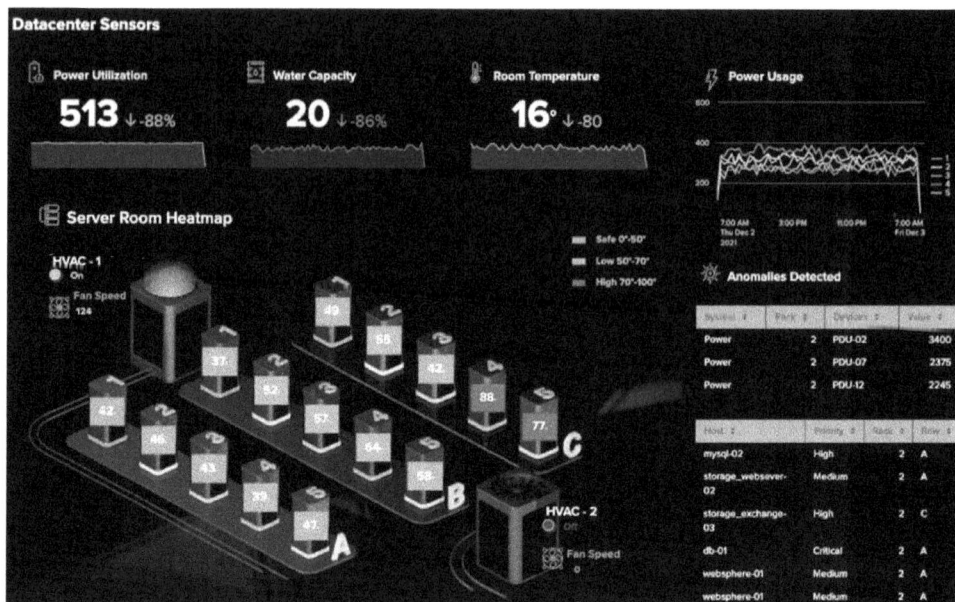

Figure 8.2: Interface of Splunk

Packet capture and analysis

The consistently evolving landscape of cybersecurity and digital forensics implies that **PCAP and analysis** play a pivotal role in uncovering critical evidence, detecting cyber threats, and understanding network behavior. This process involves intercepting, storing, and scrutinizing network packets to extract meaningful insights about data transmissions, potential intrusions, and malicious activities. The network packets are the fundamental units of digital communication, as they carry everything from web requests and emails to encrypted transactions and unauthorized access attempts. **PCAP and analysis** refer to the process of intercepting, collecting, and examining network traffic at the packet level to gain insights into data transmission, security incidents, and potential cyber threats. A **packet** is a fundamental unit of network communication that contains data along with metadata, such as source and destination IP addresses, protocol information, and payload. The capturing and analysis of these packets lead forensic investigators and cybersecurity professionals to **trace** network activity, detect malicious behavior, and reconstruct the cyberattacks.

The significance of PCAP and analysis in digital forensics relates to effective incident investigation and evidence collection. This is because it helps forensic analysts to reconstruct security incidents by analyzing network traffic logs. The range of significances further relates to reconstructing cyberattacks that allow analysts to track attacker movements and behaviors across the network.

The fundamentals of network packets include their structure as Header, Payload, and Trailer. The TCP/IP layers are segregated, and thereby, packet transmission takes place. The types of Network packets include TCP, **User Datagram Protocol (UDP)**, **Internet Control Message Protocol (ICMP)**, **Domain Name System (DNS)**, and HTTP. The application of different methods and techniques for PCAP includes active and passive. The active PCAP relates to the real-time capturing of packets from the network. The passive PCAP resembles the analysis of stored packets from a network. The PCAP relates to port mirroring and network taps for monitoring network traffic. The inline mode of PCAP relates to monitoring the entire traffic of a network. This is opposed by the promiscuous mode in terms of focusing on specific hosts within the network of devices.

The digital forensic investigators use the following specific tools for PCAP and analysis:

- **Wireshark:** The benefit of this tool relates to the graphical analysis of captured packets. Wireshark enables DPI, filtering, and visualization of network packets, making it invaluable for security professionals, network administrators, and forensic analysts. Wireshark uses **Berkeley Packet Filters (BPF)** to limit captured packets based on IP Address, protocol, port number, and network range. Wireshark can apply filters before capturing as capture filters and after capturing as display filters.

- **tcpdump/tshark:** It is a powerful, command-line-based network PCAP tool widely used in digital forensics, cybersecurity, and network troubleshooting. This tool encourages command-line PCAP and filtering from a network of devices. The tool displays detailed header information for network packets, such as source and destination IP addresses, port numbers and sequence numbers, TCP flags, protocol type, and payload data. The tool helps in analyzing network anomalies, security incidents, and protocol behavior. *(Figure 8.3)*

Figure 8.3: Interface of tcpdump

- **Zeek (Bro):** This is a powerful open-source **network security monitoring** (**NSM**) tool that goes beyond simple PCAP. This tool encourages NSM and behavioral analysis. This is owing to its ability to analyze, log, and detect security threats in real time by extracting metadata and higher-level insights from network traffic. The real-time PCAP relates to capturing packets in real time from network interfaces such as Ethernet, VLANs, VPNs, and loopback interfaces.

- **Suricata/Snort:** Suricata and Snort are IDS, IPS, and NSM tools designed to analyze network traffic for threats, anomalies, and malicious activities. Both tools offer real-time packet capturing and DPI to detect and prevent cyber threats. *(Figure 8.4)*

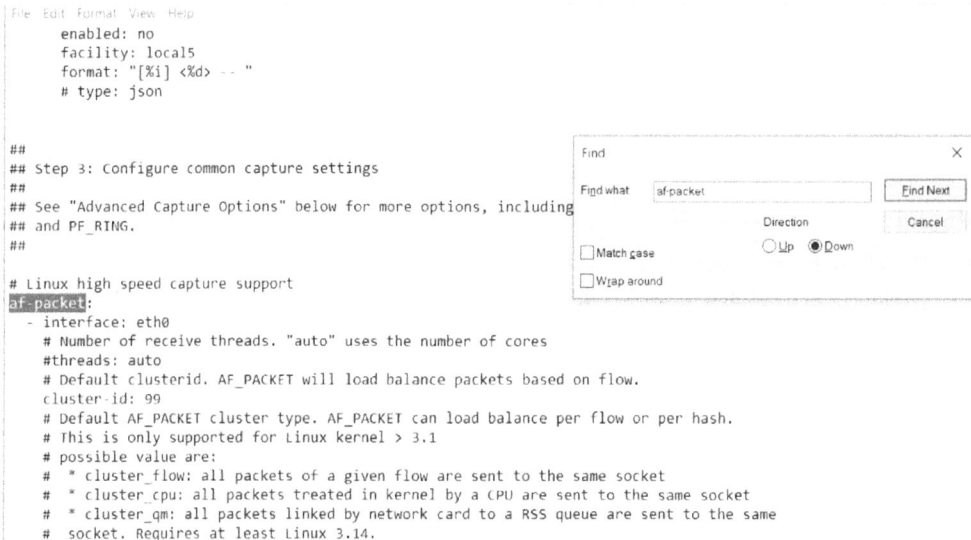

```
File  Edit  Format  View  Help
    enabled: no
    facility: local5
    format: "[%i] <%d> -- "
    # type: json


##
## Step 3: Configure common capture settings
##
## See "Advanced Capture Options" below for more options, including
## and PF_RING.
##

# Linux high speed capture support
af-packet:
  - interface: eth0
    # Number of receive threads. "auto" uses the number of cores
    #threads: auto
    # Default clusterid. AF_PACKET will load balance packets based on flow.
    cluster-id: 99
    # Default AF_PACKET cluster type. AF_PACKET can load balance per flow or per hash.
    # This is only supported for Linux kernel > 3.1
    # possible value are:
    #  * cluster_flow: all packets of a given flow are sent to the same socket
    #  * cluster_cpu: all packets treated in kernel by a CPU are sent to the same socket
    #  * cluster_qm: all packets linked by network card to a RSS queue are sent to the same
    #    socket. Requires at least Linux 3.14.
```

Find window:
```
Find                                                      ×
Find what    af-packet                                  [ Find Next ]
                                    Direction             [ Cancel  ]
☐ Match case                        ○ Up ◉ Down
☐ Wrap around
```

Figure 8.4: Interface of Suricata

Log analysis

The landscape of cybersecurity and digital forensics is consistently changing, and thus, network logs serve as invaluable sources of evidence. The relevant logs are generated by firewalls, routers, IDS, servers, endpoint devices, and other network components, providing a chronological record of network activity. Network logs serve as critical pieces of evidence in **digital forensics investigations**, providing a detailed and time-stamped record of activities occurring within a network. These logs, generated by various network devices and security systems, play a crucial role in detecting, analyzing, and responding to cyber incidents. However, the related challenges in log analysis include vast data volume, inconsistencies in log format, and log encryption. The different types of network logs are stated as follows:

- **System logs:** The system logs are the events from operating systems and applications.

- **Firewall logs:** The Firewall logs are the Traffic filtering, allowed/blocked connections, and rule violations.

- **Intrusion Detection/Prevention System (IDS/IPS) logs:** The alerts from IDS/IPS logs on potential intrusions and attacks.

- **Domain Name System (DNS) logs:** The DNS logs indicate domain name resolution records for tracking malicious domains.

- **Web server logs:** The Web server logs imply relevant user access details, requests, and HTTP status codes.

The log collection and parsing relate to the following areas:

- **Centralized vs. decentralized logging:** This aspect relates to the benefits of SIEM solutions.

- **Common log formats:** The generation of logs from different digital devices relates to formats such as Syslog, JSON, CSV, Windows Event Logs, and Apache logs.

- **Parsing tools:** The digital forensic investigators use a wide range of tools for parsing logs, such as Logstash, Splunk, ELK Stack, and custom scripts that are written in Python and Bash.

The digital forensic investigators use the following wide range of log correlation and analysis techniques:

- **Pattern recognition:** This technique relates to identifying anomalies, repeated failed logins, and suspicious IPs from logs of different devices.

- **Timeline reconstruction:** The effective log analysis results in creating an event timeline to trace the activities of the attacker.

- **Keyword and regex searches:** The target of effective log analysis relates to extracting specific patterns such as error codes, IP addresses, and MAC addresses.

- **Threat intelligence (TI) integration:** The effective log analysis is catalyzed by using relevant external threat feeds to identify known bad actors.

The effective classification of digital forensic tools for log analysis relates to **Security Information and Event Management** (**SIEM**), open-source log analysis tools, network traffic and log analysis tools, Windows and Linux log analysis tools, threat intelligence and correlation tools, and log forensics and investigation frameworks. The tools for log analysis classified across these areas are stated as follows *(Table 8.1)*:

Classification factors	Log analysis tools	Features of tool
Security Information and Event Management (SIEM)	• Splunk	Indexing and searching log data from various sources
	• IBM QRadar	Correlating log events to identify security incidents.
	• ArcSight (by OpenText)	Real-time log collection and event correlation
	• Microsoft Sentinel	Cloud-native SIEM solution for Microsoft environments
Open-source log analysis tools	• Elasticsearch, Logstash, Kibana Stack (ELK)	Storing and Indexing, Parsing and Visualizing log data
	• Graylog	Real-time log search
	• **Open Source HIDS (OSSEC)**	Monitoring logs for suspicious activities
Network traffic and log analysis tools	• Wireshark	Capturing and inspecting network packets
	• Bro (Zeek)	Converting raw network traffic into structured logs
	• NetFlow Analyzer	Monitoring and analyzing network traffic patterns
Windows and Linux log analysis tools	• Windows Event Viewer	Analyses Windows system logs for failed logins, access attempts and system errors
	• Sysmon (System Monitor by Microsoft)	Provides detailed Windows event logs for security monitoring
	• Logwatch	Log analysis tool for Linux/Unix-based systems
	• GoAccess	Real-time web log analyzer for Linux servers
Threat intelligence (TI) and correlation tools	• **Malware Information Sharing Platform (MISP)**	Correlating logs with known threat indicators
	• YARA	Identifying suspicious log entries related to malware activity
	• Cortex (TheHive Project)	Correlates forensic logs with known attack patterns

Log forensics and investigation frameworks	• Plaso (log2timeline)	Creates detailed timelines from logs
	• Timesketch	Visualizing event sequences from logs
	• Redline (by FireEye)	Analyses registry, event logs and memory dumps

Table 8.1: Details of log analysis tools

Network device forensics

Network devices such as routers, switches, firewalls, and IDS/IPS are critical components of an organization's IT infrastructure. These devices control and monitor network traffic, enforce security policies, and generate logs that provide valuable forensic evidence. Investigating these devices helps forensic analysts reconstruct cyber incidents, trace attackers, and strengthen security defenses. The network devices proceed with different activities such as logging network activity, monitoring network traffic, controlling network traffic. The logging network activity relates to network devices generating and storing logs that record key events and traffic flows thereby helping administrators and forensic investigators track network activity. The aspect of monitoring network traffic relates to different techniques used by network devices such as packet inspection, traffic analysis, real-time alerts. The controlling network traffic resembles traffic control functions of network devices. The digital forensic investigators tend to face multiple challenges while conducting network device-related investigations. These challenges include volatile memory, data encryption, proprietary firmware and log retention policies. The common devices examined by digital forensic investigators include the following:

- **Routers and Switches**: These devices store routing tables, MAC address logs and **Access Control Lists** (**ACLs**).

- **Firewalls**: These devices maintain logs of blocked/allowed traffic, intrusion attempts, and rule modifications. *(Figure 8.5)*

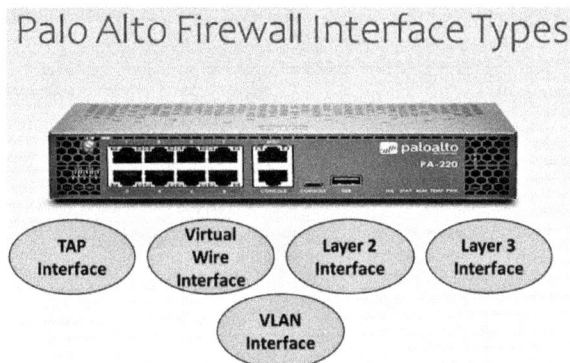

Figure 8.5: Interface types of palo alto firewall

- **IDS/IPS**: These devices detect and log malicious network activities.

- **Network-Attached Storage (NAS) and VPN Servers**: These devices contain access logs and user authentication data.

The key forensic data sources in network devices include:

- **Configuration files**: The configuration files are key forensic data sources in network devices that store device settings, user credentials and security policies.

- **Network logs**: The network logs are considered as key forensic data sources in network devices as they capture connection attempts, failed authentications and firewall rule changes.

- **Memory and packet captures**: The memory and PCAPs tend to contain volatile forensic artifacts such as active sessions and live network traffic.

- **Metadata and timestamps**: The metadata and timestamps help in reconstructing attack timelines and tracking user activities.

The tools used for network device forensics are elaborated in *Table 8.2*:

Classifying factor	Tool	Features
Log collection and analysis tools	• Splunk	Collects and indexes logs from network devices
	• ELK Stack	Collection, Indexing and Visualization of logs
	• Graylog	Open-source log management tool
	• Syslog-ng	Centralized logging tool for network devices
Network traffic analysis tools	• Wireshark	Industry-standard PCAP and analysis tool
	• Zeek (Bro)	Monitors network traffic and logs detailed activity
	• Tcpdump	Lightweight command-line PCAP tool
	• NetFlow Analyzer	Monitors and analyses network traffic flows
Firewall and IDS/IPS log analysis tools	• Firewall Analyzer (ManageEngine)	Collects and analyses firewall logs from multiple vendors
	• Suricata	Captures and analyzes network traffic for forensic investigation
	• Snort	Detects suspicious activity and generates alerts for forensic analysis
	• Security Onion	All-in-one threat detection and network forensics platform

Router and switch forensics tools	• RouterOS (MikroTik) Log Analyzer	Collects and analyses logs from MikroTik routers
	• Cisco NetFlow and PCAP tools	Supports NetFlow, which helps monitor and analyse network flows
	• Nipper (Titania)	Audits and analyzes network device configurations of Routers, firewalls, switches)
	• Config Parser Tools	Extracts and analyzes device configurations for security flaws
Threat intelligence and log correlation tools	• Malware Information Sharing Platform (MISP)	Helps forensic teams correlate network logs with known attack patterns
	• YARA	Used for malware detection and log forensics
	• Cortex (TheHive Project)	Automates threat intelligence correlation for forensic analysis.
Network device memory and firmware analysis tools	• Volatility Framework	Helps extract and analyze memory dumps from network devices.
	• Binwalk	Used for reverse-engineering router and firewall firmware.
	• FTK Imager	Captures forensic disk images of network storage devices (NAS, VPN servers).

Table 8.2: Tools of network device forensics

Malware analysis and detection

Network-based malware is a type of malicious software that spreads, operates or communicates over a network to infect systems, steal data or disrupt services. Contrary to traditional malware that targets individual devices, network-based malware leverages network protocols, vulnerabilities, and internet connectivity to propagate and execute attacks. The popular types of network-based malware are listed as follows:

- **Worms**: This self-replicating malware spreads through network vulnerabilities without human intervention. *(Figure 8.6)*

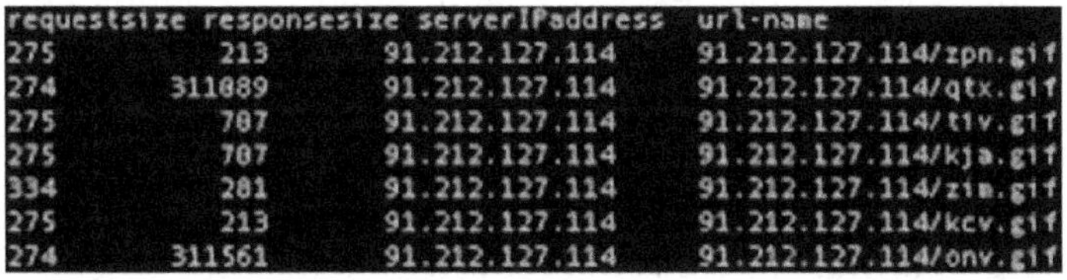

requestsize	responsesize	serverIPaddress	url-name
275	213	91.212.127.114	91.212.127.114/zpn.gif
274	311889	91.212.127.114	91.212.127.114/qtx.gif
275	787	91.212.127.114	91.212.127.114/tiv.gif
275	787	91.212.127.114	91.212.127.114/kja.gif
334	281	91.212.127.114	91.212.127.114/zim.gif
275	213	91.212.127.114	91.212.127.114/kcv.gif
274	311561	91.212.127.114	91.212.127.114/onv.gif

Figure 8.6: Interface of worm infected device

- **Botnets**: The botnets are network of compromised devices that are controlled remotely to conduct attacks such as DDoS and Spam distribution.

- **Ransomware**: This malware encrypts data and spreads across networks, demanding payment for decryption. *(Figure 8.7)*

Figure 8.7: Interface of ransomware-infected device

- **Rootkits and trojans**: These are hidden malware used for persistent backdoor access.

- **Spyware and Keyloggers**: Spyware and keyloggers are used to monitor network activity and steal credentials.

The relevant indicators of network-based malware infection include unusual network traffic spikes due to botnet activity and data exfiltration. This is further to unrecognized outbound connections to malicious IPs or domains. The **Indicators of Compromise** (**IoC**) of a Malware attack include increased failed login attempts due to brute-force attacks. Furthermore, unauthorized changes in firewall or router configurations lead to potential malware attacks on the device network. Digital forensic investigators tend to deploy the following techniques for proceeding with malware analysis:

- **Static analysis**: The procedure of static analysis relates to examining malware code without its execution in terms of file hashes, signatures, and metadata.

- **Dynamic analysis**: The process of dynamic analysis resembles executing malware in a controlled environment, such as sandboxing and behavior monitoring.

- **Memory forensics**: The aspect of memory forensics relates to extracting malware artifacts from infected system memory.

- **Reverse engineering**: The concept of reverse engineering resembles disassembling malware to study its behavior and code structure.

Digital forensic investigators tend to apply suitable network-based malware detection methods such as the following:

- **Signature-based detection:** Antivirus, IDS/IPS, YARA rules.

- **Heuristic and anomaly-based detection:** Machine learning, behavior analysis.

- **Traffic analysis using PCAP tools:** Wireshark, Zeek, Snort. *(Figure 8.8)*

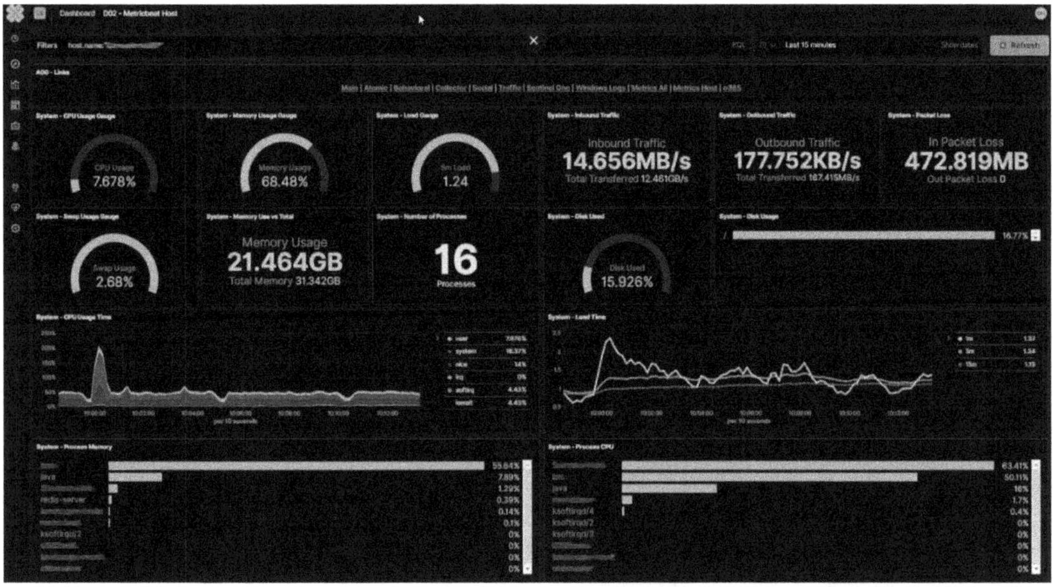

Figure 8.8: Interface of Zeek

- **Threat intelligence integration:** MISP, VirusTotal, ThreatFeeder.

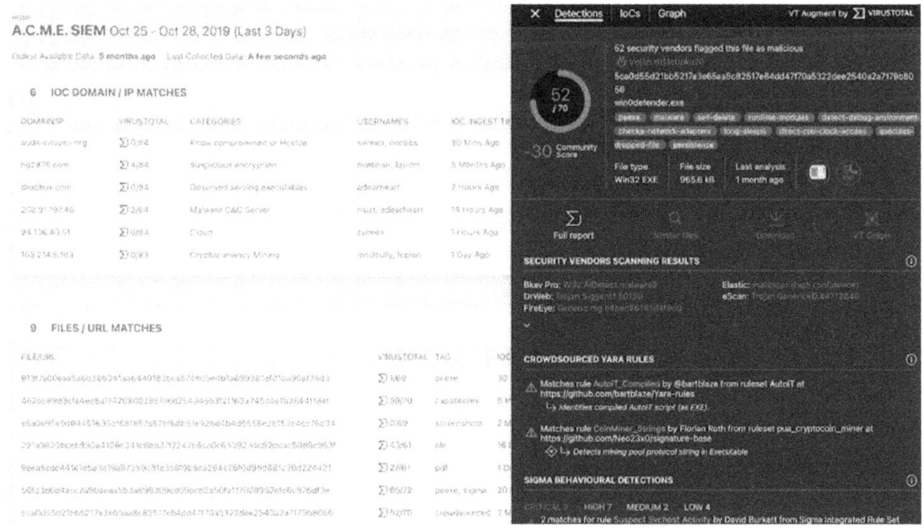

Figure 8.9: Interface of Virustotal

The deployment of relevant forensic tools for malware detection includes the following:

- **Network traffic analysis**: Wireshark, Zeek (Bro), and NetFlow Analyzer.

- **Malware sandboxing**: Cuckoo Sandbox and Any.Run Hybrid Analysis.

- **Reverse engineering**: IDA Pro, Ghidra, and Radare2.

- **Threat intelligence and log analysis**: Splunk, ELK Stack, and MISP.

Role of network forensics in incident response

Network forensics is the process of capturing, recording, and analyzing network traffic and logs to investigate cyber threats, security breaches, and malicious activities. Network forensics involves examining data packets, connection logs, and network flow records to detect, trace, and respond to cyber incidents. The key aspect of network forensics is stated as follows:

- **Traffic analysis**: The concept of traffic analysis implies monitoring and analyzing data flows for suspicious activities.

- **Log examination**: The process of log examination relates to investigating logs from firewalls, routers, IDS/IPS, and servers.

- **Attack attribution**: The aspect of attack attribution that identifies the source, method, and intent of an attack.

- **Incident response (IR)**: The IR provides forensic evidence to mitigate and prevent future attacks.

Network forensics plays a crucial role in cybersecurity investigations by detecting cyber threats in real-time. This relates to the identification of unusual traffic spikes, unauthorized access, and malware activity. This is further to helping to recognize attack techniques such as Brute-force attempts, **Denial of Service** (**DoS**) attacks, and data exfiltration. Network forensics involves tracing attack origins and identifying adversaries by tracking IP addresses, domains, and **Command and Control** (**C2**) Communications. This further assists in attributing cyberattacks to specific threat actors such as APTs, hackers, and insiders. The key network forensics artifacts for IR are listed as follows:

- **Firewall logs**: The logs generated from the Firewall reveal unauthorized access attempts and traffic anomalies. *(Figure 8.10)*

```
#Version: 1.5
#Software: Microsoft Windows Firewall
#Time Format: Local
#Fields: date time action protocol src-ip dst-ip src-port dst-port size tcpflags tcpsyn tcpack tcpwin icmptype icmpcode info path

2015-07-16 11:35:26 ALLOW TCP 10.40.4.182 10.40.1.11 63064 135 0 - 0 0 0 - - - SEND
2015-07-16 11:35:26 ALLOW TCP 10.40.4.182 10.40.1.14 63065 49156 0 - 0 0 0 - - - SEND
2015-07-16 11:35:26 ALLOW TCP 10.40.4.182 10.40.1.11 63066 65386 0 - 0 0 0 - - - SEND
2015-07-16 11:35:26 ALLOW TCP 10.40.4.182 10.40.1.11 63067 389 0 - 0 0 0 - - - SEND
2015-07-16 11:35:26 ALLOW UDP 10.40.4.182 10.40.1.14 62292 389 0 - - - - - - SEND
2015-07-16 11:35:26 ALLOW TCP 10.40.4.182 10.40.1.11 63068 389 0 - 0 0 0 - - - SEND
2015-07-16 11:35:26 ALLOW TCP 10.40.4.182 10.40.1.11 63069 445 0 - 0 0 0 - - - SEND
2015-07-16 11:35:26 ALLOW UDP 10.40.4.182 10.40.1.13 62293 389 0 - - - - - - SEND
2015-07-16 11:35:26 ALLOW TCP 10.40.4.182 10.40.1.13 63070 88 0 - 0 0 0 - - - SEND
2015-07-16 11:35:26 ALLOW TCP 10.40.4.182 10.40.1.11 63071 445 0 - 0 0 0 - - - SEND
2015-07-16 11:35:26 ALLOW TCP 10.40.4.182 10.40.1.11 63072 445 0 - 0 0 0 - - - SEND
2015-07-16 11:35:26 ALLOW TCP 10.40.4.182 10.40.1.11 63073 445 0 - 0 0 0 - - - SEND
2015-07-16 11:35:26 ALLOW TCP 10.40.4.182 10.40.1.13 63074 88 0 - 0 0 0 - - - SEND
2015-07-16 11:35:26 ALLOW TCP 10.40.4.182 10.40.1.13 63075 88 0 - 0 0 0 - - - SEND
2015-07-16 11:35:26 ALLOW TCP 10.40.4.182 10.40.1.13 63076 88 0 - 0 0 0 - - - SEND
2015-07-16 11:35:27 ALLOW UDP 10.40.4.182 10.40.1.11 55053 53 0 - - - - - - SEND
2015-07-16 11:35:27 ALLOW UDP 10.40.4.182 10.40.1.11 50845 53 0 - - - - - - SEND
2015-07-16 11:35:30 ALLOW UDP fe80::29ea:1a3c:24d6:fb49 ff02::1:3 57333 5355 0 - - - - - - RECEIVE
2015-07-16 11:35:30 ALLOW UDP 10.40.4.252 224.0.0.252 59629 5355 0 - - - - - - RECEIVE
2015-07-16 11:35:30 ALLOW UDP fe80::4c2e:505d:b3a7:caaf ff02::1:3 58846 5355 0 - - - - - - SEND
2015-07-16 11:35:30 ALLOW UDP 10.40.4.182 224.0.0.252 58846 5355 0 - - - - - - SEND
2015-07-16 11:35:31 ALLOW UDP 10.40.4.182 224.0.0.252 137 137 0 - - - - - - SEND
2015-07-16 11:35:31 ALLOW UDP fe80::4c2e:505d:b3a7:caaf ff02::1:3 63504 5355 0 - - - - - - SEND
2015-07-16 11:35:31 ALLOW UDP 10.40.4.182 224.0.0.252 63504 5355 0 - - - - - - SEND
```

Figure 8.10: Firewall logs

- **Intrusion Detection System (IDS) logs**: The logs from the IDS detect known attack patterns and signatures.

- **NetFlow records**: This tool tracks unusual data transfers and potential exfiltration.

- **DNS logs**: The DNS logs identify malicious domains used in phishing or C2 attacks.

- **Packet Captures (PCAPs):** The PCAPs provide granular details of network communications (*Figure 8.11*).

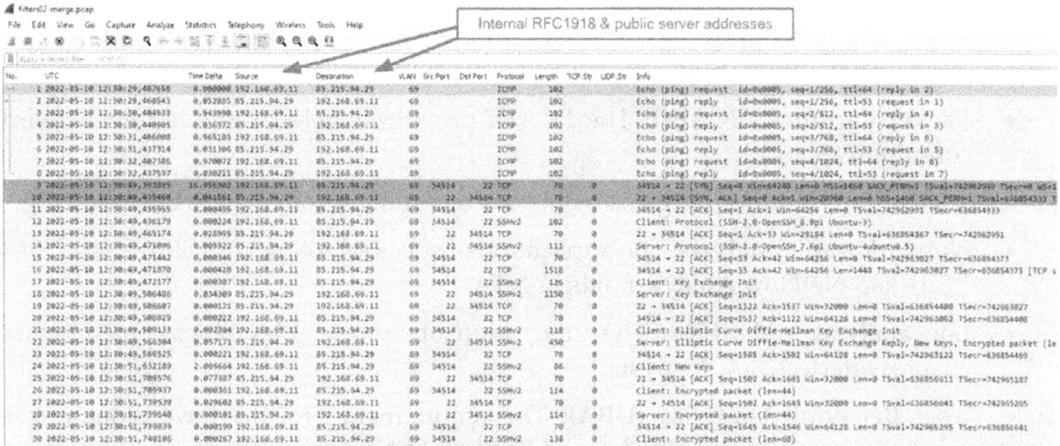

Figure 8.11: Packet Capture files

Application of network forensics in insider threat investigations

Insider threats relate to employees, contractors, or partners misusing access. The relevant types of insider threats include negligent insiders, malicious insiders, and compromised insiders. The importance of network forensics in detecting, investigating, and mitigating internal security violations relates to detecting insider threats and security violations. This is in terms of identifying unauthorized access to sensitive data, systems, or applications. This is in addition to investigating internal security breaches by reconstructing malicious activities by analyzing network logs and traffic patterns. This correlates to network events with user actions to pinpoint suspicious behavior. The effective investigation of internal security breaches results in providing forensic evidence such as timestamps, IP addresses, and access logs for legal or disciplinary action. The required mitigation of insider threats and prevention of similar incidents in the future relates to enabling real-time monitoring to detect and respond to threats before data is stolen. The relevant mitigation process involves strengthening security policies by identifying gaps and refining access controls. The mitigation further involves enhancing **User Behavior Analytics** (**UBA**) to detect anomalies early. The process of insider threat investigation involves the following key network forensic artifacts:

- **Firewall and Virtual Private Network (VPN) logs**: Logs from Firewall and VPN aids the digital forensic investigators to identify remote access attempts and policy violations.

- **Domain Name System (DNS) and Web Proxy Logs**: The logs from DNS and Web Proxy reveal connections to suspicious or unauthorized sites.

- **File access logs**: The relevant file access logs detect unusual downloads, deletions, or modifications.

- **Email and messaging logs**: The logs from email and messaging identify leaks of confidential information.

- **Packet Captures (PCAPs)**: The PCAPs provide detailed insights into network communications.

The associated tools used for progressing insider threat detection include the following:

- **Network traffic analysis:** The application of specific tools such as Wireshark, Zeek (Bro), and NetFlow Analyzer aids in NTA.

- **Log analysis and SIEM:** The integration of Splunk, ELK Stack, and Graylog ensures effective Log Analysis.

- **User Behavior Analytics (UBA):** The requirement of UBA for Insider risk is fulfilled by tools such as Exabeam, Microsoft Defender.

- **Endpoint and cloud monitoring:** The requirement of endpoint and cloud monitoring relates to enterprises using CrowdStrike, Varonis, and Digital Guardian.

Network forensics in data breach investigations

A data breach is an incident where sensitive, confidential, or protected information is accessed, stolen, or exposed without authorization. This can occur due to cyberattacks, insider threats, or accidental leaks. Data breaches often involve personal data, financial records, intellectual property, or trade secrets. The usual causes of data breaches include different cyberattacks such as hacking, phishing, ransomware, and malware. This is apart from insider threats, as the employees or contractors misusing access privileges. The relevant indicators of data exfiltration include unusual spikes in outbound traffic to external or suspicious destinations, along with unauthorized access to sensitive files or databases. The digital forensic investigators consider the following key network artifacts for data breach investigations:

- **Firewall and proxy logs:** The analysis of Firewall and Proxy Logs results in identifying unusual outbound connections.

- **DNS and VPN logs:** The analysis of DNS and VPN Logs tracks domain requests and remote access activities.

- **NetFlow and Packet Captures (PCAPs):** The detailed analysis of NetFlow and PCAPs reveals data movement and attacker communications.

- **Endpoint and file access logs:** The effective assessment of endpoint and file access logs determines which files were accessed or transferred within the device network.

The digital forensic investigators proceed with identifying breach indicators through logs and alerts. This aids them in correlating network events to pinpoint initial compromise. The analysis of attack paths and data transfer destinations reveals the extent of data loss and affected systems. Digital forensic investigators tend to preserve evidence and report findings for legal action.

Conclusion

The current chapter presented adequate details about network forensics in terms of different tools and techniques, along with widely selected methodologies by the digital forensic investigators. The chapter implied the importance of indulging in Log Analysis to detect the source of a data breach within the digital device network of an organization. The chapter implies that network forensics is crucial for strengthening the security of modern-day enterprises. The underlying areas of network forensics include NTA, which focuses on overall network communication patterns. Digital forensics investigators tend to face a wide range of challenges while dealing with network forensics investigation that requires them to select suitable tools and techniques for generating effective results that can enhance the resilience of enterprise security.

The upcoming chapter will focus on a detailed analysis of memory forensics.

Join our book's Discord space

Join the book's Discord Workspace for Latest updates, Offers, Tech happenings around the world, New Release and Sessions with the Authors:

https://discord.bpbonline.com

CHAPTER 9
Demystifying Memory Forensics

Introduction

Memory forensics is a crucial discipline in cybersecurity and digital investigations, allowing digital forensic investigators to examine volatile memory, such as RAM, for retrieving digital evidence of malicious activity. Contrary to disk forensics, which focuses on persistent storage, memory forensics provides a real-time snapshot of a system state, thereby revealing running processes, open network connections, encryption keys, and potential malware. The current chapter focuses on different areas of memory forensics that ensure relevant benefits for the digital forensic investigators from the perspective of generating expected results.

Structure

The chapter covers the following topics:

- Introduction to memory forensics
- Memory acquisition techniques
- Volatility framework
- Memory analysis fundamentals
- Detecting and analyzing malware in memory

- Identifying and investigating memory-based attacks
- Best practices and emerging trends

Objectives

The current chapter introduces memory forensics in terms of indicating its importance in enterprise network security. The chapter details relevant memory acquisition techniques for extracting memory data for forensic analysis. The chapter details the volatility framework in terms of exploring one of the most powerful memory forensics tools. The chapter implies memory analysis fundamentals as examining memory artifacts and structures. The chapter includes details about detecting and analyzing malware in memory, including uncovering memory-based threats. The chapter identifies and investigates different memory-based attacks, indicating the benefits of memory forensics for **incident response** (**IR**). The chapter indicates the advantages of memory forensics for insider threat investigations. This is in terms of detecting and responding to internal security breaches. The chapter attempts to establish memory forensics in data breach investigations. This is in terms of uncovering evidence of data theft in memory. The chapter details memory forensics in **Advanced Persistent Threat** (**APT**) investigations to trace sophisticated attacks. The chapter includes relevant best practices and emerging trends in memory forensics for enterprise network security.

Introduction to memory forensics

The concept of memory forensics involves analyzing volatile memory (RAM) to extract digital evidence. The focus of memory forensics tends to be on investigating live system artifacts such as processes, network activity, and credentials. The process of memory forensics differs from that of disk forensics as the latter deals with persistent storage, while memory forensics provides real-time system insights. The importance of memory forensics in enterprise network security relates to the following areas:

- **Incident response (IR):** Memory forensics helps detect and analyze security breaches in real-time. *(Figure 9.1)*

```
root@NeilFoxDellXPS:~/volatility# python vol.py -f win7-32-memory-raw.001 --profile=Win7SP1x86 pslist
Volatility Foundation Volatility Framework 2.6.1
Offset(V)   Name                      PID   PPID   Thds    Hnds   Sess  Wow64 Start

----------  ------------------  ------  ------  ------  --------  ------ ------ ------------------------------
----------------
0x85c50958  System                      4      0     105     532  ------     0 2012-04-04 11:47:29 UTC+0000

0x86ecaa70  smss.exe                  280      4       3      32  ------     0 2012-04-04 11:47:29 UTC+0000

0x86cfa540  csrss.exe                 412    404       9     756      0      0 2012-04-04 11:47:41 UTC+0000

0x87d85d40  wininit.exe               464    404       3      74      0      0 2012-04-04 11:47:44 UTC+0000

0x86e7f030  csrss.exe                 472    456       9      75      1      0 2012-04-04 11:47:44 UTC+0000

0x87d8fd40  winlogon.exe              520    456       3      91      1      0 2012-04-04 11:47:44 UTC+0000

0x87f68030  services.exe              564    464       7     243      0      0 2012-04-04 11:47:45 UTC+0000

0x87f79600  lsass.exe                 592    464       8     888      0      0 2012-04-04 11:47:46 UTC+0000

0x87f8c030  lsm.exe                   600    464      10     248      0      0 2012-04-04 11:47:46 UTC+0000

0x87fc5590  svchost.exe               704    564      11     358      0      0 2012-04-04 11:47:48 UTC+0000

0x87fee6d0  svchost.exe               780    564       6     277      0      0 2012-04-04 11:47:51 UTC+0000

0x88000d40  svchost.exe               820    564      18     469      0      0 2012-04-04 11:47:51 UTC+0000

0x8800e178  LogonUI.exe               880    520       7     197      1      0 2012-04-04 11:47:51 UTC+0000
```

Figure 9.1: Memory forensics for IR

- **Malware analysis:** Memory forensics identifies sophisticated threats, such as fileless malware and rootkits.

- **Insider threats:** Memory forensics detects unauthorized access and privilege escalation attempts.

- **Threat hunting:** Memory forensics proactively searches for hidden adversaries within an enterprise network.

The following key artifacts are considered by digital forensic investigators in memory forensics:

- **Running processes:** Memory forensics identifies malicious or suspicious executables within the running processes.

- **Network connections:** Memory forensics unveils unauthorized communications and **Command and Control (C2)** activity within network connections.

- **Credential harvesting:** Memory forensics extracts passwords, authentication tokens, and encryption keys as a means of credential harvesting.

- **Injected code and rootkits:** Memory forensics detects stealthy malware techniques used to bypass security measures by analyzing injected code and rootkits.

The underlying challenges in memory forensics include the following:

- **Data volatility:** The issue of data volatility occurs when RAM data is lost on power-off and thereby requires immediate acquisition by digital forensic investigators.

- **Anti-forensic techniques:** The modern-day sophisticated attackers use complicated anti-forensics techniques such as encryption and obfuscation to evade detection during digital forensic investigation.

- **Voluminous data analysis:** Processing enterprise-scale memory dumps is complex and resource-intensive, as it involves voluminous data analysis as a part of memory forensics.

Memory acquisition techniques

Memory acquisition is the process of capturing the volatile memory (RAM) of a system for forensic analysis. The importance of memory acquisition techniques for digital forensic investigation relates to providing a real-time snapshot of system activity, revealing running processes, network connections, and potential threats. The relevant use cases of memory acquisition techniques relate to critical IR, malware analysis, and detecting APTs. The aspect of memory acquisition techniques relates to a wide range of the following considerations:

- **Live vs. offline acquisition:** The memory of a digital device must be captured by the digital forensic investigators while the system is running as the associated RAM is volatile.

- **Integrity and minimal interference:** The selected memory forensics tools used by the digital forensic investigators must have a low footprint on the concerned digital device to avoid alerting adversaries or altering evidence.

- **Chain of custody:** The digital forensic investigators tend to consider proper documentation of digital evidence to ensure forensic validity and legal admissibility.

The process of memory acquisition requires the concerned digital forensic investigators to consider the relevant tools for proceeding with the investigation process across Windows systems, Linux systems, macOS systems, and virtualized environments. The suitable memory acquisition tools for Windows system are stated as follows:

- **DumpIt**: This is a lightweight tool for quick memory capture and is thus widely selected by the digital forensic investigator. The tool can be effortlessly executed from a USB drive or other removable media. The tool is ideal for quick memory acquisition in IR scenarios. *(Figure 9.2)*

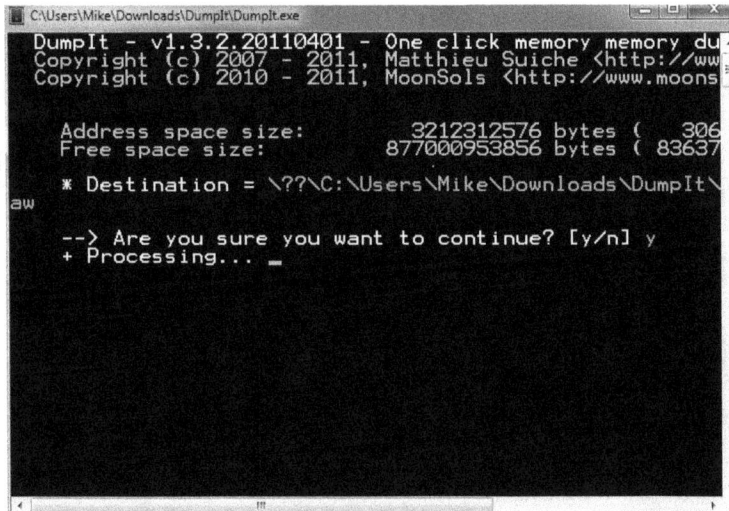

Figure 9.2: Interface of DumpIt

- **FTK Imager**: This is a forensic imaging tool that has relevant memory acquisition capabilities. The tool captures volatile memory (RAM) and live disk data without shutting down the system. It supports the imaging of entire drives, including hard drives, SSDs, USBs, and external media. It allows investigators to extract specific files or directories instead of creating full disk images, saving time and storage space. *(Figure 9.3)*

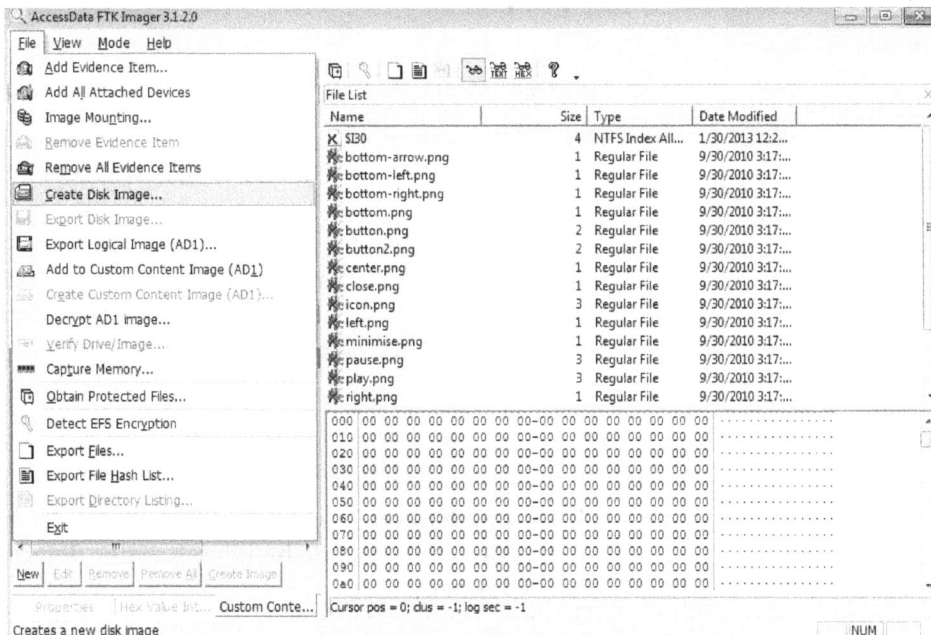

Figure 9.3: Interface of FTK Imager

- **WinPMEM**: This tool is a part of the Rekall framework, optimized for forensic extraction. The tool captures volatile memory while ensuring minimal interference with system operations. It preserves the integrity of memory dumps for forensic analysis and legal investigations. This ensures the forensically sound memory acquisition requirement of a digital forensics investigation. The tool proceeds with live memory dumping with a kernel driver in terms of using a signed kernel driver to extract memory from running Windows systems. *(Figure 9.4)*

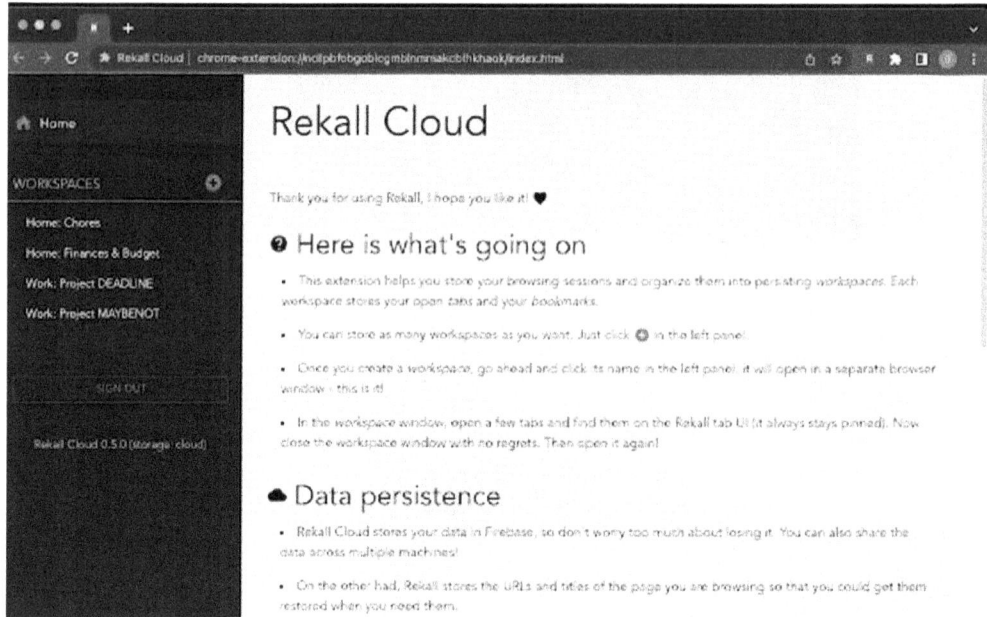

Figure 9.4: Interface of Rekall

Volatility framework

Volatility is an open-source memory forensics tool used to analyze volatile memory (RAM) dumps. The purpose of this tool is to help forensic analysts investigate security incidents, detect malware, and uncover hidden system artifacts. It encourages cross-platform support by working with Windows, Linux, macOS, and Android memory dumps. The underlying features and capabilities of this tool are listed as follows:

- **Process analysis**: The aspect of process analysis identifies running processes, including hidden or suspicious ones, during digital forensic investigations.

- **Dynamic Link Library (DLL) and handle inspection**: The DLL and handle inspection analyzes loaded libraries and system handles for the detection of anomalies during digital forensic investigations.

- **Registry and configuration extraction**: The registry and configuration extraction recover Windows registry keys and system configurations from the digital devices.

- **Network connection analysis**: The network connection analysis investigates open network ports, active connections, and potential C2 activity.

- **Malware detection**: The process of malware detection aids the digital forensic investigators in detecting injected code, rootkits, and persistence mechanisms.

- **File system and memory mapping**: The procedure of file system and memory mapping recovers in-memory files and mapped DLLs.

- **Credential and encryption key recovery**: The process of credential and encryption key recovery proceeds with the extraction of stored passwords, hashes, and cryptographic keys. *(Figure 9.5)*

```
????????????????????????????????????
????????????????????????????????????????????????????????????????????????
????????????????????????????????????????????????????????????????????????
????????????????????????????????????????????????????????????????????????
????????????????????????????????????????????????????????????????????????
????????????????????????????????????????????????????????????????????????
????????????????????????????????????????????????????????????????????????
????????????????????????????????????????????????????????????????????????
????????????????????????????????????????????????????????????????????????
XC45tNYivI72oxuIKP12q1PuoU7/fVyspFECQFFZUfiEMFb7H7fo3aWnoWFcLkjR
lVtNXO4vVL11c4oYK2XwcAxMnxr65+XsBcVcwR0Q4u9/x8+VrBtKYvp+sNcCQE1O
W4ewXTvj87uu8UAu60N2xdSwawFF5OBiRFXMSKOYtYEaqPy1p+YQvrlwom29myHd
00kOUGEdJNLG+ICGn8ECQQDUyI4oTF9N4gc9vs+19RlqdzsX6nRj2nBn8fI3y6nu
LIHsFctL38ItRE0+j4YsPs4NqRrd7glq880xlqaLIMgv
-----END RSA PRIVATE KEY-----
```

Figure 9.5: Encryption key recovery

The volatility can work with raw dumps, crash dumps, hibernation files, and **Advanced Forensic Format 4** (**AFF4**) to support multiple memory dump formats. This tool can integrate with DumpIt, FTK Imager, WinPMEM, and LiME. The uses of the volatility framework are stated as follows:

- **Command-Line Interface (CLI)**: The benefit of the CLI is that it provides powerful plugins for detailed memory analysis.

- **Common commands and plugins**: The use of CLI relates to using relevant commands and plugins as listed in the following tabular structure *(Table 9.1)*:

Command and plugins	Function
pslist, pstree	Lists running processes and their hierarchy
netscan	Displays active and historical network connections
malfind	Detects hidden or injected code segments
hashdump	Extracts password hashes from memory
cmdscan, consoles	Recovers command-line history

Table 9.1: CLI commands and plugins

The relevant advantages of the volatility framework relate to its availability as a free and open-source forensic tool. This encourages its active development by the digital forensic community. The lightweight and portable nature of the volatility framework requires no installation, thereby making it easy to deploy in digital forensic investigations. The tools encourage the development of custom plugins for specialized analysis. The tool is trusted by cybersecurity professionals and forensic analysts worldwide and is thereby used widely in IR. Volatility is a powerful and essential tool for memory forensics that provides deep insights into system activity, malware infections, and cyber threats. Mastering its capabilities enhances the overall ability of a forensic digital investigator. *(Figure 9.6)*

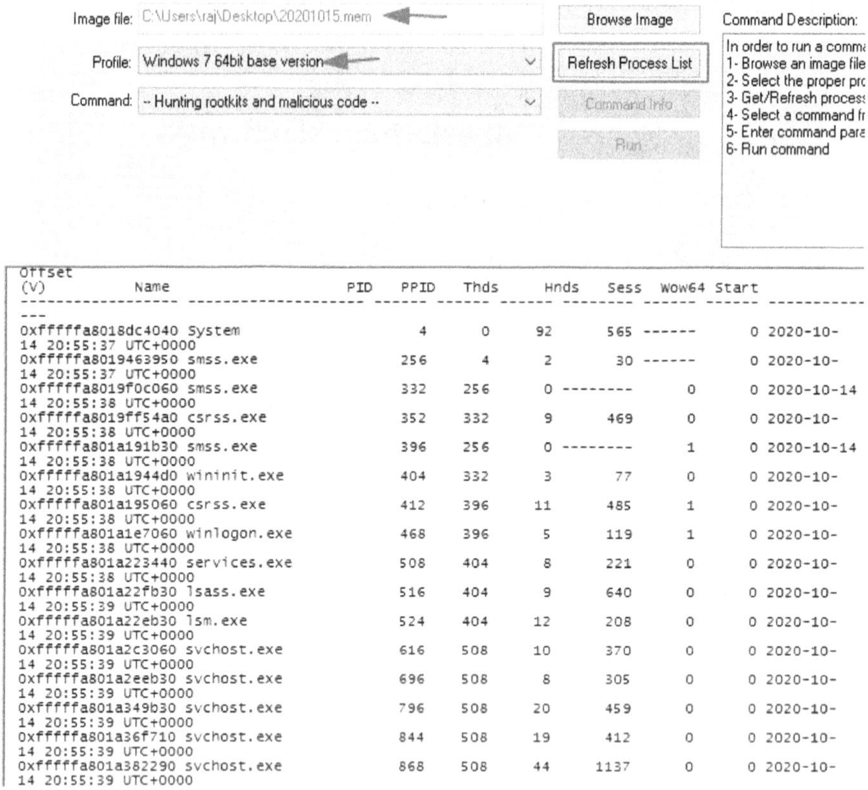

Figure 9.6: Interface of volatility framework

Memory analysis fundamentals

Memory analysis is the process of examining volatile memory (RAM) to uncover digital evidence. Its importance for digital forensic analysis includes providing real-time insights into the state of a system, including running processes, network activity, and security incidents. The procedure of memory analysis is used in malware detection, IR, insider threat investigations, and forensic casework. The key memory artifacts are stated as follows:

- **Processes and threads**: This resembles identifying active processes, terminated processes, and hidden/malicious executions.

- **Network connections**: This reveals open connections, active ports, and potential C2 channels.

- **System handles and objects**: This relates to investigating file handles, mutexes, and registry entries used by malware.

- **Kernel modules and drivers**: This relates to detecting rootkits, unauthorized kernel modifications, and injected code.

- **Registry and configuration data**: This process resembles extracting registry keys, startup items, and system preferences.

- **Credential and authentication artifacts**: This relates to recovering passwords, hashes, and authentication tokens.

The different memory structures and their roles in digital forensic investigations are stated as follows:

- **Page tables and virtual memory**: This memory structure relates to understanding how the OS manages memory allocation and paging for digital forensics.

- **Heap and stack analysis**: This memory structure relates to identifying process memory usage, potential buffer overflows, and injected shellcode.

- **Memory mapped files**: The memory mapped files relate to analyzing executable files loaded in memory for stealth malware persistence.

The following tools are used for memory analysis:

- **Volatility framework**: The volatility framework is widely used for extracting and analyzing memory artifacts.

- **Rekall**: This is an advanced forensic framework used for deep memory investigation.

- **Memoryze**: This tool is used for detecting malware and suspicious memory activity. *(Figure 9.7)*

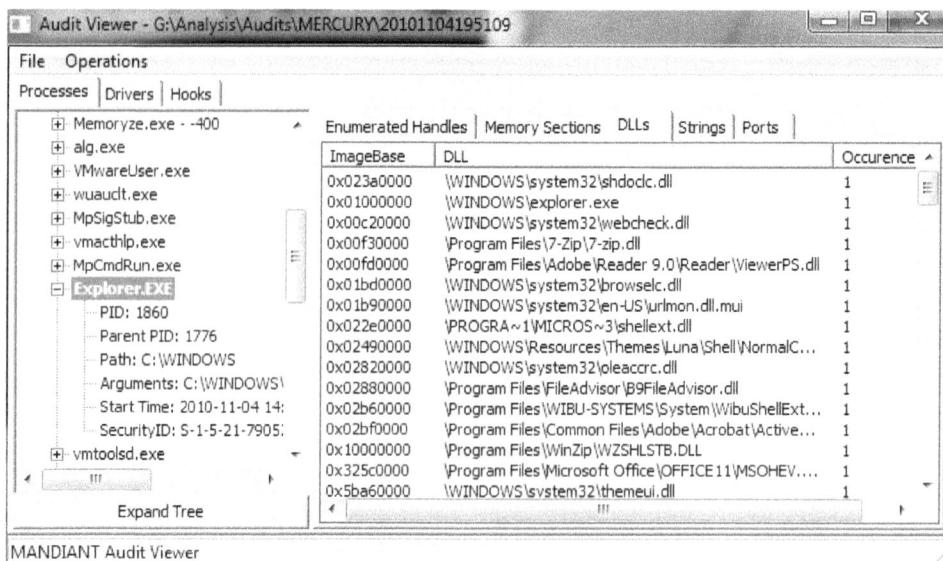

Figure 9.7: *Interface of Memoryze*

Detecting and analyzing malware in memory

Memory-based malware operates in the RAM of a system without leaving traces on disk. The importance of detecting and analyzing malware in memory relates to traditional antivirus solutions often miss in-memory threats as they do not rely on persistent storage. The common examples of malware in memory include fileless malware, rootkits, **Remote Access Trojans** (**RATs**), and APTs. The memory-based malware proceeds with the following methodologies for evading detection:

- **Code injection**: The process of code injection relates to injecting malicious code into legitimate processes such as process hollowing and DLL injection.

- **Reflective loading**: Reflective Loading relates to executing malware in memory without touching disk storage.

- **Obfuscation and encryption**: The obfuscation and encryption relate to concealing malicious activity by encrypting payloads and hiding execution traces.

- **Hooking and API manipulation**: Hooking and API manipulation relate to modifying system calls to intercept or manipulate memory activities.

The key **Incident of Compromise** (**IoCs**) in memory are related to the following:

- **Unusual running processes**: The suspicious or unsigned processes getting executed in the memory results in disrupting the performance of a system.

- **Hidden or terminated processes**: Hidden or terminated processes are pointing towards malware that hides itself or creates ghost processes.

- **Injected gts**: The memory regions of a system containing injected shellcode or executable payloads.

- **Abnormal network connections**: The unexpected outbound connections are created by the adversaries to known malicious domains.

- **Anomalous DLLs and kernel modules**: The presence of unauthorized or unsigned dynamic libraries and kernel drivers within the memory of a system implies an IoCs.

The appropriate tools for detecting and analyzing memory-based malware are detailed as follows:

- **Volatility framework**: The volatility framework analyzes memory dumps to detect injected code, hidden processes, and network activity.

- **Rekall**: Rekall provides deep forensic insights into system memory, kernel structures, and rootkits.

- **Memoryze**: Memoryze detects malware, rootkits, and hooks within memory dumps.

- **YARA Rules**: The YARA Rules help identify known malware patterns in memory by scanning for specific signatures. *(Figure 9.8)*

```
rule Linux_Ransomware_GwisinLocker : tc_detection malicious
{
    meta:

        author              = "ReversingLabs"

        source              = "ReversingLabs"
        status              = "RELEASED"
        sharing             = "TLP:WHITE"
        category            = "MALWARE"
        malware             = "GWISINLOCKER"
        description         = "Yara rule that detects GwisinLocker ransomware."

        tc_detection_type   = "Ransomware"
        tc_detection_name   = "GwisinLocker"
        tc_detection_factor = 5
```

Figure 9.8: Interface of Yara Rules

Identifying and investigating memory-based attacks

The characteristics of memory-based attacks relate to exploiting system RAM to execute malicious code, often without leaving traces on disk. The significance of identifying and investigating memory-based attacks relates to traditional forensic techniques that may miss these attacks, making memory forensics crucial for their detection. The common instances of memory-based attacks include fileless malware, credential theft (Mimikatz), process injection, and APTs. The key indicators of memory-based attacks include the following:

- **Suspicious or hidden processes**: The aspect of suspicious or hidden processes indicates the malware that masquerades as legitimate system processes or runs covertly.

- **Unusual network connections**: The unusual network connections imply unexpected outbound traffic, particularly to C2 servers.

- **Injected or hollowed code**: The injected or hollowed code is the malware that manipulates or replaces the memory space of legitimate processes.

- **Credential and token theft**: The aspect of credential and token theft relates to unauthorized access to authentication data stored in memory, such as LSASS dumps.

- **Unusual API calls and hooks**: The occurrence of unusual API calls and hooks relates to system functions that are modified to bypass security controls or intercept data.

Memory forensics in IR relates to the following:

- **Immediate memory capture**: The target of immediate memory capture relates to using tools such as WinPMEM, DumpIt, or FTK Imager to acquire RAM before shutdown.

- **Analyzing memory dumps**: The process of analyzing memory dumps relates to extracting forensic artifacts using Volatility, Rekall, or Memoryze.

- **Investigating running processes**: The aspect of investigating running processes relates to detecting anomalies using pslist, pstree, and malfind commands.

- **Network forensics in memory**: The significance of network forensics in memory resembles identifying suspicious connections with netscan and connection plugins.

- **Detecting rootkits and hooks**: The process of detecting Rootkits and Hooks relates to scanning for hidden kernel modules and API manipulations.

The following tools are used for memory-based attack investigation:

- **Volatility framework**: The volatility framework is a comprehensive tool for memory analysis and malware detection.

- **Rekall**: Rekall is an advanced forensic tool for deep system memory inspection.

- **Redline**: Redline detects malicious activity in memory, including unauthorized processes and connections.

- **YARA**: The YARA scans memory dumps for known malware signatures and behavioural indicators. *(Figure 9.9)*

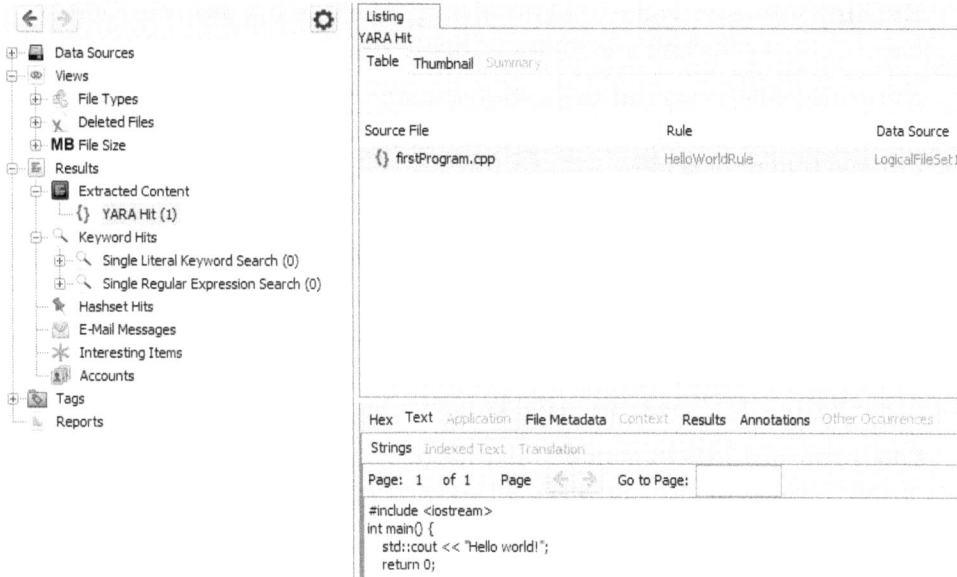

Figure 9.9: *Interface of Yara*

Memory forensics for insider threat investigations

The concept of insider threats involves employees, contractors, or trusted individuals misusing access to compromise security. The significance of memory forensics for insider threat investigation relates to the fact that traditional security tools may fail to detect malicious insider activities, making memory forensics essential. The related scenarios include data exfiltration, privilege abuse, credential theft, unauthorized access, and sabotage. The aspect of identifying insider threat indicators in memory relates to the following:

- **Suspicious process activity**: The suspicious process activity relates to unusual system processes, unauthorized software, or remote access tools.

- **Unauthorized credential usage**: The unauthorized credential usage relates to extracting passwords, authentication tokens, or encryption keys from memory.

- **Data exfiltration attempts**: The process of data exfiltration attempts relates to large file transfers, email attachments, or suspicious cloud uploads.

- **Unauthorized privilege escalation**: The unauthorized privilege escalation relates to the abnormal use of admin rights or system modifications.

- **Covert communication channels**: The covert communication channels resemble unexpected network connections, VPN tunnelling, or C2 interactions.

The digital forensic investigators consider the following key memory artifacts for investigating instances of insider threats:

- **Running processes and execution history**: The running processes and execution history aid in detecting unauthorized applications using pslist and cmdscan.

- **Network connections and exfiltration attempts**: The relevant network connections and exfiltration attempts can be assessed by using netscan to trace suspicious external communication.

- **Clipboard and file access history**: Recovering copied data and transferred files by the digital forensic investigators relates to considering the clipboard and file access history.

- **Registry and system configuration changes**: The digital forensic investigators proceed with assessing registry and system configuration changes to track unauthorized modifications in the Windows registry.

- **Email and chat logs in memory**: Extracting communication records from volatile memory relates to focusing on email and chat logs.

The digital forensic investigators focus on the following tools for responding to internal security breaches in memory forensics:

- **Volatility framework:** This framework extracts key memory artifacts such as processes, network connections, and credentials.

- **Rekall:** This tool helps detect stealthy insider activities using deep system memory analysis.

- **Redline:** This tool provides insights into active processes and suspicious user behavior.

- **YARA Rules:** This tool identifies insider threats by scanning for malicious patterns in memory.

Memory forensics in data breach investigations

Memory forensics involves analyzing volatile memory (RAM) to uncover evidence of unauthorized data access and exfiltration. Many cybercriminals use in-memory techniques to steal sensitive data while avoiding traditional disk-based detection. The key indicators of data theft in memory include processing of unusual network activity, such as unexpected outbound connections, especially to unknown IPs or external cloud services. The relevant clipboard and session data extraction relates to evidence of copied sensitive data, passwords, or credit card details. The digital forensic investigators apply process and thread analysis to identify malicious activities using pslist, pstree, and malfind. This is further to processing network and connection analysis to examine live connections and historical network traffic with netscan. The target of detecting injected or hidden code relates to using malfind and ldrmodules to uncover stealthy in-memory malware. The relevant tools used by digital forensic investigators to proceed with memory forensics in data breach investigations include the following:

- **Volatility framework:** A powerful digital forensic tool for extracting APT-related artifacts from memory dumps.

- **Rekall:** This tool provides in-depth memory analysis and helps detect advanced threats.

- **Wireshark:** This tool monitors memory-resident network traffic for APT communication patterns.

- **YARA Rules:** This tool identifies known APT malware signatures and behaviour patterns in memory.

Memory forensics in APT investigations

The APTs are long-term, stealthy cyberattacks targeting specific organizations or governments. The APTs use sophisticated evasion techniques, making disk-based forensics insufficient; memory forensics helps uncover hidden activity. The common tactics deployed by the adversaries to proceed with engaging APTs include fileless malware, process injection, credential theft, rootkits, and C2 communication. The digital forensics investigators utilize the following techniques for APT Investigations:

- **Live memory acquisition**: The process of live memory acquisition relates to capturing volatile memory using tools such as WinPMEM or FTK Imager.

- **Process and thread analysis**: The process and thread analysis relate to identifying rogue processes with pslist, pstree, and malfind.

- **DLL and code injection detection**: The relevant DLL uses ldrmodules, dlllist, and malfind to trace injected libraries.

- **Network connection analysis**: The concept of network connection analysis implies detecting APT backdoors and C2 Activity with netscan.

- **Credential and token extraction**: The process of credential and token extraction relates to recovering stolen authentication data with hashdump and creds.

Best practices and emerging trends

The best practices in memory forensics for enterprise network security are stated here:

- **Proactive memory acquisition:** The procedure of proactive memory acquisition regularly captures and analyzes memory snapshots to detect early-stage threats.

- **Standardized IR procedures:** The standardized IR procedures develop clear protocols for memory acquisition and analysis during security incidents.

- **Use of automated forensic tools:** The leveraging of automated forensic tools such as Volatility, Rekall, and Redline ensures streamlining analysis.

- **Threat intelligence integration:** The effective threat intelligence integration correlates memory forensics data with threat intelligence feeds to identify known attack patterns.

- **Forensic readiness:** The aspect of forensic readiness implies training security teams in memory analysis techniques and maintaining updated forensic toolkits.

The emerging trends in memory forensics for enterprise network security are stated here:

- **AI-powered memory analysis**: Machine learning models are being integrated to detect anomalies and automate malware classification.

- **Cloud memory forensics**: With cloud adoption, forensic tools are evolving to analyze memory dumps from virtual environments.

- **Live memory forensics**: Real-time memory scanning without full system dumps is gaining traction for faster threat detection.

- **Memory forensics in Zero Trust security**: Continuous monitoring of volatile memory aligns with Zero Trust principles.

- **Quantum-resistant forensic techniques**: Advancements in cryptographic security are being explored to protect forensic data integrity.

Conclusion

This chapter provides a detailed analysis of memory forensics as an integral part of digital forensics. The chapter includes adequate details about memory acquisition techniques, along with focusing on specific tools such as the Volatility framework. The detailed analysis of different memory forensic tools and artifacts encourages a detailed understanding of malware in memory. The chapter indicates that memory forensics plays a crucial role in responding to specific cyber incidents such as data breaches and insider threats. This is owing to the accumulation of adequate intelligence that can boost the cyber resilience level of an organization to similar attacks in the future.

The upcoming chapter relates to exploring mobile device forensics as a critical requirement for enterprise security.

Join our book's Discord space

Join the book's Discord Workspace for Latest updates, Offers, Tech happenings around the world, New Release and Sessions with the Authors:

https://discord.bpbonline.com

CHAPTER 10
Exploring Mobile Device Forensics

Introduction

The increasing dependency on smartphone devices nowadays results in their becoming potential targets by the adversaries. Modern-day cybercrimes are heavily related to considering smartphone devices as the primary point of origin of the cyberattack on the targeted entity. This encourages the emergence of mobile device forensics as a crucial part of digital forensics. Mobile device forensics is a branch of digital forensics that focuses on the recovery, analysis, and preservation of data from mobile devices, such as smartphones, tablets, and GPS devices. It plays a crucial role in criminal investigations, cybersecurity incidents, and corporate security. The current chapter focuses on exploring mobile device forensics from the perspective of evidence acquisition and their analysis by deploying different tools and techniques.

Structure

The chapter covers the following topics:

- Introduction to mobile device forensics
- Mobile device acquisition techniques
- Mobile operating systems and file systems
- Mobile app forensics

- Call log and message analysis

- Location data and GPS analysis

- Social media and messaging app forensics

- Mobile device encryption and password cracking

- Mobile device forensics in BYOD environments

- Case studies

Objectives

The current chapter focuses on introducing mobile device forensics in terms of understanding its significance in enterprise investigations. The chapter includes different mobile device acquisition techniques for extracting data from smartphones and tablets. The chapter focuses on mobile **operating systems** (**OS**) and file systems in terms of understanding the structure of mobile devices. The current chapter looks into details about mobile app forensics to investigate applications for evidence collection. The chapter includes details about call logs and message analysis to extract communication data from mobile devices. The chapter focuses on location data and **Global Positioning System** (**GPS**) Analysis in terms of tracking mobile device movements. The chapter includes adequate details about social media and messaging app forensics in terms of uncovering digital footprints in social networking apps. The chapter includes adequate details about mobile device encryption and password cracking to overcome security measures in forensic investigations. The chapter talks about how recovering deleted data from mobile devices is possible by deploying multiple techniques for data restoration. It also implies that mobile device forensics is emerging as a crucial factor in present **Bring Your Own Device** (**BYOD**) Environments. This is in terms of addressing challenges in employee-owned devices. The chapter includes multiple case studies to further establish the importance of mobile device forensics as per modern-day dependency on smartphone devices.

Introduction to mobile device forensics

Mobile device forensics is a branch of digital forensics focusing on mobile devices such as smartphones, tablets, and **Internet of Things** (**IoT**) devices. Mobile device forensics plays a crucial role in enterprise security in terms of investigating data breaches, insider threats, and policy violations. The importance of mobile device forensics in enterprise investigations relates to a wide range of factors, such as data sensitivity. This relates to mobile devices storing critical business information, emails, and corporate documents. The importance further relates to effective **incident response** (**IR**) in terms of helping to detect unauthorized access, malware attacks, and data leaks. The associated legal and compliance aspect of mobile device forensics ensures adherence to different data protection laws, such as the **General Data Protection Regulation** (**GDPR**), the **California Consumer Privacy Act** (**CCPA**), and the **Health Insurance Portability and Accountability Act**

(**HIPAA**). The significance of mobile device forensics for enterprise security investigation relates to detecting fraudulent activities, intellectual property theft, and unauthorized communications. The best practices for mobile device forensics include preservation of data integrity to avoid altering evidence and maintaining a **Chain of Custody** (**CoC**). The following methods are deployed by the digital forensic investigators to proceed with mobile device forensics:

- **Logical extraction**: The concept of Logical Extraction relates to accessing accessible data without bypassing security measures.

- **Physical extraction**: The aspect of physical extraction relates to creating full memory dumps for deeper forensic analysis.

- **Network and cloud forensics**: The importance of network and cloud forensics for mobile device forensics indicates investigating synced accounts, enterprise cloud storage, and **Virtual Private Network** (**VPN**) logs.

The selection of these methods for mobile device forensics relates to selecting relevant forensic tools from the following classification by the digital forensic investigators:

- **Commercial solutions**: Commercial forensic tools are proprietary software developed by companies specializing in digital forensics. These tools are widely used by law enforcement agencies, enterprises, and cybersecurity professionals due to their advanced capabilities, technical support, and regular updates. The commercial solutions include Cellebrite UFED, Magnet AXIOM, and Oxygen Forensics. *(Figure 10.1)*

Figure 10.1: Interface of oxygen forensics

- **Open-source tools**: Open-source forensic tools are freely available software developed by cybersecurity communities and researchers. These tools are often used for academic research, independent investigations, and situations where budget constraints prevent the use of commercial solutions. The open-source tools include Autopsy, **Mobile Verification Toolkit** (**MVT**), and Andriller.

Mobile device acquisition techniques

The concept of mobile device acquisition relates to the process of extracting, preserving, and analyzing data from mobile devices for forensic investigations. The significance of this procedure relates to helping to recover crucial evidence such as messages, call logs, app data, and location history. The associated challenges include data encryption, hardware differences, OS security updates, and cloud storage integration. The relevant types of mobile data acquisition methods are stated as follows:

- **Manual acquisition**: This mobile device acquisition technique implies inspecting the device screen and manually recording evidence, such as taking screenshots and notes. The advantages of this procedure include not requiring special tools and the process being quick and simple. However, the related disadvantages include a high risk of data alteration and incomplete data extraction. *(Figure 10.2)*

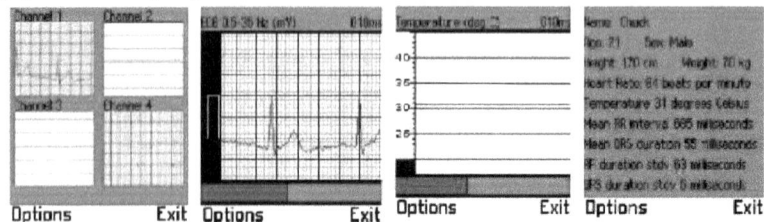

Figure 10.2: Data acquisition interface

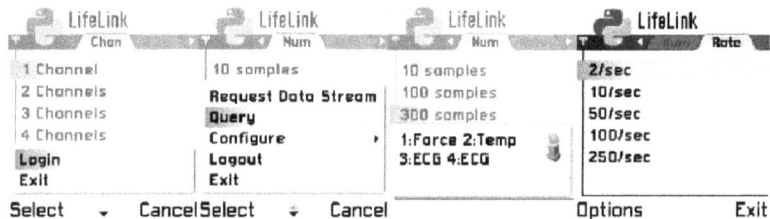

- **Logical acquisition**: This process relates to extracting accessible data using built-in **Application Programming Interfaces** (**APIs**) and forensic tools.

- **Physical acquisition**: The process creates a bit-by-bit copy of the entire device storage, including deleted and hidden data.

- **File system acquisition**: This technique of mobile device acquisition relates to extracting a file system of a device and thereby allowing user access to app data and system logs. The benefit of this approach relates to its being more comprehensive than logical acquisition but less invasive than physical acquisition.

- **Cloud-based acquisition**: This technique of mobile device acquisition relates to retrieving data from cloud backups such as Google Drive, iCloud, and OneDrive. However, this process requires proper credentials and legal authorization.

The relevant best practices for mobile device acquisition relate to maintaining a proper CoC to ensure data integrity. The digital forensic investigators use write-blockers to prevent accidental data modification within the device. They need to follow legal guidelines such as warrant requirements and privacy laws. The relevant best practices imply validating extracted data using forensic tools.

Mobile operating systems and file systems

Mobile OS are defined as the software that manages hardware, applications, and user interactions on mobile devices. The importance of a mobile OS in digital forensics relates to determining data storage, security mechanisms, and forensic extraction methods. The popular mobile OS used nowadays include Android, iOS, KaiOS, HarmonyOS, and Windows Mobile. Among these, Android is open-source and is used by multiple manufacturers. On the other side, iOS is cloud-based and exclusively used across Apple devices. The other mobile OS tends to be less common but relevant in different cases. The prime differences between Android and iOS are stated in the following tabular structure:

Attributes	Android	iOS
Primary file systems	Ext4 and F2FS	Apple File System (APFS)
Partitions	<ul><li>**/boot:** Bootloader and kernel.</li><li>**/system:** OS core files.</li><li>**/data:** User data (apps, messages, contacts, etc.).</li><li>**/cache:** Temporary files, logs.</li><li>**/sdcard:** User-accessible storage (optional, external).</li></ul>	<ul><li>**Root Partition (/):** System and OS files (read-only)</li><li>**User Data Partition (/var or /private/var):** Contains app data, messages, and logs.</li></ul>
Security	Full-disk and file-based Data Encryption (FBE)	Hardware Encryption, Secure Enclave and Sandboxing
Key artifacts for forensics	SQLite Databases, Log Files, APKs and XML Configurations	Plist Files, Keychain Data, iCloud Backups and System Logs

Table 10.1: Difference between Android and iOS

Digital forensic investigators tend to face a wide range of file system challenges while proceeding with mobile forensics. These challenges are listed as follows:

- **Encryption and security features:** The digital forensic investigators are required to bypass Lock screens, biometrics, and hardware encryptions that restrict access to mobile devices such as smartphones and tablets.

- **Data fragmentation:** The digital forensic investigators observe that versions of different mobile OS tend to store data in varying formats.

- **App sandboxing:** The extensive usage of app sandboxing tends to limit access to other data of applications for security reasons.

The prevalence of such challenges encourages digital forensic investigators to select relevant forensic techniques for proceeding with file system analysis. These techniques are stated as follows:

- **Logical extraction:** This technique of logical extraction relates to gaining access to accessible data of mobile devices using forensic tools by digital forensic investigators.

- **Physical dump:** The process of physical dump relates to digital forensic investigators' bit-by-bit imaging of digital evidences to recover deleted or hidden files from it.

- **Jailbreaking and rooting (advanced):** This advanced method is extensively used by the Digital Forensic Investigators to gain elevated privileges to access the restricted data of a digital device, despite it being legally restricted.

- **Cloud data extraction:** Digital forensic investigators tend to analyze backups of mobile devices stored on specific platforms such as iCloud, Google Drive, or OneDrive to proceed with their digital investigation.

Mobile app forensics

Mobile app forensics resembles the process of extracting, analyzing, and interpreting data from mobile applications for forensic investigations. The importance of this procedure relates to applications of a mobile storing critical user data, including messages, call logs, transactions, and location history. However, the concerned challenges in this regard include data encryption, app sandboxing, cloud synchronization, and frequent app updates affecting forensic techniques. The relevant types of mobile applications considered for analysis by the digital forensic investigators are stated as follows:

- **Messaging and communication apps:** The relevant communication and messaging applications installed in smartphone devices include WhatsApp, Telegram, Signal, and iMessage.

- **Social media and networking apps:** The increasing popularity of social media encourages smartphone users to install various applications such as Facebook, Instagram, Twitter, and TikTok.

- **Financial and banking apps:** The increasing dependency on digital currency led to extensive usage of various applications such as PayPal, Venmo, Google Pay, and Apple Pay.

- **Email and cloud storage apps:** The extensive requirement of continuous communication requires the use of effective applications such as Gmail, Outlook, Google Drive, and iCloud.

- **Navigation and ride-sharing apps:** The requirement of seamless travel encourages users to use specific applications such as Google Maps, Uber, and Lyft.

Identifying the app data storage locations is crucial for digital forensic investigators and refers to the following areas:

- **Local device storage:** The local device storage includes SQLite databases, specifically the **.db** files for chat history and contacts. This is apart from Log files and cache that are stored at **/data/data/** for Android and **/private/var/mobile/Containers/Data/Application/** for iOS. The types of local device storage further extend to shared preferences and configuration files, such as XML and Plist.

- **Cloud storage and synchronization:** The cloud storage and synchronization result in the storage of data in iCloud, Google Drive, or app-specific servers. However, accessing data across such areas requires legal authorization in the form of subpoenas and warrants.) for access.

- **Encrypted and deleted data:** Some smartphones use end-to-end encryption to ensure the data privacy of their users. These apps include Signal and Telegram Secret Chats. The recovery of deleted app data is possible for digital forensic investigators using forensic tools.

The digital forensic investigators deploy the following techniques for mobile app data extraction:

- **Logical extraction:** The process of logical extraction implies extracting accessible user data via OS APIs (less intrusive).

- **File system acquisition:** The procedure of file system acquisition relates to retrieving deeper app data, including logs and databases.

- **Physical acquisition:** The process of physical acquisition resembles bit-by-bit cloning of data fragments for full data recovery, including deleted files.

- **Cloud-based analysis:** The process of cloud-based analysis investigates data synced with cloud services from digital devices.

- **App-specific forensics:** The app-specific forensics resembles applying reverse engineering apps to extract hidden artifacts.

Apart from the relevant techniques, the digital forensic investigators select suitable tools for mobile app investigations:

- **Commercial tools:** The relevant commercial tools for Mobile App Forensics include Cellebrite UFED, Oxygen Forensics, and Magnet AXIOM.

- **Open-source tools:** The wide requirement of applying mobile app forensics encourage application of open-source tools such as Autopsy, Andriller, and MVT.

Call log and message analysis

Communication data forensics resembles the process of extracting, analyzing, and interpreting call logs and message data from mobile devices. The overall importance of this practice relates to helping in criminal investigations, corporate security cases, and legal disputes. The associated challenges in this regard include data encryption, deleted data recovery, cloud synchronization, and app-specific security features. The relevant types of communication data on mobile devices include the following:

- **Call logs:** This includes the incoming, outgoing, and missed calls apart from call duration, timestamps, and associated contact details. This classification further includes voicemail and call recordings (if available).

- **SMS and MMS messages:** The SMS and MMS Messages are stored in SQLite databases such as `mmssms.db` on Android and `sms.db` on iOS. Along with this, metadata such as sender, recipient, timestamps, and message status, such as sent, received, and deleted, acts as a reliable source of evidence for the digital forensic investigators.

- **Instant messaging apps:** The instant messaging apps that are widely used nowadays include WhatsApp, Telegram, Signal, Facebook Messenger, iMessage, etc. The associated challenge in this regard includes end-to-end encryption that complicates extraction of data from apps such as Signal and WhatsApp-encrypted backups. The digital forensic investigators tend to consider chat attachments, deleted messages, and timestamps.

Digital forensic investigators tend to apply the following techniques for the extraction of call logs and messages:

- **Logical extraction:** The process of logical extraction relates to accessing call logs and messages from backups or device APIs.

- **Physical acquisition:** The tactics of physical acquisition resemble bit-by-bit imaging to recover deleted call logs and messages.

- **Cloud-based extraction:** The cloud-based extraction indicates retrieving data from iCloud, Google Drive or app servers (requires legal authorization).

- **Database analysis:** The process of database analysis includes extracting communication data from SQLite databases and log files.

- **Decryption and password recovery:** The recovery of encrypted messages and app-specific data is progressed by the digital forensic investigators using forensic tools.

The dedicated application of techniques requires the Digital Forensic Investigators to consider the following tools:

- **Commercial tools:** The relevant commercial tools include Cellebrite UFED, Magnet AXIOM, and Oxygen Forensics.

- **Open-source tools:** The open-source tools include Andriller, MVT, and SQLite Browser. *(Figure 10.3)*

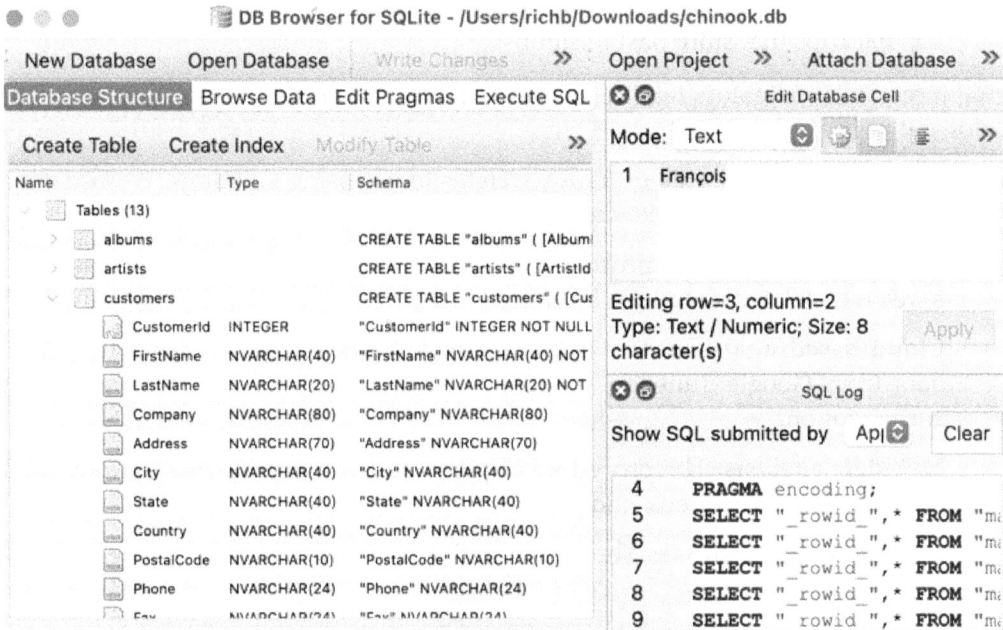

Figure 10.3: Interface of DB Browser for SQLite

Location data and GPS analysis

The concept of location data forensics relates to the process of extracting and analyzing location data from mobile devices to track movements and activities. The process of location data forensics helps in criminal investigations, missing person cases, fraud detection, and verifying alibis. Contrarily, the associated challenges include data encryption, GPS accuracy, cloud synchronization, and Privacy laws. The relevant sources of location data on mobile devices are stated as follows:

- **GPS data:** The GPS data includes data captured via built-in GPS receivers in smartphones and tablets. The data implies the store's latitude, longitude, altitude, and timestamps.

- **Wi-Fi and cell tower data:** The Wi-Fi and cell tower data include mobile devices log, nearby Wi-Fi networks, and cell towers for location approximation. Such data is used when GPS signals are weak, such as when indoors.

- **App-based location logs:** The app-based location logs include Google Maps Timeline, Apple Location Services, and app-specific location history such as Uber, Snapchat, and Facebook. The benefit of such data relates to its tendency to store user movements, visited locations, and timestamps.

- **EXIF metadata in media files:** This includes photos and videos that may contain embedded GPS coordinates in metadata.

- **Cloud and backup data:** Such data relates to iCloud, Google Location History, and app backups that store past locations.

Digital forensic investigators tend to apply the following techniques for the extraction of location data:

- **Logical extraction:** This procedure relates to accessing GPS logs, Wi-Fi data, and location history using relevant forensic tools.

- **Physical extraction:** The process of physical extraction relates to bit-by-bit imaging to recover deleted or hidden location data.

- **Cloud-based analysis:** The cloud-based analysis relates to retrieving location data from Google Timeline, iCloud, or third-party apps, as they require legal authorization.

- **Metadata analysis:** The procedure of metadata analysis relates to extracting GPS data from photos, videos, and similar multimedia files.

- **Triangulation methods:** The triangulation method relates to using cell tower records to approximate device movements.

The digital forensic investigators are required to apply the following tools for proceeding with such techniques:

- **Commercial tools:** The appropriate commercial tools include Cellebrite UFED, Magnet AXIOM, and Oxygen Forensics. *(Figure 10.4)*

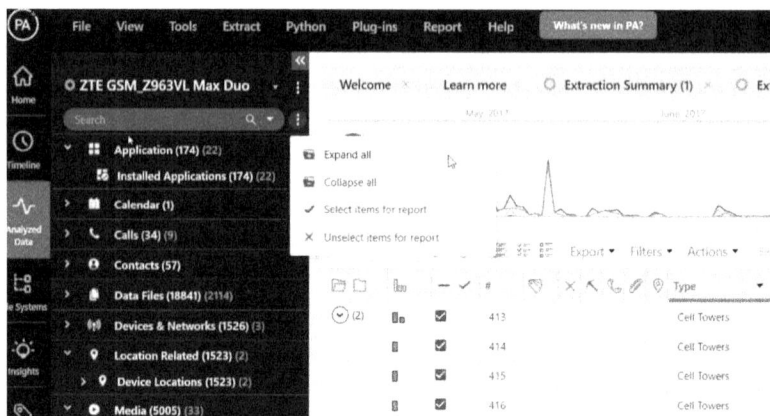

Figure 10.4: Interface of Cellebrite UFED

- **Open-source tools:** The relevant open-source tools include Google Takeout Analyzer, ExifTool, and GPSBabel.

Social media and messaging app forensics

The concept of social media and messaging app forensics is defined as the process of extracting, analyzing, and preserving digital evidence from social media and messaging applications. The importance of this practice relates to the observation that social networking platforms store vast amounts of user-generated data, including chats, images, videos, posts, and location history. The related challenges include end-to-end encryption, cloud storage, frequent app updates, and data privacy regulations. Social media and messaging app forensics considers the following platforms for forensic investigation:

- **Social media apps:** The specific social media apps include Facebook, Instagram, Twitter, TikTok, LinkedIn, and Snapchat.

- **Messaging apps:** The widely popular messaging apps include WhatsApp, Telegram, Signal, iMessage, Facebook Messenger, and WeChat.

- **Hybrid apps:** The hybrid apps imply the platforms having both social networking and messaging features such as Discord and Reddit.

The following data types are closely associated with social media and messaging apps:

- **User profile data:** The concept of user profile data includes Username, email, phone number, and account creation details.

- **Chat and messaging history:** The chat and messaging history includes text messages, timestamps, message deletions, and media attachments.

- **Multimedia files:** The wide range of multimedia files includes Photos, videos, voice messages, and their metadata.

- **Location data:** The relevant location data includes check-ins, shared locations, and tagged locations in posts/photos.

- **Posts and comments:** The posts and comments include relevant Timeline posts, stories, likes, shares, and interactions.

- **Contacts and connections:** The contacts and connections include Friend lists, followers, and group memberships.

The digital forensic investigators proceed with the following techniques for social media and messaging app forensics:

- **Logical extraction:** This procedure is for retrieving accessible data via app APIs and device backups.

- **Cloud-based acquisition:** This procedure of acquisition relates to extracting data from iCloud, Google Drive, or app servers that require legal authorization.

- **Physical acquisition:** This process of acquisition indicates bit-by-bit imaging to recover deleted messages and media.

- **Network traffic analysis:** The process of network traffic analysis relates to capturing real-time data transmission from social media apps.

- **App-specific forensic analysis:** The deployment of app-specific forensic analysis relates to relevant reverse engineering apps for hidden artifacts.

The widely used forensic tools for social media and messaging app investigations are stated as follows:

- **Commercial tools:** The suitable commercial tools include Cellebrite UFED, Magnet AXIOM, and Oxygen Forensics. *(Figure 10.5)*

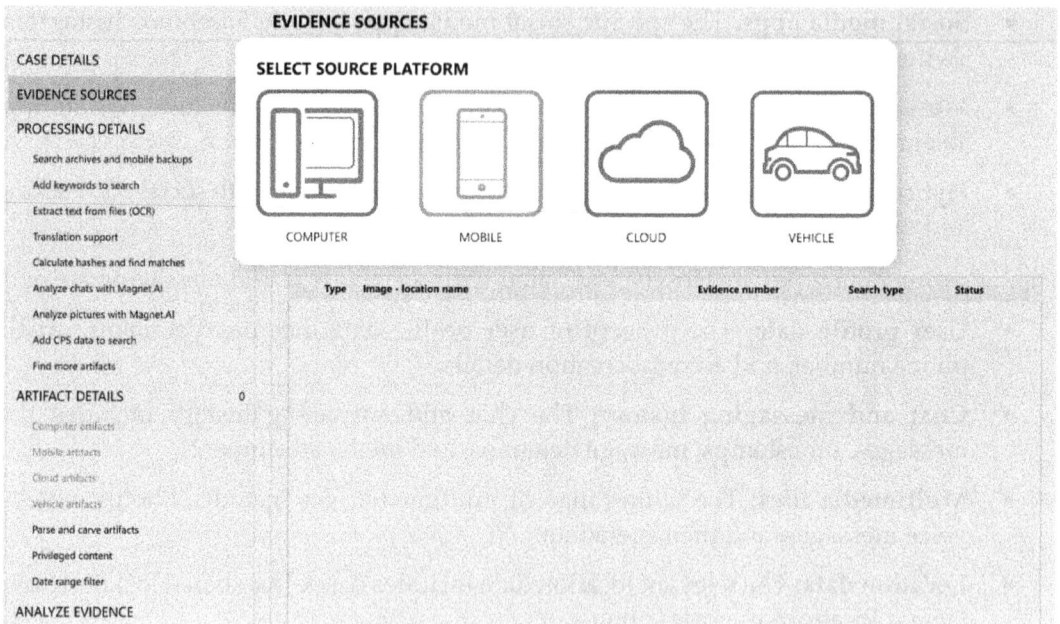

Figure 10.5: Interface of Magnet AXIOM

- **Open-source tools:** The open-source tools used by the digital forensic investigators include **Social Media Intelligence** (**SOCMINT**) tools such as the OSINT framework, Hunchly, and MVT.

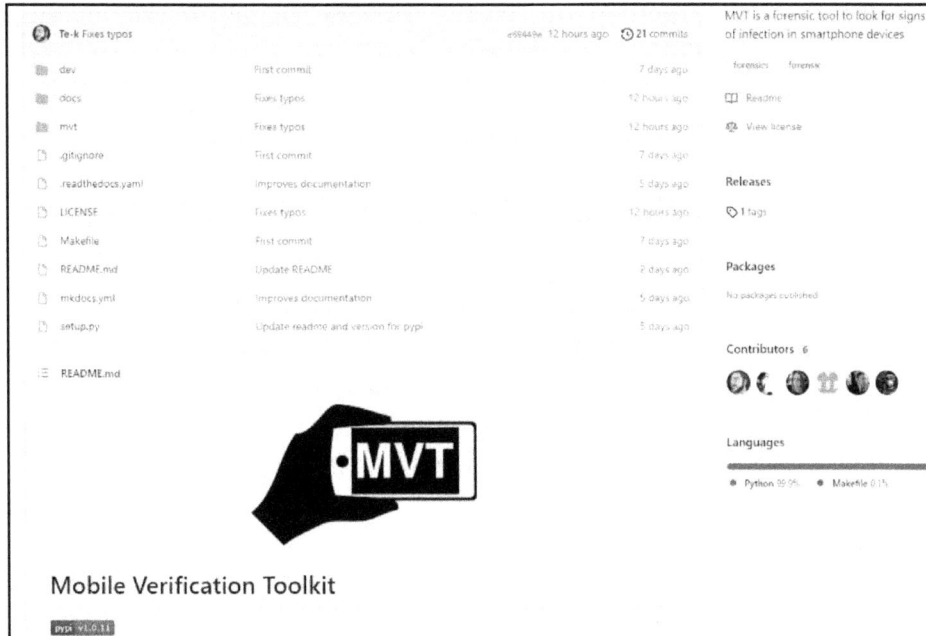

Figure 10.6: Interface of MVT

Mobile device encryption and password cracking

Mobile device security measures relate to mobile devices using encryption and password protection to secure user data. Its importance in forensics relates to investigators needing to bypass or decrypt security measures to access evidence. The related challenges during such forensic investigations include strong encryption algorithms, biometric authentication, and legal restrictions. The relevant types of mobile device encryption include the following:

- **Full-disk encryption (FDE):** This encryption method encrypts the entire storage (Android pre-10, older iOS versions) of a digital device.

- **File-based encryption (FBE):** This encryption technique proceeds with encrypting files individually and thereby allows different security levels for Android 10+ and iOS.

- **End-to-end encryption (E2EE):** This encryption procedure is used in messaging apps like WhatsApp, Signal, and Telegram.

- **Hardware-based encryption:** This encryption process relates to Secure Enclave (iOS) and TrustZone (Android) to protect sensitive data.

The digital forensic investigators use the following encryption and authentication bypassing methods:

- **Jailbreaking and rooting:** This process aids the digital forensic investigator in elevating privileges to access restricted data.

- **Chip-off forensics:** The digital forensic investigators proceed with physically extracting data by removing the memory chip.

- **Joint Test Action Group (JTAG) analysis:** This process encourages accessing data via debugging ports.

- **Cloud data acquisition:** This process relates to extracting encrypted backups from iCloud or Google Drive that require legal access.

This is apart from using the following forensic tools for password cracking and encryption bypassing:

- **Commercial tools:** The suitable tools for such an investigation include Cellebrite UFED, GrayKey, and Passware Kit Mobile.

- **Open-source tools:** The effective tools for similar investigations include Hashcat, John the Ripper, and MVT.

Recovering deleted data from mobile devices

The relevant techniques for deleted data recovery from mobile devices imply the following:

- **Logical recovery:** This process relates to extracting data from backups across iCloud, Google Drive, and local backups. This further includes recovering deleted files from SQLite databases such as chat logs and call history. The tool is used for examining app caches and temporary files.

- **Physical recovery:** This process implies bit-by-bit imaging of device storage using forensic tools. The relevant extraction of raw data from NAND memory relates to chip-off or JTAG techniques.

- **Cloud-based recovery:** The retrieval of synced data from cloud storage services including Google Photos and iCloud Drive. This process further relates to analysing metadata and timestamps of recovered files.

- **Forensic artifact analysis:** This analytical method indicates recovering deleted SMS, call logs, and chat messages from system logs. The relevant extraction of metadata from images, videos, and documents aids digital forensic investigation.

Mobile device forensics in BYOD environments

The relevant challenges for the BYOD environment include the following:

- **Legal and privacy concerns:** Employees tend to retain ownership rights over personal data. This relates to the prevalence of legal restrictions on accessing personal information without consent.

- **Data segmentation issues:** The tendency to mix personal and corporate data makes targeted extraction difficult. This encourages the use of separate work profiles or **Mobile Device Management (MDM)** solutions.

- **Limited access to devices:** The employers tend to lack the authority to seize or analyse personal devices. Furthermore, encryption and passcode protections further restrict access to devices for digital forensic investigators.

- **Cloud and third-party app storage:** The sensitive company data may be stored on third-party apps such as Google Drive, Dropbox, and WhatsApp. The cloud synchronization complicates local data recovery.

- **Remote wiping and anti-forensics measures:** The employees tend to use factory resets, encryption tools, or self-wiping apps to erase data.

The forensic techniques for aiding BYOD investigations relate to the following:

- **Selective data acquisition:** This relates to extracting only work-related data to protect employee privacy. The logical extraction methods as a part of selective data acquisition relates to avoiding full-device imaging.

- **Mobile Device Management (MDM) logs:** These log files are Access logs, app usage, and security alerts from MDM solutions. This verifies compliance with company policies.

- **Cloud-based data retrieval:** This relates to obtaining relevant data from enterprise cloud services with legal authorization. This examines syncing work emails, documents, and messaging platforms.

- **Network and endpoint analysis:** This analytical process investigates corporate network logs for device activity. This process relates to using endpoint detection tools to analyze security incidents.

Case studies

The following case studies imply the importance of mobile device forensics for modern situations:

- **San Bernardino Terrorist Attack (2015): Federal Bureau of Investigation (FBI) vs. Apple:**

  The FBI investigated a mass shooting involving an individual and his wife. The iPhone 5C was locked, and the FBI requested assistance from Apple to unlock it. The relevant challenges in this regard relate to iPhone encryption and security features that prevent brute-force unlocking. Apple refused to create a backdoor, citing privacy concerns. The FBI hired a third-party security firm (reportedly Cellebrite) to crack the phone. The resolution-related data was successfully extracted, though it reportedly provided minimal additional intelligence. The impact of this case on digital forensics sparked global debate on privacy vs. national security. This highlighted the need for legal frameworks on encrypted devices in investigations.

- **Enron Scandal (2001): Early mobile forensics in corporate fraud:**

  The Enron executives engaged in corporate fraud, hiding financial losses through illegal accounting. The concerned digital forensic investigators examined mobile devices, emails, and text messages to uncover fraudulent activities. The relevant challenges include early mobile devices that lacked encryption but had limited data storage. The other challenges include concerned data that had to be correlated with corporate emails and call logs. The investigators recovered incriminating SMS messages and call records linking executives to fraud. The case led to the creation of the **Sarbanes-Oxley Act** (**SOX**) to improve corporate accountability. The impact of this case indicated the importance of mobile device records in corporate investigations. The occurrence of this case led to stricter data retention policies in financial institutions.

Conclusion

This chapter proceeds with realizing the significance of mobile device forensics within enterprise investigations. The chapter indicated that both commercial solutions and open-source tools are crucial for digital forensic investigators to resolve the complexities of cyberattacks. The chapter indicated multiple techniques for evidence acquisition. The chapter stated the appropriate differences between Android and iOS. The aspect of investigating multiple applications relates to digital forensic investigators selecting suitable techniques and deploying them with suitable tools and frameworks. The associated areas of mobile forensics include location data and GPS Analysis that aid in tracking mobile device movements.

The upcoming chapter corresponds to deciphering virtualization and hypervisor forensics.

Join our book's Discord space

Join the book's Discord Workspace for Latest updates, Offers, Tech happenings around the world, New Release and Sessions with the Authors:

https://discord.bpbonline.com

CHAPTER 11

Deciphering Virtualization and Hypervisor Forensics

Introduction

The process of virtualization relates to enabling multiple operating systems to run on a single physical machine using a hypervisor. This implies its sheer importance in digital forensics investigations. This is because multiple operating systems run on a single physical machine using a hypervisor. The importance of deciphering virtualization and hypervisor forensics relates to virtualized environments, complicating forensic investigations due to layered data storage, shared resources, and live migration. The related common use cases include cloud computing, enterprise IT infrastructure, and cybersecurity sandboxes. The current chapter looks in detail at the importance of effectively deciphering virtualization and hypervisor forensics to aid digital forensic investigators in resolving cyberattacks seamlessly.

Structure

The topics covered are as follows:

- Introduction to virtualization and hypervisor technology
- Virtual machine forensics
- Hypervisor forensics
- Virtual disk forensics

- Snapshot analysis
- Network forensics in virtualized networks
- Hypervisor security considerations
- Best practices
- Case studies

Objectives

This chapter provides a basic understanding of virtualization and hypervisor technology. The chapter focuses on **virtual machine** (**VM**) forensics in terms of investigating digital evidence within virtual environments. The chapter relates to hypervisor forensics in terms of uncovering evidence from the virtualization layer. The chapter indicates that virtual disk forensics relates to extracting and analyzing data from virtual hard drives. The chapter introduces the concept of snapshot analysis in terms of leveraging VM snapshots for forensic investigations. The chapter includes adequate details about network forensics in virtualized networks in terms of investigating network traffic within virtualized environments. The chapter includes adequate details about hypervisor security considerations in terms of addressing vulnerabilities and exploits. The chapter lists several best Practices in virtualization and hypervisor forensic investigations that can benefit the digital forensic investigators seamlessly. The chapter includes an adequate number of case studies to establish the importance of deciphering virtualization and hypervisor forensics.

Introduction to virtualization and hypervisor technology

The concept of virtualization relates to a process of creating virtual instances of computing resources (e.g., OS, storage, network) on a single physical system. Its sheer importance in modern computing relates to enhancing resource efficiency, scalability, and security in enterprise IT environments. The common applications of this technology include cloud computing, server consolidation in data centers, and development and testing environments. The specific instances of cloud computing include **Amazon Web Services** (**AWS**) *(Figure 11.1)*, Azure, and Google Cloud.

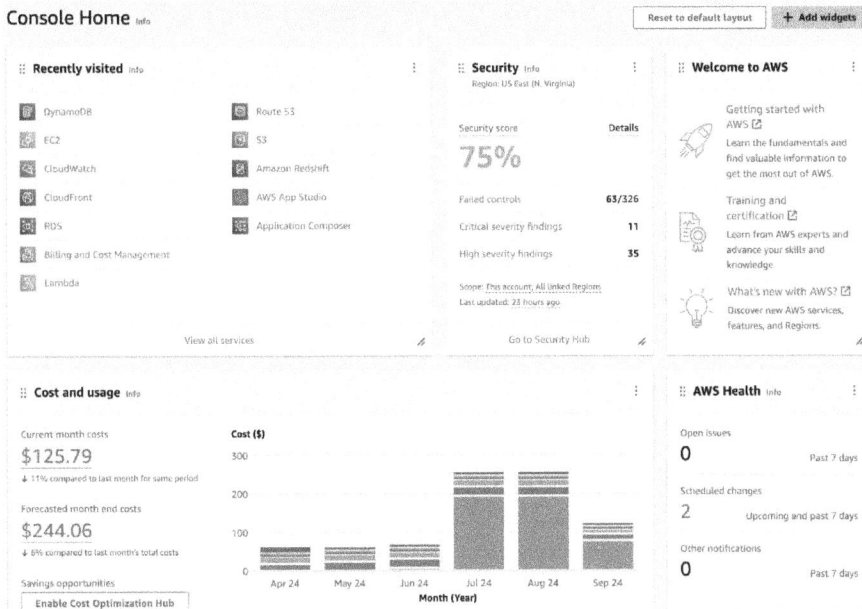

Figure 11.1: *Interface of AWS*

The detailed overview of hypervisor technology relates to it being a software solution that enables multiple VMs to run on a single physical host. The relevant types of hypervisors are listed as follows:

- **Type 1 (Bare-Metal):** The Type 1 Hypervisors run directly on hardware such as VMware ESXi, Microsoft Hyper-V, and Xen.

- **Type 2 (Hosted):** The Type 2 Hypervisors run within an operating system such as VirtualBox, VMware Workstation, and KVM.

The key functions of a hypervisor include the creation of a VM and the allocation of **Central Processing Unit** (**CPU**), memory, and storage. The key functions of a hypervisor further imply isolation between VMs for security. The hypervisor further ensures effective management of VM snapshots, cloning, and migration.

The components of a virtualized environment include the following:

- **Host machine:** The host machine is the physical hardware running the hypervisor.

- **Guest VMs:** The guest VMs are the virtualized operating systems running on top of the hypervisor. *(Figure 11.2)*

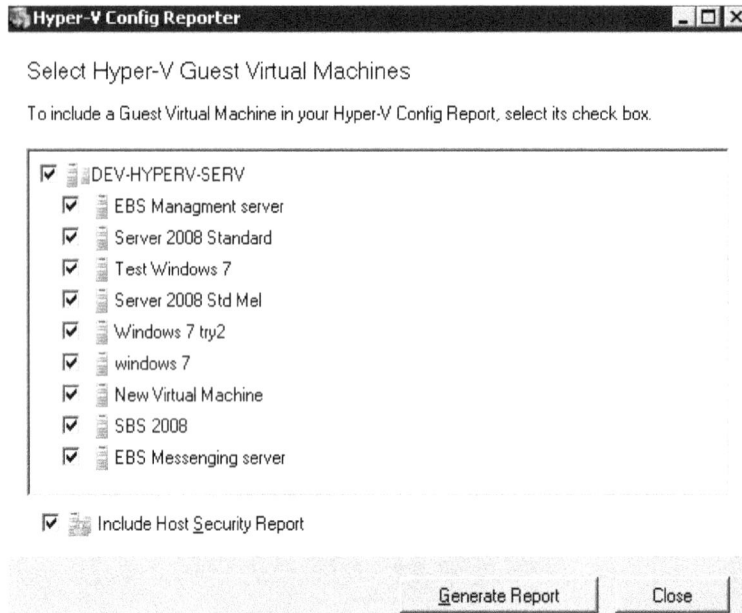

Figure 11.2: Interface of Hyper-V Guest VMs

- **Virtual disks and storage:** The virtual disks and storage indicate the VMs using **virtual hard disk** (**VHD**) files (VMDK, VDI, VHD) that simulate physical storage.

- **Virtual network adapters:** The virtual network adapters enable network communication between VMs and external networks. *(Figure 11.3)*

Figure 11.3: Interface of the hypervisor

Virtual machine forensics

The concept of VM forensics refers to the process of identifying, collecting, analyzing, and preserving digital evidence from virtualized environments. The increasing importance of VM forensics includes multiple enterprises and cloud services relying on the process of virtualization. Contextually, cybercriminals use VMs to evade detection and forensic investigations. *(Figure 11.4)*

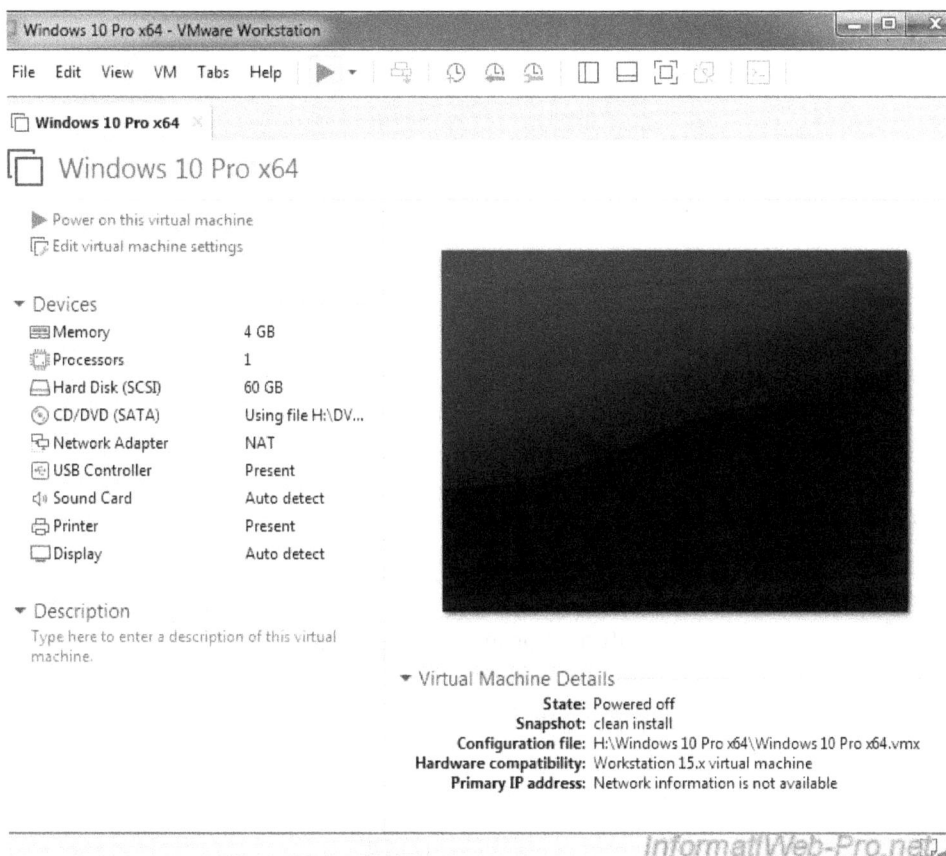

Figure 11.4: Interface of VM

The related VM artifacts are stated as follows:

- **Virtual disk files:** The virtual disk files contain all data stored in a VM (e.g., VMDK for VMware, VDI for VirtualBox, VHD for Hyper-V).

- **VM configuration files:** The VM configuration files store settings, hardware allocations, and snapshots.

- **Snapshot and memory dumps:** The snapshot and memory dumps capture VM states and RAM contents for forensic analysis. *(Figure 11.5)*

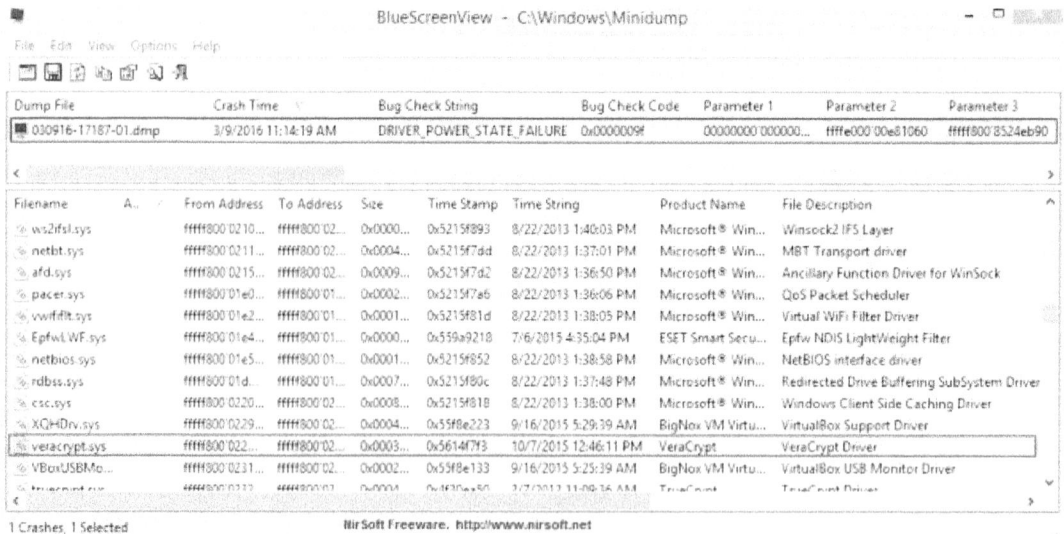

Figure 11.5: Memory dumps

- **Hypervisor logs:** The hypervisor logs aid in tracking VM activity, boot times, and interactions with the host system.

The techniques deployed for investigating VMs include:

- **Live forensics:** This forensic procedure aids in capturing volatile memory using tools like Volatility or LiME. This is apart from aiding the extraction of running processes and network activity from VMs.

- **Offline analysis:** This analytical procedure aids in acquiring virtual disk images for forensic examination using tools such as FTK Imager and Autopsy. This procedure further aids in mounting and analyzing VM snapshots for deleted files and system logs.

- **Network traffic analysis:** This analytical procedure aids in monitoring inter-VM communications for malicious activities. The process tends to use packet capture tools (Wireshark, Zeek) to detect covert channels.

The following tools are selected by the digital forensic investigators to proceed with the required investigation:

- **Commercial tools:** The range of commercial tools includes EnCase, Magnet AXIOM, and X-Ways Forensics.

- **Open-source tools:** The open-source tools include Volatility, Autopsy, FTK Imager, and VMDK/VDI mount tools. *(Figure 11.6)*

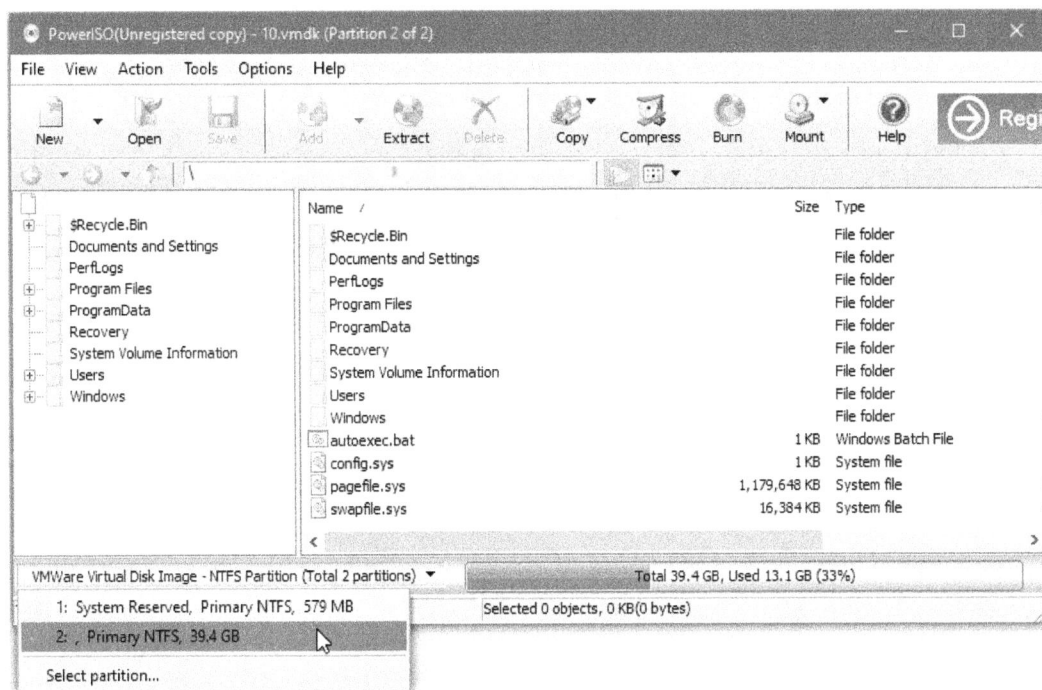

Figure 11.6: *Interface of VMDK*

Hypervisor forensics

The concept of hypervisor forensics relates to the process of analyzing hypervisors to identify, collect, and preserve digital evidence in virtualized environments. The importance of such forensic investigation relates to cybercriminals tending to exploit hypervisors to create hidden VMs. Contextually, forensic analysis of hypervisors helps to uncover unauthorized VM activities, system breaches, and security violations. The relevant hypervisor logs and artifacts include the following:

- **VM creation logs:** The VM creation logs track the deployment of virtual instances.

- **System snapshots and memory dumps:** The system snapshots and memory dumps capture system states for forensic analysis.

- **Virtual disk files (VMDK, VHD, VDI):** The specific virtual disk files, such as VMDK, VHD, and VDI, store VM data that may contain forensic evidence.

The relevant techniques for hypervisor forensic analysis include the following:

- **Live forensics:** The process of live forensics relates to capturing hypervisor logs to track system events and VM activity. This process further aids in analyzing memory dumps from hypervisors for running processes and malicious code.

- **Offline analysis:** This analytical procedure aids in extracting and mounting virtual disk files to examine stored data. This process relates to investigating hypervisor configuration files for evidence of unauthorized VMs.

- **Network and traffic analysis:** The network and traffic analysis aids in monitoring VM network communications for anomalies or security threats. This procedure further proceeds with using specific packet analysis tools such as Wireshark and Zeek to detect covert channels.

The associated forensic tools for hypervisor analysis are stated as follows:

- **Commercial tools:** The commercial tools appropriate for hypervisor forensics include Magnet AXIOM, EnCase, and X-Ways Forensics. *(Figure 11.7)*

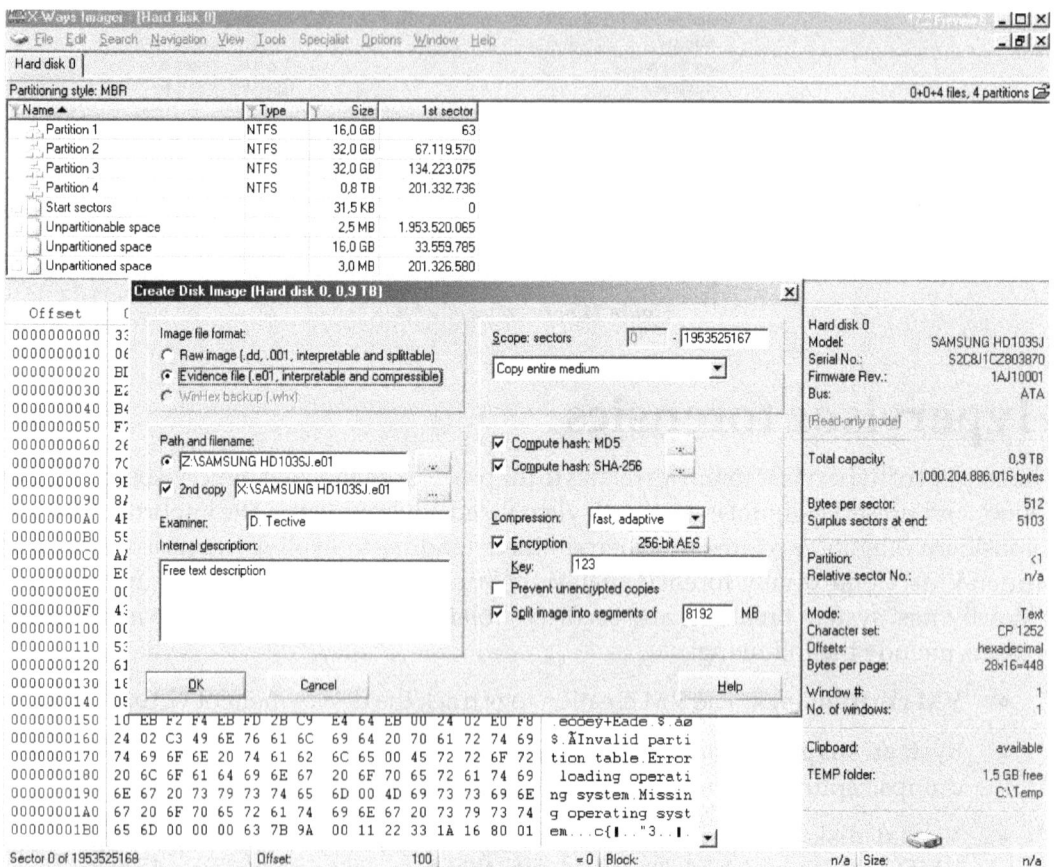

Figure 11.7: Interface of X-Ways imager

- **Open-source tools:** The open-source tools for aiding digital forensic volatility are FTK Imager and Autopsy.

Virtual disk forensics

The perspective of virtual disk forensics implies the process of identifying, extracting, and analyzing data stored within VHD files used by VMs. The sheer importance of virtual disk forensics in digital investigations includes virtual disks storing OS files, applications, logs, and user data, thus making them critical sources of forensic evidence. Thus, cybercriminals tend to use virtual disks to hide illicit activities or avoid detection. The different virtual disk formats include the following:

- **VMware Virtual Disk (VMDK):** The VMDK is used by VMware Workstation, ESXi, and Fusion.

- **Virtual Hard Disk (VHD/VHDX):** The VHD/VHDX is used by Microsoft Hyper-V.

- **Virtual Disk Image (VDI):** The VDI is used by Oracle VirtualBox.

- **QEMU Copy-On-Write (QCOW/QCOW2):** The QCOW/QCOW2 is used in KVM and QEMU environments.

The structure of a virtual disk resembles the underlying provisions of either dynamic allocation or fixed size. The aspect of dynamic allocation resembles effective expansion as per requirement. The structure of the virtual disk further conforms to storing system partitions, file systems, and deleted data remnants.

The digital forensic investigators apply the following forensic techniques for virtual disk analysis:

- **Mounting and extracting virtual disks:** This relates to using forensic tools to mount virtual disks as read-only images, apart from recovering deleted files and analyzing metadata.

- **File system analysis:** This resembles examining NTFS, FAT, ext4, and other file systems within virtual disks. This process further aids in searching for artifacts such as logs, registry files, and browser history.

- **Memory and snapshot analysis:** This analytical procedure proceeds with extracting RAM snapshots to analyze running processes. This aids in investigating VM snapshots for historical evidence.

The relevant tools extensively used by digital forensic investigators for Virtual Disk Forensics resemble the presence of both commercial and open-source tools. These tools are stated as follows: *(Table 11.1)*

Commercial tools	**Open-source tools**
• EnCase • Magnet AXIOM • X-Ways Forensics	• FTK Imager *(Figure 11.8)* • Autopsy • Volatility • Sleuth Kit

Table 11.1: Commercial and open-source tools for virtual disk forensics

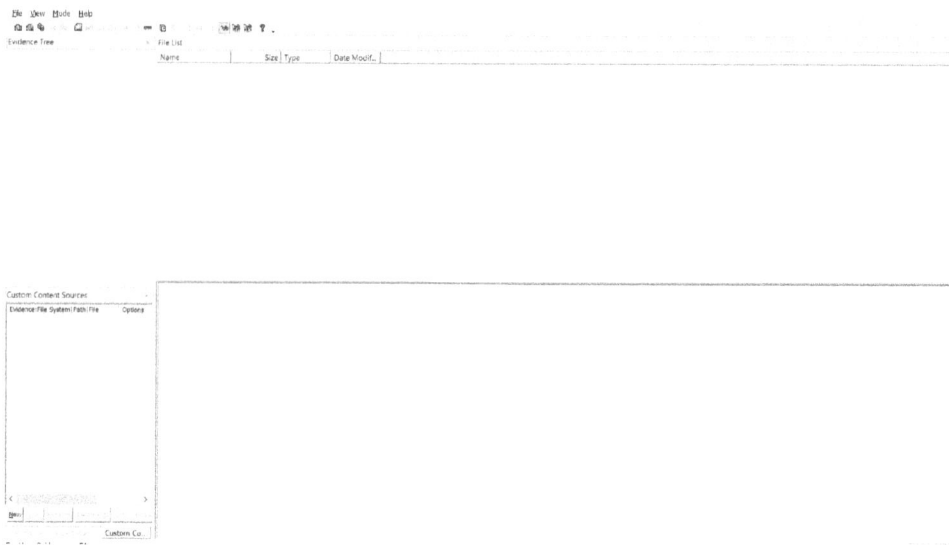

Figure 11.8: Interface of FTK Imager

The legal and compliance consideration of virtual disk forensics include assurance of forensic integrity when handling virtual disk evidence. This is apart from adhering to data privacy regulations such as General Data GDPR and HIPAA.

Snapshot analysis

The concept of VM snapshots relates to point-in-time disk copies of a VM, memory, and settings. The forensic significance of VM snapshots includes preserving evidence of system states at different times. This process aids in rollback analysis to track changes and deleted data. The snapshot analysis is useful in cyberattack investigations, malware infections, and insider threats. The relevant types of VM snapshots are stated here:

- **Full snapshots:** The concept of full snapshots implies capturing the entire VM, including disk and memory states.

- **Delta snapshots:** The delta snapshots indicate storing only changes since the last snapshot and thereby reducing storage size.

- **Memory snapshots:** The memory snapshots imply saving the RAM of the system and thereby allowing forensic recovery of active processes.

The snapshot artifacts and evidence sources are listed as follows:

- **Virtual disk files:** The virtual disk files contain stored files, applications, and potentially deleted data.

- **Memory dumps:** The memory dumps capture running processes, network activity, and encryption keys.

- **Configuration files:** The configuration files tend to store metadata, VM Settings, and Timestamps useful for forensic timelines.

The digital forensic investigators tend to apply the following multiple techniques for analyzing VM snapshots:

- **Mounting and extracting snapshots:** This process relates to using forensic tools to access and analyze virtual disk images. This process is suitable for recovering deleted files and logs from historical snapshots.

- **Memory analysis:** This procedure is ideal for identifying active processes, malware, and encryption keys. This procedure relates to using tools such as Volatility and Rekall for deep memory forensics.

- **Timeline reconstruction:** The process of timeline reconstruction relates to comparing multiple snapshots to identify unauthorized system changes. This process is suitable for detecting persistence mechanisms used by attackers.

The digital forensic investigators tend to use both commercial and open-source tools for snapshot analysis. These tools are accordingly segregated here:

- **Commercial tools:** The appropriate commercial tools for snapshot analysis include Magnet AXIOM, EnCase, X-Ways Forensics, and VMware Workstation. (*Figure 11.9*)

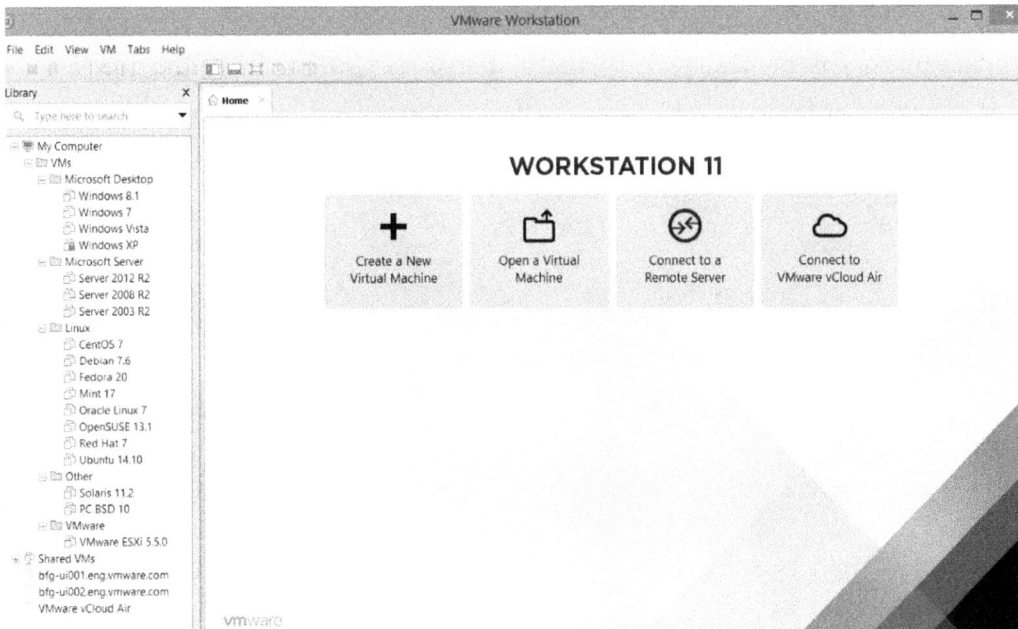

Figure 11.9: Interface of VMware Workstation

- **Open-source tools:** The appropriate open-source tools are Volatility, FTK Imager, The Sleuth Kit, and Autopsy.

Network forensics in virtualized networks

The concept of virtualized network forensics relates to the process of capturing, analyzing, and interpreting network traffic within virtualized environments. The importance of virtualized network forensics in digital investigations includes virtualized networks being widely used in cloud computing, enterprise data centers, and cybersecurity research. The significance further relates to attackers exploiting virtualized networks to conceal malicious activities. The associated challenges of virtualized network forensics include limited visibility into internal VM-to-VM traffic apart from dynamic network configurations in cloud environments, and encrypted communications complicate data analysis. The underlying components of Virtualized Network Infrastructure include the following:

- **Virtual Switches (vSwitches):** The vSwitches imply the software-based switches that control traffic between VMs.

- **Software-Defined Networking (SDN):** The SDN decouples network control from hardware, making forensic investigation more complex.

- **Network Function Virtualization (NFV):** The NFV replaces physical network devices (firewalls, IDS, routers) with virtualized components.

- **Overlay networks and tunneling:** The overlay networks and tunnelling imply the use of VXLAN, GRE, and SDN to manage traffic flow between virtual instances.

The relevant sources of evidence in virtualized networks include the following:

- **Packet Captures (PCAP):** The PCAP relates to capturing real-time network traffic for analysis. *(Figure 11.10)*

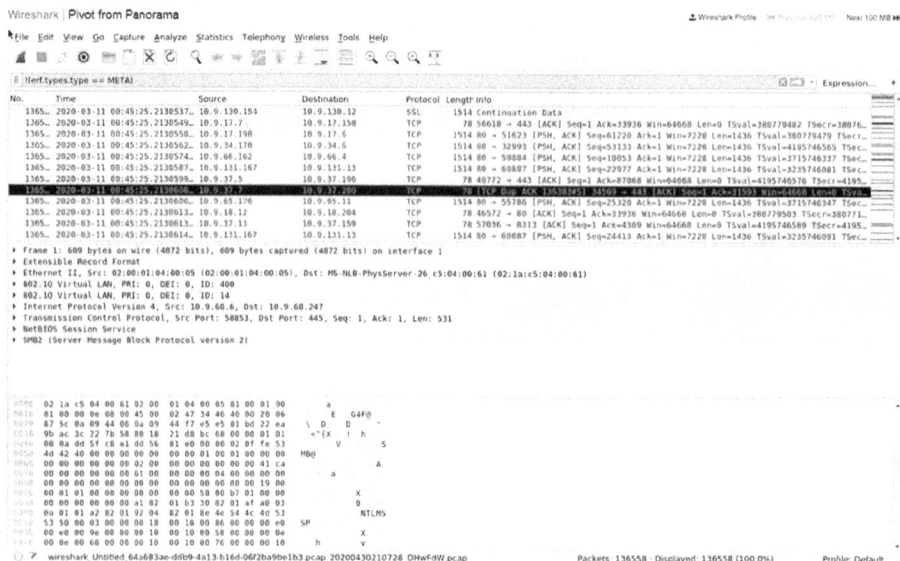

Figure 11.10: Interface of PCAP Files

- **VM Logs and network flow records:** The VM logs and network flow records indicate monitoring VM communication and connection patterns.

- **Hypervisor-level monitoring:** Hypervisor-level monitoring relates to analyzing traffic at the virtualization layer, such as VMware NSX and Open vSwitch logs.

- **Firewall and Intrusion Detection System /Intrusion Prevention System (IDS/ IPS) Logs:** The Firewall and IDS/IPS Logs refer to extracting security-related information from virtualized security devices.

The relevant techniques for investigating virtual network traffic include the following:

- **Traffic capture and packet analysis:** The traffic capture and packet analysis relate to using tools such as Wireshark and Zeek to inspect packets within virtualized environments. This analytical process proceeds with identifying suspicious network activity, **Command-and-Control (C2)** Communications, and data exfiltration.

- **Network flow analysis:** The process of network flow analysis relates to leveraging NetFlow and IPFIX to analyze traffic behavior and detect anomalies.

- **Correlation with host-based forensics:** This forensic process relates to mapping network activity to specific VMs and processes.

- **Intrusion detection in virtual networks:** This process relates to using virtual IDS/ IPS solutions such as Suricata and Snort to detect security breaches.

The relevant tools for virtualized network forensics include both commercial tools and open-source tools that are segregated below:

- **Commercial tools:** The commercial tools include Magnet AXIOM, EnCase, X-Ways Forensics, and VMware vRealize Log Insight.

- **Open-source tools:** The open-source tools include Wireshark, Zeek, Suricata, tcpdump, and Open vSwitch.

Hypervisor security considerations

The concept of hypervisor security relates to ensuring the security of the hypervisor, which manages VMs and acts as the virtualization layer between hardware and guest operating systems. The importance of hypervisor security for digital forensics indicates that a compromised hypervisor can lead to full system compromise, affecting all hosted VMs. Specifically, attackers exploit hypervisor vulnerabilities to gain unauthorized access, deploy malware, or escape VMs. The common hypervisor vulnerabilities are stated as follows:

- **VM escape attacks:** The VM escape attacks relate to exploiting flaws that allow an attacker to break out of a VM and access the host system.

- **Privilege escalation:** The process of privilege escalation relates to gaining higher access rights within the hypervisor to manipulate or control VMs.

- **Side-channel attacks:** The side-channel attacks relate to extracting sensitive information by analyzing shared hardware resources such as CPU cache and memory.

- **Hyperjacking:** The process of Hyperjacking relates to installing a rogue hypervisor to take full control of virtualized environments.

- **Misconfigurations and weak access controls:** The misconfigurations and weak access controls imply poorly configured hypervisors that can expose sensitive data and allow unauthorized access.

The exploits targeting hypervisors are stated as follows:

- **Zero-day vulnerabilities:** The zero-day vulnerabilities include exploiting unknown security flaws before patches are available.

- **Attack on virtual network infrastructure:** The attack on virtual network infrastructure relates to compromising virtual switches and network interfaces to intercept VM communications.

- **Malicious VM injection:** Malicious VM injection relates to deploying rogue VMs within a virtualized environment to launch attacks.

The relevant security measures to protect hypervisors are stated as follows:

- **Regular patching and updates:** The practice of regular patching and updates relates to applying security patches to prevent the exploitation of known vulnerabilities.

- **Strong access controls and authentication:** The strong access controls and authentication resemble implementing **Multi-Factor Authentication** (**MFA**) and **Role-based Access Control** (**RBAC**).

- **Isolation and sandboxing:** The effective isolation and sandboxing relates to ensuring VMs are properly isolated to prevent their unauthorized data access.

- **Monitoring and logging:** The process of monitoring and logging relates to capturing hypervisor logs to detect suspicious activity.

- **Hardware-assisted security:** Hardware-assisted security relates to using technologies like Intel VT-x and AMD-V to enhance virtualization security. *(Figure 11.11)*

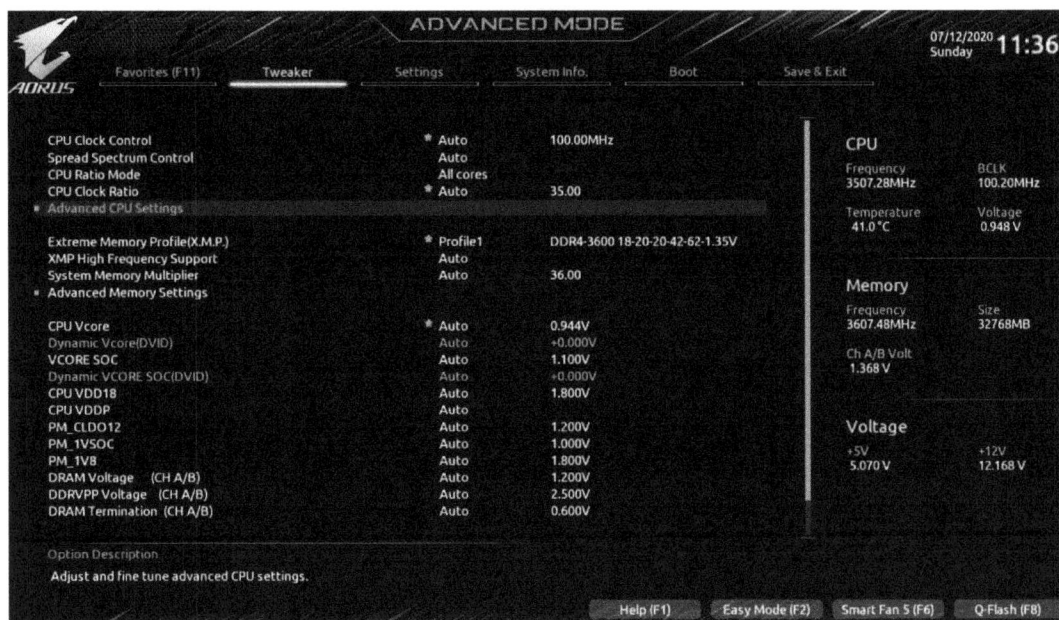

Figure 11.11: Enabling AMD-V

The digital forensic investigators tend to deploy the following relevant forensic techniques for proceeding with hypervisor security investigations:

- **Log analysis:** The process of log analysis relates to examining hypervisor and VM logs to detect unauthorized activities.

- **Memory forensics:** The procedure of memory forensics involves analyzing hypervisor memory dumps for signs of exploitation.

- **Network traffic analysis:** The process of network traffic analysis relates to identifying unusual VM-to-VM or VM-to-host communications.

- **Snapshot and disk analysis:** Investigating hypervisor snapshots for examining saved VM states to analyze historical changes and detect past compromises. The process relates to investigating virtual disk files such as VMDK, VHD, and QCOW2 to recover deleted files, malware, or hidden data. *(Figure 11.12)*

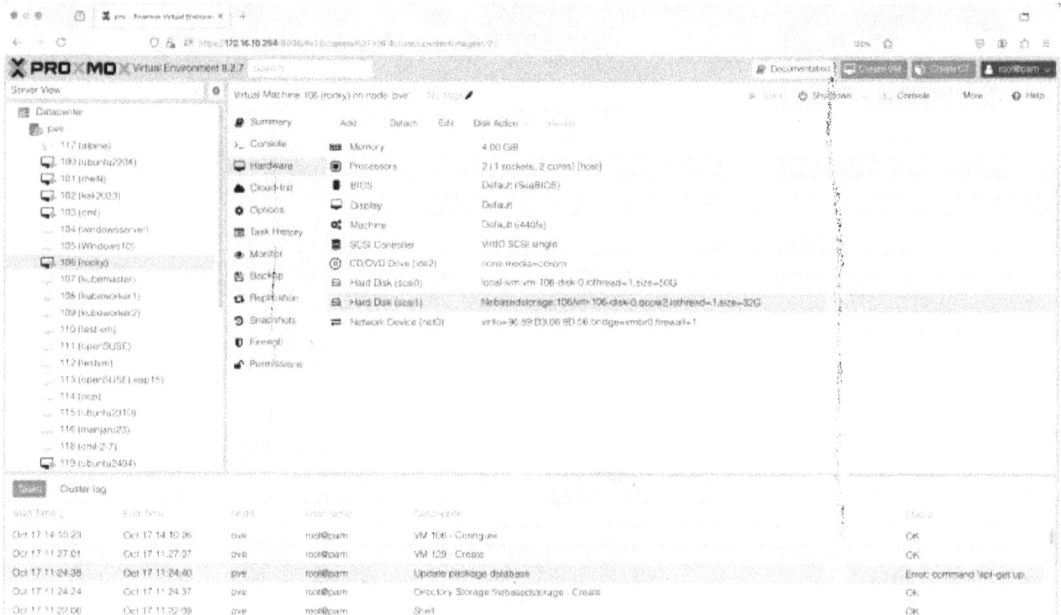

Figure 11.12: Interface of QCOW2

The result of investigating snapshot and disk analysis relates to identifying unauthorized VM rollback to conceal malicious actions. This relates to examining differences between snapshots for forensic reconstruction.

The associated tools for hypervisor security analysis include the following:

- **Commercial solutions:** The commercial solutions for hypervisor security analysis include VMware vShield, Microsoft Defender for Endpoint, and Citrix Hypervisor Security. *(Figure 11.13)*

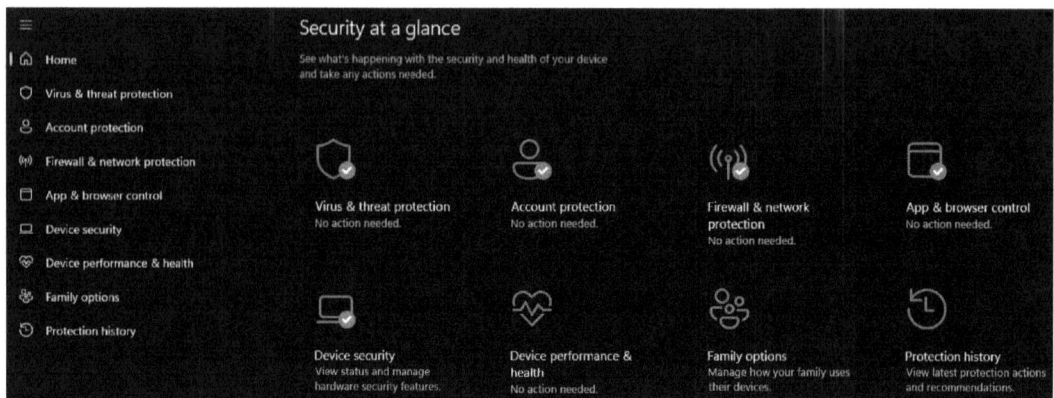

Figure 11.13: Interface of Microsoft Defender

- **Open-source tools:** The open-source tools for hypervisor security analysis include XenForensics, Volatility, Snort, and Suricata.

Best practices

The best practices are as follows:

- **Dedicated evidence collection and preservation:** The process of acquiring hypervisor logs relates to collecting logs from VMware ESXi, Microsoft Hyper-V, Xen, or KVM for traces of unauthorized access. The preservation of VM snapshots relates to securely copying VM snapshots to retain system states for analysis. The performing live memory capture relates to using forensic tools to dump hypervisor and VM memory before shutting down systems. The securing virtual disk images relates to creating forensic copies of virtual disk files such as VMDK, VHD, and QCOW2 for data recovery. The associated tools that can be used for this best practice include FTK Imager, The Sleuth Kit, Volatility, and Autopsy. *(Figure 11.14)*

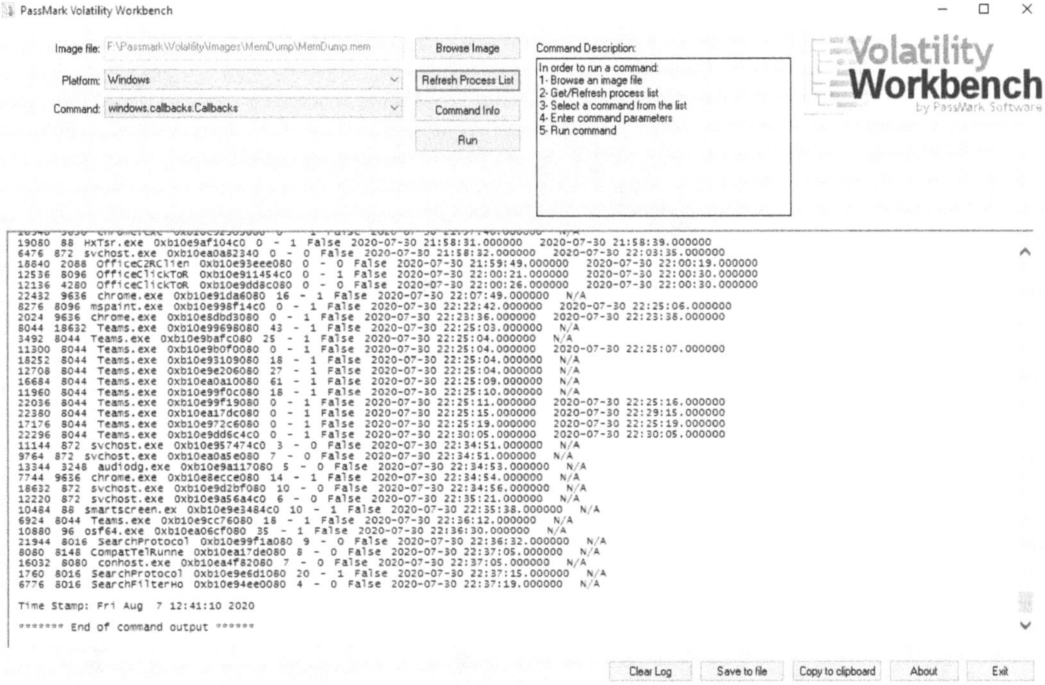

Figure 11.14: Interface of Volatility Workbench

- **Maintaining Chain of Custody (CoC) and adhering to legal compliance:** The perspective of maintaining CoC and adhering to legal compliance implies maintaining logs of data acquisition, access permissions, and forensic procedures. The legal compliance relates to following regulatory requirements to ensure compliance with GDPR, HIPAA, NIST 800-53, and ISO 27001 when handling sensitive data. The effective working with legal teams implies verifying the admissibility of virtualized forensic evidence in court proceedings.

- **Hardening hypervisor security for future prevention:** Hardening hypervisor security for future prevention leads to enforcing least privilege access, apart from enabling secure logging and monitoring inter-VM communication. The enforcement of least privilege access implies restricting administrative permissions to hypervisor management interfaces. The enabling of secure logging relates to configuring hypervisor logs for detailed auditing of system events. The monitoring of inter-VM communication relates to using virtual network monitoring tools to detect unauthorized traffic between VMs. This is in addition to regular patching and updating in terms of applying vendor security patches to mitigate hypervisor vulnerabilities. The relevant tools used in this regard include VMware vRealize Log Insight, OSSEC, Zeek, and Suricata. *(Figure 11.15)*

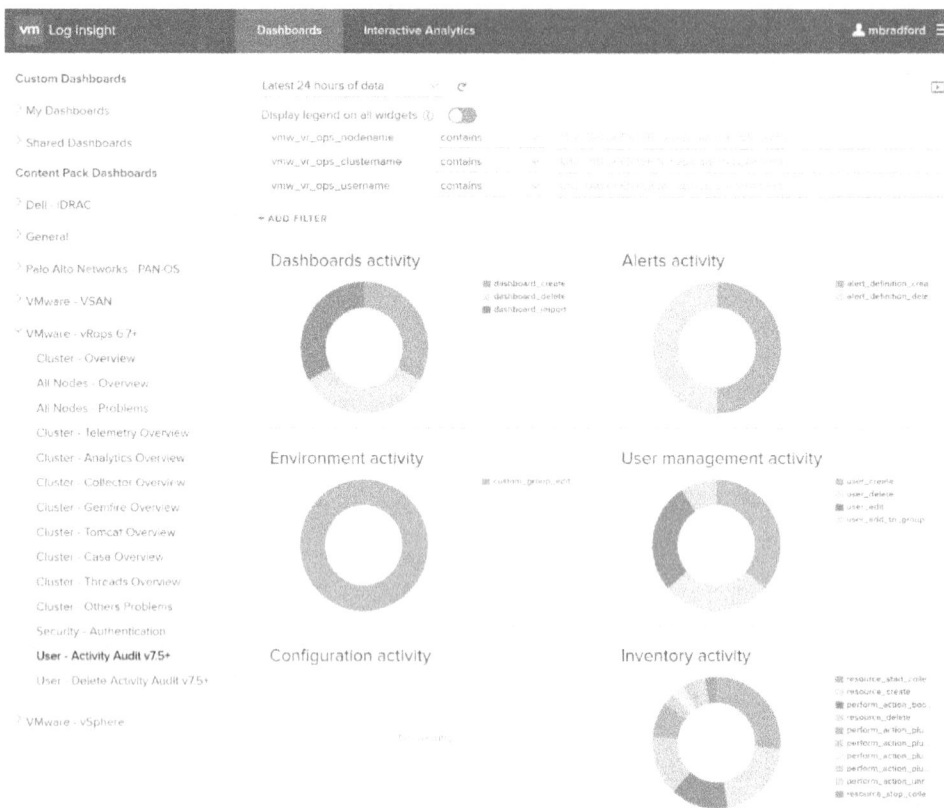

Figure 11.15: Interface of VMware vRealize Log Insight

- **Comprehensive forensic analysis techniques:** The comprehensive forensic analysis techniques relate to analyzing hypervisor and VM memory, investigating network traffic, detecting hidden VMs, and identifying side-channel attacks. The analysis of hypervisor and VM memory resembles detecting running malware, rootkits, and encryption keys using RAM forensics. The process of network traffic investigation relates to inspecting VM-to-VM and hypervisor traffic for anomalies. The detection of hidden VMs relates to identifying unauthorized VMs running outside normal configurations. The identifying side-channel attacks relate to monitoring CPU and cache behavior to detect hypervisor-based exploits such as Spectre and Meltdown. The associated tools in this regard include Wireshark, Volatility, Rekall, and Snort.

- **Incident response and remediation:** The incident response and remediation relate to isolating affected systems, performing post-incident analysis, strengthening security controls, and training forensic teams. The isolation of affected systems relates to quarantining compromised VMs and hypervisors to prevent further attacks. The performance of post-incident analysis relates to reconstructing attack timelines and identifying exploited vulnerabilities. The strengthening of security controls relates to implementing **Host-based Intrusion Detection** (**HIDS**) and enforcing MFA for hypervisor access. The effective training of forensic teams relates to ensuring investigators are well-versed in hypervisor-specific forensic methodologies.

Case studies

The following case studies are related to virtualization forensics:

- **Cloud Hopper Attack (2016-2018): Chinese APT targeting virtualized systems:**

  Cloud Hopper was a sophisticated cyber-espionage campaign attributed to APT10, a Chinese state-sponsored group. The attackers targeted **Managed Service Providers** (**MSPs**) that hosted virtualized environments for multiple clients. The impact of this attack relates to multiple Fortune 500 companies suffering data exfiltration, with stolen information including intellectual property and trade secrets. This is apart from the attack, highlighting vulnerabilities in multi-tenant cloud environments where compromised hypervisors could affect multiple organizations. The elaborate forensic investigation revealed that attackers exploited weak remote access protocols and credentials to gain access to hypervisors in cloud environments. The attackers compromised virtualized systems using malware embedded in VMs. The related log analysis revealed lateral movement between virtual networks and unauthorized hypervisor access. The concerned investigators used hypervisor memory dumps and virtual network forensics to trace malicious activities.

- **ESXi Rootkit Incident: Undetectable hypervisor malware:** A financial institution noticed irregular transactions originating from VMs hosted on VMware ESXi hypervisors. Initial endpoint security scans detected no malware, leading investigators to suspect hypervisor-level tampering. The outcome of this attack relates to millions of dollars being siphoned off before the institution detected the breach. Accordingly, the investigators had to rebuild the compromised VM from clean snapshots to restore integrity. The detailed investigation reveals the presence of a hypervisor rootkit within VMware ESXi that allowed attackers to intercept and modify VM operations and yet remain undetected. The live memory forensics of the hypervisor revealed malicious code injected into the **virtual CPU (vCPU)**. The virtual disk analysis indicated unauthorized modifications in system files across multiple VMs. The attackers exploited a hypervisor escape vulnerability, enabling them to control virtualized banking servers.

Conclusion

The current chapter engages in an in-depth analysis of hypervisor forensics in terms of effectively deciphering virtualization. The detailed understanding of a VM from the perspective of the current chapter implies the presence of multiple layers. The process of hypervisor forensics is implicated in the recovery of digital evidence from virtualization layers. The process of hypervisor forensics further indicated the extraction and analysis of data from virtual hard drives. The related case studies implied that digital forensic investigators are required to deploy effective tools and techniques to tackle critical cases of hypervisor forensics. The chapter states different tools that can be used by digital forensic investigators to benefit their investigations appropriately.

The upcoming chapter focuses on integrating incident response with digital forensics.

Join our book's Discord space

Join the book's Discord Workspace for Latest updates, Offers, Tech happenings around the world, New Release and Sessions with the Authors:

https://discord.bpbonline.com

CHAPTER 12

Integrating Incident Response with Digital Forensics

Introduction

The increasing dependence on the networking of digital devices leads to modern-day organizations facing frequent cybersecurity incidents. The complex nature of such incidents and, thereby, the requirement of complicated investigation procedures, leads to the relevant involvement of digital forensics. Contextually, integrating **incident response (IR)** with digital forensics ensures a more comprehensive approach to handling cybersecurity incidents. The outcome of involving digital forensics for IR results in the accumulation of adequate **threat intelligence (TI)** that can resist the occurrence of similar incidents in the future. The current chapter proceeds by focusing on the integration of IR with digital forensics.

Structure

The chapter covers the following topics:

- Improving IR through digital forensics
- Proactively preparing for IR with forensic readiness
- Preserving digital evidence for forensic analysis
- Leveraging digital forensics tools and methods
- Utilizing digital forensics findings

- Bridging the gap between IRs and DF investigators
- Case studies

Objectives

The current chapter targets to indicate relevant strategies for improving IR through digital forensics. The current chapter proceeds with proactively preparing for IR with forensic readiness. The chapter focuses on preserving digital evidence for forensic analysis during incident containment and preservation. The current chapter indicates leveraging digital forensics tools and methods for forensic analysis in IR. The current chapter implies utilizing digital forensics findings for effective incident mitigation and recovery. The current chapter indicates the importance of bridging the gap between incident responders and digital forensics investigators through collaboration and communication.

Improving IR through digital forensics

The increasingly sophisticated nature of cyber threats leads to modern-day organizations facing critical challenges in securing their data. This encourages organizations to enhance their ability to detect, respond to, and recover from security incidents. Contextually, digital forensics plays a crucial role in strengthening IR by providing accurate evidence, uncovering attack vectors, and helping organizations prevent future incidents. The relevant aspects of digital forensics enhancing IR are stated as follows:

- **Accurate and timely evidence collection:** Digital forensics enables organizations to collect and preserve digital evidence systematically. This timely evidence collection helps security teams understand the root cause of an incident, including the source of the attack, the extent of the breach, and the attack timeline.

- **Faster incident detection and containment:** Specific forensic techniques, such as log analysis, network forensics, and malware reverse engineering, help IR teams identify threats faster. The underlying benefits of real-time forensic analysis lead security teams to detect anomalies and **Indicators of Compromise (IoCs)**, apart from isolating infected systems to prevent further damage. The outcome of this aspect relates to assessing attack patterns to mitigate future risks.

- **Enhancing response strategies with deep insights:** Digital forensics provides valuable insights into attackers' **tactics, techniques, and procedures (TTPs)**. This intelligence helps security teams refine their IR strategies by understanding whether the attack was targeted or opportunistic. This relates to identifying vulnerabilities exploited by attackers and thereby strengthening defensive mechanisms to prevent their recurrence.

- **Legal and compliance considerations:** Forensics ensures that evidence collected during an incident is admissible in court or regulatory investigations. Proper documentation and **Chain of Custody (CoC)** help organizations comply with relevant Data protection laws such as GDPR and CCPA. This is along with relevant Industry standards such as ISO 27037 and NIST guidelines. The legal consideration further relates to effective legal proceedings where cybercrime needs to be established at the Court of Law by the associated **digital forensic investigators (DFIs)**.

- **Enabling post-incident analysis and continuous improvement:** The occurrence of a cyber incident encourages forensic analysis to allow security teams to conduct a detailed investigation to determine details of attackers gaining access to the digital assets. This is beneficial as it encourages plugging the existing gap and improvement of future responses.

The integration of digital forensics with IR leads an organization to build a more proactive and intelligence-driven security posture, thereby minimizing the impact of cyber threats and improving its resilience against future attacks.

Proactively preparing for IR with forensic readiness

The consistent evolution of cyber threats results in organizations adopting proactive strategies to detect, respond to, and mitigate security incidents effectively. Forensic readiness plays a crucial role in modern cybersecurity by ensuring that digital evidence is systematically collected, preserved, and analyzed when an incident occurs. The impact of proactively preparing for IR with forensic readiness includes the following:

- **Faster incident detection and response:** A well-prepared forensic strategy enables organizations to detect security breaches quickly. The readily available logs, audit trails, and system snapshots allow security teams to analyze and contain threats in real-time. This process reduces downtime and disruption by streamlining investigative processes.

- **Strengthening legal and regulatory compliance:** Modern-day industries are required to maintain digital evidence for compliance with regulations such as GDPR, HIPAA, and ISO 27037. Contextually, effective forensic documentation ensures that collected data is admissible in legal proceedings. The relevant strengthening of legal and regulatory compliance results in avoiding legal penalties and reputational damage by demonstrating due diligence in cybersecurity practices.

- **Preserving digital evidence integrity:** The forensic readiness plan ensures that evidence is collected, stored, and handled securely. The proper CoC procedures prevent tampering, alteration, or corruption of critical data. The strengthening ability of an organization to prove the source and impact of an attack.

- **Enhancing TI and incident prevention:** The historical forensic data aids in identifying attack patterns, vulnerabilities, and recurring threats. It provides valuable insights into cybercriminal TTPs. This is apart from supporting proactive security enhancements by addressing system weaknesses before exploitation occurs.

- **Reducing financial and operational impact:** The occurrence of cyber incidents can lead to significant financial losses, including remediation costs, legal fees, and reputational harm. Thus, forensic readiness minimizes recovery time and prevents prolonged system downtime. The organizations save costs by avoiding expensive post-incident investigations due to lack of evidence.

- **Facilitating coordination between security teams and law enforcement:** The well-prepared forensic data enables collaboration with cybersecurity authorities, regulatory bodies, and law enforcement agencies. The occurrence of cybercrime leads organizations to provide concrete evidence to support investigations. It increases the likelihood of identifying and prosecuting cybercriminals.

- **Building a strong cybersecurity culture:** The effort of building a strong cybersecurity culture encourages continuous security monitoring and documentation. This process enhances awareness among employees and IT teams about the importance of secure data management. This is further to aligning security operations with business continuity and risk management strategies.

Forensic readiness is a critical component of modern cybersecurity as it encourages organizations to respond efficiently to cyber threats, preserve digital evidence for legal proceedings, and improve their overall security posture.

Preserving digital evidence for forensic analysis

Digital evidence plays a critical role in cybersecurity investigations, helping organizations identify, analyze, and respond to cyber threats effectively. Proper collection and preservation of digital evidence ensure that security incidents are handled efficiently, legally, and accurately. The timely identification of digital evidence relates to identifying the nature and scope of cyber incidents. This is because digital evidence helps determine the type of attack in terms of malware, phishing, insider threats, and data breaches. Proper preservation of digital evidence is critical in forensic analysis and legal proceedings, ensuring that cybersecurity incidents are thoroughly investigated and, when necessary, legally prosecuted. Digital evidence, if not handled correctly, can be easily altered, destroyed, or rendered inadmissible in court. The key principles of digital evidence preservation include the following:

- **Integrity:** The aspect of Integrity relates to ensuring data is not altered or corrupted during collection.

- **Authenticity:** The perspective of authenticity relates to maintaining the originality and credibility of digital evidence.

- **Chain of Custody:** The CoC relates to relevant documentation of evidence handling from the phase of collection to analysis. *(Figure 12.1)*

Description of Evidence		
Item #	Quantity	Description of Item (Model, Serial #, Condition, Marks, Scratches)

Chain of Custody				
Item #	Date/Time	Released by (Signature & ID#)	Received by (Signature & ID#)	Comments/Location

Figure 12.1: Snapshot of Chain of Custody

- **Volatility consideration:** The volatility consideration of digital evidence relates to capturing volatile data, such as RAM and network connections, before it is lost.

The DFIs tend to apply the following relevant steps for preserving digital evidence during incident containment:

- **Isolating affected systems:** The timely isolation of affected systems prevents further evidence tampering by disconnecting compromised devices.

- **Capturing live data:** The capturing of live data relates to extracting volatile information such as running processes, network activity, and open ports.

- **Taking forensic disk images:** This relates to creating bit-by-bit copies of storage devices to maintain the integrity of original evidence. *(Figure 12.2)*

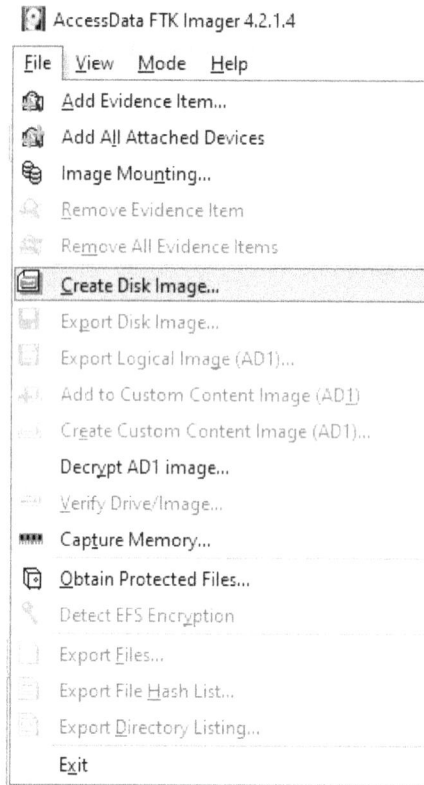

Figure 12.2: Disk image creation

- **Preserving logs and metadata:** The preservation of logs and metadata resembles secure system logs, access records, and timestamps.

- **Encrypting and storing evidence securely:** The process of encrypting and storing evidence securely relates to protecting collected data from unauthorized access.

The DFIs tend to select the following tools and techniques for digital evidence collection:

- **Forensic imaging tools:** The imaging of digital evidence relates to deploying forensic imaging tools such as FTK Imager, EnCase, and Autopsy.

- **Memory analysis tools:** The requirement of memory analysis is fulfilled by tools such as Volatility and Rekall.

- **Log and network forensics tools:** The forensic tools for log and network analysis include Wireshark, Splunk, and ELK Stack.

- **Malware analysis platforms:** DFIs tend to apply relevant malware analysis platforms such as Cuckoo Sandbox and IDA Pro.

In addition to the deployment of the abovementioned tools and techniques, DFIs tend to apply multiple best practices from the following:

- **Use write-blockers:** The extensive use of write-blockers prevents accidental modification of evidence. *(Figure 12.3)*

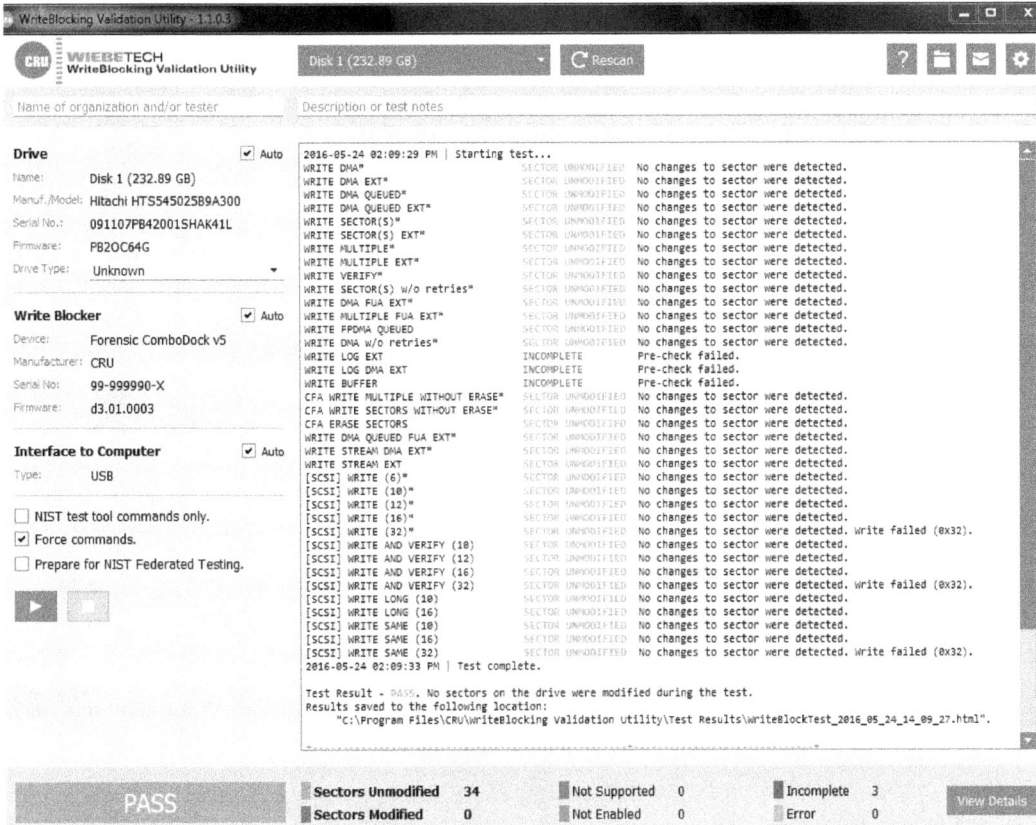

Figure 12.3: *Write-blockers*

- **Follow IR playbooks:** The effective following of IR playbooks results in ensuring standardized collection methods.

- **Train IR teams:** The effective training of IR teams improves expertise in forensic procedures.

- **Regularly test forensic tools:** The regular testing of forensic tools verifies their overall accuracy and reliability.

Proper digital evidence preservation is essential for effective forensic analysis and legal proceedings. This is in terms of maintaining evidence integrity, following CoC protocols, ensuring compliance, and preventing tampering, organizations and law enforcement agencies can accurately investigate cyber incidents, support legal actions, and strengthen overall cybersecurity resilience.

Leveraging digital forensics tools and methods

Digital forensics plays a critical role in strengthening IR by enabling organizations to detect, investigate, and mitigate cyber threats effectively. By leveraging forensic techniques, security teams can analyze attacks in detail, preserve evidence, and enhance overall cybersecurity resilience. The importance of digital forensics in enhancing IR relates to rapid and accurate incident detection. This is because digital forensics helps identify unauthorized access, system intrusions, and suspicious activities. Specifically, forensic tools analyze logs, network traffic, and system events to detect IoCs. The timely threat detection enables faster containment and response to cyber incidents. Digital forensic tools and methodologies play a crucial role in detecting, investigating, and mitigating cyber threats. These tools help organizations collect, preserve, and analyze digital evidence, enabling IR teams to respond swiftly and effectively to security incidents. The process of threat identification relates to the timely detection of cyber threats by monitoring system activities, network traffic, and digital artifacts. This encourages the DFIs to use the following key methods and tools for **TI**:

- **Log analysis:** The process of Log Analysis relates to SIEM solutions such as Splunk, ELK Stack, and Graylog to analyze system logs for anomalies and suspicious activities. *(Figure 12.4)*

Figure 12.4: Log analysis

- **Network forensics:** The concept of network forensic tools such as Wireshark *(Figure 12.5)*, Zeek (Bro), and TCPDump helps detect network intrusions and malware communication.

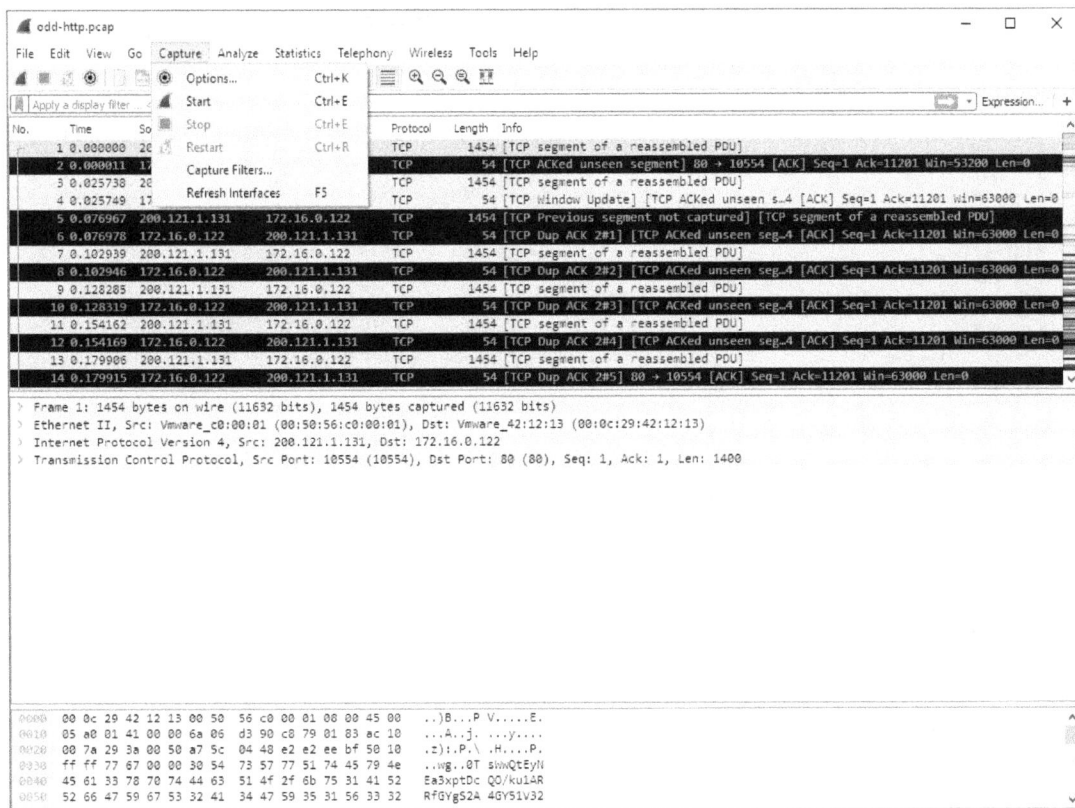

Figure 12.5: Interface of Wireshark

- **Endpoint detection:** The process of endpoint detection relates to the deployment of solutions such as Carbon Black, CrowdStrike, and OSSEC to monitor endpoint behaviors for malicious activities.

- **Memory forensics:** The process of memory forensics relates to utilizing Volatility and Rekall to analyze live memory (RAM) to detect hidden processes, malware injections, and rootkits.

- **Malware detection:** The requirement of malware detection relates to using Cuckoo Sandbox and IDA Pro *(Figure 12.6)* that aid in dynamic and static analysis of malicious files.

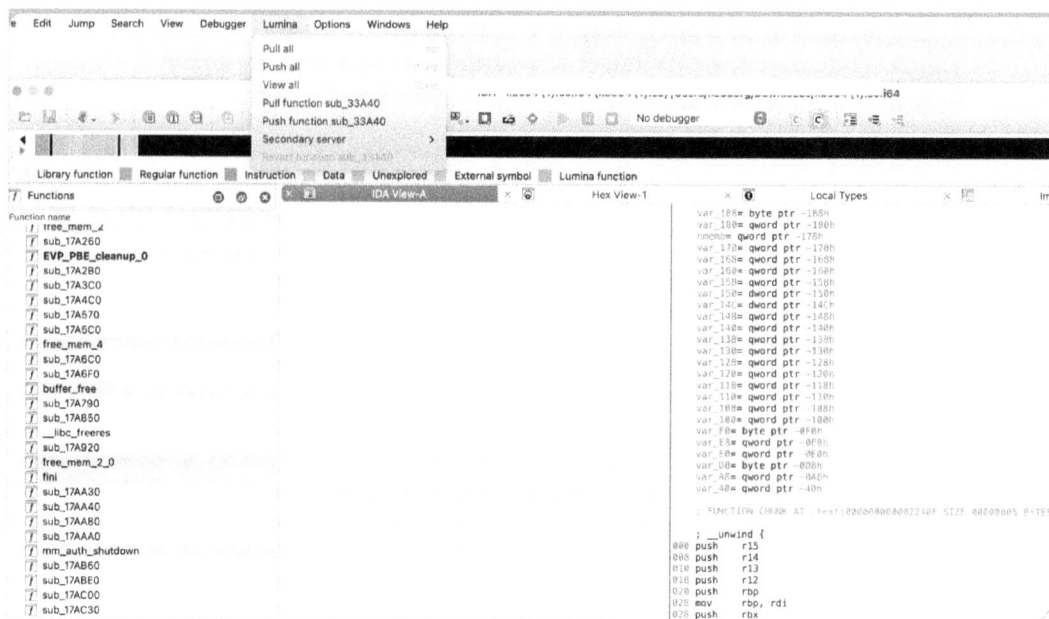

Figure 12.6: Interface of IDA Pro

The key phases of forensic analysis in IR include the following:

- **Identification:** The process of identification relates to detecting anomalies, unauthorized access, and system breaches.

- **Collection:** The process of collection relates to acquiring digital evidence without altering data integrity.

- **Analysis:** The phase of analysis relates to examining logs, network traffic, and system artifacts to determine responsible attack vectors.

- **Preservation:** The phase of preservation relates to maintaining evidence integrity for legal and investigative use.

- **Reporting:** The phase of reporting relates to documenting findings for IR teams and legal authorities.

The essential digital forensics tools for IR include the following:

- **Disk forensics:** The process of disk forensics relates to using tools such as Autopsy, EnCase, and FTK Imager for disk imaging and file recovery.

- **Memory forensics:** The concept of memory forensics relates to using tools such as Volatility and Rekall for analyzing RAM and detecting malware.

- **Network forensics:** The procedure of network forensics resembles using Wireshark and Zeek (Bro) for monitoring and analyzing network traffic.

- **Log analysis:** The requirement of log analysis is fulfilled by Splunk and ELK Stack for detecting anomalies in system logs.

- **Malware analysis:** The malware analysis is preceded by Cuckoo Sandbox *(Figure 12.7)* and IDA Pro for reverse engineering malicious code.

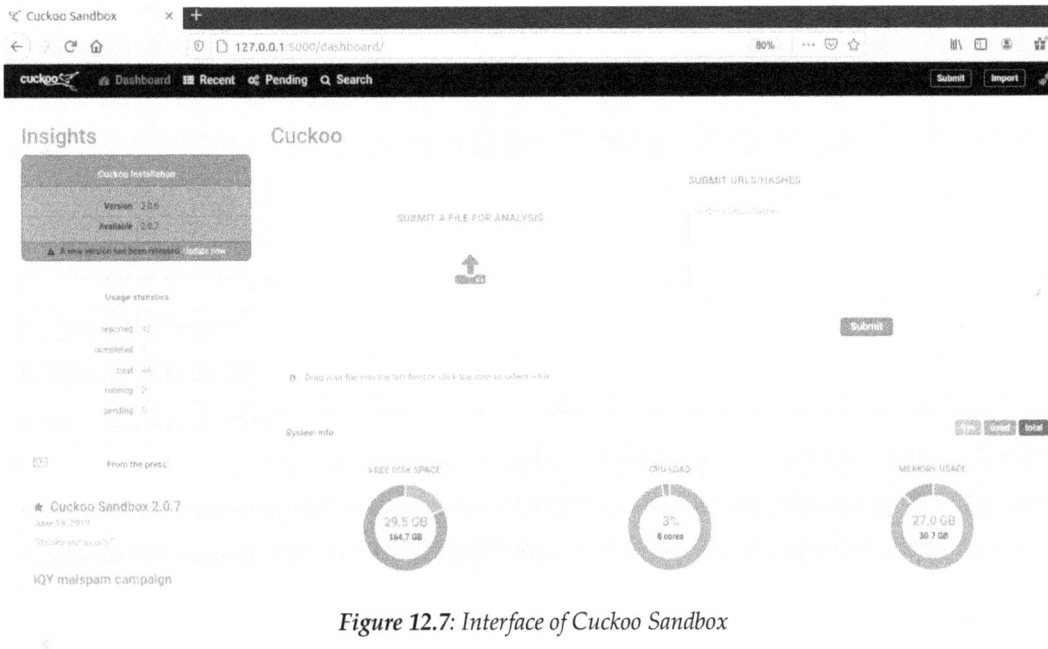

Figure 12.7: Interface of Cuckoo Sandbox

- **Cloud forensics:** The process of cloud forensics relates to using AWS CloudTrail and Google Chronicle for investigating cloud-based incidents.

Forensic tools and methodologies are indispensable for identifying, analyzing, and mitigating cyber threats. The leveraging of advanced forensic techniques, real-time monitoring, and investigative tools aids an organization in enhancing its IR capabilities, minimizing cyber risks, and complying with regulatory requirements.

Utilizing digital forensics findings

Digital forensics plays a crucial role in post-IR, ensuring that organizations can effectively mitigate threats, recover operations, and prevent future attacks. The occurrence of a cyber incident encourages forensic analysis that helps identify the root cause, attack methods, and security vulnerabilities that led to the breach. This intelligence enables organizations to develop targeted mitigation strategies and improve their overall cybersecurity posture. Forensic findings play a crucial role in post-incident analysis, enabling organizations to understand the how, why, and where of a cyberattack. The examination of digital evidence leads forensic investigations to provide clear insights into the root cause, attack vectors, and security weaknesses, allowing for targeted mitigation and prevention strategies. The key forensic insights for Incident Mitigation include the following:

- **Attack timeline reconstruction:** The procedure of attack timeline reconstruction resembles understanding when and how the breach occurred.

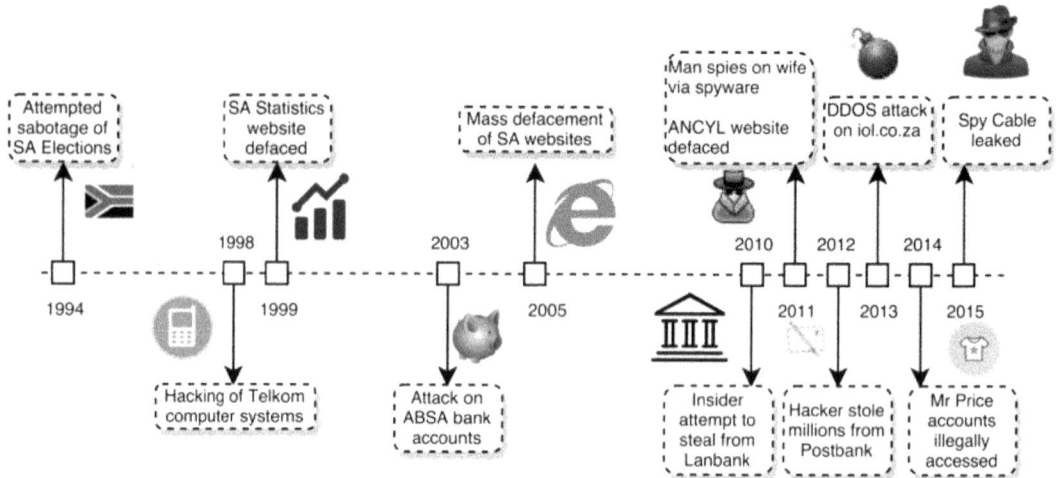

Figure 12.8: Attack timeline reconstruction

- **Indicators of Compromise (IoCs):** The concept of IoCs relates to identifying malicious files, IPs, and behaviors to contain threats.

- **Threat attribution:** The concept of threat attribution resembles analyzing forensic evidence to trace attackers, irrespective of internal or external threats.

- **Forensic log analysis:** Forensic log analysis aids in detecting anomalies in system, application, and network logs for incident correlation.

Implementing forensic findings for containment and eradication relates to the following aspects:

- **Isolating affected systems:** Using forensic reports to quarantine compromised endpoints.

- **Removing persistent threats:** Forensic malware analysis to eliminate hidden backdoors and rootkits.

- **Closing security gaps:** Applying patches and security controls based on forensic recommendations.

The effective leveraging of forensic evidence for incident recovery relates to the following:

- **Data restoration:** Data restoration relates to recovering deleted or corrupted data using forensic imaging and backup validation.

- **System integrity checks:** The system integrity checks relate to verifying system and file integrity before resuming operations.

- **Strengthening security policies:** The strengthening security policies relates to updating access controls, network monitoring, and forensic readiness plans.

The relevant continuous improvement and future prevention relate to the following:

- **Lessons learned analysis:** The analysis of lessons learned from a cybersecurity incident relates to using forensic findings to enhance cybersecurity strategies.

- **Threat intelligence (TI) sharing:** The sharing of TI relates to contributing forensic insights to industry and government cybersecurity networks.

- **Forensic-driven training:** The engagement of forensic-driven training relates to educating security teams on IR best practices based on past findings.

Bridging the gap between IRs and DF investigators

The IRs and DFIs play distinct but complementary roles in the field of cybersecurity. While IR teams focus on identifying, containing, and mitigating threats, DFIs specialize in evidence collection, forensic analysis, and root cause investigation. Effective collaboration between these two teams is essential for efficient threat response, accurate forensic analysis, and long-term security improvements. The importance of seamless collaboration between incident responders and DFIs relates to faster and more effective incident containment. This is because the concerned IR teams rely on forensic insights to quickly detect and isolate threats. Forensic investigators provide critical intelligence on malware, attacker methods, and compromised systems. Well-defined communication channels ensure that IRs and DFIs can coordinate quickly during an active security breach. The aspect of effective communication relates to clearly defined roles to prevent delays caused by uncertainty about who handles containment, mitigation, and forensic analysis. Continuous communication between IRs and DFI teams helps track attacker activity, system vulnerabilities, and incident progression. The effective improvement of evidence handling and integrity implies avoiding accidental data loss. This is because poor communication can lead to responders unintentionally overwriting or destroying forensic evidence during containment efforts. The assurance of proper CoC relates to well-documented communication that ensures that digital evidence remains admissible in legal proceedings.

The roles of IRs relate to focusing on real-time threat containment, mitigation, and system recovery. The roles of incident responders further extend to work on minimizing operational disruption and restoring business functions. The roles of DFIs resemble specializing in evidence collection, preservation, and in-depth attack analysis. This relates to ensuring forensic integrity for legal and compliance purposes. The common challenges in collaboration between IRs and DFI are as follows:

- **Siloed operations:** The siloed operations relate to a lack of information sharing between the IR and forensic teams.

- **Conflicting priorities:** The conflicting priorities relate to IRs prioritizing quick containment, whereas DFIs require detailed evidence preservation.

- **Lack of communication protocols:** The lack of communication protocols results in siloed operations technology and tool gaps. The outcome of this relates to different teams using varied forensic and security tools making their integration difficult.

The following strategies for effective collaboration ensure effective working between IRs and DFI:

- **Developing a unified IR and forensic framework:** This relates to implementing joint workflows that balance rapid response and forensic integrity. This requires defining transparent **Standard Operating Procedures** (**SOPs**) for evidence handling. This is further enhancing Communication channels by establishing secure real-time communication platforms, resulting in the sharing of relevant findings. The conduction of cross-team debriefs after major incidents.

- **Utilizing integrated tools:** The deployment of SIEM (*Figure 12.9*), EDR, and other forensic tools facilitates shared insights such as Splunk, CrowdStrike, and Magnet Axiom.

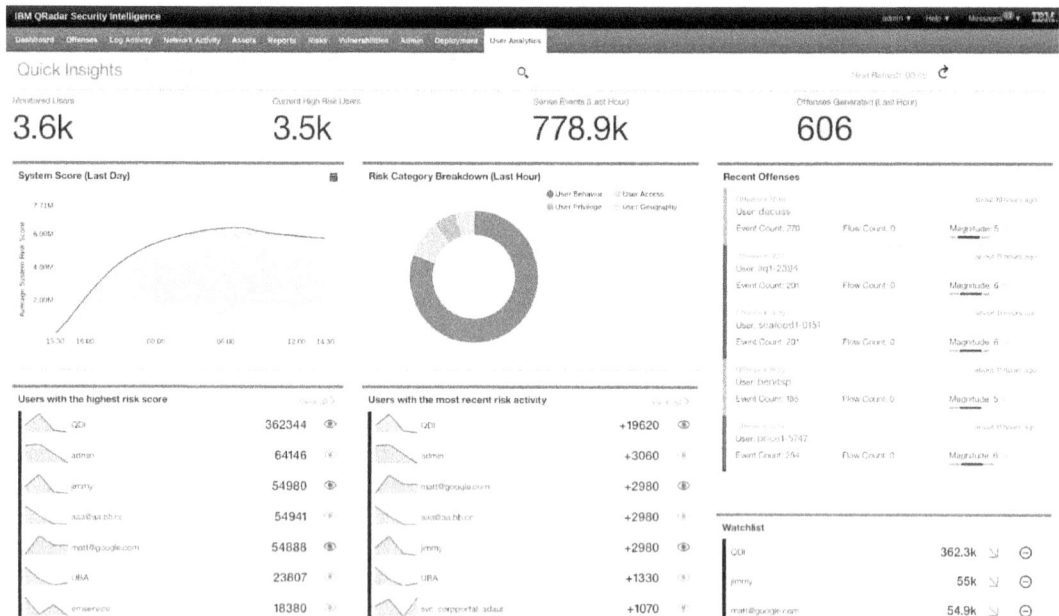

Figure 12.9: Interface of SIEM

- **Regular training and tabletop exercises:** The regular training and tabletop exercises relates to conducting joint training sessions on forensic readiness and IR best practices. The effective simulation of real-world cyber incidents to improve teamwork and role clarity.

Case studies

The related case studies are stated as follows:

- **Target Data Breach (2013), forensic investigation uncovered attack vectors:** Target is one of the largest U.S. retailers, which suffered a massive data breach in 2013 that compromised 40 million credit card details and 70 million personal records of customers. The attackers gained access to the target's network through a third-party HVAC vendor, leveraging stolen credentials to move laterally and extract sensitive data. The combined effort of IR and digital forensics resulted in IR teams detecting unusual network activity and **Point-of-Sale (PoS)** anomalies. The team applied relevant containment strategies despite the progressing state of data exfiltration. The digital forensic teams analyzed logs and malware samples to identify the attack vector. The digital forensic team further discovered that attackers installed memory-scraping malware on PoS terminals.

- **Sony Pictures Hack (2014), cyber espionage and threat attribution:** Sony Pictures was hacked by a suspected nation-state group (allegedly North Korea) in retaliation for a movie release. The attackers stole internal emails, employee records, and unreleased films, eventually destroying critical IT infrastructure using malware. The IR team attempted to contain the attack but discovered that the hackers had already gained persistent access. The team further observed that systems were locked, and critical data was being wiped by a destructive malware strain called Shamoon. The concerned digital forensics teams retrieved logs, malware signatures, and communication traces to identify the attackers. The team further analyzed the attack and indicated similarities to previous attacks by the Lazarus Group. The generated evidence was used to attribute the attack to North Korea, leading to U.S. government sanctions.

Conclusion

The current chapter relates to improving IR through digital forensics. The chapter indicated that proactive preparation for IR with forensic readiness relates to generating effective results from digital forensic investigations. The effective preservation of digital evidence during incident contamination relates to the application of suitable strategies by DFIs. The preservation of digital evidence for forensic analysis during incident containment and preservation relates to abiding by relevant standards and guidelines. The chapter indicates that effectively bridging the gap between IR and DFIs encourages fast progress in digital forensic investigations.

The upcoming chapter focuses on detailing relevant advanced tactics in digital forensics.

Join our book's Discord space

Join the book's Discord Workspace for Latest updates, Offers, Tech happenings around the world, New Release and Sessions with the Authors:

https://discord.bpbonline.com

CHAPTER 13

Advanced Tactics in Digital Forensics

Introduction

The increasing complexity of modern-day cyber-attacks results in the introduction of advanced tactics in digital forensics to cater to the relevant needs. Digital forensics has evolved beyond traditional methods due to sophisticated cyber threats, encrypted data, and anti-forensic techniques used by attackers. Advanced tactics in digital forensics help investigators uncover hidden evidence, analyze complex cyber incidents, and strengthen legal cases. The current chapter proceeds with listing advanced tactics in digital forensics.

Structure

The chapter covers the following topics:

- Memory forensics
- Anti-forensic techniques
- Steganography analysis
- Mobile device chip-off forensics
- Advanced data analysis
- Cryptocurrency forensics
- Data fragmentation and reconstruction

- Artificial intelligence and machine learning in digital forensics
- Case studies

Objectives

The chapter details memory forensics from the perspective of examining volatile data for advanced insights. The chapter indicates that anti-forensic techniques is effective for uncovering and countering attempts to obfuscate digital evidence. The chapter proceeds with steganography analysis in terms of detecting and decoding hidden information in digital files. The chapter implies that mobile device chip-off forensics is the process of extracting data from mobile devices at the hardware level. The chapter further implies that advanced data analysis is the application of statistical and data mining techniques to digital forensic investigations. The chapter looks into details about cryptocurrency forensics in terms of investigating transactions and wallets in the digital currency space. The chapter includes adequate details about data fragmentation and reconstruction as a strategy for piecing together shredded or fragmented digital evidence. The current chapter proceeds with artificial intelligence and machine learning in digital forensics in terms of leveraging AI for advanced analysis and automation. The chapter includes case studies about advanced tactics in digital forensics.

Memory forensics

Memory forensics is a crucial technique in digital forensics, allowing investigators to extract real-time evidence from volatile memory (RAM). Contrary to traditional disk-based forensics, memory analysis provides deep insights into running processes, malware behavior, and attack traces that disappear upon system shutdown. The sheer importance of memory forensics in cyber investigation includes capturing live system activity, including running applications, open network connections, and encryption keys. Digital forensic investigators proceed with memory forensics during cyber investigations in terms of detecting fileless malware, rootkits, and **Advanced Persistent Threats** (**APTs**) that do not leave artifacts on disk. Effective memory forensics aids in **incident response** (**IR**), cybercrime investigation, and threat attribution. For instance, memory forensics helped detect TrickBot malware, which operated in memory to evade traditional antivirus solutions. The well-known volatile artifacts and their forensic value are stated as follows:

- **Running processes and hidden threads:** The running processes and hidden threads identify active programs including suspicious or injected processes.

- **Network connections and open ports:** The network connections and open ports track **Command and Control** (**C2**) communication used by attackers.

- **Encryption keys and credentials:** The deployment of encryption keys and credentials recovers decryption keys and passwords used in ransomware cases.

- **Registry hives and event logs:** The assessment of registry hives and event logs results in the analysis of system configurations, execution history, and forensic timestamps.

For instance, memory analysis helped uncover ransomware decryption keys before attackers could delete them.

The digital forensic investigators consider the following tools and techniques for performing memory analysis:

- **Volatility framework**: The volatility framework is an open-source tool for extracting process lists, network activity, and injected code. The benefits of this tool relate to its ability to detect Mimikatz in RAM, revealing attacker's attempts to steal Windows credentials. *(Figure 13.1)*

```
  .#####.    mimikatz 2.2.0 (x64) #19041 Sep 19 2022 17:44:08
 .## ^ ##.   "A La Vie, A L'Amour" - (oe.eo)
 ## / \ ##   /*** Benjamin DELPY `gentilkiwi` ( benjamin@gentilkiwi.com )
 ## \ / ##        > https://blog.gentilkiwi.com/mimikatz
 '## v ##'        Vincent LE TOUX             ( vincent.letoux@gmail.com )
  '#####'         > https://pingcastle.com / https://mysmartlogon.com ***/

mimikatz #
```

Figure 13.1: *Interface of Mimikatz*

- **Rekall**: Rekall is an advanced memory analysis tool with cross-platform compatibility.

- **MemProcFS**: The MemProcFS implies live forensic analysis of Windows process memory.

- **DumpIt and FTK Imager**: Both DumpIt and FTK Imager are ideal tools for acquiring full memory dumps for offline investigation.

The seamless detection of malware and advanced threats using the procedure of memory forensics relates to identifying fileless malware running entirely in memory. The procedure of memory forensics relates to extracting packed or obfuscated code used in advanced attacks. The procedure of memory forensics recovers injected shellcode and rootkits that evade disk-based detection. For instance, forensic analysts used memory dumps to analyze Cobalt Strike payloads, helping organizations block post-exploitation techniques.

Anti-forensic techniques

Anti-forensic techniques are methods used by cybercriminals to hide, alter, or destroy digital evidence, thus making forensic investigations more challenging. Attackers use anti-forensics to evade detection, delay investigations, and destroy incriminating evidence. The widely used anti-forensics techniques range from data hiding and encryption to metadata manipulation and log wiping. Accordingly, effective digital forensics requires detecting, analyzing, and countering these obfuscation methods. For instance, the Sony Pictures Hack of 2014 resembles that the attackers wiped logs and altered timestamps to confuse digital forensics investigators. The widely used anti-forensics techniques are stated as follows:

- **Data hiding and obfuscation:** The relevant data hiding and obfuscation techniques include steganography, **Alternate Data Streams (ADS)**, hidden partitions, and encrypted containers. Steganography is a procedure of hiding files within images, videos, or other media. The ADS relates to concealing data within NTFS file system attributes. The hidden partitions and encrypted containers relate to using TrueCrypt and VeraCrypt to obscure sensitive files. However, expert digital forensic investigators tend to apply appropriate countermeasures such as StegExpose, ADS Spy, and other forensic carving tools to help detect hidden data.

- **Data deletion and destruction:** The requirement of data deletion and destruction relates to using secure deletion tools, disk wiping and formatting, and memory scrubbing. The range of secure deletion tools includes CCleaner, BleachBit, and SDelete to erase files beyond recovery. The process of disk wiping and formatting relates to overwriting entire drives to prevent their forensic analysis. The process of memory scrubbing relates to attackers clearing RAM dumps before shutdown to remove volatile evidence. However, digital forensic investigators use tools such as Magnet AXIOM, Autopsy, and FTK Imager that can recover deleted files and detect tampering.

- **Metadata and log manipulation:** The metadata and log manipulation relate to Timestamp Forgery (Timestamping), event log tampering, and process hollowing. The timestamp forgery relates to modifying file creation, access, and modification times. The event log tampering relates to deleting or modifying Windows, Linux, or cloud security logs. Process hollowing relates to injecting malicious code into legitimate processes to avoid detection. Contrary to these anti-forensics techniques, digital forensic investigators use log correlation, event reconstruction, and forensic timeline analysis to aid in detecting inconsistencies.

Furthermore, digital forensic investigators use the following advanced countermeasures to these anti-forensics' techniques and incident detection techniques:

- **Disk and memory forensics:** Disk and memory forensics relates to analyzing RAM and disk images to recover hidden data.

- **Log correlation and timeline analysis:** Log correlation and timeline analysis relate to identifying discrepancies in system and network logs. *(Figure 13.2)*

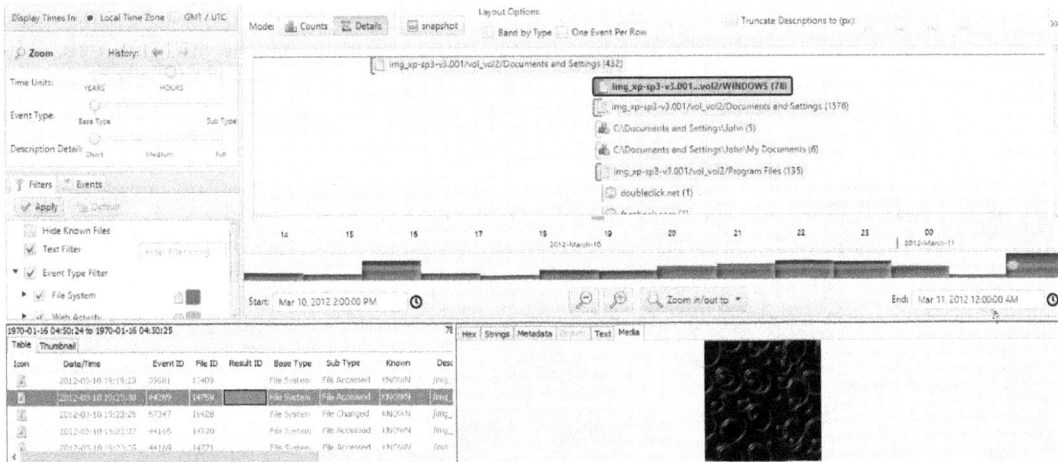

Figure 13.2: Timeline analysis

- **File system analysis:** File system analysis relates to detecting abnormal file system changes, hidden partitions, and ADS usage.

- **AI-powered forensic tools:** The AI-powered forensic tools relate to using machine learning to spot data obfuscation patterns. For instance, AI-driven forensic tools helped reconstruct deleted messages from an encrypted messaging app used in cybercrime cases.

Anti-forensic techniques pose a significant challenge to digital investigations and IR. By leveraging advanced forensic tools, AI-driven detection, and proactive monitoring, forensic investigators can effectively counter data obfuscation, log manipulation, and evidence destruction.

Steganography analysis

Steganography is a covert technique used to hide data within digital files, such as images, videos, audio, or text, making it difficult to detect unauthorized communication or cybercriminal activity. This detailed analysis of various steganographic methods, forensic detection techniques, and countermeasures implies the overall importance of uncovering concealed information. The procedure of steganography is used by adversaries for covert communication, cyber espionage, malware distribution, and data exfiltration. The attackers embed malicious payloads within media files to bypass security mechanisms. Digital forensics must analyze suspicious files to uncover hidden data and prevent information leaks. For instance, the Duqu malware used image steganography to exfiltrate sensitive data without detection. The well-known and commonly used steganographic techniques are stated as follows:

- **Image steganography (LSB encoding):** LSB encoding is a type of image steganography that hides data in the **Least Significant Bits** (**LSB**) of pixel values in JPEG, PNG, or BMP images. This process of image steganography maintains visual integrity, making modifications imperceptible to the human eye. The countermeasures applied by the Digital Forensic Investigators to tackle the issue of image steganography include StegExpose, OpenStego, and pixel analysis tools that aid in identifying hidden patterns. *(Figure 13.3)*

```
Microsoft Windows [Version 10.0.19044.1586]
(c) Microsoft Corporation. All rights reserved.

C:\Users\uchen>cd \

C:\>cd C:\Users\uchen\PycharmProjects\HDLMSteganography\StegExpose

C:\Users\uchen\PycharmProjects\HDLMSteganography\StegExpose>cd C:\Users\uchen\PycharmProjects\HDLMSteganography
\StegExpose

C:\Users\uchen\PycharmProjects\HDLMSteganography\StegExpose>java -jar StegExpose.jar HDLMImages default 0.5 ste
ganalysisReport.csv

C:\Users\uchen\PycharmProjects\HDLMSteganography\StegExpose>java -jar StegExpose.jar testFolder default default
 steganalysisOfTestFolder
```

Figure 13.3: Interface of StegExpose

- **Audio and video steganography:** Audio and video steganography relates to echo hiding, phase coding, and frequency masking that tend to embed data in MP3, WAV, or MP4 files. This relates to attackers using these formats to smuggle **command-and-control** (**C2**) instructions in malware campaigns. However, digital forensic investigators use tools such as *Audacity* and *DeepSound* to analyze abnormal signal distortions. *(Figure 13.4)*

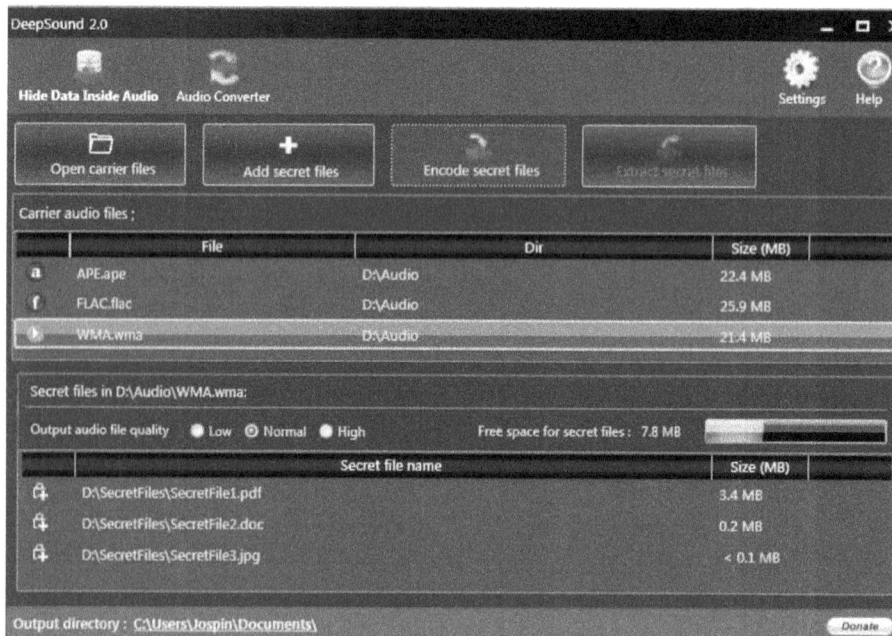

Figure 13.4: Interface of DeepSound

- **Text steganography and whitespace encoding:** The text steganography and whitespace encoding conceals information using invisible characters, Unicode manipulation, or formatting tricks. The procedure of text steganography and whitespace encoding is widely exploited in phishing emails, dark web forums, and insider threats. Accordingly, digital forensic investigators use Stegdetect and NLP-based anomaly analysis to identify unusual text patterns. *(Figure 13.5)*

```
C:\work\Ch-6\stegdetect>stegdetect -tjopi -s10.0 *.jpg
4486077256132177_n.jpg : negative
Corrupt JPEG data: 13 extraneous bytes before marker 0xd9
Nihad_Hassan_FirstBook.jpg : jphide(**)  ◀━━━
Corrupt JPEG data: 1 extraneous bytes before marker 0xd9
Nihad_pix.jpg : negative
Corrupt JPEG data: bad Huffman code
_5074146228339284407.jpg : negative
Corrupt JPEG data: 7 extraneous bytes before marker 0xd9
output.jpg : negative

C:\work\Ch-6\stegdetect>
```

Figure 13.5: *Interface of Stegdetect*

- **Network steganography (Covert channels):** The network steganography (covert channels) tends to embed data in TCP/IP packet headers, DNS requests, or HTTP payloads. This is thereby used by adversaries in data exfiltration and botnet communication. Contrarily, the digital forensic investigators use Wireshark and Zeek (Bro) for deep packet inspection. *(Figure 13.6)*

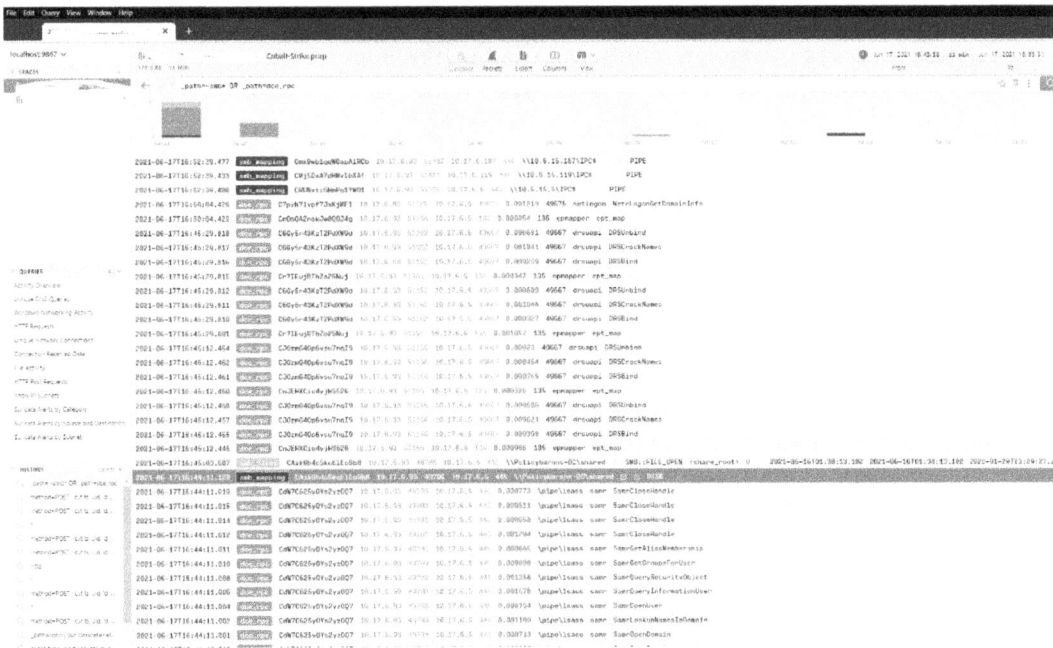

Figure 13.6: *Interface of Zeek*

The counter-steganographic techniques used by digital forensic investigators to decode and detect steganographic data include the following:

- **Histogram and statistical analysis:** The histogram and statistical analysis detect color distortions and irregular frequency patterns. For instance, investigators uncovered hidden terrorist messages embedded in images using histogram analysis.

- **Steganalysis tools and machine learning:** The steganalysis tools and machine learning relate to formulating AI-based detection models to analyze pixel deviations.

- **Reverse engineering and brute-force extraction:** Reverse engineering and brute-force extraction attempt to decode encryption keys or hidden payloads.

- **Comparative image analysis:** The comparative image analysis compares original media files with modified media files to highlight alterations.

Steganography poses a significant challenge to digital forensics and cybersecurity. Detecting and decoding hidden data requires advanced analytical tools, AI-driven forensic techniques, and deep media analysis to counter covert cyber threats effectively.

Mobile device chip-off forensics

Chip-off forensics is an advanced digital forensic technique used to extract data directly from the memory chip of a mobile device when traditional software-based methods fail. This process involves physically removing the flash memory chip and using specialized tools to retrieve and analyze stored data. The importance of chip-off forensics relates to recovering data from locked, damaged, or encrypted devices where software-based forensics is ineffective. The chip-off forensics extracts deleted messages, call logs, app data, and multimedia files from non-functional or water-damaged devices. Chip-off forensics is used in criminal investigations, corporate espionage cases, and intelligence gathering. Specifically, law enforcement used chip-off forensics to recover deleted messages from a suspect's phone in a financial fraud case.

The underlying stages of the chip-off forensics process and techniques are stated as follows:

- **Device preparation and chip removal:** Device preparation and chip removal relate to disassembling the mobile device to access the **Embedded MultiMediaCard (eMMC)** or **Universal Flash Storage (eUFS)** chip. The process involves using hot air rework stations, infrared heat, or laser tools to carefully desolder the chip from the motherboard. The associated challenge in this regard relates to the risk of the chip overheating or physical damage during extraction.

- **Data dumping and extraction:** The process of data dumping and extraction relates to using chip programmers, NAND readers, and forensic imaging tools to create a bit-for-bit dump of the memory. The process aids in recovering deleted, hidden and fragmented data using forensic tools. Digital forensic investigators use relevant tools such as RIFF Box, Z3X Pro, Cellebrite UFED, and JTAG adapters.

- **Data parsing and analysis:** The procedure of data parsing and analysis relates to converting raw binary dumps into readable file formats. This process further relates to extracting SMS, call logs, and app data from various communication applications such as WhatsApp, Signal, and Telegram and location history. The process further relates to conducting timeline reconstruction and metadata analysis for case investigation. For instance, chip-off forensics helped decrypt an encrypted Android phone in a cybercrime investigation.

Chip-off forensics is a powerful but complex investigative method for retrieving critical evidence from inaccessible mobile devices. Chip-off forensics is powered by specialized tools, careful handling, and advanced data recovery techniques, and thereby aids forensic experts in recovering and analyzing key digital artifacts that are crucial for criminal and cybersecurity investigations.

Advanced data analysis

The increasingly complex nature of cybercrimes encourages digital forensics to leverage statistical analysis and data mining techniques to extract meaningful patterns, detect anomalies, and strengthen investigations. This advanced data analysis enhances forensic investigations, key methodologies, tools, and real-world applications. This is in terms of aiding the identification of hidden patterns, correlations, and anomalies in large forensic datasets. The advanced data analysis enhances timeline reconstruction, event correlation, and malware behavior analysis. The advanced data analysis supports fraud detection, insider threat investigations, and cybersecurity breach analysis. For instance, data mining helped uncover a hidden network of cybercriminals laundering money through cryptocurrency transactions.

The key data analysis techniques in digital forensics are stated as follows:

- **Statistical analysis for anomaly detection:** The statistical analysis for anomaly detection relates to using probability distributions, standard deviations, and clustering methods to detect irregular activity. This technique further helps in identifying suspicious login attempts, data access anomalies, and fraudulent transactions. Statistical modeling detected unusual spikes in data transfers, revealing an ongoing data exfiltration attack.

- **Data mining for pattern recognition:** The data mining for pattern recognition relates to using machine learning algorithms such as decision trees, k-means clustering, and neural networks to classify forensic data. This method also identifies malware signatures, phishing attacks, and financial fraud trends. Data mining techniques helped detect previously unknown ransomware variants through behavior analysis.

- **Timeline reconstruction and event correlation:** The timeline reconstruction and event correlation relate to using log file analysis, time-series data, and sequence alignment techniques to reconstruct cyber incidents. This process helps in tracking attack timelines, root causes, and compromised user accounts. forensic analysts used event correlation to link multiple breach attempts to a single APT group.

- **Social network and link analysis:** The social network and link analysis examines relationships between digital entities such as users, devices, and IP addresses to uncover cybercriminal networks. The process can be applied in dark web investigations, organized cybercrime cases, and terrorist activity tracking. The link analysis revealed connections between fraudulent e-commerce sites and money laundering accounts.

The tools for advanced forensic data analysis are stated as follows:

- **Autopsy and EnCase**: Autopsy and EnCase are forensic suites with built-in data mining capabilities.

- **Splunk and ELK Stack**: Splunk and ELK Stack are log analysis tools for detecting anomalies in security events.

- **Weka and RapidMiner**: Weka and RapidMiner are machine learning platforms for forensic data classification.

- **Maltego and Linkurious**: The Maltego and Linkurious graph-based analysis for cybercrime and fraud detection. the digital forensic investigators used Maltego to map a cybercriminal network operating on the dark web.

Advanced data analysis techniques enhance the accuracy, speed, and depth of digital forensic investigations. The integration of statistical models, machine learning algorithms, and data mining approaches leads investigators to uncover hidden patterns, detect anomalies, and strengthen cybercrime investigations.

Cryptocurrency forensics

The increasing relevance of cryptocurrency leads cybercriminals to use it for money laundering, fraud, and illicit transactions. Thus, cryptocurrency forensics is essential for tracing blockchain transactions, identifying wallet owners, and uncovering financial crimes. This detailed analysis of cryptocurrency forensics explores relevant forensic techniques, challenges, tools, and real-world applications in cryptocurrency investigations. The importance of cryptocurrency forensics in digital investigations relates to identifying suspicious transactions, money laundering schemes, and illicit financial activities. This is further to tracing funds across Bitcoin, Ethereum, Monero, and other cryptocurrencies. The benefits of cryptocurrency forensics further assist law enforcement in seizing illegal funds and prosecuting cybercriminals. For instance, investigators tracked stolen Bitcoin from a ransomware attack to an exchange where it was converted into fiat currency.

The concept of blockchain transaction tracking relates to public blockchains providing immutable transaction records and allowing forensic tracking. This tracking further reveals bitcoin addresses, transaction hashes, and wallet movements to help reconstruct financial trails. Authorities traced illicit silk road funds through multiple Bitcoin wallets using forensic tools.

The concept of Wallet identification and address attribution relates to cryptocurrency wallets that have unique public addresses, but owners often remain anonymous. Accordingly, investigators use heuristic clustering, transaction patterns, and metadata analysis to link wallets to individuals. Specifically, the exchange **Know Your Customer (KYC)** regulations helped identify a cybercriminal cashing out Bitcoin proceeds.

The increasing impact of the dark web and associated privacy coins challenges relate to cyber criminals using Monero, Zcash, and privacy-enhancing tools to hide transaction trails. The cybercriminals at the dark web marketplaces use mixing services (tumblers) and coin swaps to launder funds. The AlphaBay takedown revealed a network of Monero transactions used for illicit trade.

The relevant tools for cryptocurrency forensics are stated as follows:

- **Chainalysis and Elliptic**: The Chainalysis and Elliptic tools are blockchain analytics platforms that are used by digital forensic investigators for tracking transactions. Chainalysis helped law enforcement recover millions in stolen crypto from ransomware payments.

- **CipherTrace and TRM Labs**: The CipherTrace and TRM Labs are used by digital forensic investigators to identify illicit crypto activities and connect addresses to real-world entities.

- **Blockchair and Bitcoin Explorer**: The Blockchair and Bitcoin Explorer are public tools for viewing blockchain transactions.

Cryptocurrency forensics is critical for tracing illicit transactions, identifying cybercriminals, and securing digital financial ecosystems. Digital forensic investigators use advanced blockchain analytics, forensic tools, and investigative techniques to unravel complex crypto-related crimes and enhance cybersecurity enforcement.

Data fragmentation and reconstruction

Digital evidence is often intentionally or unintentionally fragmented, making forensic reconstruction essential for retrieving lost, deleted, or manipulated data. The importance of data reconstruction in digital forensics relates to enabling the recovery of shredded, deleted, or corrupted digital evidence. The process of data fragmentation and reconstruction relates to assisting in reconstructing partial files, disk images, and fragmented database records. The process of data fragmentation and reconstruction supports cybercrime investigations by retrieving logs, financial transactions, and communication records. For instance, law enforcement successfully reconstructed shredded files from the hard drive of a fraud suspect, thereby uncovering key evidence.

The causes of data fragmentation and loss are as follows:

- **File system behavior:** The file system behavior relates to operating systems storing files in non-contiguous sectors, leading to fragmentation.

- **File deletion and overwriting:** The process of file deletion and overwriting relates to deleted files that may be partially recoverable until overwritten. A hacker used secure file deletion tools, but forensic methods recovered partial logs.

- **Disk formatting and partitioning:** Disk formatting and partitioning imply that formatting does not erase data but removes index references.

- **Encryption and obfuscation:** Cybercriminals use data shredding tools, encryption, and compression to hide evidence as part of encryption and obfuscation.

- **RAM and volatile storage:** The RAM and volatile storage relate to memory dumps containing temporary data that may vanish upon shutdown.

The following techniques for data fragmentation analysis and reconstruction are used by digital forensic investigators:

- **File carving and signature analysis:** The file carving and signature analysis relates to identifying file headers and footers to extract recoverable fragments. This process is useful for retrieving JPEGs, PDFs, and documents without relying on file system metadata. Investigators used file carving to reconstruct deleted emails from **Solid State Drives (SSD)**.

- **Hash matching and similarity analysis:** The hash matching and similarity analysis relate to comparing fragmented data to known hash signatures for file identification. The process uses fuzzy hashing (e.g., SSDeep) to detect altered or partially recovered files. Partial document fragments were matched against a classified intelligence report to confirm leaks.

- **Disk image analysis and virtual reconstruction:** Disk image analysis and virtual reconstruction relate to using disk imaging to analyze fragmented sectors in a forensically sound manner. This process reassembles partitions and logical volumes to recover missing data. A forensic team reconstructed a damaged RAID system to extract hidden financial records.

- **RAM and network packet reconstruction:** The process of RAM and network packet reconstruction recovers session data, encryption keys, and volatile artifacts from memory dumps. The process reconstructs fragmented network traffic for cybercrime and malware analysis. The digital forensic Investigators recovered passwords from volatile memory before the system shutdown.

The tools for data fragmentation and reconstruction are as follows:

- **Autopsy and Scalpel**: Autopsy and Scalpel are tools used for file carving and forensic analysis. A forensic team used Scalpel to recover image fragments from a cyberstalker's deleted archives.

- **TestDisk and PhotoRec**: TestDisk and PhotoRec are tools used by digital forensic investigators for data recovery from formatted disks.

- **Recuva and R-Studio**: Recuva and R-Studio are specific tools used for recovering deleted files from storage devices.

- **Wireshark and Volatility**: Wireshark and Volatility are specific tools used for Network and memory reconstruction.

Data fragmentation and reconstruction are critical for recovering vital digital evidence in cybersecurity investigations. With the usage of advanced forensic techniques such as machine learning and specialized tools, investigators can piece together missing data, detect tampering, and strengthen digital forensic capabilities.

Artificial intelligence and machine learning in digital forensics

The evolution of cyber threats implies **artificial intelligence** (**AI**) and **machine learning** (**ML**) transforming digital forensics by enhancing efficiency, automating processes, and detecting anomalies at scale. The inherent importance of AI and ML in digital forensics includes automating data analysis, pattern recognition, and anomaly detection in large datasets. The combination of AI and ML speeds up evidence processing, malware analysis, and cybercrime investigations. This combination enhances **threat intelligence** (**TI**), fraud detection, and intrusion forensics. AI helped identify ransomware variants by analyzing malicious code behavior in real-time.

The AI and ML applications in digital forensics are stated as follows:

- **Automated threat detection and anomaly analysis:** Automated threat detection and anomaly analysis use ML to identify unusual patterns in network traffic, logs, and user behavior. This analytical tool detects malware, insider threats, and data exfiltration attempts. AI flagged anomalous login attempts linked to a credential-stuffing attack.

- **Predictive analysis for cybercrime prevention:** The predictive analysis for cybercrime prevention relates to predicting potential security breaches by analyzing historical attack data. The process helps security teams to take proactive measures to prevent incidents. AI-driven predictive models forecast a phishing campaign based on email patterns.

- **Intelligent data processing and evidence classification:** Intelligent data processing and evidence classification use **Natural Language Processing** (**NLP**) and image recognition to analyze forensic data. This process classifies emails, documents, and encrypted files based on forensic relevance. AI helped analyze thousands of chat logs to detect human trafficking networks.

- **AI in malware and reverse engineering:** The AI in malware and reverse engineering identifies zero-day malware by analyzing code structures and execution patterns. This process further automates reverse engineering of obfuscated or polymorphic malware. ML algorithms uncovered a new form of fileless malware bypassing traditional detection.

The AI-powered forensic tools are stated as follows:

- **IBM Watson for cybersecurity**: The IBM Watson for cybersecurity is the AI-driven TI.

- **Darktrace**: **Darktrace** uses ML for real-time anomaly detection. Investigators used Darktrace to detect unauthorized data transfers from compromised systems.

- **Autopsy with AI plugins**: The Autopsy with AI plugins automates forensic data analysis.

- **VirusTotal AI**: The VirusTotal AI is an AI-powered malware analysis and classification.

AI and ML are revolutionizing digital forensics by automating complex investigations, detecting threats, and enhancing forensic intelligence. As AI-powered tools advance, forensic professionals must adapt to evolving AI-driven cybercrime tactics while ensuring ethical and legal considerations.

Case studies

The real-life case studies about using advanced tactics in digital forensics are listed as follows:

- **AI-based dark web investigation of Europol:** Criminals use the dark web and encrypted platforms to conduct illegal activities, such as human trafficking and drug sales. Europol leveraged AI-powered NLP and deep learning to analyze vast amounts of chat logs, forums, and transaction patterns. AI identified hidden links between criminal groups and flagged suspicious transactions in cryptocurrency. Law enforcement dismantled multiple dark web networks. AI-driven language processing helps forensic teams analyze dark web conversations and track cybercriminal activities faster.

- **FBI uses AI to trace Bitcoin ransomware payments:** Cybercriminals behind a ransomware attack demanded payment in Bitcoin, making tracking difficult. The FBI utilized AI-powered blockchain forensics such as Chainalysis and Elliptic to analyze cryptocurrency transactions. AI helped trace the Bitcoin payments through multiple wallets and exchanges, ultimately leading to the arrest of the ransomware operators. AI-powered blockchain analytics is crucial for tracking cryptocurrency transactions linked to cybercrime.

Conclusion

The current chapter focused on including relevant details about advanced techniques that are deployed in modern-day digital forensics investigation. The outcomes of the current chapter indicated that engagement of advanced techniques encouraged the fast resolution of cybersecurity investigations in terms of aiding the associated digital forensics investigators. The relevant areas of the chapter implied the application of relevant tools by digital forensic investigators to proceed with required investigations. The chapter implied that the combination of AI and ML tends to simplify the overall process of cybersecurity investigation.

The upcoming chapter proceeds with introducing digital forensics in industrial control systems in terms of protecting critical infrastructure.

Join our book's Discord space

Join the book's Discord Workspace for Latest updates, Offers, Tech happenings around the world, New Release and Sessions with the Authors:

https://discord.bpbonline.com

CHAPTER 14
Introduction to Digital Forensics in Industrial Control Systems

Introduction

Digital transformation significantly influences multiple critical sectors such as energy, manufacturing, water treatment, and transportation. The adoption of digital forensics across **industrial control systems (ICS)** relates to their emergence as prime targets for cyber threats. The current chapter proceeds with a dedicated introduction to digital forensics across ICS in terms of protecting critical infrastructure. The chapter includes relevant details about vulnerabilities that can disrupt the functionality of ICS. Such disruption can result in adversely impacting the associated stakeholders of such critical sectors.

Structure

The chapter covers the following topics:

- Introduction to ICS and its vulnerabilities
- Digital forensics for protecting critical infrastructure
- Investigation standards and guidelines in digital forensics
- NIST Cybersecurity Framework
- NIST SP 800-61
- NIST SP 800-86

- NIST SP 800-53
- Digital forensics challenges and considerations
- Incident response and digital forensics workflow
- Case studies

Objectives

The current chapter introduces ICS and their associated vulnerabilities. The chapter states the overall importance of digital forensics in protecting critical infrastructure. The chapter presents an overview of investigation standards and guidelines in digital forensics. The chapter includes adequate details about the NIST **Cybersecurity Framework (CSF)** in terms of applying it to ICS. The chapter states the underlying provisions of the NIST CSF in terms of applying it to ICS. The chapter engages in a detailed analysis of NIST SP 800-61 as an effective computer security incident handling guide. The chapter proceeds with detailing NIST SP 800-86 as a guide to integrating forensic techniques into **incident response (IR)**. The chapter details NIST SP 800-53 in terms of security and privacy controls for federal information systems and organizations. The chapter relates to different digital forensics challenges and considerations in ICS. The chapter includes details about IR and digital forensics workflow for ICS. The chapter states multiple case studies that establish the importance of digital forensics for the smooth functionality of ICS.

Introduction to ICS and its vulnerabilities

The adoption of digital forensics in ICS environments is crucial to detecting, analyzing, and mitigating cyber incidents that can have severe operational and safety consequences. The sheer importance of digital forensics in ICS relates to protecting critical infrastructure from cyberattacks such as malware infections, insider threats, and state-sponsored attacks. Digital forensics identifies attack vectors, malicious activities, and compromised control system components. Digital forensics helps ensure compliance with industry regulations such as NERC CIP (for energy) and IEC 62443 (for industrial cybersecurity). The integration of digital forensics enhances IR and forensic readiness for mitigating operational disruptions. A forensic investigation in an energy plant identified malware (TRITON) designed to manipulate safety controllers, preventing a major disaster. ICS are critical components of modern infrastructure, managing essential processes in power grids, manufacturing, transportation, water treatment, and oil and gas industries. As ICSs become more interconnected, they face increasing cybersecurity threats, making digital forensics and IR crucial for protecting these systems. ICS refers to computer-based systems that monitor and control industrial processes. *(Figure 14.1)*

Figure 14.1: Industrial control systems

ICS traditionally prioritized reliability and availability over security, making them vulnerable to cyber threats. Its underlying components are stated as follows:

- **Supervisory Control and Data Acquisition (SCADA):** The SCADA controls large-scale industrial operations remotely. Power grids rely on SCADA systems for real-time control of electricity distribution. *(Figure 14.2)*

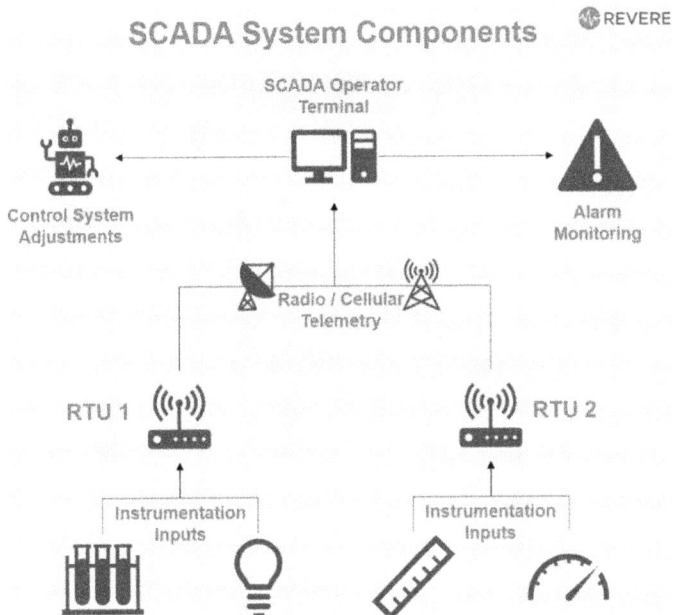

Figure 14.2: Overview of SCADA

- **Distributed Control Systems (DCS):** The DCS manages continuous production processes within plants.

- **Programmable Logic Controllers (PLC):** The PLC automates specific industrial tasks. *(Figure 14.3)*

Figure 14.3: Overview of Programmable Logic Controllers

- **Human-Machine Interfaces (HMI):** The HMI interfaces for operators to monitor system status. *(Figure 14.3)*

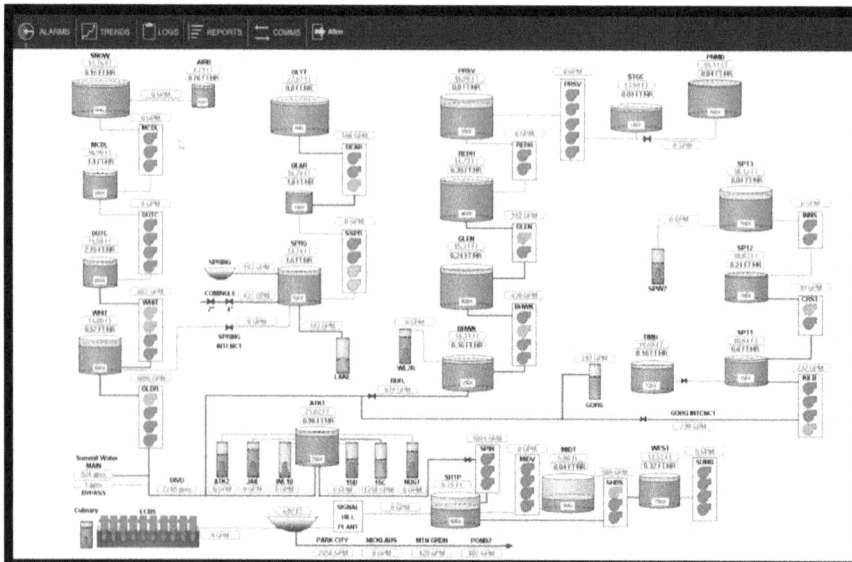

Figure 14.4: Human-Machine Interfaces

- **Remote Terminal Units (RTU)**: The RTU collects and transmits data from sensors. *(Figure 14.5)*

Figure 14.5: *Remote Terminal Units*

ICSs are increasingly targeted by cybercriminals due to legacy systems, lack of encryption, and remote connectivity. The vulnerabilities in ICS are stated as follows:

- **Legacy systems and outdated software:** The legacy systems and outdated software relate to multiple ICS components running decades-old software with no security updates. This implies that the vulnerabilities cannot be easily patched due to operational constraints. The TRITON malware attack exploited outdated safety controllers in an energy plant.

- **Lack of network segmentation:** The ICS often interconnects with corporate IT networks, exposing them to ransomware, phishing, and remote access threats. The Colonial Pipeline attack (2021) started as an IT breach but impacted ICS operations.

- **Weak authentication and default credentials:** The weak authentication and default credentials relate to multiple ICS using default or weak passwords, making them easy targets for brute-force attacks. The integration of **multi-factor authentication (MFA)** is often absent across such critical sectors. Attackers accessed a water treatment plant in Florida using a shared password on TeamViewer.

- **Industrial protocol vulnerabilities:** The relevant ICS protocols, such as Modbus, DNP3, and OPC UA, were designed for functionality and not for security. Many areas of critical sectors lack encryption and authentication, making them vulnerable to man-in-the-middle attacks. Attackers intercepted and modified Modbus traffic to manipulate PLC commands.

- **Supply chain attacks:** The ICS components from third-party vendors may contain pre-installed malware or backdoors. The SolarWinds attack allowed hackers to infiltrate ICS networks through compromised software updates.

The overall importance of ICS cybersecurity and forensics relates to the following aspects:

- **Incident response (IR):** The IR quickly identifies and contains threats in ICS environments.

- **Digital forensics:** The benefit of digital forensics lies in investigating ICS breaches through log analysis, network forensics, and malware reverse engineering.

- **Proactive security measures:** The proactive security measures relate to implementing firewalls, **Intrusion Detection Systems** (IDS), and network segmentation. *(Figure 14.6)*

ICS cybersecurity is evolving, with AI-driven anomaly detection, zero-trust security models, and industrial threat intelligence playing a key role.

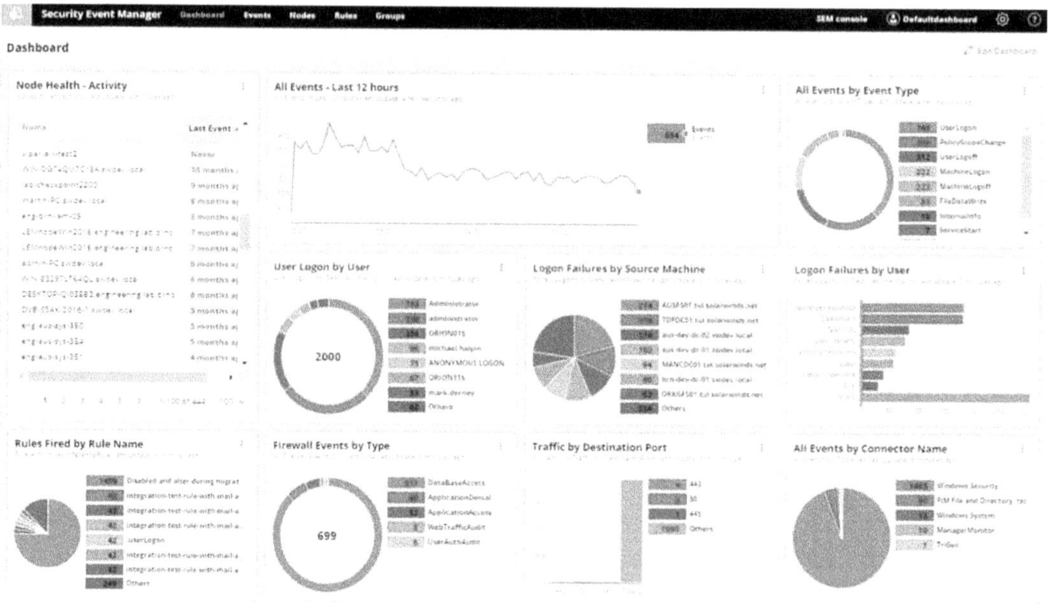

Figure 14.6: Intrusion Detection System

ICSs are foundational to critical infrastructure, but their vulnerabilities pose serious risks. Securing industrial environments and mitigating cyber threats relates to understanding ICS components, attack surfaces, and forensic investigation methods by digital forensic investigators.

Digital forensics for protecting critical infrastructure

Critical infrastructure is a prime target for cyber threats as it includes power grids, water treatment facilities, transportation networks, healthcare systems, and industrial plants. The role of digital forensics in protecting these essential systems has become more crucial as cyberattacks grow in sophistication and scale. Critical infrastructure relies on ICS, SCADA systems, and IoT devices, all of which have cybersecurity vulnerabilities. Attacks on these systems can lead to operational disruptions, economic losses, and threats to public safety. Digital forensics provides the ability to investigate, analyze, and prevent cyber incidents affecting these infrastructures. A cyberattack on Colonial Pipeline in 2021 disrupted fuel supplies across the U.S., highlighting the need for robust forensic capabilities.

Digital forensics helps identify breaches early by analyzing system logs, network traffic, and unauthorized access patterns. Digital forensics uses memory forensics, malware analysis, and event correlation to determine how an attack occurred. Digital forensics aids in containment and recovery by pinpointing compromised assets and restoring normal operations. Forensic investigation of the Industroyer malware attack on the power grid of Ukraine helped security teams understand how hackers manipulated ICS protocols.

The common threats to critical infrastructure are stated as follows:

- **Ransomware attacks:** The ransomware attacks relate to encrypting operational data and demanding a ransom, leading to downtime. The forensic analysis traces ransom demands, identifies malware signatures, and helps decrypt data. The WannaCry ransomware attack crippled hospitals and transportation systems worldwide, emphasizing the role of forensic analysis in tracing malware origins.

- **Nation-State and Advanced Persistent Threat (APT) attacks:** The Nation-State and APT attacks imply highly sophisticated attacks that target national security, utilities, and defense industries. Forensic analysis helps attribute attacks to threat actors and strengthens cyber defenses. Stuxnet (2010) targeted the nuclear centrifuges of Iran, demonstrating how digital forensics can uncover cyber espionage.

- **Insider threats:** Insider threats refer to employees or contractors who may intentionally or unintentionally cause security breaches. The forensic analysis detects unauthorized access, data leaks, and policy violations. Forensic evidence in a water treatment plant breach revealed an insider attempting to manipulate chemical levels remotely.

Digital forensics is a key pillar in defending critical infrastructure from cyber threats. The enabling of rapid detection, investigation, and mitigation of security incidents and forensic techniques helps ensure business continuity, public safety, and national security.

Investigation standards and guidelines in digital forensics

Digital forensic investigations require structured methodologies, legal compliance, and standardized procedures to ensure the integrity, admissibility, and accuracy of digital evidence. Various international and industry-specific standards provide a framework for conducting forensic examinations systematically. The importance of standards and guidelines in digital forensics relates to ensuring consistency and reliability in forensic investigations. They further extend to maintaining evidence integrity and admissibility in legal proceedings. Standards and guidelines in digital forensics establish best practices for data acquisition, analysis, and reporting. It helps investigators collaborate across jurisdictions and agencies. A forensic investigation following ISO/IEC 27037 guidelines ensures that evidence collection is valid for court use.

The key international standards for digital forensics are stated as follows:

- **ISO/IEC 27037:** This standard relates to the identification, collection, acquisition, and preservation of digital evidence. The standard defines best practices for handling digital evidence while ensuring integrity. The standard covers guidelines for **chain of custody (CoC)** and data preservation.

- **ISO/IEC 27042:** This standard relates to analyzing and interpreting digital evidence. The standard provides principles for examining and interpreting forensic data. Adherence to this standard ensures results are repeatable and scientifically valid.

- **ISO/IEC 27043:** This standard relates to relevant incident investigation principles that define the structure and flow of a digital forensic investigation. The standard further covers steps from incident detection to reporting and remediation.

- **NIST Special Publications (SP 800-86, SP 800-101):** This standard provides technical guidelines for forensic data collection, memory forensics, and mobile forensics. This standard helps law enforcement and corporate security teams to follow a systematic investigation approach. Specifically, NIST SP 800-101 outlines forensic methods for extracting data from mobile devices.

The relevant digital forensics methodologies are stated as follows:

- **Association of Chief Police Officers, UK (ACPO) guidelines:** This is a four-step forensic model for law enforcement investigations that restricts altering original digital evidence during analysis. These guidelines further encourage documenting all processes and actions taken. These guidelines ensure that qualified forensic experts handle evidence. The provision of this guideline relates to maintaining a clear audit trail for court presentations.

- **NIST Cybersecurity Framework (CSF):** This framework relates to providing a forensic roadmap under five phases in terms of identifying, protecting, detecting, responding, and recovering.

- **Locard's exchange principle in digital forensics:** This principle relates to any digital interaction leaving traces such as logs, metadata, and deleted files. This principle is used in forensic investigations to trace cybercriminals and reconstruct events. This principle helped investigators track hackers through hidden system logs in a financial fraud case.

Investigation standards and guidelines ensure structured, legally compliant, and scientifically valid digital forensic investigations. Adherence of companies to ISO, NIST, ACPO, and legal frameworks aids associated forensic professionals appropriately.

NIST Cybersecurity Framework

The NIST CSF is a widely recognized set of guidelines for managing cybersecurity risks. ICS, which operate critical infrastructure such as power plants, water treatment facilities, and manufacturing systems, require a tailored approach to cybersecurity due to their unique vulnerabilities and operational constraints. Applying the NIST CSF to ICS enhances threat detection, IR, and resilience against cyber threats. ICS plays a critical role in power grids, water treatment plants, manufacturing, and transportation. These systems face unique cybersecurity challenges, including outdated technology, limited security controls, and increasing cyber threats. The NIST CSF provides a structured approach to securing ICS environments by helping organizations identify, protect, detect, respond to, and recover from cyber threats.

ICSs are high-value targets for cyberattacks that can disrupt critical infrastructure. Many ICSs rely on legacy systems that lack built-in cybersecurity features. ICS prioritizes availability and reliability over security, requiring a balanced cybersecurity approach. This requires complying with industry regulations such as NERC CIP and IEC 62443, which aligns with NIST CSF principles. The Triton malware attack on a Saudi petrochemical plant (2017) highlighted the need for robust ICS cybersecurity.

The NIST CSF is developed by NIST to enhance cyber resilience. It provides a risk-based, adaptable approach for ICS to improve cybersecurity. It consists of five core functions: identify, protect, detect, respond, and recover. A power grid operator applying NIST CSF ensures continuous monitoring and rapid response to cyber threats. The importance of the NIST CSF for ICS relates to it being a high-value target for cyberattacks, leading to disruptions in critical infrastructure. Contrary to IT systems, ICS prioritizes availability and safety over security, requiring customized cybersecurity measures. ICS often uses legacy systems, unpatched software, and unsecured remote access, making them vulnerable. Compliance with NIST CSF improves risk management, regulatory adherence, and incident mitigation for ICS. The 2015 Ukrainian power grid attack exploited weak ICS security, demonstrating the need for NIST CSF adoption.

The core functions of NIST CSF and their application to ICS are detailed below:

- **Identify:** The function of identification relates to understanding risks and assets apart from mapping out critical ICS components such as SCADA, PLCs, HMIs, and sensors. This core function relates to conducting risk assessments to identify vulnerabilities. This function relates to developing an ICS asset inventory to track devices and software. A manufacturing plant using NIST CSF classifies PLCs as high-risk assets requiring additional security.

- **Protect:** This core function relates to implementing security controls apart from network segmentation to isolate ICS from IT networks. The use of MFA for remote access as a part of this function relates to enforcing patch management and endpoint security for ICS devices. A water treatment facility applies firewall rules to prevent unauthorized access to SCADA systems.

- **Detect:** This core function relates to monitoring for anomalies and threats and deploying IDS for real-time monitoring. The utilization of behavioral analytics and AI-driven anomaly detection is a part of this core function. This core function relates to continuously logging and auditing ICS network activity. The SIEM system of the power plant detects unauthorized PLC modifications, triggering an alert.

- **Respond:** The core function of responding relates to managing and mitigating incidents to develop an ICS-specific IR plan. This aids in conducting forensic analysis of cyber incidents for root cause identification. The outcome of this results in the implementation of automated threat containment mechanisms. A gas pipeline operator isolates an infected HMI during a cyberattack, preventing system-wide compromise.

- **Recover:** The core function of recovering relates to restoring systems after an attack. This is further to maintain ICS backup and recovery plans for operational continuity. The conduct of post-incident analysis is to improve security posture. The implementation of lessons learned from an incident relates to future cybersecurity improvements. A manufacturing plant restores compromised PLC configurations using offline backups.

Applying the NIST CSF to ICS strengthens cyber resilience, risk management, and IR for critical infrastructure. Following the identify, protect, detect, respond, and recover model, ICS operators can proactively defend against cyber threats while ensuring operational continuity.

NIST SP 800-61

NIST **Special Publication (SP)** 800-61 provides guidelines for IR planning, detection, analysis, containment, eradication, and recovery. It helps organizations build an effective IR capability to minimize damage, reduce recovery time, and strengthen cybersecurity resilience. NIST SP 800-61 in IR in terms of establishing best practices for managing security incidents. The application of NIST SP 800-61 during IR further ensures consistent and repeatable incident handling processes. The deployment of NIST SP 800-61 during IR helps organizations comply with cybersecurity regulations and standards. The integration of NIST SP 800-61 during IR reduces the impact of security incidents through efficient response and recovery. A financial institution successfully contained and mitigated a ransomware attack by following NIST SP 800-61 guidelines.

The key phases of incident handling in NIST SP 800-61 are stated as follows:

- **Preparation:** The phase of Preparation relates to building an **incident response plan (IRP)** in addition to developing an IR policy and team. This phase encourages implementing several security monitoring tools such as SIEM, IDS/IPS, and log management. This phase encourages conducting employee training and awareness programs. A healthcare provider creates an IR playbook for responding to phishing attacks.

- **Detection and analysis:** The phase of detection and analysis relates to identifying and investigating incidents by using security logs, IDS, and endpoint monitoring. This phase further categorizes incidents based on severity and impact. This phase encourages conducting forensic analysis to determine the root cause. A SOC team detects unusual traffic patterns, signaling a potential data breach.

- **Containment, eradication, and recovery:** This phase of containment, eradication, and recovery relates to limiting damage and restoring operations. The process of short-term containment relates to isolating compromised systems to prevent lateral movement. The process of eradication relates to removing malware, patching vulnerabilities, and closing existing security gaps. The phase of recovery relates to restoring systems from clean backups and verifying integrity. A retail company isolates infected POS systems after a credit card data breach.

- **Post-incident activity:** The post-incident activity relates to learning from the Incident by conducting a post-mortem analysis and documenting lessons learned. The phase further articulates updating IR policies to improve future handling. This phase encourages implementing new security measures to prevent similar incidents. A government agency revises its email filtering policies after a spear-phishing attack.

NIST SP 800-61 provides a structured approach to IR, ensuring organizations can quickly detect, contain, and recover from cyber incidents. With the effective following of its preparation, detection, containment, and post-incident analysis principles, critical sectors can strengthen their cyber resilience and minimize disruption.

NIST SP 800-86

NIST SP 800-86 provides a framework for incorporating digital forensic techniques into IR. Forensic investigations are crucial for identifying cyber threats, minimizing downtime, and ensuring operational continuity at the ICS. The application of NIST SP 800-86 encourages organizations to effectively collect, analyze, and preserve digital evidence while responding to security incidents in ICS environments. The benefit of this framework relates to providing a structured approach to forensic data collection, analysis, and reporting. This framework is essential for securing ICS and other critical infrastructure environments.

The importance of digital forensics in ICS IR relates to ICS networks being highly sensitive, as cybersecurity incidents can disrupt power grids, water treatment plants, and manufacturing lines. Thus, traditional forensic techniques must be adapted to real-time, always-on ICS environments. Contrarily, digital forensics emphasizes minimizing operational disruption while conducting investigations. The key phases of digital forensics, as per NIST SP 800-86, are stated as follows:

- **Collection**: The phase of the collection relates to identifying and acquiring relevant forensic data, such as logs, network traffic, and device memory, from relevant ICS components such as SCADA, PLCs, and RTUs.

- **Examination**: The phase of examination relates to processing collected data to extract relevant information while ensuring CoC.

- **Analysis**: The phase of analysis relates to identifying anomalies, correlating evidence, and determining the root cause of an incident.

- **Reporting**: The phase of reporting relates to documenting findings, recommending remediation steps, and ensuring compliance with regulatory frameworks.

The best practices for implementing NIST SP 800-86 in ICS relate to using passive forensics to avoid system disruption, such as network-based monitoring instead of direct system access. The assurance of continuous logging and SIEM solutions tailored for ICS can aid in relevant digital forensics investigations as per NIST SP 800-86. The integration of NIST SP 800-86 within ICS implies the development of IR playbooks specific to ICS environments. The assurance of digital forensic investigators having ICS-specific expertise beyond traditional IT security knowledge indicates adhering to the provisions of NIST SP 800-86.

NIST SP 800-86 provides a structured approach to integrating forensic techniques into IR, which is crucial for securing ICS and protecting critical infrastructure. Contrary to traditional IT environments, ICS requires specialized forensic methods due to its real-time operations, unique protocols, and system uptime requirements. This framework outlines four key phases of collection, examination, analysis, and reporting to ensure proper forensic investigations while maintaining system integrity.

NIST SP 800-53

The overview of NIST SP 800-53 resembles a comprehensive CSF developed by NIST to establish security and privacy controls for federal information systems. The integration of NIST SP 800-53 indicates providing a risk-based approach to selecting and implementing security controls. The NIST SP 800-53 is primarily designed for federal agencies, but it is widely adopted by critical infrastructure sectors, including ICS. The relevance of NIST SP 800-53 to ICS relates to ICS environments, including its underlying components, such as SCADA, DCS, PLCs, and other **operational technologies (OT)**, which tend to face unique cybersecurity risks. The integration of NIST SP 800-53 within the ICS offers tailored controls that can help mitigate threats such as ransomware, insider threats, and supply chain attacks. The relevance of NIST SP 800-53 with ICS ensures compliance with regulatory frameworks such as NERC CIP, ISA/IEC 62443, and DHS CISA guidelines. The key security control families within NIST SP 800-53 for ICS are stated as follows:

- **Access Control (AC):** The AC is the key security family that enforces strict authentication and least privilege access to ICS components.

- **Audit and Accountability (AU):** The AU is the key security family that ensures logging and monitoring of ICS network activity for forensic investigations.

- **Incident response (IR):** The IR is the key security function that is responsible for developing ICS-specific response plans and integrating forensic techniques.

- **System and Communications Protection (SC):** The SC is the key security family that secures ICS communication protocols such as Modbus and DNP3 and implements encryption in feasible areas.

- **System and Information Integrity (SI):** The SI is the key security family that indicates continuous monitoring and patch management to prevent cyber threats.

The relevant best practices for applying NIST SP 800-53 to ICS include the following:

- **Risk-based approach**: The risk-based approach is a best practice as it prioritizes security controls based on threat impact and operational criticality.

- **Segmentation strategies**: The segmentation strategies are the best practice as they implement network segmentation, such as the Purdue Model, to isolate ICS from external threats.

- **Zero Trust Architecture (ZTA)**: The ZTA is the best practice as it encourages adopting Zero Trust principles to limit unauthorized access and prevent lateral movement of threats.

- **Regular assessments and audits**: Regular assessments and audits are the best practice as they indicate conducting periodic vulnerability assessments to ensure compliance with evolving threats and regulations.

- **Training and awareness**: Training and awareness are the best practices as they relate to educating personnel on ICS-specific cyber threats and enforcing security best practices.

NIST SP 800-53 provides a structured approach to securing federal information systems, but its principles are highly applicable to ICS. It defines a risk-based control framework that addresses key security areas such as AC, IR, and system integrity. However, ICS environments present unique challenges, including legacy systems, operational constraints, and limited cybersecurity resources. The effective implementation of NIST SP 800-53 in ICS encourages an organization to focus on risk prioritization, network segmentation, Zero Trust principles, and continuous security assessments. The integration of these controls leads ICS operators to enhance resilience, prevent cyber threats, and protect critical infrastructure from emerging risks.

Digital forensics challenges and considerations

The application of digital forensics in ICS is essential for investigating cyber incidents and protecting critical infrastructure. The forensic process in ICS differs from traditional IT environments due to real-time operations, proprietary protocols, and system uptime requirements. The primary goal is to detect, analyze, and mitigate cyber threats while ensuring minimal disruption to industrial processes. The presence of legacy systems and limited built-in security features complicates forensic investigations. The relevant challenges in conducting forensic investigations imply that the real-time nature of ICS makes traditional forensic methods difficult, as systems cannot be easily shut down for investigation. Furthermore, the challenges expand to the use of proprietary ICS protocols such as Modbus, DNP3, and IEC 60870-5-104, limiting the effectiveness of standard forensic tools. The lack of comprehensive logging and auditing in legacy ICS devices makes evidence collection challenging. The volatility of ICS data leads to difficulties in preserving forensic evidence, as logs and memory states change rapidly. The need for compliance with regulatory frameworks such as NERC CIP, ISA/IEC 62443, GDPR, and CISA guidelines introduces additional constraints.

The relevant forensic considerations in an ICS include the use of passive forensic techniques, including network traffic monitoring, to help minimize system disruption. The collection and preservation of forensic artifacts such as controller logs, network captures, and memory dumps is crucial. Adherence to the CoC principles ensures the integrity and legal admissibility of forensic evidence. The integration of forensic capabilities into ICS-specific SIEM solutions enables real-time threat detection and analysis. The requirement for ICS cybersecurity expertise is critical, as traditional IT forensics training is often insufficient.

The relevant best practices for digital forensics in ICS include the development of forensic readiness plans to ensure ICS environments are prepared for cyber incidents. The implementation of continuous logging and centralized monitoring enhances visibility into security events. The collaboration between IT and OT security teams strengthens forensic investigations and response efforts. The use of air-gapped forensic analysis environments prevents contamination of live ICS networks during investigations. The periodic testing and refinement of forensic strategies ensures ICS forensic readiness evolves with emerging threats.

The digital forensics of ICS presents unique challenges due to real-time operational constraints, proprietary protocols, and limited forensic tools. The forensic investigation process must balance security and system availability, as ICS environments cannot afford downtime. The lack of comprehensive logging, volatile data, and compliance requirements further complicates evidence collection. The use of passive forensic techniques, strict CoC protocols, and ICS-specific SIEM solutions is essential for effective investigations. The adoption of forensic readiness plans, continuous monitoring, and IT-OT collaboration enhances the ability to detect, analyze, and respond to cyber threats in ICS environments.

Incident response and digital forensics workflow

The IR process in ICS must be tailored to minimize operational disruptions while addressing cyber threats. The integration of digital forensics into ICS IR enhances the detection, investigation, and remediation of security incidents. The real-time nature of ICS requires a well-coordinated IR strategy to avoid downtime or safety hazards. The key phases of IR in ICS are stated as follows:

- **Preparation:** The phase of preparation relates to the development of IRPs, forensic readiness strategies, and training programs tailored for ICS.

- **Detection and identification:** The detection and identification phase relates to the use of ICS-specific IDS, SIEM, and continuous monitoring to identify anomalies.

- **Containment:** The containment phase relates to the rapid isolation of affected systems to prevent lateral movement of threats while maintaining system availability.

- **Eradication:** The phase of eradication relates to the removal of malicious artifacts, backdoors, or vulnerabilities without disrupting ICS processes.

- **Recovery:** The phase of recovery relates to the restoration of affected systems with minimal downtime using backups, redundancy, and resilience planning.

- **Lessons learned:** The lessons learned phase relates to post-incident review to improve forensic techniques, update IR plans, and strengthen ICS security.

The relevant digital forensics workflows in ICS are as follows:

- **Evidence collection**: The evidence collection relates to the acquisition of critical forensic data such as controller logs, network captures, system memory, and endpoint artifacts.

- **Forensic analysis**: The phase of forensic analysis relates to the examination of logs, traffic patterns, and malware artifacts to determine attack vectors and root causes.

- **Chain of Custody (CoC)**: The CoC relates to the documentation and secure handling of forensic evidence to ensure legal admissibility.

- **Incident correlation**: The incident correlation relates to cross-referencing of collected forensic data with threat intelligence sources to identify attack patterns.

- **Reporting and documentation**: The phase of reporting and documentation relates to the generation of detailed reports outlining attack impact, forensic findings, and recommended mitigations.

The best practices for IR and forensics in ICS include the development of ICS-specific IR playbooks tailored to industrial processes and regulatory requirements. The implementation of continuous monitoring with network anomaly detection and forensic logging. The collaboration between IT and OT teams to create an effective, unified response strategy. The use of passive forensic techniques to gather evidence without impacting real-time processes. The regular testing of IR plans is to improve readiness and response efficiency.

The IR and digital forensics workflow for ICS must be carefully designed to balance security and operational continuity. The phased IR approach, including detection, containment, eradication, and recovery, ensures a structured response to security incidents. The forensic investigation process requires specialized tools, passive evidence collection, and strict CoC procedures. The adoption of ICS-specific IR playbooks, continuous monitoring, IT-OT collaboration, and proactive testing enhances the overall cybersecurity posture of industrial environments.

Case studies

The relevant case studies of digital forensics across ICS are detailed as follows:

- **Stuxnet (2010), The first ICS cyber weapon:** The overview of the attack implied that the Stuxnet worm was a highly sophisticated cyberattack targeting Iran's nuclear centrifuges at the Natanz facility. This malware exploited zero-day vulnerabilities and used PLC manipulation to alter centrifuge speeds, thereby causing physical damage. The attack remained undetected for months due to its ability to hide malicious activities from operators. The forensic investigation revealed multiple zero-day exploits and stolen digital certificates, indicating a Nation-State attack. The IR process included malware reverse engineering, which uncovered Modbus protocol manipulation within infected PLCs. The attack highlighted the need for ICS-specific monitoring tools since traditional IT security mechanisms failed to detect Stuxnet. The digital forensics investigation implied the importance of air-gapped security controls for critical ICS environments. This is further to the necessity of anomaly detection in PLC behavior and network traffic monitoring. The value of forensic analysis in uncovering complex multi-stage attacks on ICS is further correlated with the digital forensic outcome of this attack.

- **Ukraine Power Grid Attack (2015 and 2016), Targeted ICS Disruption:** The overview of the incident revealed that this 2015 cyberattack targeted Ukrainian power substations, causing a blackout for over 230,000 people. The concerned adversaries used BlackEnergy malware to gain access and remotely disable circuit breakers. The subsequent 2016 attack on the transmission network of Ukraine used Industroyer malware that directly manipulated IEC 104 and OPC protocols to disrupt grid operations. The forensic investigation traced the origin of the attack to spear-phishing emails, which deployed **Remote Access Trojans (RATs)**. The associated IR involved isolating infected systems, restoring manual control, and forensic reconstruction of malware behavior. The attack exposed weaknesses in operator awareness, network segmentation, and endpoint security. The outcome of the attack implied the overall importance of strong authentication and endpoint security for ICS operators. The need for network segmentation to prevent malware from spreading across industrial networks. The role of forensic analysis in identifying attack vectors and improving future response strategies.

Conclusion

The integration of digital forensics into ICS is essential for safeguarding critical infrastructure from cyber threats. The unique challenges of ICS environments, such as real-time operational constraints, proprietary protocols, and legacy systems, require specialized forensic techniques and IR strategies. The implementation of NIST guidelines (SP 800-86, SP 800-53) provides a structured approach to integrating forensics into CSFs, ensuring regulatory compliance and operational security. The exploration of key forensic challenges highlights the need for passive evidence collection, strict CoC protocols, and ICS-specific forensic tools. IR workflows must be tailored to industrial environments, balancing threat containment with operational continuity. Case studies, including Stuxnet and the Ukraine power grid attacks, illustrate real-world attacks that underscore the importance of forensic readiness, network segmentation, and IT-OT collaboration.

The upcoming chapter focuses on venturing into IoT forensics and thereby includes relevant details.

Join our book's Discord space

Join the book's Discord Workspace for Latest updates, Offers, Tech happenings around the world, New Release and Sessions with the Authors:

https://discord.bpbonline.com

CHAPTER 15

Venturing into IoT Forensics

Introduction

The rapid expansion of the **Internet of Things (IoT)** has revolutionized various industries, connecting billions of devices across homes, healthcare, transportation, industrial systems, and smart cities. However, the increasing reliance on IoT devices introduces new security vulnerabilities and forensic challenges, making IoT forensics a critical field in digital investigations. Contrary to traditional computing systems, IoT ecosystems involve a vast array of interconnected devices with diverse hardware, operating systems, and communication protocols. These complexities make data acquisition, evidence preservation, and forensic analysis more challenging for digital forensic investigators. Additionally, the limited storage, processing power, and transient data nature of many IoT devices further complicate forensic investigations. The current chapter explores the fundamentals of IoT forensics, including forensic challenges, methodologies, legal considerations, and real-world case studies. The chapter highlights best practices and tools for conducting forensic investigations across smart environments, ensuring that digital evidence from IoT devices, cloud services, and network logs is effectively collected and analyzed by digital forensic investigators.

Structure

The chapter covers the following topics:

- Understanding the significance of IoT forensics

- Exploring the IoT device landscape and technologies
- Investigating IoT architecture and communication protocols
- Mastering IoT forensic acquisition techniques
- Analyzing IoT traffic and communication
- Analyzing firmware, logs, and configuration data
- Real-world case studies
- Navigating privacy and legal considerations in IoT forensics
- Case studies

Objectives

The chapter begins with a detailed introduction that focuses on understanding the significance of IoT forensics. The chapter proceeds to explore the IoT device landscape and technologies. The chapter attempts a detailed investigation of IoT architecture and communication protocols. The chapter implies mastering IoT forensics in terms of acquisition techniques. The chapter implies analyzing IoT traffic and communication through network forensics. The chapter unveils the secrets within firmware, logs, and configuration data. The chapter includes real-world case studies in terms of detailed lessons learned from IoT forensic investigations. The chapter proceeds with navigating privacy and legal considerations in IoT forensics. The chapter includes relevant case studies to establish the importance of IoT forensics.

Understanding the significance of IoT forensics

The IoT is rapidly expanding across industries, including smart homes, healthcare, transportation, and industrial automation. *(Figure 15.1)*

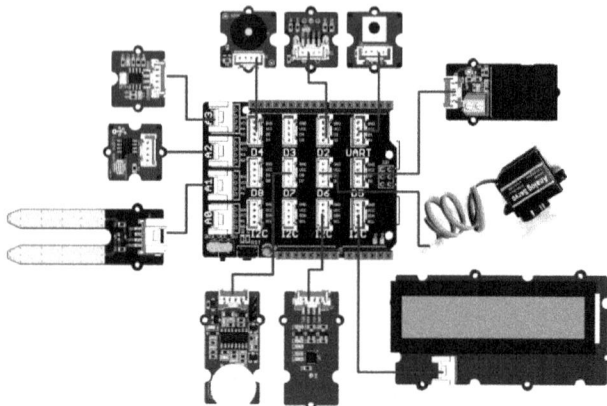

Figure 15.1: Internet of Things (IoT)

The increased interconnectivity of IoT devices generates massive volumes of data, which can serve as critical evidence in forensic investigations. The presence of IoT devices in cybercrime cases has made IoT forensics a crucial component of modern digital investigations. IoT devices are increasingly targeted in cyberattacks, fraud, and criminal activities, requiring forensic analysis to trace the associated threat actors. Digital forensic investigators can extract key digital evidence from IoT sensors, logs, and network data to reconstruct events in cybercrime, physical crimes, and fraud investigations. The overall volatile nature of IoT data, often stored in the cloud, volatile memory, or overwritten quickly, makes timely forensic intervention essential. The underlying challenges of IoT forensics include the following:

- **Diversity of IoT devices:** The IoT ecosystems involve various hardware, operating systems, and proprietary protocols, making standardized forensic procedures difficult.

- **Data volatility:** The data volatility resembles multiple IoT devices storing only limited data and thereby evidence can be lost due to frequent data overwriting or power loss.

- **Distributed data storage:** Distributed data storage relates to IoT data being stored in cloud environments, edge computing nodes, or remote servers, thereby complicating evidence collection.

- **Encryption and privacy concerns:** The encryption and privacy concerns relates to securing forensic access to IoT devices requires compliance with legal frameworks, privacy laws and data protection regulations.

The role of IoT forensics in cybercrime investigation relates to helping investigators analyze hacked IoT cameras, manipulated smart home devices, and compromised **Industrial IoT (IIoT)** systems. The Forensic analysis of IoT logs and network traffic assists in detecting data breaches, unauthorized access, and malware infections. IoT forensics plays a key role in critical infrastructure protection, ensuring the security of smart grids, industrial systems, and healthcare devices. The rise of **artificial intelligence (AI)** and **machine learning (ML)** in forensic automation will improve IoT evidence analysis. The adoption of blockchain-based security models for IoT devices could enhance forensic integrity. Stronger legal and regulatory frameworks will define best practices and compliance requirements for IoT forensic investigations.

Exploring the IoT device landscape and technologies

The IoT consists of interconnected smart devices that collect, process, and exchange data. IoT devices operate in diverse environments, including smart homes, healthcare, industrial automation, and critical infrastructure. The architecture of IoT includes edge devices (sensors, actuators), gateways, cloud platforms, and data analytics systems. The different categories of IoT devices are stated as follows:

- **Consumer IoT:** The consumer IoT relates to wide range of smart home devices such as smart locks, thermostats, cameras and wearables.

- **Industrial IoT (IIoT):** The IIoT includes sensors, robotic systems, SCADA devices, and smart grids. *(Figure 15.2)*

Figure 15.2: Sensors

- **Healthcare IoT:** The healthcare IoT relates to medical implants, remote patient monitoring systems, and smart insulin pumps.

- **Smart cities:** The smart cities include traffic management systems, smart lighting, and environmental monitoring.

- **Automotive IoT:** The automotive IoT relates to connected vehicles, fleet tracking **vehicle-to-vehicle (V2V)** communication.

The key technologies powering IoT devices include the following:

- **Communication protocols:** The communication protocols relate to IoT devices using specific protocols like MQTT, CoAP, Zigbee, Z-Wave, **Bluetooth Low Energy (BLE)**, NFC, and 5G.

- **Cloud and edge computing:** Cloud and edge computing relate to IoT, relying on cloud platforms (AWS IoT, Microsoft Azure IoT, and Google Cloud IoT) for data storage and processing. *(Figure 15.3)*

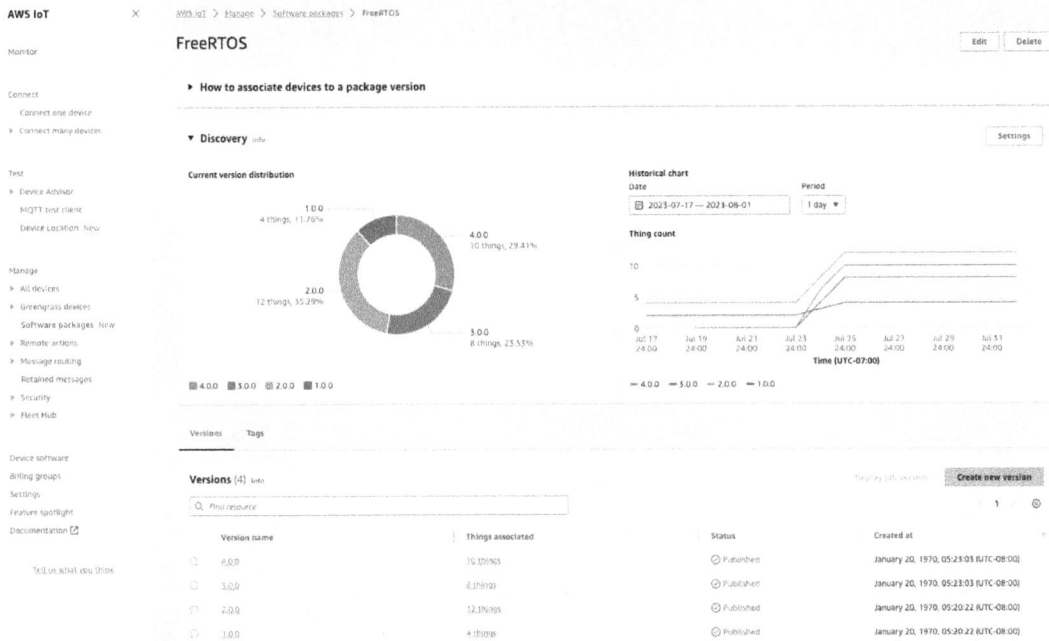

Figure 15.3: *Interface of AWS IoT*

Edge computing enables local data processing to reduce latency.

- **Security technologies:** The security technologies include IoT security mechanisms, including encryption, authentication protocols, blockchain, and Zero Trust security models.

- **AI and ML:** The AI/ML helps in predictive analytics, anomaly detection, and automated threat mitigation in IoT systems.

Forensic investigators need specialized tools to extract data from varied hardware, firmware, and communication protocols. Understanding IoT communication patterns by digital forensic investigators is essential for analyzing network traffic, detecting anomalies, and tracing cyber incidents. Cloud forensics and edge forensics play a key role in retrieving and preserving digital evidence from distributed IoT ecosystems. The IoT landscape consists of diverse devices, communication protocols, and computing technologies that make forensic investigations more complex. Forensic experts must adopt specialized tools and methodologies to extract digital traces from IoT devices, cloud platforms, and network logs.

Investigating IoT architecture and communication protocols

The architecture and communication protocols of IoT devices play a crucial role in how data is collected, transmitted, and processed within an IoT ecosystem. Understanding these components is essential for forensic investigators seeking to analyze digital evidence from IoT networks. IoT systems are built on a multi-layered architecture and consist of the following components:

- **Perception layer (Device layer):** The perception layer includes sensors, actuators, RFID tags, cameras, and embedded devices to collect data.

- **Network layer:** The network layer facilitates communication between devices using Wi-Fi, Bluetooth, Zigbee, LoRa, 5G, and LPWAN protocols.

- **Edge layer:** The edge layer performs local data processing on IoT gateways or edge servers to reduce latency before sending data to the cloud.

- **Cloud/processing layer:** The cloud/processing layer stores, processes, and analyses IoT data using platforms such as AWS IoT, Google Cloud IoT, and Microsoft Azure IoT. *(Figure 15.4)*

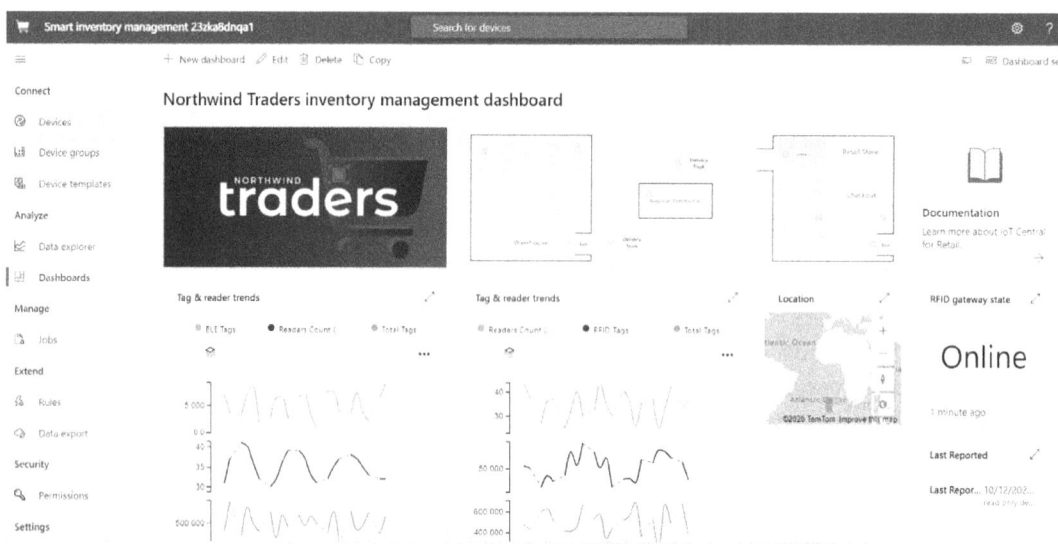

Figure 15.4: Interface of Azure IoT

- **Application layer:** The application layer provides user interfaces, mobile applications, and AI-based analytics for IoT system management.

IoT devices rely on a variety of communication protocols depending on range, power consumption, and use cases. The communication protocols in IoT include the following:

- **Short-range communication protocols:** These protocols are BLE, Zigbee, Z-Wave and **Near Field Communication** (**NFC**). BLE is used in wearables, medical devices and smart home appliances for low-power wireless communication. The usage of Zigbee and Z-Wave is common in smart home automation systems for low-power and mesh-network communication. The NFC is used for contactless payments and access control systems.

- **Medium to long-range protocols:** The medium to long-range protocols include Wi-Fi, cellular (3G, 4G, 5G), and **Low Power Wide Area Network** (**LoRaWAN**). The Wi-Fi protocol is common in home and office IoT networks but has higher power consumption than other protocols. The cellular (3G, 4G, 5G) is used for IoT applications requiring mobility, such as connected cars and IIoT. The LoRaWAN is used in smart cities and environmental monitoring due to its long-range and low-power capabilities.

- **IoT-specific messaging protocols:** The IoT-specific messaging protocols include **Message Queuing Telemetry Transport** (**MQTT**), **Constrained Application Protocol** (**CoAP**), and **Open Platform Communications Unified Architecture** (**OPC UA**). MQTT is a lightweight messaging protocol used for low-bandwidth IoT communication. The CoAP is designed for resource-constrained IoT devices, enabling low-power communication over networks. The OPC UA is used in industrial automation and SCADA systems for secure and standardized communication.

The investigative approaches for IoT forensics are the following:

- **Packet capture and traffic analysis:** The **packet capture** (**PCAP**) and traffic analysis monitor network traffic logs to trace IoT device activities and detect anomalies. *(Figure 15.5)*

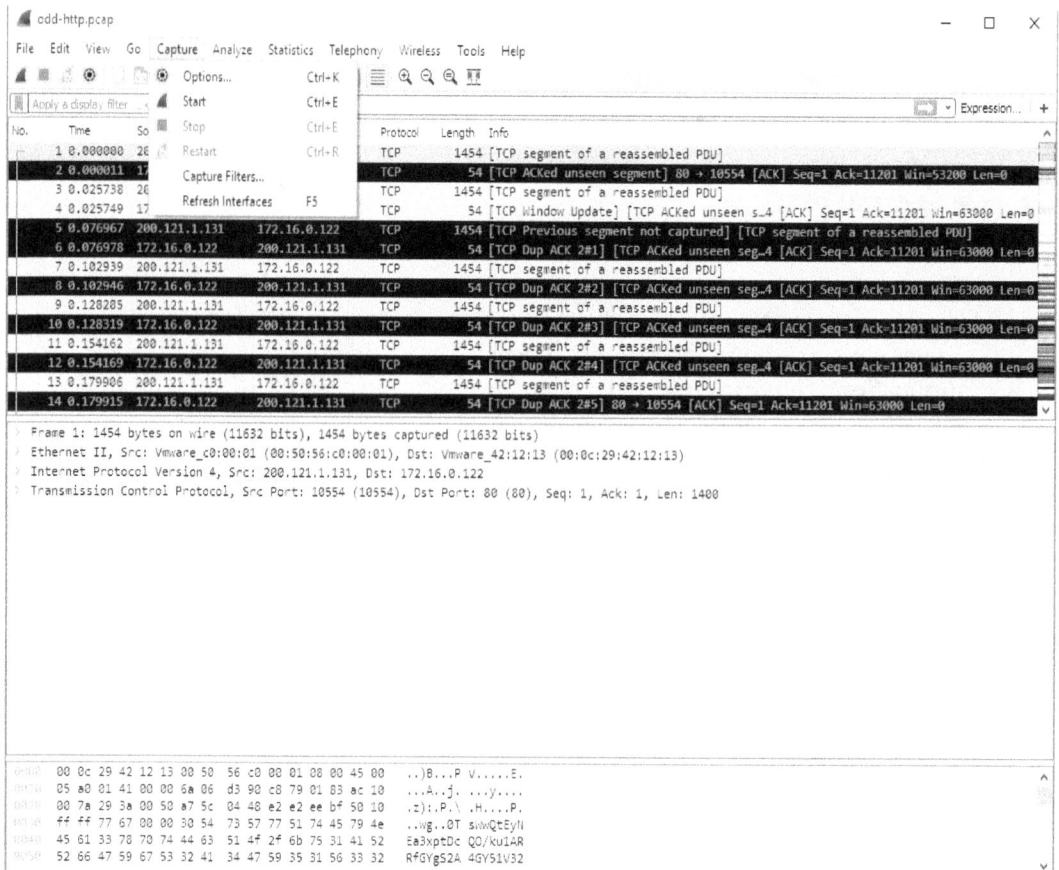

Figure 15.5: Packet capture

- **Log analysis:** The log analysis investigates device logs, gateway logs, and cloud storage records to reconstruct events.

- **Reverse engineering IoT firmware:** The reverse engineering of IoT firmware extracts data from IoT device firmware and embedded systems to retrieve forensic artifacts.

- **Cloud forensics:** Cloud forensics accesses IoT cloud platforms to retrieve stored data, logs, and access records.

IoT forensics requires a deep understanding of IoT architectures and communication protocols to effectively analyze device behavior and extract evidence. The diversity of network layers, messaging protocols, and data storage mechanisms introduces challenges in forensic investigations. Forensic investigators must leverage network analysis, log extraction, and cloud forensics to reconstruct cyber incidents and ensure the integrity of IoT-based evidence.

Mastering IoT forensic acquisition techniques

The acquisition of digital evidence from IoT devices is a fundamental step in forensic investigations. Contrary to traditional computing systems, IoT environments involve diverse hardware, real-time data transmission, and distributed storage across edge and cloud platforms, thereby making forensic acquisition more complex. IoT forensic acquisition involves retrieving data from physical devices, network traffic, and cloud storage, each requiring specialized tools and methodologies. However, challenges such as data encryption, volatile memory, and proprietary device architectures often limit direct access to forensic evidence. The progress of IoT forensics relates to collecting data from a variety of digital evidence. Identifying where data is stored and how it is transmitted is crucial for forensic acquisition. The relevant types of digital evidence are listed as follows:

- **IoT devices:** The IoT devices include smart cameras, wearables, and industrial sensors.

- **Network infrastructure:** Network infrastructure includes routers, gateways, and firewalls.

- **Cloud platforms:** Cloud platforms are the areas where IoT data is stored remotely.

- **Mobile applications:** The mobile applications and web dashboards control IoT devices.

The various types of IoT data acquisition methods are listed as follows:

- **Physical acquisition:** This acquisition method relates to direct extraction from IoT device memory using hardware interfaces such as JTAG, UART, and SPI. The physical acquisition is suitable for embedded devices and proprietary hardware.

- **Logical acquisition:** The collecting files, logs and system data through software-based access such as SSH, ADB for Android-based IoT. The provides access to user data, logs, and configurations without modifying the device.

- **Network traffic acquisition:** Network traffic acquisition relates to capturing real-time data packets using network sniffers such as Wireshark, Zeek, or tcpdump. The tool helps to track device communications, unauthorized access and cyberattacks.

- **Cloud acquisition:** This acquisition method proceeds with extracting logs, user activity and stored data from cloud services including AWS, Google Cloud and Microsoft Azure IoT. This type of acquisition requires legal authorization and compliance with cloud provider policies.

The following tools are used for IoT forensic acquisition:

- **Firmware extraction:** Tools such as Binwalk, JTAGulator, and FTK Imager aid in firmware extraction. *(Figure 15.6)*

```
DECIMAL        HEXADECIMAL        DESCRIPTION
- - - - - - - - - - - - - - - - - - - - - - - - - - - - - - - - - - - - - - - - - - - - - - - - -
7383740        0x70AABC           Certificate in DER format (x509 v3), header
                                  length: 4, sequence length: 1643
16068292       0xF52EC4           CRC32 polynomial table, little endian
16069628       0xF533FC           SHA256 hash constants, little endian
16097980       0xF5A2BC           Microsoft executable, portable (PE)
16100092       0xF5AAFC           Microsoft executable, portable (PE)
16101556       0xF5B0B4           Microsoft executable, portable (PE)
16104484       0xF5BC24           Microsoft executable, portable (PE)
16106780       0xF5C51C           LZMA compressed data, properties: 0x5D,
                                  dictionary size: 16777216 bytes, uncompressed
                                  size: 9542 bytes
```

Figure 15.6: *Interface of Binwalk*

- **Network forensics:** The tools, such as Wireshark, Zeek, and Nmap encourage network forensics. *(Figure 15.7)*

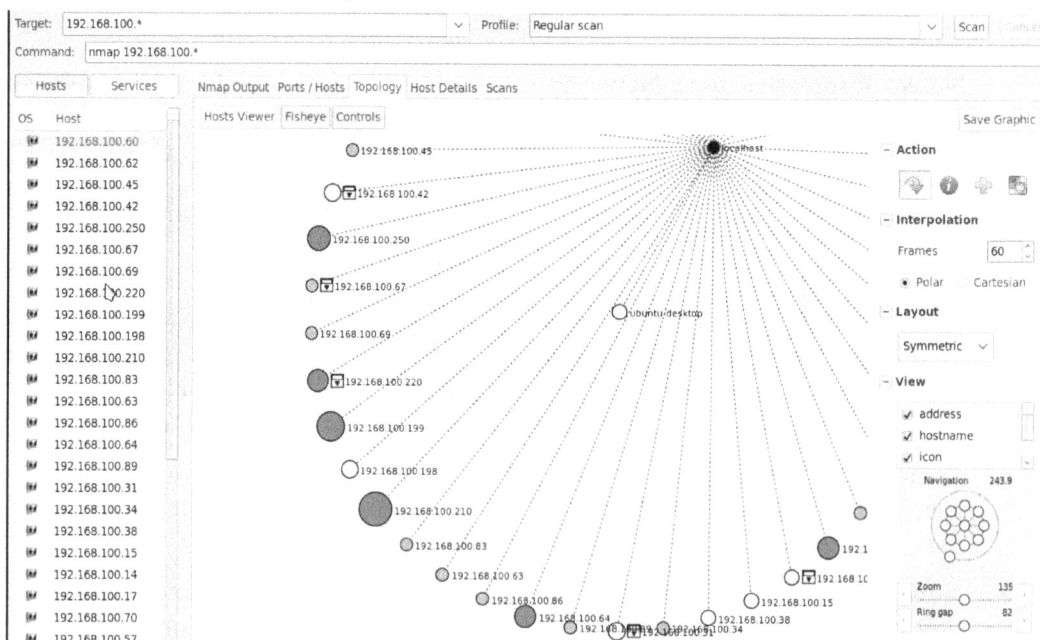

Figure 15.7: *Interface of Nmap*

- **Cloud forensics:** Tools such as AWS CloudTrail, Google Cloud Logging, and Magnet AXIOM encourage cloud forensics.

- **Mobile and IoT analysis:** The tools including Autopsy, Cellebrite UFED, and IoTInspector aids in mobile and IoT analysis.

IoT forensic acquisition involves retrieving data from devices, networks, and cloud environments using specialized tools and techniques. Challenges such as device heterogeneity, encryption, and volatile data require forensic investigators to adopt customized acquisition strategies. The effective mastering of physical, logical, network, and cloud acquisition methods encourages forensic professionals to effectively collect and preserve digital evidence from IoT environments.

Analyzing IoT traffic and communication

The analysis of IoT network traffic is a crucial aspect of forensic investigations, as IoT devices constantly exchange data over wired and wireless networks. Contrary to traditional computing environments, IoT ecosystems involve diverse communication protocols, real-time data transmissions, and cloud-based interactions, making network forensics both challenging and essential. IoT devices rely on continuous data exchange over various network protocols, making network forensics crucial for monitoring, detecting anomalies, and collecting digital evidence. Cyberattacks, unauthorized access, and data breaches in IoT ecosystems can often be traced through network traffic analysis. Forensic investigators analyze PCAP, communication logs, and encrypted transmissions to reconstruct cyber incidents.

The key IoT network traffic analysis techniques include the following:

- **Packet capture and Deep Packet Inspection (DPI):** The requirement of PCAP and DPI implies multiple tools such as Wireshark, Zeek, and tcpdump that help capture real-time traffic for forensic analysis. These tools identify malicious traffic, unauthorized connections, and device communications.

- **Log and metadata analysis:** The requirement of log and metadata analysis relates to examining firewall logs, router logs and **Security Information and Event Management (SIEM)** alerts to detect security incidents. This analytical technique provides insights into failed authentication attempts, unusual traffic spikes and botnet activity.

- **Anomaly detection and intrusion analysis:** The anomaly detection and intrusion analysis relates to several AI-driven forensic techniques used by the Digital Forensic Investigators such as ML models to detect IoT-specific threats such as **Distributed Denial of Service (DDoS)** attacks and Ransomware. The associated behavioral analysis can identify compromised IoT devices communicating with malicious servers.

The associated tools for IoT network forensics include the following:

- **Wireshark and Zeek:** Wireshark and Zeek aid in PCAP and deep network analysis.

- **Nmap and Shodan:** Nmap and Shodan aid in scanning IoT devices for vulnerabilities.

- **Suricata and Snort:** Suricata and Snort can be used as intrusion detection for detecting IoT threats.

- **Elasticsearch and Splunk:** Elasticsearch and Splunk act as SIEM solutions for analyzing IoT network logs.

IoT network forensics plays a critical role in tracking cyber incidents, detecting malicious activities, and preserving forensic evidence. Investigators must analyze PCAPs, network logs, and anomalies while overcoming challenges such as encrypted traffic and protocol diversity. With the effective leveraging of advanced forensic tools and AI-driven analysis, professionals can effectively monitor, investigate, and secure IoT environments.

Analyzing firmware, logs, and configuration data

Firmware, logs, and configuration files are critical forensic artifacts that store device settings, security policies, and operational data. Investigating these components helps uncover device compromises, unauthorized modifications, malware injections, and security misconfigurations. These elements provide insights into system operations, user interactions, and potential vulnerabilities exploited in cyberattacks.

Extracting and analyzing IoT firmware relates to firmware being the backbone of IoT devices, containing the operating system, applications, and embedded security controls. The relevant methods of firmware acquisition include:

- **Direct extraction:** The process of direct extraction relates to using JTAG, UART, or SPI interfaces for low-level access.

- **Over-the-Air (OTA) updates:** The process of OTA Updates relates to capturing firmware updates sent to the device.

- **File system analysis:** The process of file system analysis relates to extracting firmware images using forensic tools.

The key tools for firmware analysis include the following:

- **Binwalk:** Binwalk is a tool that extracts and analyzes firmware file structures.

- **Ghidra and IDA Pro:** Ghidra and IDA Pro are reverse-engineering firmware for malware detection.

- **Firmwalker:** Firmwalker scans for security vulnerabilities in firmware.

Logs serve as a timeline of device activities, network connections, and security events. The different types of IoT Logs for forensic analysis relate to the following:

- **System logs:** The system logs relate to document firmware updates, crashes, and error messages.

- **Authentication logs:** The authentication logs relate to recording login attempts and failed authentication events.

- **Network logs:** The network logs relate to capturing device communication patterns and suspicious traffic.

- **Cloud logs:** The cloud logs store remote access records and interactions with cloud platforms.

The different log analysis tools are listed here:

- **Splunk and Elasticsearch, Logstash, Kibana Stack (ELK):** The Splunk and ELK relate to log aggregation and anomaly detection.

- **Graylog:** Graylog is an open-source log management tool for forensic auditing.

- **Wireshark:** Wireshark examines network logs for unusual traffic.

Configuration files dictate how IoT devices operate, manage security settings, and handle data storage. Specifically, misconfigured settings can lead to weak authentication mechanisms, such as default passwords and open ports. This is apart from unsecured remote access, such as exposed SSH, Telnet, or API keys, and a lack of encryption in data transmissions. The forensic techniques for configuration analysis relate to extracting config files from embedded devices using forensic tools. This is apart from comparing default vs. modified configurations to detect unauthorized changes. The appropriateness of relevant forensic techniques relates to identifying malicious scripts or hidden backdoors in configuration files. Firmware, logs, and configuration data provide valuable forensic evidence that can reveal cyber intrusions, unauthorized modifications, and system vulnerabilities in IoT devices. Investigators must use specialized tools and techniques to extract, analyze, and interpret these components while overcoming challenges like encryption, tampering, and proprietary formats.

Real-world case studies

The relevant real-world case studies implying learning lessons from IoT forensic investigations are provided here:

- **Mirai Botnet Attack (2016):** The Mirai botnet infected hundreds of thousands of IoT devices, including IP cameras and routers, to launch massive DDoS attacks. The attackers exploited default credentials and weak security settings in IoT devices. The relevant forensic investigation and findings relate to IoT forensic analysts identifying malware signatures in firmware and network traffic logs. The digital forensic investigators analyzed **command-and-control (C2)** Traffic using tools like Wireshark and Zeek. The reverse-engineered Mirai malware was used to understand propagation techniques. The lessons learned from this incident relate to the importance of changing default passwords and disabling unnecessary services. This is apart from the need for real-time IoT network monitoring and anomaly detection.

- **Stuxnet Worm Targeting Industrial IoT (2010):** Stuxnet was a sophisticated malware designed to sabotage Iran's nuclear centrifuges by exploiting IIoT systems. It spread via USB drives and targeted Siemens PLCs. The relevant forensic investigation and Findings imply that investigators analyze malicious firmware updates and PLC logs to trace the attack. The investigation related to using firmware reverse-engineering tools such as IDA Pro and Ghidra to deconstruct malware. The investigation discovered zero-day vulnerabilities in **industrial control systems** (**ICS**). The investigation revealed the need for air-gapped security in critical infrastructure. The investigation focused on the importance of firmware integrity checks and behavioral anomaly detection.

Navigating privacy and legal considerations in IoT forensics

IoT forensics involves collecting, analyzing, and preserving digital evidence from interconnected devices, often containing sensitive personal or corporate data. Legal and privacy concerns arise due to data ownership, consent, and cross-jurisdictional challenges in forensic investigations. Compliance with regional and global regulations is essential to ensure the admissibility of evidence and the ethical handling of personal data. The key legal frameworks impacting IoT Forensics include the following:

- **General Data Protection Regulation (GDPR) (EU):** This legal framework emphasizes on data protection, user consent and right to privacy in forensic investigations. This legal framework requires forensic teams to minimize data collection and anonymize sensitive information.

- **California Consumer Privacy Act (CCPA) (US):** This framework grants consumers the right to know, access, and delete personal data, affecting IoT forensic data retention.

- **Electronic Communications Privacy Act (ECPA) (US):** This framework restricts unauthorized interception of electronic communications, including IoT device transmissions.

- **Computer Fraud and Abuse Act (CFAA) (US):** This framework criminalizes unauthorized access to IoT networks and computing systems, impacting forensic investigations.

The best practices for privacy-conscious IoT forensics are stated as follows:

- **Obtaining proper legal authorization:** The aspect of obtaining proper legal authorization always ensures court approval or organizational consent before conducting forensic analysis.

- **Following data minimization principles:** The following data minimization principles relate to collecting only the necessary forensic data to avoid privacy violations.

- **Ensuring secure evidence handling:** The assurance of Secure Evidence Handling relates to using tamper-proof storage, access logs, and encryption to protect forensic data integrity.

- **Staying updated with legal and regulatory changes:** The target of staying updated with legal and regulatory changes relates to keeping track of new cybersecurity laws, data protection policies and compliance frameworks that are relevant to IoT investigations.

IoT forensic investigations must balance security, privacy, and legal compliance while handling sensitive data. Investigators face challenges in data access, jurisdictional conflicts, and evidence integrity, requiring adherence to privacy laws and forensic best practices. The effective integration of legal expertise, ethical forensic methods, and data protection measures encourages forensic professionals to navigate the complexities of IoT investigations while ensuring lawful evidence collection.

Case studies

The relevant case studies are detailed here:

- **Amazon Ring Camera Breaches (2019-2020):** Attackers gained unauthorized access to Ring security cameras, spying on homeowners and even harassing individuals. Weak security practices, such as reusing passwords and a lack of **multi-factor authentication** (**MFA**), led to breaches. The digital forensic investigators examined access logs and cloud storage metadata to track unauthorized logins. The digital forensic investigators used relevant log analysis tools such as Splunk and Graylog to detect compromised accounts. The course of the investigation indicated that credentials were leaked in dark web forums due to credential stuffing attacks. The outcome of the digital forensic investigation revealed the importance of MFA and strong password policies for IoT devices. The investigation further indicated the need for continuous monitoring of IoT authentication logs.

- **Smart Car Hacking (Jeep Cherokee, 2015):** Security researchers remotely took control of a Jeep Cherokee's braking and acceleration system via vulnerabilities in its infotainment system. The attack exploited a weakly secured Uconnect system, allowing hackers to send malicious commands over the CAN bus network. The forensic investigation and findings relate to analyzing vehicle log data and network traffic for remote access traces. The investigation revealed underlying zero-day vulnerabilities in the telemetry and control systems of the car. The course of investigation revealed the usage of CAN bus forensic tools such as ICSim and Kayak to replicate and analyze attack vectors. The detailed analysis of the investigation revealed the need for stronger encryption in in-vehicle communication protocols.

Conclusion

The rapid expansion of IoT technologies has introduced both opportunities and challenges in the field of digital forensics. The increasingly integrated nature of IoT devices results in their presence in personal, industrial, and critical infrastructure environments, encouraging forensic professionals to develop specialized methodologies to investigate security incidents effectively. As IoT technology continues to advance, the field of IoT forensics must evolve accordingly, integrating AI, ML, and automated forensic tools to enhance investigative capabilities.

The upcoming chapter focuses on setting up digital forensics labs and tools.

Join our book's Discord space

Join the book's Discord Workspace for Latest updates, Offers, Tech happenings around the world, New Release and Sessions with the Authors:

https://discord.bpbonline.com

CHAPTER 16
Setting Up Digital Forensics Labs and Tools

Introduction

The establishment of a well-equipped digital forensics lab is essential for conducting efficient, reliable, and legally admissible investigations. A properly structured lab provides forensic analysts with the necessary tools, infrastructure, and security controls to examine digital evidence while maintaining integrity, **chain of custody (CoC)**, and compliance with legal standards. Understanding the capabilities and limitations of these tools enables forensic professionals to select the most suitable solutions for different types of digital evidence and investigative scenarios. The current chapter focuses on the detailed steps of setting up digital forensics labs and tools.

Structure

The chapter covers the following topics:

- Understanding the importance of digital forensics labs
- Designing and planning a digital forensics lab
- Hardware and software requirements
- Setting up workstations and servers in the lab
- Network infrastructure for digital forensics investigations

- Forensic imaging tools and equipment
- Data storage and backup solutions
- Mobile device forensics tools and equipment
- Forensic analysis software and tools
- Network forensics tools and appliances
- Open source and commercial tools for digital forensics

Objectives

The current chapter focuses on understanding the importance of digital forensics labs. The chapter proceeds with designing and planning a digital forensics lab. The chapter includes relevant hardware and software requirements for a digital forensics lab. The chapter indicates setting up workstations and servers in the lab. The chapter details network infrastructure for digital forensics investigations. The chapter indicates forensic imaging tools and equipment. The current chapter proceeds with stating data storage and backup solutions for digital forensics labs. The current chapter lists mobile device forensics tools and equipment. The chapter indicates forensic analysis software and tools. The chapter lists network forensics tools and appliances. The chapter states different open-source and commercial tools for digital forensics.

Understanding the importance of digital forensics labs

A dedicated forensic lab ensures that digital evidence is analyzed in a controlled and secure setting, reducing the risk of tampering, contamination, or data loss. The forensic lab provides isolation from external networks to prevent unauthorized access or malware contamination during investigations. Forensic labs follow standardized procedures to maintain the CoC, ensuring that evidence remains legally admissible in the Court of Law. The required compliance with regulatory standards such as ISO/IEC 17025, NIST guidelines, and GDPR ensures the integrity of forensic findings.

A well-structured lab provides specialized hardware and software tools to streamline data acquisition, analysis, and reporting. Such labs further encourage forensic teams to process large volumes of digital evidence efficiently, thereby improving incident response times. Digital forensics labs cater to various investigative needs, including cybercrime investigations, corporate fraud, insider threats, and national security cases. Digital forensics labs can be tailored for specialized forensic disciplines, such as mobile forensics, IoT forensics, cloud forensics, and memory forensics. Efficient investigations help reduce case backlogs, improve response times, and ensure timely legal action. Several factors contribute to enhancing efficiency within a digital forensics lab, including advanced tools, standardized workflows, automation, and skilled personnel. A forensic lab is equipped with high-performance forensic workstations designed to handle large datasets, high-speed processing, and advanced cryptographic analysis. Specialized forensic software suites allow investigators to quickly extract and analyze digital evidence from various devices. These forensic software suites include EnCase, Autopsy, FTK, and X-Ways Forensics. The use of dedicated forensic duplicators and write-blockers ensures that data is acquired in a forensically sound manner without modifying the original evidence.

Digital forensics labs can act as a hub for forensic research and skill development, allowing digital forensic investigators to test new forensic methodologies, tools, and techniques. Digital forensics labs provide a structured environment for law enforcement agencies, academic institutions, and cybersecurity professionals to train in real-world forensic scenarios. The successful establishment of a forensic lab ensures adherence to best practices, frameworks, and legal mandates for conducting digital investigations. The presence of a well-equipped forensic lab helps organizations avoid legal pitfalls by ensuring forensic processes align with industry-recognized compliance standards.

A digital forensics lab is the backbone of modern forensic investigations, providing a secure, efficient, and legally compliant environment for analyzing digital evidence. With the effective integration of cutting-edge forensic tools, rigorous protocols, and skilled professionals, forensic labs play a crucial role in solving cybercrimes, mitigating security threats, and upholding justice.

Designing and planning a digital forensics lab

Setting up a digital forensics lab requires careful planning, infrastructure design, and resource allocation to ensure effective investigations, evidence preservation, and compliance with legal and security standards. A well-structured lab provides forensic investigators with the necessary environment, tools, and protocols to analyze digital evidence systematically. The establishment of a digital forensics lab relates to having clearly defined objectives. The relevant objectives include law enforcement investigations, corporate incident response, academic research, and cybersecurity threat analysis. The lab will focus on specific forensic disciplines such as computer forensics, mobile forensics, cloud forensics, or IoT forensics. The digital forensics lab can serve as a dedicated facility or operate as a portable or remote forensics setup for field investigations.

Selecting a secure and access-controlled facility ensures that digital evidence is protected from unauthorized access, theft, or tampering. The effective prevention of hardware damage relates to implementing environmental controls such as temperature regulation, dust-free zones, and **Electrostatic Discharge (ESD)** protection. The progress of uninterrupted forensic operations relates to the lab being equipped with high-speed network connectivity, sufficient power supply, and data backup solutions.

The effective establishment of security and access controls relates to implementing strict access controls, allowing only authorized forensic personnel to enter the lab. This is further to using biometric authentication, surveillance cameras, and **Intrusion Detection Systems (IDS)** to secure the facility. The establishment of secure evidence storage with lockable cabinets, fireproof safes, and offsite backup solutions for preserving forensic data integrity. The selection of hardware and software for forensic analysis at the lab relates to equipping the lab with high-performance forensic workstations capable of processing large datasets, disk images, and encrypted files. The process of evidence acquisition relates to utilizing specialized forensic hardware such as write blockers, forensic duplicators, and portable forensic kits. Contextually, the installation of the following tools relates to setting up the digital forensics lab:

- **Disk and file forensics:** Disk and file forensics relates to EnCase, Autopsy, FTK, and X-Ways.

- **Mobile forensics:** The tools for mobile forensics include Cellebrite UFED, MOBILedit, and Magnet AXIOM.

- **Memory and malware analysis:** The memory and malware analysis relates to using Volatility, Rekall, and Cuckoo Sandbox.

- **Cloud forensics:** Effective cloud forensics includes AWS CloudTrail, Google Takeout, and Azure Security Center.

Designing and planning a digital forensics lab requires a strategic approach, considering security, infrastructure, hardware, software, and compliance requirements. A well-equipped lab enhances investigative efficiency, ensures evidence integrity, and enables forensic teams to handle complex cyber incidents. Effectively adhering to legal standards, implementing strong security measures, and fostering continuous learning, organizations can create a forensically sound environment that supports modern cybercrime investigations and digital forensic research.

Hardware and software requirements

A digital forensics lab must be equipped with specialized hardware and software tools to effectively acquire, analyze, and preserve digital evidence. The selection of these resources depends on the scope of forensic investigations, the types of cases handled, and the volume of digital evidence processed.

The essential hardware components include:

- **Forensic workstations:** The forensic workstations imply high-performance computers designed for data processing, disk imaging, and forensic analysis. These are equipped with multi-core processors, large RAM (32GB or more), high-speed SSDs, and GPU acceleration for faster forensic processing.

- **Write blockers (hardware and software):** The write blockers in both hardware and software forms prevent accidental modification of evidence by allowing read-only access to storage devices. The well-known write blockers include Tableau T8-R2, CRU WiebeTech USB WriteBlocker, and OpenText Blocker.

- **Forensic duplicators and imaging devices:** Forensic duplicators and imaging devices are used to create bit-by-bit forensic images of hard drives, SSDs, USB devices, and SD cards. These include Logicube Falcon, Tableau TD3, and Atola Insight Forensic.

- **Storage solutions for evidence preservation:** The high-capacity RAID/NAS/SAN storage servers for long-term storage of forensic images and case data. The benefit of these storage solutions for evidence preservation includes secure, encrypted external hard drives for portable evidence storage.

- **Mobile device forensic tools:** Mobile device forensic tools resemble dedicated tools for extracting data from iOS, Android, and other mobile devices. The relevant tools include Cellebrite UFED, MSAB XRY, and Oxygen Forensics Suite. *(Figure 16.1)*

Figure 16.1: Imaging of mobile devices

- **Network forensic equipment:** The network forensic equipment includes packet-capturing devices for analyzing network traffic, detecting intrusions, and identifying malicious activity. The relevant examples in this regard include Wireshark, Zeek (formerly Bro), and Arkime (formerly Moloch).

- **Live forensics and memory analysis tools:** The tools for capturing RAM and volatile data for malware detection, insider threats, and incident response. These tools include Volatility, Rekall, and Magnet RAM Capture.

- **Hardware for IoT and embedded device forensics:** The relevant hardware for IoT and embedded device forensics includes the devices that interface with IoT devices, smart appliances, and ICS. The relevant tools include JTAG adapters, Chip-Off tools, Bus Pirate, and Shikra.

- **Secure evidence storage and physical security:** Secure evidence storage and physical security relate to fireproof safes, access-controlled lockers, and evidence bags to securely store seized devices. The surveillance systems and biometric access control are used to ensure effective lab security.

The essential software tools for digital forensics include the following:

- **Disk and file forensic software:** These are used for disk imaging, file system analysis, and deleted file recovery. The concerned tools are listed below:

  o **EnCase (OpenText):** This is an industry-standard forensic tool.

  o **Autopsy (Sleuth Kit):** This is an open-source forensic analysis suite.

  o **Forensic Toolkit (FTK):** This is a fast indexing and case management tool.

  o **X-Ways forensics:** This is a lightweight but powerful forensic suite. *(Figure 16.2)*

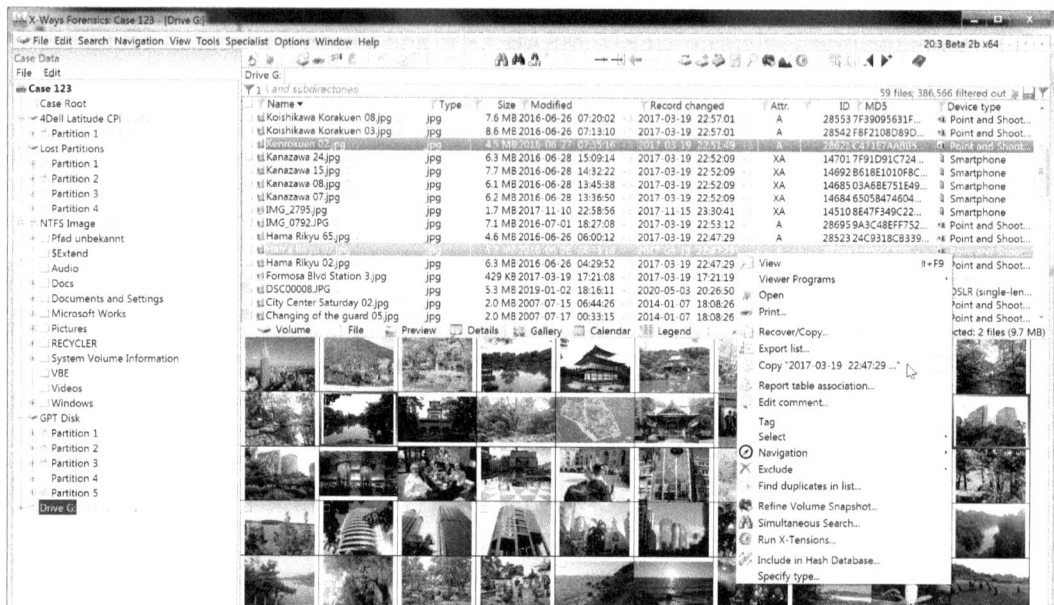

Figure 16.2: Interface of X-Way forensics

- **Mobile device forensics software:** Mobile device forensics software is used for data extraction, decryption, and analysis of smartphones and tablets. The concerned tools are listed here:

  o **Cellebrite UFED:** This tool is an industry-leading mobile forensics tool.

  o **MSAB XRY:** This tool is used for mobile forensic analysis and report generation.

  o **Magnet AXIOM:** This tool is used as a unified forensic tool for mobile, cloud, and computer forensics.

- **Network and cloud forensic tools:** The network and cloud forensic tools capture and analyze network traffic, cloud logs, and intrusion data. The relevant tools are listed below:

- o **Wireshark:** This is a tool for effective network packet analysis.

- o **Zeek (formerly Bro):** This is a tool for effective network security monitoring.

- o **AWS CloudTrail, Google Takeout, and Microsoft Azure Security Center:** These tools are used for effective cloud forensics.

- **Memory and malware analysis tools:** These tools are used for analyzing volatile memory (RAM), malware behavior, and rootkits. The relevant examples include:

  - o **Volatility:** This is an open-source memory forensics framework.

  - o **Rekall:** This is a memory forensics and incident response tool.

  - o **Cuckoo Sandbox:** This is an automated malware analysis.

- **Log analysis and SIEM tools:** These tools are used for examining system logs, security logs, and event monitoring records. The relevant examples include the following:

  - o **Splunk:** Log analysis and threat detection.

  - o **Graylog:** Open-source SIEM solution.

  - o **Elasticsearch, Logstash, Kibana (ELK Stack):** Log correlation and visualization.

- **Hashing and data integrity tools:** These tools are used to verify evidence integrity using cryptographic hashing. The relevant examples include the following:

  - o MD5, SHA-1, SHA-256 Hash Calculators

  - o Hashdeep, FTK Imager

- **Steganography and hidden data detection:** This tool attempts to detect hidden or obfuscated data within images, audio, and files. The relevant tools in this category include the following:

  - o **StegExpose**: This tool detects LSB steganography in images.

  - o **OutGuess, OpenStego**: These are steganography detection tools used by digital forensic investigators.

- **Cloud and IoT forensics software:** The cloud and IoT forensics software relates to extracting and analyzing forensic data from cloud storage and IoT ecosystems. The relevant examples include the following:

  - o **Magnet AXIOM Cloud:** This tool aids digital forensic investigators in cloud data extraction.

  - o **AWS CloudTrail:** The AWS CloudTrail relates to forensic logging for AWS environments.

  - o **IoT inspector:** The IoT inspector is a forensics tool for IoT traffic analysis.

Setting up workstations and servers in the lab

A well-designed digital forensics lab requires properly configured workstations and servers to handle intensive forensic investigations, data processing, and secure evidence storage. The setup must ensure high performance, data integrity, and security while supporting multiple forensic disciplines, such as computer, network, mobile, and cloud forensics. The workstation requirements for digital forensics are stated here:

- **Selecting high-performance hardware:** The selection of high-performance hardware includes the following factors:

    o **Processor:** The selection of multi-core CPUs such as Intel i9, Xeon, or AMD Ryzen Threadripper is crucial for fast data processing.

    o **RAM:** The minimum RAM requirement is 32GB, and preferably 64GB or more for handling large forensic images and memory dumps.

    o **Storage:** The selection of adequate storage in terms of the following factors is crucial for setting up workstations and servers in the digital forensics lab:

        ▪ **NVMe SSD (1TB or more):** This storage is ideal for fast forensic data processing.

        ▪ **HDD (4TB or more):** This storage is ideal for evidence storage.

        ▪ **RAID-configured storage:** This storage is ideal for redundancy and data integrity.

    o **Graphics Processing Unit (GPU):** A high-end NVIDIA or AMD GPU is crucial for password cracking and accelerated forensic analysis.

    o **Multiple monitors:** The presence of multiple monitors in terms of dual or triple-screen setups is ideal for multitasking forensic tasks.

- **Operating system considerations:** The following **operating systems (OS)** can be considered for digital forensic analysis:

    o **Windows 10/11 Professional:** This OS is compatible with most forensic tools such as FTK, EnCase, and X-Ways.

    o **Linux (Ubuntu, Kali, SIFT Workstation):** These OSs are used for open-source forensic tools and security analysis.

    o **macOS (For Apple Forensics):** This OS is essential for investigating Mac devices.

    o **Virtualization software (VMware, VirtualBox, Hyper-V):** This software solution is suitable for analyzing malware and running forensic simulations.

- **Essential forensic software and tools:** The essential forensic tools are as follows:
  - **Disk imaging tools:** The relevant disk imaging tools include FTK Imager, EnCase, and Autopsy.
  - **Memory analysis tools:** The relevant memory analysis tools include Volatility and Rekall.
  - **Mobile forensics tools:** The relevant mobile forensics tools include Cellebrite UFED and Oxygen Forensics.
  - **Network forensics tools:** The relevant network forensics tools include Wireshark and Zeek.
  - **Cloud forensics tools:** The relevant cloud forensics tools include Magnet AXIOM Cloud and AWS CloudTrail.
  - **Password recovery tools:** The relevant password recovery tools include Hashcat and John the Ripper.
  - **Forensic analysis suites:** The appropriate forensics analysis suites include X-Ways Forensics, Autopsy, and Magnet AXIOM.

The setting up of forensic servers relates to the following:

- **Server role in a digital forensics lab:** The role of a server in a digital forensics lab includes centralized evidence storage and case management. It supports multi-user collaboration for forensic teams. It hosts database-driven forensic tools such as Splunk, ELK Stack, and Magnet REVIEW.

- **Hardware requirements for servers:** The hardware requirement for servers relates to the following areas:
  - **Processor:** Dual Xeon or AMD EPYC processors are suitable for high-end forensic computing.
  - **Memory (RAM):** Approximately 128GB or more of RAM is suitable for handling multiple forensic workloads.
  - **Storage:** The aspect of Storage relates to the following:
    - **RAID 5/6/10 configurations:** This configuration is ideal for redundancy and speed.
    - **NAS/SAN solutions:** This solution is ideal for centralized forensic evidence storage.
    - **Encrypted external drives:** The encrypted external drives are suitable for long-term evidence preservation.
    - **Network interface:** The selection of 10GbE network adapters is suitable for fast data transfer.

- o **Server software and tools:** The relevant server software and tools include the following:

  - **Case management systems:** The case management systems include Magnet REVIEW and Cellebrite Pathfinder.

  - **Forensic data management:** Forensic data management relates to tools such as X1 Social Discovery and Paladin.

  - **Network monitoring and logging:** The requirement of network monitoring and logging relates to tools such as Zeek, Splunk, and Graylog.

  - **Secure backup solutions:** The secure backup solutions include Veeam and Acronis Cyber Protect.

  - **Cloud forensics support:** The cloud forensics support includes AWS, Azure, and Google Cloud security tools.

Setting up workstations and servers in a digital forensics lab is crucial for efficient data acquisition, analysis, and evidence management. High-performance hardware, specialized forensic tools, secure storage solutions, and strong access controls ensure the integrity and reliability of forensic investigations. A well-structured lab setup enables investigators to handle large volumes of digital evidence, conduct multi-layered forensic analysis, and support collaborative case management in compliance with legal and cybersecurity standards.

Network infrastructure for digital forensics investigations

A robust network infrastructure is essential for digital forensics labs to facilitate secure evidence collection, analysis, and collaboration while maintaining the integrity of forensic data. Properly designed network infrastructure ensures efficient data transfer, centralized logging, remote forensic analysis, and secure access controls.

The key components of a network infrastructure in a forensics lab include the following:

- **Secure forensic network architecture:** The Isolated forensic network (Air-Gapped or VLAN) is relevant to prevent external threats. The separate subnets are used for forensic analysis, evidence storage, and administrative tasks. The **Intrusion Detection and Prevention Systems (IDS/IPS)** are used to monitor unauthorized activity. The dedicated VPN and remote access solutions are ideal for secure forensic investigations.

- **High-speed networking equipment:** The high-speed networking equipment relates to 10GbE or higher network switches for fast data transfers. This is apart from opting for a fiber-optic backbone for high-speed forensic data exchange.

The extensive use of load balancers relates to optimizing forensic application performance. The network segmentation is ideal for separating forensic workstations, evidence storage, and analysis servers.

- **Centralized log management and SIEM solutions:** The centralized log management and SIEM solutions relate to **Security Information and Event Management** (**SIEM**) for monitoring forensic activities. The relevant examples include Splunk, ELK Stack, and Graylog. Contextually, the Syslog servers collect logs from forensic workstations and servers.

- **Secure data storage and backup solutions:** The secure data storage and backup solutions relate to using **Network-Attached Storage** (**NAS**) or **Storage Area Network** (**SAN**) for centralized evidence storage. The relevant RAID-configured storage solutions are suitable for redundancy and reliability. Contextually, the cloud-based forensic storage solutions are suitable for off-site evidence backups. The automated backup policies is used to prevent data loss.

The network forensics capabilities in a forensic lab are as follows:

- **Network packet capture and analysis:** Network packet capture and analysis relate to the following tools:

  o **Wireshark, Zeek (Bro), and TCPDump:** These tools are used for real-time traffic analysis.

  o **Deep Packet Inspection (DPI) tools:** These tools are ideal for detecting hidden threats.

- **Traffic monitoring and anomaly detection:** The requirement of traffic monitoring and anomaly detection relates to the following tools:

  o **Network Behavior Analysis (NBA) tools:** These tools are ideal for detecting malicious traffic. The relevant examples include SolarWinds, NetFlow, and PRTG network monitor.

A well-structured network infrastructure is a critical component of any digital forensics lab, enabling secure and efficient evidence acquisition, storage, and analysis. The effective implementation of isolated forensic networks, high-speed data transfer solutions, centralized log management, and secure access controls encourages investigators in the integrity and confidentiality of forensic data. Additionally, integrating network forensics tools enhances the capability of the digital forensics lab to monitor traffic, detect anomalies, and trace cyber threats effectively. As digital forensics continues to evolve, maintaining a resilient and adaptable forensic network infrastructure will be crucial for addressing modern cybersecurity challenges.

Forensic imaging tools and equipment

Forensic imaging is a critical first step in digital investigations, ensuring that an exact, bit-by-bit copy of digital evidence is preserved for analysis while maintaining the integrity of the original data. Proper forensic imaging tools and equipment help investigators acquire data from hard drives, **solid-state drives** (**SSDs**), mobile devices, network storage, and volatile memory without altering or corrupting the evidence. The process of forensic imaging relates to maintaining data integrity through cryptographic hashing such as MD5, SHA-1, and SHA-256. The aspect of forensic imaging relates to preventing contamination of digital evidence by ensuring write-protected acquisitions. Forensic imaging allows the safe analysis of digital evidence without modifying the original source. Forensic Imaging supports legal admissibility by preserving metadata and timestamps. The different types of forensic imaging are stated here:

- **Disk imaging (Full Bit-by-Bit Copy):** This process creates an exact replica of a storage device, including deleted and unallocated space. The common formats include EnCase (E01), Raw Image (DD), and **Advanced Forensic Format** (**AFF**). The relevant tools include FTK Imager, EnCase, X-Ways, dd, and Guymager.

- **Live memory (RAM) imaging:** This process relates to capturing volatile data from RAM, including running processes, encryption keys, and open network connections. The relevant tools used include Magnet RAM Capture, Volatility, and Belkasoft Live RAM Capturer.

- **Mobile device imaging:** The process of mobile device imaging relates to extracting full logical or physical copies of smartphones and tablets. The relevant tools used include Cellebrite UFED, Oxygen Forensics, and Magnet GrayKey.

- **Cloud storage and virtual machine imaging:** Cloud storage and **virtual machine** (**VM**) imaging relate to capturing evidence from cloud services such as AWS, Google Drive, and OneDrive. This process acquires forensic images of VMs used in cloud environments. The relevant tools used include Magnet AXIOM Cloud, AWS CloudTrail, and FTK Imager for VMs.

The essential forensic imaging tools include the following:

- **Software-based imaging tools:** The relevant software-based imaging tools include the following:

- **FTK imager:** The FTK imager creates forensic disk images, and verifies integrity.

- **Autopsy and Sleuth Kit:** The Autopsy and Sleuth Kit are open-source forensic imaging and analysis toolsets.

- **X-Ways forensics:** X-Ways forensics is an advanced forensic imaging and evidence extraction.

- **Guymager:** The Guymager is a Linux-based imaging tool with high-speed acquisition.

- **Magnet AXIOM:** The Magnet AXIOM is an imaging and analysis tool for multiple digital sources.

- **Hardware-based imaging tools:** The relevant hardware-based imaging tools include the following:

    o **Tableau Forensic Duplicators (TX1, TD4, TD3):** Tableau Forensic Duplicators (TX1, TD4, TD3) aids in standalone forensic disk imaging.

    o **Logicube Falcon Neo:** Logicube Falcon Neo is a high-speed imaging system with multiple hashing algorithms.

    o **Ditto DX Forensic Duplicator:** Ditto DX Forensic Duplicator supports imaging of encrypted and damaged drives.

Forensic imaging tools and equipment play a vital role in digital forensics by ensuring accurate and legally admissible evidence acquisition. The choice of software-based or hardware-based imaging solutions depends on the type of media, speed requirements, and security considerations. The following best practices, such as using write blockers, verifying hashes, and maintaining CoC, encourage forensic investigators to safeguard the integrity of digital evidence and conduct thorough investigations.

Data storage and backup solutions

Digital forensics labs handle large volumes of sensitive data, including forensic images, case files, and investigative reports. Ensuring secure, scalable, and redundant storage is essential to maintain data integrity, prevent loss, and comply with legal and regulatory requirements. Effective backup solutions further protect against hardware failures, cyber threats, and accidental deletions. Storage solutions must support high-volume forensic images (in terabytes per case). Capacity and Scalability further relate to preferring scalable architectures such as SAN or NAS. Reliable cloud-based forensic storage options can provide on-demand scalability. The concept of data integrity and security relates to **write-once, read-many** (**WORM**) storage that prevents tampering of evidence. The application of Encryption techniques such as AES-256 and TLS ensures data confidentiality. The deployment of relevant access control mechanisms, such as RBAC and MFA, restricts unauthorized access. The implementation of techniques such as hashing and checksums, such as MD5 and SHA-256, verifies data integrity. The high-speed access and performance relate to SSDs and NVMe storage for faster forensic analysis. This is apart from relevant RAID configurations such as RAID 5, RAID 6, and RAID 10 for redundancy and performance. This is further to the connection of dedicated forensic workstations via 10GbE or fiber-optic networks for efficient data transfer.

The relevant backup strategies for digital forensics labs are stated here:

- **On-site backups:** This relates to using redundant storage systems (RAID, NAS, and SAN) for immediate access. This further extends to automated backup scheduling to reduce manual errors. The deployment of air-gapped backup servers results in additional security.

- **Off-site and cloud backups:** The cloud-based forensic backup solutions (AWS S3, Azure, Google Cloud) are used for disaster recovery. Cold storage (tape backups, offline disks) is used for long-term archival. The usage of hybrid cloud storage results in balancing cost and accessibility effectively.

- **Incremental vs. full backups:** Full backups capture entire forensic datasets but require more storage. The Incremental backups store only changed data, optimizing space. The versioning and snapshot capabilities ensure data recovery options.

- **Compliance and CoC preservation:** The Backup logs and metadata tracking are beneficial for forensic audit trails. The relevant legal compliance with NIST, ISO 27040, and GDPR is beneficial for data handling. The immutable storage options are used to prevent unauthorized modifications.

The appropriate storage solutions are stated here:

- **Synology NAS, QNAP NAS**: The Synology NAS, QNAP NAS a scalable NASs.

- **Dell EMC Isilon and NetApp FAS**: The Dell EMC Isilon and NetApp FAS an enterprise-grade forensic storage.

- **Veritas NetBackup and IBM Spectrum Protect**: The Veritas NetBackup and IBM Spectrum Protect resemble high-performance backup solutions.

The backup and disaster recovery tools are as follows:

- **Veeam backup and replication:** The Veeam backup and replication are associated with VM and cloud backups.

- **Acronis cyber backup:** The Acronis cyber backup implies secure forensic data protection.

- **AWS Glacier and Google Vault:** AWS Glacier and Google Vault a cost-effective long-term storage.

A well-planned data storage and backup strategy is critical for forensics labs to ensure data integrity, security, and accessibility. The implementation of scalable storage solutions, secure access controls, and multi-tiered backup strategies encourages forensic teams to safeguard critical evidence against data loss, cyber threats, and compliance violations. The relevant investment in redundant, encrypted, and legally compliant storage solutions ensures that forensic investigations remain efficient, reliable, and legally defensible.

Mobile device forensics tools and equipment

Mobile devices play a crucial role in digital forensic investigations, containing valuable evidence such as call logs, messages, emails, GPS data, app data, and multimedia files. Extracting and analyzing this data requires specialized forensic tools and equipment that can handle different OSs, encryption mechanisms, and data recovery challenges while preserving evidence integrity. The mobile device forensics indicates that Android, iOS, Windows, and legacy mobile OSes require platform-specific forensic approaches. However, the process of Device fragmentation in terms of varied manufacturers, hardware, and OS versions complicates data extraction. The relevant data acquisition challenges include Encrypted storage, such as file-based encryption and full-disk encryption, that restricts access. Furthermore, locked devices and passcode protections prevent direct forensic analysis. Cloud storage and remote wiping can erase evidence before extraction. The associated legal and compliance issue relates to search warrants and legal permissions that are necessary before the acquisition of digital evidence. The associated data privacy laws, such as GDPR, CCPA, CFAA, and ECPA, regulate mobile forensics practices. The CoC documentation ensures that the evidence is admissible in the Court of Law.

The relevant mobile forensic acquisition techniques include the following:

- **Logical acquisition:** This acquisition technique extracts accessible data such as contacts, messages, call logs, and media. Such an acquisition technique is less intrusive but does not recover deleted or hidden files. The associated tools include Cellebrite UFED, Oxygen Forensic Detective, and Magnet AXIOM.

- **Physical acquisition:** This acquisition technique relates to creating a bit-by-bit copy of the entire device memory, including deleted data. The process requires specialized hardware and bypassing encryption/security mechanisms. The associated tools include GrayKey (for iOS), JTAG and Chip-Off techniques, and MSAB XRY.

- **Cloud forensics:** This tool extracts data from cloud backups such as Google Drive, iCloud, and OneDrive. The application of this tool requires legal authorization and credentials for access. The associated tools include Elcomsoft Cloud eXplorer and Magnet AXIOM Cloud.

- **SIM and SD card analysis:** This tool retrieves deleted texts, contacts, and network logs from SIM cards. The tool extracts multimedia files, documents, and hidden data from SD cards. The associated tools include SIM Analyzer and Belkasoft Evidence Center.

The essential mobile forensics tools include the following:

- **Commercial mobile forensics tools:** The Cellebrite UFED is an Industry-leading tool for extracting data from mobile devices. The GrayKey is an advanced iOS forensic tool for password bypass and data extraction. The MSAB XRY supports logical and physical extractions from various devices. The Oxygen Forensic Detective resembles a comprehensive tool for app analysis and cloud forensics.

- **Open-source and free mobile forensics tools:** The **Android Debug Bridge (ADB)** extracts app data, logs, and system information from Android devices. The Autopsy with mobile modules is an open-source forensic suite supporting mobile data analysis. The Magnet AXIOM Free Edition is the Basic version of Magnet AXIOM for preliminary mobile analysis. The **Linux Memory Extractor (LiME)** captures live memory from Android devices for forensic analysis. The iLEAPP and ALEAPP are the tools that extract and analyze applications and log data from iOS and Android devices.

The best practices for mobile device forensics include ensuring legal authorization before performing any forensic acquisition. The use of Faraday bags and isolation tools prevents remote access or tampering with data. The list of best practices further relates to always creating a forensic image first before analyzing the device. The effective verification of extracted data integrity relates to using cryptographic hashes such as SHA-256 and MD5. The best practices further relate to documenting the CoC to maintain evidence admissibility. Mobile device forensics is a complex but essential part of digital investigations, requiring specialized tools and techniques to handle diverse OSs, encryption challenges, and data acquisition methods.

Forensic analysis software and tools

Forensic analysis software and tools play a crucial role in identifying, extracting, and analyzing digital evidence from various sources, including computers, mobile devices, networks, and cloud environments. These tools help forensic investigators conduct in-depth data examinations, recover deleted files, trace cybercrimes, and ensure legal compliance while preserving evidence integrity. Forensic analysis tools are required to be accurate and reliable as they must extract evidence without altering original data. The forensic analysis tools require supporting hash verification, such as MD5 and SHA-256, to ensure integrity. The forensic analysis tools are required to comply with industry standards such as NIST and ISO 27037. The multi-platform compatibility aspect of forensic analysis tools relates to supporting Windows, Linux, macOS, and specific mobile OSes such as Android and iOS. The tools required to analyze data from physical, virtual, and cloud environments.

The relevant categories of forensic analysis tools are listed as follows:

- **Disk and file system forensics:** This relates to extracting and analyzing deleted files, partitions, and metadata. This is apart from recovering corrupt, hidden, and encrypted data from storage devices. The popular tools include the following:

  o **Autopsy and Sleuth Kit:** The Autopsy and Sleuth Kit are open-source forensic suites for effective disk analysis.

  o **X-Ways forensics:** X-Ways forensics is an advanced disk and memory forensics tool.

  o **EnCase Forensic:** EnCase Forensic is an industry-standard tool for deep file system analysis.

- **Memory and live system forensics:** This category of forensic tools implies extracting RAM dumps, running processes, and volatile data from live systems.

These tools further help in the investigation of malware infections, rootkits, and cyber intrusions. The well-known tools in this regard are listed here:

- o **Volatility framework:** The volatility framework is an open-source tool for RAM analysis.

- o **Rekall:** Rekall is a memory forensics tool for extracting volatile data.

- o **Belkasoft RAM Capturer:** The Belkasoft RAM Capturer captures live system memory for forensic analysis.

- **Network forensics tools:** This category of forensic tools captures and analyzes network traffic, logs, and communications. Such forensic tools help in detecting intrusions, data exfiltration, and insider threats. The popular tools in this context are stated here:

  - o **Wireshark:** Wireshark is a leading network packet analysis tool.

  - o **Xplico:** The Xplico extracts and reconstructs network sessions.

  - o **NetworkMiner:** The NetworkMiner passively captures network packets for forensic analysis.

- **Mobile forensics tools:** This category of tools extracts app data, call logs, SMS, GPS history, and deleted files from mobile devices. This category of tool works with Android, iOS, and cloud backups. The well-known tools in this regard are listed here:

  - o **Cellebrite UFED:** This is an Industry-standard tool for mobile data extraction.

  - o **MSAB XRY:** This tool captures and analyses data from mobile devices.

  - o **Magnet AXIOM:** This tool recovers mobile, cloud, and computer evidence.

- **Cloud and internet forensics tools:** These forensic tools extract evidence from cloud storage, emails, social media, and web browsing history. These forensic tool helps recover deleted cloud data and encrypted communications. The popular tools in this category include the following:

  - o **Magnet AXIOM Cloud:** This tool analyses cloud-based data and backups.

  - o **Elcomsoft Cloud Explorer:** This tool recovers data from Google, Apple, and Microsoft cloud accounts.

  - o **X1 Social Discovery:** This tool captures and analyses social media and web content.

- **Log and event analysis tools:** This category of forensic tools analyses system logs, security events, and audit trails for forensic investigations. This category of forensic tools helps to identify unauthorized access, system anomalies, and cyberattacks.

The popular tools in this context include the following:

o **Splunk:** Splunk is a centralized log analysis and forensic investigation tool.

o **ELK Stack (Elasticsearch, Logstash, Kibana):** ELK Stack is an open-source log management solution.

o **EventLog Analyzer:** EventLog Analyzer is a tool that automates event log collection and analysis.

• **Malware and reverse engineering tools:** This category of forensic tools identifies and analyzes malicious software, exploits, and vulnerabilities. These tools are used for reverse engineering malware behavior. The extensively used tools of this category are listed here:

o **IDA Pro:** IDA Pro is an advanced reverse engineering and disassembly tool.

o **Ghidra:** Ghidra is an open-source reverse engineering suite by the NSA.

o **Cuckoo Sandbox:** Cuckoo Sandbox is an automated malware analysis tool.

Forensic analysis software and tools are indispensable in digital investigations, enabling forensic experts to extract, analyze, and present critical evidence from various digital sources. The right combination of disk, memory, network, mobile, and malware forensics tools leads digital forensic investigators to uncover digital footprints, track cyber threats, and ensure legal compliance. Thus, adopting best practices and proper tool selection strengthens the reliability and accuracy of forensic investigations, thus ensuring that findings are court-admissible and technically sound.

Network forensics tools and appliances

Network forensics is a critical branch of digital forensics that focuses on monitoring, capturing, and analyzing network traffic, logs, and communications to detect cyber threats, intrusions, data breaches, and other security incidents. Specialized network forensics tools and appliances help investigators reconstruct network events, analyze anomalies, and trace malicious activities while preserving forensic integrity.

The real-time tools provide live monitoring and alerting for active threats. The post-incident tools focus on reconstructing historical network traffic for forensic analysis. The network forensics tools need to capture full packet data (PCAP), metadata, and session logs, apart from log correlation across multiple network devices to enhance visibility. The network forensics tools are required to analyze common protocols (TCP, UDP, HTTP, DNS, SMTP, and FTP), apart from handling encrypted traffic analysis such as TLS/SSL, VPN, and SSH. The network forensics tools need to scale for enterprise networks, cloud environments, and IoT ecosystems. This is in terms of integrating with SIEM systems to enhance efficiency.

The different categories of network forensics tools are stated here:

- **Packet capture and traffic analysis tools:** These tools capture and analyze network packets, traffic flow, and communications. These tools help in identifying malware activity, unauthorized access, and data exfiltration. The well-known tools in this regard include the following:

  o **Wireshark:** Wireshark is an industry-leading open-source packet analysis tool.

  o **Tcpdump:** Tcpdump is a command-line tool for capturing and filtering network packets.

  o **TShark:** TShark is a terminal-based version of Wireshark for deep packet analysis.

Network forensics tools and appliances are essential for identifying cyber threats, reconstructing attack timelines, and securing digital infrastructures. By leveraging packet capture tools, IDS/IPS solutions, flow analyzers, and cloud forensics platforms, investigators can detect intrusions, trace malicious activities, and respond to incidents effectively. Adopting scalable forensic solutions and best practices ensures that network investigations are comprehensive, reliable, and legally admissible.

Open source and commercial tools for digital forensics

Digital forensics investigators rely on a wide range of open-source and commercial tools to acquire, analyze, and report digital evidence from various devices, including computers, mobile phones, networks, and cloud environments. The choice between open-source and commercial tools depends on factors such as budget, functionality, legal admissibility, and ease of use.

The open-source forensics tools are freely available and widely used for investigations. These tools are preferred for their transparency, community-driven development, and flexibility, but they may require technical expertise and lack official support. Open-source digital forensics tools are as follows:

- **Disk and file system forensics:** The relevant tools include Autopsy and Sleuth Kit, TestDisk and PhotoRec, and X-Ways WinHex (Free Version). These tools are described as follows:

  o **Autopsy and Sleuth Kit:** The Autopsy and Sleuth Kit is a GUI-based forensic suite for file system analysis and evidence recovery.

  o **TestDisk and PhotoRec:** TestDisk and PhotoRec are disk partition recovery and file recovery tools.

  o **X-Ways WinHex (Free Version):** The free version of X-Ways WinHex is a Low-level disk editor for raw data analysis.

- **Memory and volatile data forensics:** The relevant memory and volatile data forensics tools include Volatility Framework, Rekall, and Belkasoft RAM Capturer. These tools are detailed as follows:

  o **Volatility framework:** The volatility framework is a leading memory forensics tool for analyzing RAM dumps.

  o **Rekall:** Rekall is an open-source tool for extracting volatile data and detecting malware in memory.

  o **Belkasoft RAM Capturer:** Belkasoft RAM Capturer captures live system memory for forensic investigations.

- **Network and packet analysis:** Network and packet analysis tools include Wireshark, Tcpdump, and Zeek (Bro). These tools are detailed as follows:

  o **Wireshark:** Wireshark is an industry-standard tool for analyzing network traffic and identifying anomalies.

  o **Tcpdump:** Tcpdump is a command-line packet capture tool for network forensic investigations.

  o **Zeek (Bro):** Zeek is a Network security monitoring and traffic analysis framework.

- **Mobile forensics:** The relevant tools for mobile forensics include **Mobile Verification Toolkit (MVT)**, Andriller and AFLogical OSE. These tools are detailed as follows:

  o **Mobile Verification Toolkit (MVT):** This is an open-source tool for analyzing mobile device security and spyware detection.

  o **Andriller:** This tool extracts data from Android devices, including passwords and PINs.

  o **AFLogical OSE:** This tool captures data from Android devices for forensic analysis.

- **Malware and reverse engineering:** The relevant tools include Ghidra, Radare2, and Cuckoo Sandbox. These are detailed as follows:

  o **Ghidra:** This open-source reverse engineering framework was developed by the NSA.

  o **Radare2:** This is an advanced reverse engineering and binary analysis tool.

  o **Cuckoo Sandbox:** This is an automated malware analysis tool that runs suspicious files in an isolated environment.

- **Log and event analysis:** The relevant tools include **Elasticsearch, Logstash, Kibana (ELK** Stack), Graylog, and Sysmon. These are listed below:

- o **Elasticsearch, Logstash, Kibana (ELK Stack):** This is an open-source log management and analysis framework.

- o **Graylog:** This is a centralized log collection and forensic investigation tool.

- o **Sysmon (Microsoft):** This tool monitors and logs system activities for forensic investigations.

Commercial forensics tools are proprietary solutions developed by cybersecurity companies, often certified for legal investigations and offering official support, automation, and advanced analytics. These tools are widely used by law enforcement, corporations, and forensic professionals due to their user-friendly interfaces, comprehensive reporting, and built-in compliance features.

- **Disk and file forensics:** The relevant tools are listed here:

  - o **EnCase forensic:** This is an industry-leading tool for forensic imaging, analysis, and evidence preservation.

  - o **AccessData FTK (Forensic Toolkit):** This is an advanced forensic suite for hard disk and registry analysis.

  - o **X-Ways Forensics:** This is a lightweight but powerful forensic software for disk analysis.

- **Memory and volatile data forensics:** The associated tools are listed here:

  - o **Magnet RAM Capture:** This tool captures live memory for forensic investigations.

  - o **Belkasoft Evidence Center:** This tool captures, extracts, and analyses RAM, hard drives, and cloud storage data.

- **Network and cloud forensics:** The associated tools are listed here:

  - o **Magnet AXIOM Cloud:** This tool captures and analyzes cloud-based digital evidence.

  - o **FireEye Helix:** This is an advanced threat detection and network forensic analysis platform.

  - o **Cellebrite Pathfinder:** This network forensic tool is suitable for reconstructing digital communication and traffic.

- **Mobile forensics:** The concerned tools include the following:

  - o **Cellebrite UFED:** This is an industry-standard tool for extracting and analyzing mobile phone data.

  - o **MSAB XRY:** This is a mobile forensic software for data extraction from locked devices.

- o **Oxygen Forensic Detective:** This is an advanced forensic tool for analyzing smartphones and IoT devices.

- **Malware and reverse engineering:** The associated tools include the following:

  - o **IDA Pro:** This commercial tool is used for disassembling and reverse engineering malware.

  - o **RE-Ghidra Pro:** This is an enhanced professional version of Ghidra with additional enterprise features.

  - o **Cuckoo Enterprise:** The premium version of Cuckoo Sandbox for large-scale malware analysis.

- **Log analysis and SIEM integration**: The relevant tools are listed here:

  - o **Splunk Enterprise Security:** This is an advanced log collection and forensic investigation platform.

  - o **IBM QRadar:** This is an AI-driven security intelligence and log analysis tool.

  - o **Microsoft Sentinel:** This cloud-native SIEM solution is for forensic log analysis and incident response.

Conclusion

Setting up a digital forensics lab is a crucial step in ensuring effective investigations, evidence preservation, and analysis. A well-designed lab incorporates specialized hardware, software, and network infrastructure to handle forensic processes efficiently while maintaining the integrity and CoC of digital evidence. The selection of forensic imaging tools, data storage solutions, and mobile forensics equipment plays a vital role in optimizing investigations across various digital environments.

The upcoming chapter focuses on advancing careers in digital forensics.

Join our book's Discord space

Join the book's Discord Workspace for Latest updates, Offers, Tech happenings around the world, New Release and Sessions with the Authors:

https://discord.bpbonline.com

CHAPTER 17

Advancing Your Career in Digital Forensics

Introduction

The field of digital forensics is rapidly evolving, driven by technological advancements, increasing cyber threats, and legal complexities. As organizations prioritize cybersecurity and digital investigations, the demand for skilled digital forensic professionals continues to grow. Building a successful career in digital forensics requires a strong technical foundation, practical experience, and continuous learning. Whether pursuing roles in law enforcement, private security firms, government agencies, or corporate cybersecurity teams, professionals must stay updated on the latest tools, investigative techniques, and legal considerations. Additionally, obtaining industry-recognized certifications and participating in hands-on forensic investigations can significantly enhance career prospects. This chapter explores career pathways, essential skills, certifications, and industry trends to help aspiring and experienced professionals advance in the digital forensics domain.

Structure

The chapter covers the following topics:

- Evolving field of digital forensics
- Digital forensics in enterprise environments
- Key skills and knowledge

- Specializing in enterprise digital forensics
- Networking and professional associations
- Mastering enterprise forensic analysis tools and techniques
- Working with legal and compliance teams
- Managing large-scale digital forensics investigations in enterprises
- Emerging technologies and trends
- Professional certifications and continuing education

Objectives

The current chapter details the evolving field of digital forensics in terms of the latest trends and opportunities. The chapter proceeds with understanding the role of digital forensics in enterprise environments. The chapter includes key skills and knowledge for enterprise digital forensics professionals. The chapter specializes in enterprise digital forensics in terms of incident response, data breaches, fraud, etc. The chapter indicates networking and professional associations in the digital forensics community. The chapter relates to mastering enterprise forensic analysis tools and techniques. The chapter relates to working with legal and compliance teams in enterprise digital forensics. The chapter implies managing large-scale digital forensics investigations in enterprises. The chapter indicates staying up-to-date with emerging technologies and trends in enterprise digital forensics. The chapter stresses developing leadership and communication skills for enterprise digital forensics professionals. The chapter includes details about professional certifications and continuing education in enterprise digital forensics.

Evolving field of digital forensics

The field of digital forensics is constantly evolving due to technological advancements, sophisticated cyber threats, and new regulatory requirements. As digital ecosystems expand, forensic professionals must adapt to emerging challenges and leverage new technologies to enhance investigations.

The key trends shaping digital forensics include the following:

- **Cloud and virtualized forensics:** With the emergence of cloud computing as a primary requirement, forensic professionals must develop effective techniques for analyzing cloud-stored data, virtual machines, and remote servers.

- **IoT and embedded device forensics:** The increasing number of IoT devices and smart technologies has created new forensic challenges, requiring digital forensic analysts to focus on firmware analysis, sensor data extraction, and networked device investigations.

- **AI and ML in forensics:** AI-powered tools assist in automating digital investigations, pattern recognition, and anomaly detection, speeding up forensic processes.

- **Cryptocurrency and blockchain investigations:** The growing use of cryptocurrencies in cybercrimes has led to the development of forensic tools to trace blockchain transactions and uncover illicit activities.

- **Automated and cloud-based forensic tools:** Digital forensics is shifting toward cloud-based solutions and automation, allowing for real-time forensic analysis and remote investigations.

- **Forensics in 5G and edge computing:** The continuous expansion of 5G networks and edge computing encourages forensic experts to develop strategies to analyze data spread across decentralized environments.

The key opportunities for shaping digital forensics relate to the following:

- **Cybersecurity integration:** The forensic professional transitions into cybersecurity roles, including threat intelligence, risk assessment, and red teaming.

- **Specialized forensics domains:** Professionals can focus on niche areas such as malware reverse engineering, vehicle forensics, **industrial control system (ICS)** forensics, and mobile device forensics.

- **International and corporate investigations:** The demand for forensic professionals in financial crime investigations, fraud detection, and compliance audits is increasing across global enterprises and multinational organizations.

- **Academia and research:** Opportunities exist in teaching, training, and forensic tool development for professionals looking to contribute to the academic side of digital forensics.

The rapid expansion of cybercrime leads to data privacy regulations and digital transformation. This implies a continuous demand increment for highly skilled forensic professionals. Staying ahead in this field requires continuous learning, advanced certifications, hands-on experience, and adapting to evolving technologies.

Digital forensics in enterprise environments

The increasing growth of complexity within cyber threats requires digital forensics to play a critical role in enterprise environments in terms of identifying, analyzing, and mitigating security incidents. Organizations rely on forensic professionals to investigate breaches, detect insider threats, ensure regulatory compliance, and strengthen cybersecurity defenses. The importance of digital forensics in enterprise environments is as follows:

- **Incident response (IR) and threat mitigation:** Forensic experts analyze cyber incidents, reconstruct attack vectors, and provide evidence for containment and recovery. This represents effective IR and threat mitigation.

- **Insider threat detection:** Forensic analysis helps detect data theft, unauthorized access, and employee misconduct within organizations. This resembles insider threat detection within an organization.

- **Fraud and financial crime investigations:** Digital forensics is used to uncover fraudulent transactions, identity theft, and corporate espionage as a part of fraud and financial crime investigations.

- **Regulatory and compliance requirements:** Enterprises must comply with standards such as GDPR, HIPAA, PCI-DSS, and ISO 27001, which often require forensic investigations following security incidents. This indicates relevant regulatory and compliance requirements of an organization within its operating sector.

The best practices for implementing forensic readiness are stated here:

- **Establishing a digital forensics policy:** Enterprises should establish clear forensic investigation procedures to ensure a timely response to incidents. This relates to establishing an effective digital forensics policy within the enterprise.

- **Deploying forensic tools and logging mechanisms:** Automated forensic tools and real-time logging enhance investigative efficiency. This is a part of deploying forensic tools and logging mechanisms.

- **Training and awareness programs:** Regular training for IT teams and employees helps improve forensic readiness and cyber hygiene. This highlights the importance of training and awareness programs.

As businesses face increasing cyber risks, the demand for forensic experts skilled in enterprise security, cloud investigations, and compliance auditing continues to rise. Professionals with expertise in incident response, malware analysis, and forensic data recovery will be highly sought after in corporate environments.

Key skills and knowledge

The target of excelling in enterprise digital forensics requires professionals to possess a combination of technical expertise, analytical skills, legal knowledge, and investigative proficiency. The increasing complexity of enterprise environments enhances the need for forensic specialists to adapt to emerging threats, cloud-based infrastructures, and evolving compliance requirements.

The core technical skills are stated as follows:

- **Operating system forensics:** The concept of operating system forensics relates to the proficiency of a digital forensics investigator in analyzing Windows, Linux, macOS, and mobile OS artifacts for forensic evidence.

- **Network forensics:** The concept of network forensics relates to understanding details of packet analysis, intrusion detection, and forensic log correlation for cyber incident investigations.

- **Cloud and virtualization forensics:** Cloud and virtualization forensics relates to the ability of a digital forensic analyst to extract and analyze data from cloud platforms such as AWS, Azure, and Google Cloud and virtual machines.

- **Malware analysis and reverse engineering:** The relevant skills in sandboxing, static and dynamic malware analysis, and thereby identifying malicious code behavior imply malware analysis and reverse engineering.

- **Cryptography and data encryption:** The aspect of cryptography and data encryption covers knowledge of encryption algorithms, cryptographic hash functions, and secure data recovery techniques.

- **Scripting and automation:** The proficiency of a digital forensic investigator relates to being skilled in Python, PowerShell, and Bash scripting to automate forensic data extraction and analysis.

The relevant investigative and analytical abilities of a digital forensic investigator relate to the following areas:

- **Evidence collection and Chain of Custody (CoC):** The process of evidence collection and CoC ensures forensic data integrity, proper documentation, and legal admissibility.

- **Timeline analysis:** The process of timeline analysis relates to reconstructing event sequences from log files, system artifacts, and user activities.

- **Behavioral analysis:** The process of behavioral analysis relates to understanding Attacker **Techniques, Tactics, and Procedures (TTPs)** to identify **advanced persistent threats (APTs)**.

The relevant legal and compliance knowledge relates to the following:

- **Cybercrime laws and regulations:** The relevant cybercrime laws and regulations relate to familiarity with GDPR, HIPAA, CCPA, PCI-DSS, and ISO 27001 requirements.

- **Digital evidence admissibility:** The perspective of digital evidence knowledge for a digital forensic investigator relates to knowledge of forensic procedures, affidavit preparation, and expert witness testimony.

- **Incident reporting and documentation:** Incident reporting and documentation is the ability of a digital forensic investigator to prepare detailed forensic reports for law enforcement, legal teams, and corporate management.

Apart from the technical skills, the digital forensic investigator is required to possess the following soft skills for the benefit of enterprise forensic requirements:

- **Critical thinking and problem-solving:** The skill of critical thinking and problem solving resembles the ability to correlate evidence, detect anomalies, and reconstruct cyber incidents.

- **Communication and reporting:** The aspect of communication and clearly presenting forensic findings to **technical and non-technical stakeholders**.

- **Collaboration and teamwork:** The aspect of collaboration and teamwork relates to working alongside IT security teams, legal departments, and law enforcement agencies.

The aspect of continuous learning and professional development relates to the following areas:

- **Certifications**: The aspect of certifications relates to earning credentials by potential digital forensic investigators, such as GCFA, EnCE, CHFI, CCFP, and CISSP.

- **Hands-on training:** The aspect of hands-on training relates to participating in cyber ranges, **Capture the Flag (CTF)** competitions, and forensic simulations.

- **Research and networking:** The research and networking aspect relates to engaging in forensic communities, conferences, and industry collaborations.

Enterprise digital forensics professionals are required to blend technical expertise, investigative abilities, legal awareness, and analytical skills to effectively handle cyber incidents and forensic investigations. Digital forensic investigators are required to consider mastery of operating system forensics, network analysis, cloud and virtualization forensics, and malware analysis, which is essential for identifying and mitigating security threats.

Specializing in enterprise digital forensics

The increasing complexity of cyber threats encourages enterprise digital forensics professionals to often specialize in specific areas of investigation to enhance their expertise and effectiveness. The process of specialization allows forensic analysts to develop in-depth knowledge of attack methods, forensic tools, and investigative techniques relevant to various enterprise security challenges.

The incident response and cyberattack investigation relate to the following:

- **Threat identification and containment:** Threat identification and containment relate to rapidly detecting and isolating threats such as ransomware, insider attacks, and APTs.

- **Memory and volatile data forensics:** Memory and volatile data forensics relate to analyzing RAM dumps, process activity, and live system artifacts to uncover active threats.

- **Incident recovery and reporting:** Incident recovery and reporting relate to developing a timeline of events, implementing mitigation strategies, and preparing detailed forensic reports.

The data breach investigation relates to the following areas:

- **Compromised system analysis:** The compromised system analysis relates to identifying relevant **Indicators of Compromise (IoCs)** in log files, network traffic, and endpoint activity.

- **Data exfiltration tracking:** Data exfiltration tracking relates to using relevant forensic tools to trace stolen data movement and determine the extent of a data breach.

- **Regulatory compliance and reporting:** The regulatory compliance and reporting relate to ensuring compliance with data protection laws such as GDPR, HIPAA, and CCPA, and thereby preparing breach notification reports.

The financial fraud and insider threat investigation relates to the following areas:

- **Forensic accounting and transaction analysis:** Forensic accounting and transaction analysis relate to investigating financial records, cryptocurrency transactions, and money laundering activities.

- **Employee misconduct and data theft:** Employee misconduct and data theft relate to detecting unauthorized access, intellectual property theft, and policy violations within the organization.

- **Behavioral analysis and threat intelligence:** Behavioral analysis and threat intelligence relate to leveraging ML and forensic profiling to detect fraudulent activities.

The related cloud and SaaS-based forensics relates to the following areas:

- **Cloud storage and virtual machine analysis:** Cloud storage and virtual machine analysis relate to extracting and analyzing relevant forensic evidence from AWS, Azure, Google Cloud, and related SaaS platforms.

- **Log aggregation and threat hunting:** The effective use of SIEM tools such as Splunk and ELK and associated forensic platforms aids digital forensic investigators in detecting anomalies across the cloud environments.

- **Legal and jurisdictional challenges:** Legal and jurisdictional challenges for digital forensic analysts include navigating cross-border data laws and cloud provider policies during the course of forensic investigations.

The Mobile and IoT forensics in enterprise environments relates to the following:

- **Enterprise mobile device investigations:** The effective analysis of mobile artifacts from **Bring Your Own Device (BYOD)** policies, corporate-issued smartphones, and encrypted messaging apps implies enterprise mobile device investigations.

- **IoT and embedded device forensics:** The investigation of smart security systems, **Industrial IoT (IIoT)**, and networked enterprise devices relates to IoT and embedded.

The relevant threat intelligence and proactive forensics include the following:

- **Dark web investigations:** The dark web investigations relates to monitoring underground forums for stolen enterprise data, credentials, and cybercrime activities as a part of dark web investigations.

- **Proactive threat hunting:** The process of proactive threat hunting relates to using forensic techniques to detect hidden malware, zero-day exploits, and persistent threats before they escalate to the next level.

- **Integration with SOC and Red Teaming:** The effective collaboration with **Security Operations Centers (SOCs)** and penetration testers to improve enterprise security posture resembles seamless integration with SOC and Red Teaming.

The aspect of career growth and specialization path relates to professionals advancing in enterprise forensics by earning certifications such as **GIAC Certified Forensic Analyst (GCFA)**, **Certified Fraud Examiner (CFE)**, and Cloud Security Certifications (CCSP and CCSK). This is apart from gaining hands-on experience with relevant incident response frameworks such as NIST and MITRE ATT&CK, and forensic tools such as Autopsy, X-Ways, and Magnet AXIOM that enhance expertise. Effective specialization in specific industries such as finance, healthcare, and government can lead to higher-demand forensic roles.

Networking and professional associations

Networking and active participation in professional associations are crucial for digital forensics professionals seeking to expand their expertise, stay updated on emerging threats, and advance their careers. The process of engaging with industry peers, attending conferences, and joining professional organizations provides opportunities for knowledge-sharing, mentorship, and career growth for the associated individuals.

The importance of networking in digital forensics relates to the following:

- **Knowledge exchange and collaboration:** The knowledge exchange and collaboration relate to engaging with experts helps forensic professionals learn new techniques, best practices, and case studies.

- **Career growth and opportunities:** Career growth and opportunities relate to effective networking, leading to job referrals, project collaborations, and professional recognition.

- **Access to exclusive resources:** Access to exclusive resources leads to multiple professional associations offering research papers, forensic toolkits, training sessions, and certifications.

- **Legal and ethical guidance:** The professionals can stay informed on new regulations, digital evidence laws, and courtroom testimony best practices in terms of legal and ethical guidance.

The leading digital forensics professional associations relate to the following:

- **International Association of Computer Investigative Specialists (IACIS):** The IACIS relates to offering training and certification for law enforcement and private-sector forensic analysts.

- **High Technology Crime Investigation Association (HTCIA):** The HTCIA is a global network for professionals specializing in cybercrime investigations and forensic analysis.

- **International Society of Forensic Computer Examiners (ISFCE):** The ISFCE provides CCE certification and supports forensic examiners worldwide.

- **SANS Institute and GIAC certifications:** The SANS Institute and GIAC Certifications offer industry-recognized certifications such as Certified Forensic Analyst (GCFA) and Reverse Engineering Malware (GREM).

- **Association of Certified Fraud Examiners (ACFE):** The ACFE focuses on financial crime investigations, fraud prevention, and forensic accounting.

- **Cloud Security Alliance (CSA):** The CSA provides guidance on cloud forensics, security controls, and incident response in cloud environments.

- **International Association of Privacy Professionals (IAPP):** The IAPP covers data protection laws, privacy regulations, and compliance in forensic investigations.

The aspect of actively networking and engaging with professional associations, forensic experts can enhance their careers, stay ahead in the field, and contribute to the advancement of digital forensics.

Mastering enterprise forensic analysis tools and techniques

Enterprise digital forensics requires professionals to leverage specialized tools and advanced techniques to efficiently investigate cyber incidents, data breaches, and insider threats. Mastery of forensic analysis tools enables digital forensics experts to collect, analyze, and interpret digital evidence while ensuring its integrity and admissibility in legal proceedings. The essential categories of enterprise forensic tools include the following:

- **Disk and file system forensics:** Disk and file system forensics relates to the usage of relevant tools for disk imaging, deleted file recovery, and forensic analysis of file systems. These tools include Autopsy, X-Ways Forensics, EnCase, FTK, and Sleuth Kit.

- **Memory and volatile data analysis:** The memory and volatile data analysis examines RAM artifacts using suitable tools to detect malware, active processes, and rootkits. These tools include Volatility, Rekall, and Redline.

- **Network forensics:** Network Forensics tools capture and analyze network traffic to investigate cyber intrusions and suspicious activities. The relevant tools include Wireshark, Zeek (Bro), NetworkMiner, and Snort.

- **Cloud and virtualization forensics:** Cloud and virtualization forensics relates to retrieving evidence from cloud environments, virtual machines, and SaaS platforms by using the benefit of suitable tools. These tools include AWS CloudTrail, Azure Security Center, and Magnet AXIOM Cloud.

- **Log and event analysis:** Examines logs from operating systems, firewalls, applications, and security appliances using the underlying benefit of relevant tools. These tools include Splunk, **Elasticsearch, Logstash, Kibana Stack (ELK)**, and Graylog.

- **Malware and reverse engineering:** Malware and reverse engineering analyze malicious code behavior and forensic indicators of malware infections using tools such as IDA Pro, Ghidra, Cuckoo Sandbox, and PEStudio.

- **Mobile and IoT forensics:** The Mobile and IoT forensics extracts data from mobile devices, embedded systems, and IoT networks using tools such as Cellebrite UFED, MOBILedit Forensic, and IoT Inspector.

The advanced enterprise forensic techniques include the following:

- **Timeline analysis:** The timeline analysis relates to reconstructing sequences of system events using timestamps from logs, registry files, and metadata.

- **Live forensics:** Live forensics conducts investigations on active systems without disrupting business operations.

- **Steganography detection:** Steganography detection identifies hidden messages or files within multimedia content.

- **Forensic hashing and integrity verification:** Forensic hashing and integrity verification use cryptographic hashes such as MD5 and SHA-256 to ensure data integrity.

- **Dark web and OSINT investigations:** Dark Web and OSINT investigations relate to conducting cyber threat intelligence gathering from relevant dark web sources.

- **AI and ML in forensics:** AI and ML in forensics automate threat detection, anomaly analysis, and log correlation.

Mastering forensic tools and techniques is essential for effectively investigating enterprise cyber threats, ensuring compliance, and enhancing organizational security posture.

Working with legal and compliance teams

Enterprise digital forensics is not just about technical investigations, as it also requires close collaboration with legal and compliance teams to ensure that forensic processes adhere to regulatory frameworks, corporate policies, and legal standards. Proper legal coordination helps organizations mitigate risks, maintain evidence integrity, and ensure admissibility in court proceedings.

Effective legal and compliance collaboration relates to ensuring investigations align with laws and regulations. This is in terms of digital forensics requiring compliance with local, national, and international laws such as GDPR, HIPAA, CCPA, and PCI-DSS. This is in terms of digital forensics requiring compliance with local, national, and international laws such as GDPR, HIPAA, CCPA, and PCI-DSS. The appropriate protection of CoC relates to forensic professionals documenting evidence collection, handling, and storage procedures to prevent legal challenges. The key legal and compliance considerations in enterprise forensics relate to the following:

- **Data privacy and protection laws:** Data privacy and protection laws relate to understanding how digital forensic investigations impact **Personally Identifiable Information (PII)**, employee data, and customer records.

- **Electronic Discovery (eDiscovery) and legal holds:** eDiscovery and legal holds ensure that electronic evidence is preserved for internal investigations, regulatory inquiries, or litigation.

- **Employee monitoring and workplace investigations:** The balancing of corporate security policies with employee privacy rights while conducting forensic investigations relates to employee monitoring and workplace investigations.

- **Intellectual property theft and insider threats:** The investigation of cases of corporate espionage, unauthorized data access, and trade secret theft while ensuring compliance with labor laws relates to intellectual property theft and insider threats.

- **Cross-border investigations and jurisdictional challenges:** The handling of forensic investigations that span multiple countries, legal systems, and data sovereignty laws relates to cross-border investigations and jurisdictional challenges.

The best practices for working with legal and compliance teams relate to the following:

- **Early legal involvement in investigations:** The early legal involvement in investigations relates to engaging legal counsel from the beginning, ensuring forensic efforts align with regulatory requirements.

- **Standardizing digital evidence documentation:** The standardizing digital evidence documentation relates to maintaining detailed forensic reports, incident log, and proper chain-of-custody records.

- **Implementing role-based access controls:** The implementation of role-based access controls relates to restricting access to forensic data to authorized personnel only to prevent legal risks.

The effective working between the legal and compliance team encourages digital forensic professionals to lawfully conduct the digital forensic investigations and thereby protects organizations from legal risks.

Managing large-scale digital forensics investigations in enterprises

Enterprise digital forensics investigations can be complex, time-sensitive, and resource-intensive, especially when dealing with large-scale cyber incidents, data breaches, or insider threats. Managing such investigations requires structured methodologies, scalable forensic solutions, and effective coordination among forensic, security, legal, and compliance teams. The existing challenges in large-scale forensic investigation include the following:

- **Massive data volume:** The massive data volume relates to the enterprises generating vast amounts of logs, emails, files, and system activity, requiring efficient data processing.

- **Distributed and hybrid IT environments:** Distributed and hybrid IT environments imply that the investigations often involve on-premises systems, cloud storage, virtualized environments, and remote endpoints.

- **Coordinating multiple teams and stakeholders:** The coordination of multiple teams and stakeholders relates to large-scale cases requiring collaboration across security teams, IT administrators, legal counsel, and law enforcement.

- **Maintaining CoC:** The maintenance of CoC relates to handling evidence integrity across multiple locations and teams, being crucial for legal admissibility of digital evidence at the Court of Law.

- **Compliance and regulatory requirements:** Large investigations must comply with global privacy laws, industry regulations, and corporate policies in terms of compliance and regulatory requirements.

The effective tools and technologies for large-scale digital forensics include the following:

- **Enterprise forensic suites:** The enterprise forensic suites include EnCase Enterprise, FTK Enterprise, and X-Ways Investigator.

- **Cloud and remote forensics:** Cloud and remote forensics include Magnet AXIOM Cloud, AWS CloudTrail, and Azure Sentinel.

- **Big data and AI-powered forensics:** Big data and AI-powered forensics include Splunk, ELK Stack, and IBM QRadar.

- **Network and endpoint monitoring:** Network and endpoint monitoring include Wireshark, Zeek, Carbon Black, and CrowdStrike Falcon.

- **Automated log analysis and SIEM:** Automated log analysis and SIEM include Splunk, ArcSight, and Microsoft Sentinel.

Managing enterprise-scale forensic investigations demands a combination of technical expertise, structured methodologies, scalable forensic tools, and strong interdepartmental coordination. Efficient management ensures rapid incident response, minimal business disruption, and compliance with legal and regulatory standards.

Emerging technologies and trends

The field of enterprise digital forensics is constantly evolving, driven by advancements in cyber threats, computing technologies, and forensic methodologies. This implies that Forensic professionals are required to continuously update their skills, tools, and investigative approaches to stay ahead of sophisticated cybercriminals and adapt to the changing digital landscape. The key emerging technologies influencing digital forensics include the following:

The key emerging technologies impacting digital forensics include the following:

- **AI and ML in forensics:** The AI and ML-driven forensic tools that aid in automating data analysis, detecting anomalies, and speeding up evidence correlation. Contextually, ML models assist in identifying previously unknown attack patterns and behavioral anomalies.

- **Cloud and remote forensics:** The rise of cloud computing, hybrid environments, and decentralized data storage requires new methods for acquiring and analyzing forensic evidence. The associated cloud forensic tools include AWS CloudTrail and Magnet AXIOM Cloud, which help in investigating data breaches and insider threats in cloud environments.

- **Blockchain and cryptocurrency forensics:** The increased usage of cryptocurrencies and blockchain technology encourages forensic investigators to track Bitcoin transactions, analyze smart contracts, and uncover financial fraud using relevant tools. These tools include Chainalysis, CipherTrac, and Elliptic, and they assist in blockchain investigations.

- **Internet of Things (IoT) and edge computing forensics:** The expansion of IoT devices in enterprises relates to creating new attack surfaces that require specialized forensic approaches. The investigators need IoT forensic frameworks to analyze smart devices, embedded systems, and industrial control networks.

- **Zero Trust and endpoint forensics:** The implication of Zero Trust security models requires forensic experts to continuously validate identities, monitor access logs, and analyze endpoint telemetry.

- **Advanced Endpoint Detection and Response (EDR) solutions:** The Advanced EDR solutions include CrowdStrike Falcon *(Figure 17.1)*, Carbon Black, to aid forensic analysis.

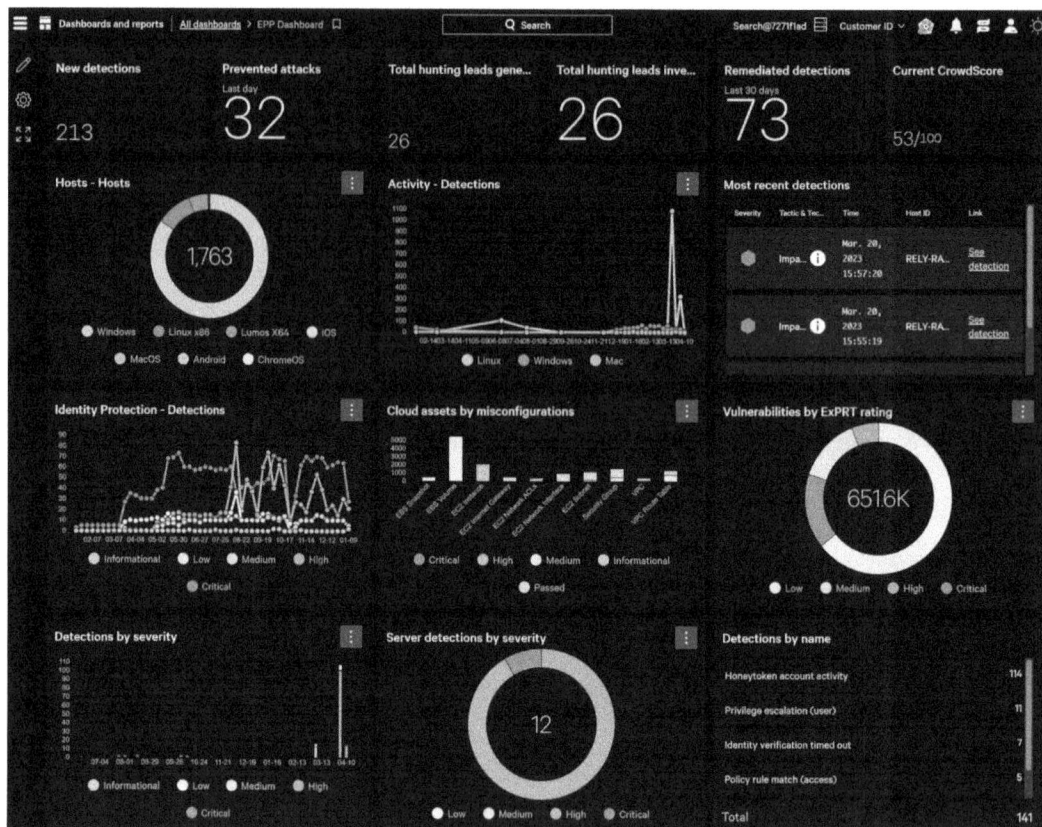

Figure 17.1: Interface of CrowdStrike Falcon

The key trends that are shaping the future of enterprise digital forensics include the following:

- **Rise of ransomware investigations:** Enterprises tend to face an increasing number of ransomware attacks, requiring specialized forensic techniques to trace attackers, decrypt files, and restore systems.

- **Integration with SOCs and IR:** Digital forensics is now a core function of SOCs, which implies working closely with incident response teams to analyze breaches in real-time. Organizations are adopting **Security Orchestration, Automation, and Response** (**SOAR**) platforms to streamline forensic workflows.

- **Dark web and threat intelligence forensics:** The investigators require leveraging **Open-Source Intelligence** (**OSINT**) and dark web monitoring tools to uncover stolen credentials, data leaks, and cybercriminal activity.

- **Automation and cloud-native forensics:** Enterprises are integrating cloud-native forensic solutions that enable real-time investigations and automated evidence gathering.

Staying updated with emerging technologies, tools, and forensic trends is essential for enhancing investigative capabilities, improving threat detection, and maintaining compliance with evolving regulations.

Leadership and communication skills

Technical expertise alone is not enough for success in enterprise digital forensics. Leadership and communication skills are crucial for effectively managing investigations, collaborating with cross-functional teams, and conveying forensic findings to executives, legal teams, and stakeholders. The development of key leadership and communication skills includes the following:

- **Enhancing problem-solving and critical thinking:** Strong analytical thinking aids forensic leaders in finalizing data-driven decisions and adapting to evolving cyber threats.

- **Gaining experience in crisis management:** The aspect of gaining experience in crisis management relates to managing high-pressure forensic cases that require resilience, adaptability, and the ability to stay composed under stress.

- **Improving public speaking and report writing:** The improvement of public speaking and report writing skills encourages engaging in professional writing courses, public speaking workshops, and forensic presentation training that enhances clarity in delivering forensic results.

Strong leadership and communication skills enable forensic professionals to effectively manage investigations, collaborate with enterprise teams, and present forensic findings with confidence.

Professional certifications and continuing education

The continuous evolution of cyber threats leads enterprise digital forensics professionals to stay updated with the latest investigative techniques, legal considerations, and technological advancements. Earning professional certifications and engaging in continuous education aids forensic experts in enhancing their credibility, refining their skills, and advancing in their careers. The top digital forensics certifications for enterprise professionals include the following:

- **GIAC Certified Forensic Analyst (GCFA):** This professional certification focuses on advanced forensic analysis, memory forensics, and incident response.

- **GIAC Network Forensic Analyst (GNFA):** This professional certification tends to specialize in network traffic analysis, intrusion detection, and network-based forensic investigations.

- **Certified Computer Examiner (CCE):** This professional certification relates to forensic evidence acquisition, analysis, and reporting methodologies.

- **EnCase Certified Examiner (EnCE):** This professional certification relates to validating expertise in using EnCase for forensic investigations, eDiscovery, and evidence analysis.

- **Certified Forensic Computer Examiner (CFCE):** This professional certification is offered by IACIS, focusing on digital forensic best practices and courtroom presentation of evidence.

- **Certified Cyber Forensics Professional (CCFP):** This professional certification relates to providing a broad understanding of cyber forensics, legal aspects, and forensic management strategies.

Continuing education in digital forensics includes the following:

- **Advanced training courses and workshops:** Organizations such as **SANS Institute, EC-Council,** and **ISFCE** offer hands-on forensic training. The specialized courses in cloud forensics, IoT forensics, and mobile device forensics help professionals stay ahead.

- **Higher education and degree programs:** Pursuing a Master's degree in Cybersecurity, Digital Forensics, or Computer Science enhances the expertise of a potential digital investigator in enterprise forensics.

- **Online learning and self-paced training:** The relevant platforms, such as Cybrary, Coursera, and Pluralsight, provide flexible forensic training options.

- **Attending conferences and industry events:** Engaging in events such as the SANS DFIR Summit, Black Hat, and RSA Conference helps forensic experts learn from real-world case studies and network with industry leaders.

- **Publishing research and contributing to the forensics community:** The writing of white papers, blogs, or case studies on forensic investigations demonstrates expertise and helps advance the field.

Obtaining professional certifications and engaging in continuous education ensures enterprise digital forensics professionals remain skilled, competitive, and prepared to handle complex forensic investigations.

Conclusion

The field of enterprise digital forensics is a dynamic and rapidly evolving discipline that requires a combination of technical expertise, leadership abilities, and continuous learning. As cyber threats become more sophisticated, forensic professionals need to adapt by mastering emerging technologies, enterprise forensic tools, and investigative methodologies. A successful career in enterprise digital forensics demands specialized skills, including incident response, fraud investigations, legal compliance, and large-scale forensic analysis. Professionals must also develop strong communication and leadership abilities to effectively collaborate with security teams, legal departments, and executive stakeholders. Staying up-to-date with the latest forensic techniques, tools, and regulatory requirements is essential for success. This can be achieved through professional certifications, continuing education, networking, and active participation in industry events. Certifications such as GCFA, CCE, EnCE, and CFCE provide industry recognition and enhance career growth opportunities.

The upcoming chapter focuses on relevant industry best practices deployed in the field of digital forensics. The chapter delves in detail into the different career scopes that are available for potential professionals in the field of digital forensics.

Join our book's Discord space

Join the book's Discord Workspace for Latest updates, Offers, Tech happenings around the world, New Release and Sessions with the Authors:

https://discord.bpbonline.com

CHAPTER 18

Industry Best Practices in Digital Forensics

Introduction

Digital forensics is a multidisciplinary field integrating cybersecurity, law enforcement, and corporate investigations. Rising cyber threats have increased reliance on digital forensics for evidence collection and security enforcement. The foundation and evolution of digital forensics relate to its comprehensive role in cybersecurity, law enforcement, and enterprise security. The evolution of digital forensics aligns with basic file recovery in traditional days to advanced forensic methodologies for investigating cybercrimes and breaches. The continuous expansion of the digital footprint links to the growing complexity of cyber threats due to cloud computing, the **Internet of Things (IoT)**, and evolving digital platforms. The current chapter attempts to focus on relevant industry best practices along with career scopes in the field of digital forensics.

Structure

The chapter covers the following topics:

- Industry best practices
- Career scopes in digital forensics

Objectives

The current chapter focusses on detailed understanding of different best practices that are utilized across the different areas of digital forensics. The chapter further points different career scopes in digital forensics.

Industry best practices

The importance of digital forensics in enterprise environments relates to enterprise applications, **incident response (IR)** integration, and regulatory and compliance needs. The enterprise applications related to digital forensics are no longer limited to law enforcement but extend to corporate security, compliance, and fraud detection. The IR integration relates to the role of forensic teams in mitigating security breaches and ensuring business continuity. Enterprises use forensics to investigate data breaches, fraud, and insider threats. The regulatory and compliance needs include adhering to GDPR, HIPAA, PCI-DSS, and other global security frameworks. Enterprises integrate forensic processes into security operations to handle cyber incidents efficiently. The legal and ethical considerations include realizing the importance of the chain of custody associated with ethical challenges and global legal frameworks. The importance of the chain of custody relates to maintaining the integrity and admissibility of digital evidence in legal proceedings. The ethical challenges are related to balancing investigative needs with privacy laws and corporate policies. The relevant global legal frameworks imply understanding the differences in digital forensic regulations across various jurisdictions. The methodologies and processes in digital forensics include forensic process stages beyond traditional approaches and standardization. The forensic process stages include collection, preservation, analysis, documentation, and reporting. The aspect of leveraging AI, automation, and cloud-based forensic solutions for efficiency relates to considering strategies beyond traditional approaches. The effective standardization includes adopting NIST, ISO 27037, and other forensic best practices.

The related historical perspective of digital forensics relates to early forensic investigations focusing on hard drives, as compared to today, as they span cloud and virtual environments. The related technological shifts relate to the introduction of sophisticated encryption techniques, cloud-based storage, and decentralized networks. The relevant future growth areas include AI-powered forensic automation and real-time forensic intelligence, which are shaping the future of the digital forensics field. The effective navigation of legal and ethical aspects is relevant to regulatory challenges, as different countries have varying digital evidence laws, thereby requiring forensic professionals to stay updated. The related ethical considerations indicate responsible handling of sensitive data to avoid privacy violations and legal conflicts. The courtroom admissibility relates to forensic evidence requiring to following proper **Chain-of-Custody (CoC)** procedures to be legally admissible. The relevant unfolding of the digital forensics process relates to a standardized approach of collection, preservation, analysis, documentation, and reporting to ensure the integrity and preservation of digital forensics investigations. The handling of digital evidence relates to using relevant forensic imaging tools to create secure copies and prevent their tampering. The reporting and presentation relate to documenting findings in a structured manner to be used in legal proceedings. The expanding toolkit of digital forensics expands beyond Kali Linux. This is in terms of a diversified toolset, specialized tools for different domains, and scalability and automation. The effective expansion of the **forensic toolkit (FTK)** relates to suitable open-source and commercial tools, such as EnCase, Autopsy, and Magnet Axiom, playing crucial roles. The diversified toolset is exploring commercial and open-source forensic tools beyond traditional Linux-based forensic suites. The specialized tools for different domains include memory forensics, mobile forensics, cloud forensics, and IoT investigations. Different tools for network forensics, memory analysis, mobile forensics, and cloud investigations. Scalability and automation relate to using **machine learning (ML)** and automation tools to enhance forensic efficiency. The integration of ML to speed up forensic data processing and anomaly detection.

The process of digital forensics aligns with the investigation, analysis, and recovery of digital evidence from collected electronic devices at a digital crime scene. The importance of deploying standardized procedures in digital forensics investigations implies ensuring the accuracy, integrity, and overall legal admissibility of digital evidence in the Court of Law. The key areas of effective digital forensics investigation include handling digital evidence, imaging of digital evidence, data analysis, legal compliance, and reporting. The procedures of digital forensics investigation resemble appropriate guidelines such as the **National Institute of Standards and Technology (NIST)**, ISO/IEC 27037, and legal regulations. Digital forensic investigators widely use the following best practices across the digital forensics field to deliver justice in cybersecurity cases at the Court of Law:

- **Evidence handling and chain of custody:** Digital evidence is critical for justice delivery in cybersecurity cases and thus requires effective handling during the entire duration of the cybercrime cases. The appropriate digital evidence handling requires the deployment of a CoC by digital forensic investigators. This document resembles detailed records of digital evidence handling by digital forensic investigators. Accordingly, digital forensic investigators use appropriate software solutions such as Write Blocker Tools to restrict the alteration of digital evidence. The digital forensic investigators store the digital evidence in secure and tamper-proof locations. The digital forensic investigators ensure maintaining proper documentation of digital evidence, such as timestamps, case numbers, and signatures. *(Figure 18.1)*

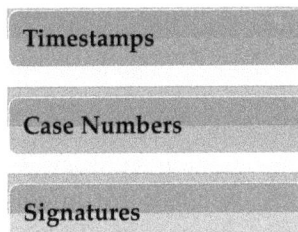

Figure 18.1: Areas of digital evidence documentation

- **Forensic acquisition and imaging:** The effective acquisition of digital evidence from the cybercrime scene requires creating forensic copies of it before initiating the process of digital forensic investigation. Digital forensic investigators use industry-approved digital evidence imaging tools such as FTK Imager, EnCase, and Autopsy. Digital forensic investigators encourage verifying the integrity of acquired digital evidence images using hashing algorithms such as MD5, SHA-1, and SHA-256. *(Figure 18.2)*

MD5	SHA-1	SHA-256
•Message Digest Algorithm 5 •Fixed Length Output •Used for File Integrity Checking	•Secure Hash Algorithm 1 •Fixed Length Output •Designed for Cryptographic Security	•Secure Hash Algorithm 256 Bit •Fixed Length Output •Used in Bitcoin

Figure 18.2: Different hash algorithms

The process of forensic evidence acquisition and imaging requires avoiding possible tampering of digital evidence to the extent possible.

- **Data analysis and examination:** The process of data analysis and examination involves following standardized forensic methodologies such as the NIST **Cybersecurity Framework (CSF)** and ISO/IEC 27037. *(Figure 18.3)*

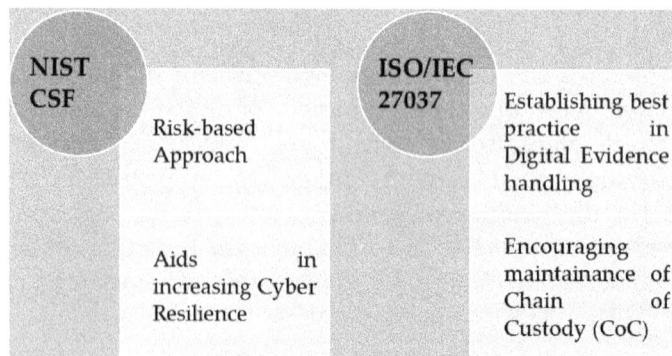

NIST CSF		ISO/IEC 27037	
	Risk-based Approach		Establishing best practice in Digital Evidence handling
	Aids in increasing Cyber Resilience		Encouraging maintainance of Chain of Custody (CoC)

Figure 18.3: Cybersecurity Frameworks

This requires following multiple forensic tools for effective cross-verification of digital evidence. These tools include Autopsy, X-Ways, and Magnet AXIOM. The entire phase of data analysis requires documenting all findings and maintaining logs of individual steps. The process of digital evidence examination resembles correlating findings with timelines, logs, and metadata for context.

- **Legal and ethical compliance:** The legal and ethical compliance of digital forensics resembles adherence to multiple legal frameworks such as the **General Data Protection Regulation (GDPR)**, **Health Insurance Portability and Accountability Act (HIPAA)**, or the **Computer Fraud and Abuse Act (CFAA)**. *(Figure 18.4)*

GDPR	General Data Protection Regulation
•Lawfulness, Fairness & Transparency	

HIPPA	Health Insurance Portability & Accountability Act
•Protecting Patient Health Information (PHI)	

CFAA	Computer Fraud & Abuse Act
•Criminalizing Unauthorized Access, Hacking & Data Theft	

Figure 18.4: Legal frameworks in cybersecurity

The legal and ethical compliance requires the concerned forensic analysis to follow court-admissible procedures. This is crucial to avoid unauthorized access to data or systems during the phase of digital forensic investigation. Ethical compliance further requires respecting privacy and confidentiality during the phase of personal and sensitive information handling in a digital forensic investigation.

- **Reporting and documentation:** The reporting and documentation imply maintaining a detailed and well-structured forensic report, having specific areas such as findings, methods, and conclusions. The detailed reporting and documentation involve considering screenshots, log files, and extracted metadata for inclusion in the report to support claims. The hallmark of an effective report relates to using clear, concise, and unbiased language that is suitable for legal proceedings. Digital forensic investigators are required to be prepared to testify in a Court of Law as per the requirement.

- **IR and collaboration:** The occurrence of a cybersecurity incident at an organization requires the initiation of effective IR and collaboration. This requires digital forensic investigators to work with cybersecurity teams to effectively contain and mitigate the threats. The outcome of IR and collaboration leads to sharing findings with relevant stakeholders, law enforcement, or legal teams. The detailed analysis of the outcomes, thus generated, encourages scheduling effective training to enhance the knowledge of organizational employees on emerging threats and technologies.

- **Continuous learning and tool validation:** The benefit of continuous learning and tool validation encourages staying updated for individuals in terms of new digital forensic tools and methodologies. The aspect of tool validation relates to regularly testing forensic software for accuracy and reliability. Such requirements encourage the involvement of individuals having professional certifications such as **Certified Cybersecurity Expert (CCE)**, GIAC **Certified Forensic Analyst (GCFA)**, **EnCase Certified Examine**r **(EnCE)**, and **Computer Hacking Forensic Investigator (CHFI)**. *(Figure 18.5)*

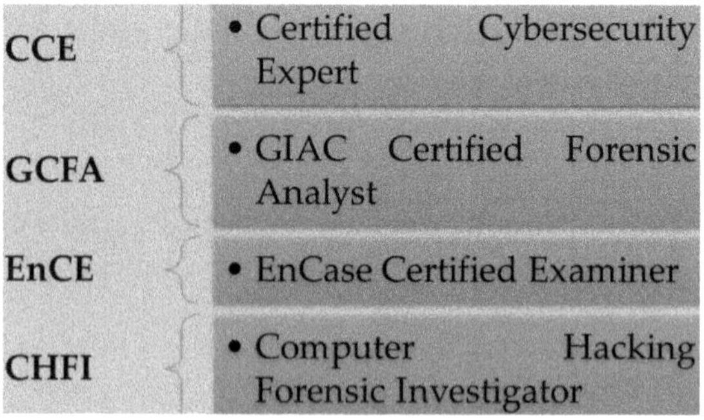

Figure 18.5: Professional certifications

The training of GCFA covers advanced IR and forensic techniques to benefit relevant organizations. The EnCE Certification is associated with focusing on the usage of EnCase for digital investigations. The CHFI certification focuses on providing expertise in forensic analysis and cybercrime investigation. The CISSP Certification is a broader cybersecurity certification that includes forensic principles. The process of continuous learning requires potential individuals to attend workshops, training programs, and hands-on experience with forensic tools such as FTK, Autopsy, and Magnet AXIOM, which are essential for career growth. *(Figure 18.6)*

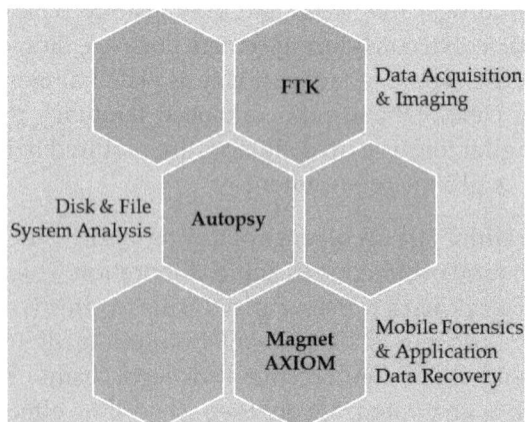

Figure 18.6: Forensic tools

The consistent participation in industry forums and training, such as SANS Institute and the **Digital Forensics Incident Response (DFIR)** community by associated individuals.

Career scopes in digital forensics

The specialized areas of digital forensics include network forensics, memory forensics, mobile device forensics, virtualization and hypervisor forensics, **industrial control systems (ICS)** forensics, and IoT forensics. The concept of network forensics includes investigating cyberattacks, intrusion detection, and traffic analysis. The concept of memory forensics indicates extracting volatile data to detect advanced malware and rootkits. The benefit of mobile device forensics relates to handling encrypted devices, cloud backups, and app-based evidence. Virtualization and hypervisor forensics relate to multiple existing challenges in the forensic analysis of virtualized and cloud-hosted environments. ICS forensics indicate investigating attacks on critical infrastructures such as power grids and transportation. IoT Forensics poses unique challenges in handling smart devices, embedded systems, and edge computing. The aspect of network traffic analysis relates to investigating logs, packet captures, and intrusion detection system alerts. The identification of malicious activity relates to tracking cybercriminals through network logs and thereby reconstructing attack paths. The dark web and deep web analysis relate to investigating illegal activities in anonymized networks. The process of extracting volatile data relates to analyzing RAM to detect malware, hidden processes, and encryption keys. The advanced threat analysis relates to identifying fileless malware and rootkits that bypass traditional security tools. The overall difference between live and post-mortem analysis relates to their differentiating acquisition process from active systems vs. analyzing memory dumps.

The challenge in mobile forensics relates to encryption, diverse **operating systems (OS)**, and locked devices, complicating investigations. This, apart from cloud and app forensics, deals with extracting data from cloud backups, app metadata, and social media platforms. The mobile threats and malware relate to analyzing spyware, Trojans, and phishing attempts targeting mobile users. The efficiency of digital forensics labs and infrastructure relates to effortlessly setting up a lab by designing it with appropriate hardware, software, and security measures. The workstations, servers, and networking needs relate to ensuring scalability and efficiency in forensic investigations. The cloud-based forensic environments resemble leveraging virtual forensic labs for distributed investigations. **Virtual machines (VMs)** and Containers relate to investigating forensic artifacts within cloud-based and virtualized environments. The hypervisor attacks relate to identifying threats such as hyperjacking and VM escape attacks. The limitation of forensic tools includes adapting traditional forensic tools to handle virtual environments effectively. IR and threat hunting relate to a proactive forensic investigation that helps prevent cyberattacks. The threat intelligence integration relates to using forensic analysis for cyber threat intelligence and proactive defense. The application of **artificial intelligence (AI)** and big data in forensics relates to automating evidence analysis to handle large-scale investigations. The fast integration of blockchain and quantum computing across different areas implies the future impact of emerging technologies on digital forensics. The process of rapid incident handling relates to using forensic data to detect, contain, and remediate security breaches. The effective collaboration with SOC teams encourages digital forensics to play a vital role in **Security Operations Centers (SOCs)** to investigate **advanced persistent threats**

(**APTs**). The incident documentation relates to ensuring legal and regulatory compliance in forensic-led IR efforts. The certifications and training relate to the importance of obtaining credentials such as GCFA, CCE, EnCE, and CFCE. The specialized career paths relate to different opportunities in corporate security, government, cybersecurity firms, and consulting. Continuous learning and research relate to staying updated with new forensic tools, methodologies, and legal frameworks.

The increasing number of different cybercrimes in modern days, such as data breaches and digital fraud, inflates the demand for cyber forensics investigators. The successful building of a career in digital forensics enhances the career development scope of an individual across various areas such as law enforcement, cybersecurity, corporate security, legal consulting, and academia. The potential digital forensic experts are required to possess specific key skills and specializations such as cybercrime investigation, malware analysis, mobile forensics, and cloud forensics. The demand for skilled individuals in digital forensics is increasing across a wide range of government agencies, private firms, and multinational corporations. The different career scopes in digital forensics are stated as follows:

- **Digital forensics investigator:** The role of a digital forensics investigator includes investigating cybercrime, fraud, and data breaches by focusing on a detailed investigation of digital evidence. The key skills required by digital forensic investigators include expertise in different areas such as computer forensics, evidence handling, IR, and data recovery. *(Figure 18.7)*

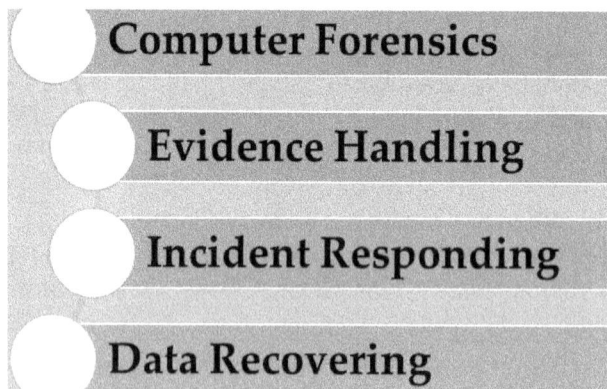

Figure 18.7: Key skills required by a digital forensic investigator

Digital forensics investigators can seamlessly work for law enforcement agencies, private investigation firms, and corporate security teams.

- **Cybercrime investigator:** The role of a cybercrime investigator includes specializing in tracking hackers, cyber fraud, identity theft, and digital scams. The fulfillment of such roles within the digital forensics field requires the concerned individuals to possess key skills such as the ability to perform network forensics, malware analysis, encryption, and **Open-Source Intelligence** (**OSINT**). *(Figure 18.8)*

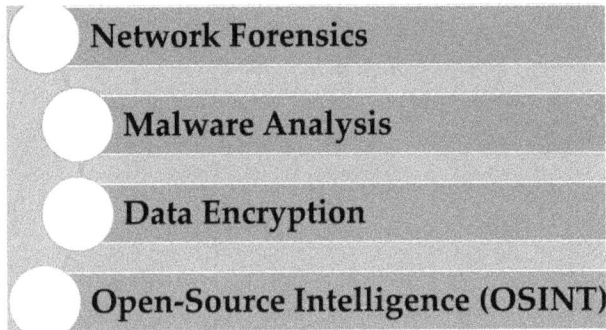

Figure 18.8: Key skills required by a cybercrime investigator

Thereby, skilled individuals can work for reputed organizations such as the FBI, Interpol, cyber police, financial institutions, and consulting firms. *(Figure 18.9)*

Figure 18.9: Reputed organizations for cybersecurity jobs

- **IR analyst:** The IR analysts are assigned the role of detecting and responding to security incidents, data breaches, and cyberattacks. The individuals targeting to become IR analysts are required to possess key skills such as Threat analysis and SIEM tools, such as Splunk and QRadar digital and Digital Evidence Collection. *(Figure 18.10* and *Figure 18.11)*

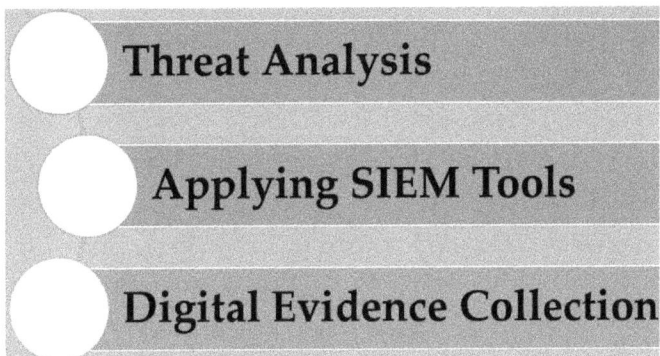

Figure 18.10: Key skills required by an IR analyst

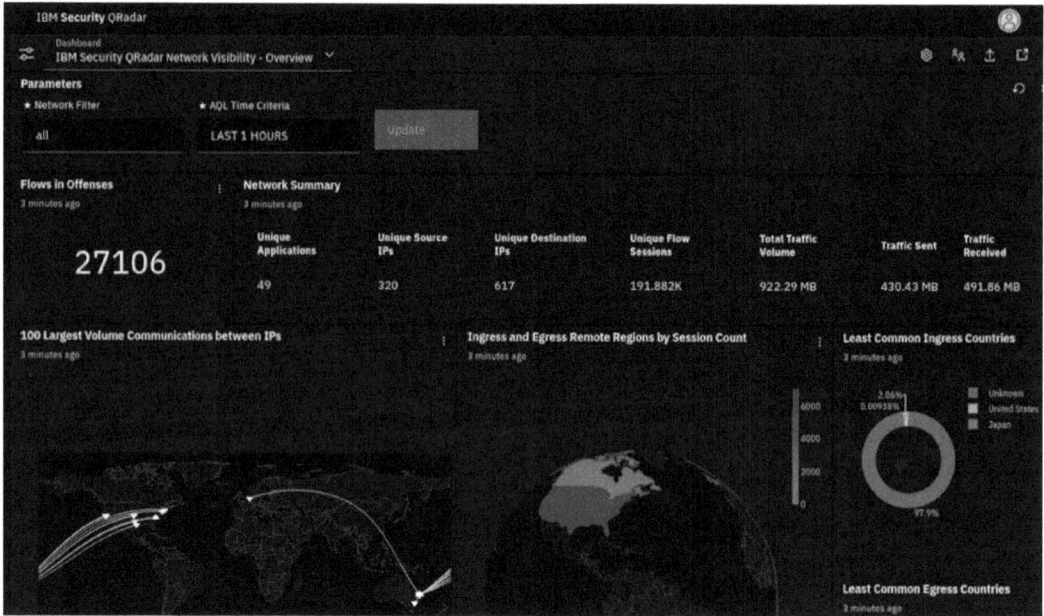

Figure 18.11: Interface of IBM QRadar

- **Digital forensics consultant:** The role of a digital forensics consultant includes providing expert advice on forensic investigations, legal cases, and cyber resilience. The required skills for timely and effective fulfillment of such goals include having the capability of using a wide variety of digital forensic tools such as EnCase, FTK, and Autopsy. *(Figure 18.12)*

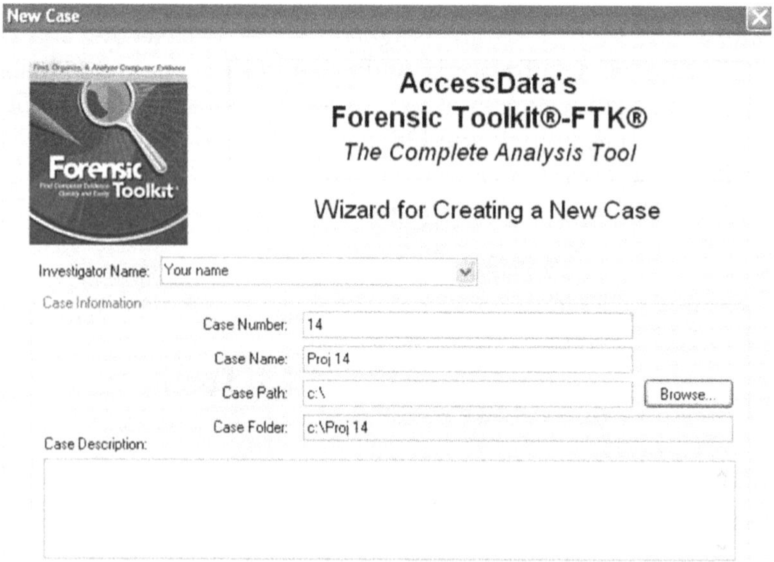

Figure 18.12: Snapshot of FTK

This is apart from possessing the capability to adhere to legal compliance and effective reporting. The digital forensics consultant tends to be seamlessly recruited across areas such as cybersecurity consulting firms, law firms, and private practice. *(Figure 18.13)*

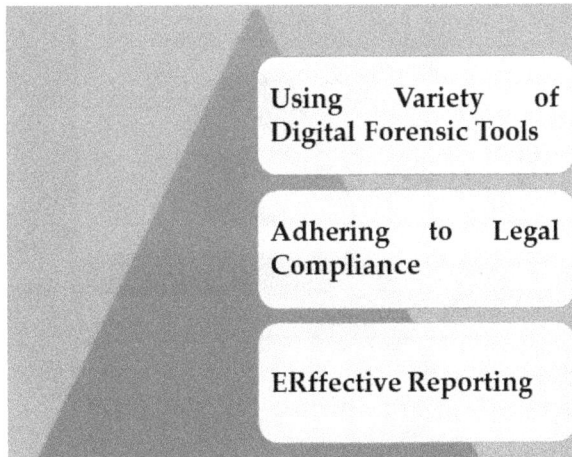

Using Variety of Digital Forensic Tools

Adhering to Legal Compliance

ERffective Reporting

Figure 18.13: Key skills required by a digital forensic consultant

- **Malware analyst/reverse engineer:** The role of a malware analyst or reverse engineer implies analyzing and dissecting malware to trace attack mechanisms and their effective mitigation. The key skills required for such roles of malware analysts include being versed in assembly language, apart from static and dynamic malware analysis, sandboxing, and YARA rules. *(Figure 18.14) (Figure 18.15)*

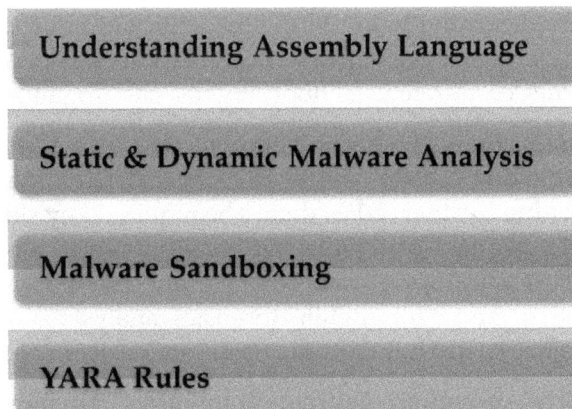

Understanding Assembly Language

Static & Dynamic Malware Analysis

Malware Sandboxing

YARA Rules

Figure 18.14: Key skills required by malware analyst

Figure 18.15: Malware Sandboxing on Any.Run

Malware analysts are in high demand across cybersecurity companies, threat intelligence firms, and government agencies.

- **E-discovery specialist:** The role of an E-discovery specialist focuses on managing electronic evidence for legal cases, including emails, documents, and metadata. The associated key skills for such a role include the application of E-discovery platforms such as Relativity and Nuix, the ability of effective data preservation, and adherence to compliance laws. The E-discovery specialist can work across various law firms, corporate legal departments, and litigation support companies.

- **Mobile forensics analyst:** The professional role of a mobile forensics analyst includes investigating mobile devices to recover deleted messages, call logs, and **Global Positioning System** (GPS) data. The required key skills for the fulfillment of such roles encompass using specific mobile forensic tools such as Cellebrite and Oxygen Forensics, apart from effective app analysis and appropriate data extraction. The demand for mobile forensics analysts is observed across law enforcement agencies, private forensic firms, and telecom security teams.

- **Cloud forensics specialist:** The cloud forensics specialists are assigned the responsibility of investigating cybercrime cases involving Cloud Storage, **Software-as-a-Service** (SaaS) platforms, and virtual environments. The key skills appropriate for this role as a cloud forensics specialist include AWS / Azure Security and various cloud forensic tools such as Magnet AXIOM Cloud and Google Vault. Cloud Forensics Specialists are in high demand for cloud service providers, cybersecurity firms, and large enterprises.

- **Ethical hacker/penetration tester (Red team):** The role of an ethical hacker or penetration tester as a Red team indicates simulating cyberattacks to test security and uncover vulnerabilities well in advance of real hackers. The required skills for an ethical hacker or penetration tester include penetration testing, exploitation techniques, and forensics-based threat hunting. Ethical hackers are in significant demand across cybersecurity firms, ethical hacking teams, and financial institutions.

- **Digital forensics trainer/educator:** The digital forensics trainer or educator plays the role of mentor to train individuals, including students and professionals, in digital forensic skills and certifications. The required key skills for this career scope include curriculum development, forensic lab setup, and relevant industry certifications such as GCFA and EnCE. The digital forensics trainer works for universities and training institutes such as SANS, EC-Council, and Government Agencies.

Conclusion

The increasing importance of digital forensics relates to the evolving cyber threats, and thereby, digital forensics remains a cornerstone of cybersecurity. The requirement of bridging technical and legal gaps resembles the need for forensic professionals to understand both technical and legal aspects. The relevant requirement of innovation and collaboration within digital forensics relates to encouraging interdisciplinary collaboration between forensic experts, legal teams, and policymakers.

Join our book's Discord space

Join the book's Discord Workspace for Latest updates, Offers, Tech happenings around the world, New Release and Sessions with the Authors:

https://discord.bpbonline.com

Index

www.ingramcontent.com/pod-product-compliance
Lightning Source LLC
Chambersburg PA
CBHW061800210326
41599CB00034B/6821